THE LIFE AND
WORKS OF
ALFRED BESTALL

THE LIFE AND WORKS OF ALFRED BESTALL

illustrator of Rupert Bear

CAROLINE G. BOTT

BLOOMSBURY

First published in Great Britain 2003
This paperback edition published 2004

Author's text copyright © Caroline Bott 2003
Diaries copyright © Caroline Bott
Rupert characters ™ and © Express Newspapers 2003

The publishers would like to thank the following
for their permission to reproduce material:

The *Daily Express* for the article by Hilda Coe that appears on pp.65-8
The *Methodist Recorder* for the articles that appear on pp.19-20, 42, 51-3
The *Observer* for the article by Anna Coote that appears on p.98 © *Observer*
The *Surrey Comet* for the articles that appear on pp.98-105
Punch for the cartoons that appear on pp.46-50 © Punch, Limited
Doris Raws for the letter that appears on pp. 84-5
Leslie Sherwood for the letter that appears on p.70
George Perry for the extracts from *Rupert: A Bear's Life* (Pavilion Books Ltd, 1985) that
appear on pp.21-3, 32

The letter from Enid Blyton that appears on p.59 is reproduced with the kind
permission of Enid Blyton Limited © 1927 Enid Blyton Limited, a Chorion company. All
rights reserved.

Bloomsbury Publishing plc, 38 Soho Square, London W1D 3HB

A CIP catalogue record for this book
is available from the British Library

ISBN 0 7475 7336 0

10 9 8 7 6 5 4 3 2 1

All papers used by Bloomsbury Publishing are natural,
recyclable products made from wood grown in well-managed forests.
The manufacturing processes conform to the
environmental regulations of the country of origin.

Typeset by Hewer Text Limited, Edinburgh
Printed by Clays Ltd, St Ives plc

www.bloomsbury.com/carolinebott

To Jonathan, Simon and Alison

CONTENTS

FOREWORD

I never had a teddy bear but, as a boy, I always turned to the Rupert column in my parents' *Daily Express* and was particularly fond of the Rupert Christmas annuals. I rediscovered him in the seventies when I started reading bedtime stories to my eldest daughter Heather.

For some reason, I tend to think of Rupert as an eleven-year-old boy – I don't know why. His attitude is very much 'It can be done'; he's very positive and always has that spark of optimism combined with a certain innocence which I think is what drew me to him in the first place.

For the British, Rupert is an institution – like the Queen. Britain just wouldn't be the same without him.

Sir Paul McCartney

PREFACE

Alfred Edmeades Bestall MBE, perhaps best known as author and illustrator of *Rupert Bear* for thirty years, was my father's first cousin. He was
also my godfather. He never married and he took his godfatherly duties
very seriously, especially as my father died in the Second World War when
I was still a baby. My first memory of him is in 1945: I was a child of five
just 'home' from Australia. We were sitting in a bus shelter in torrential rain
in Torrington, North Devon. 'Uncle Fred' was making paper models and
flying them across the shelter to pass the time while we waited for one of
the infrequent buses back to Northam where my grandparents lived. In
1951 he introduced me to his beloved North Wales and, when he died in
1986, he left me his tiny cottage in Snowdonia, complete with much of his
early artwork, diaries and journals.

My aim in this book has been to let him tell his own story, using his own
words as much as possible. In this spirit, I have done minimal editing,
though I have changed some of the place names to adopt more modern
spellings. In my view, what emerges is a picture of a versatile artist and an
endearing man who, though very much of his own time, still has great
resonance for people of all ages at the beginning of the twenty-first century.

Caroline Bott
Milford
2003

ACKNOWLEDGEMENTS

I am enormously grateful to Emma Matthewson and to everybody at Bloomsbury who has made this publication possible. I have been treated with the utmost generosity and the whole project has been delightful.

I am also greatly indebted to R.E. Head for all the painstaking care he has taken in photographing so many pictures for publication.

I would like to thank the *Daily Express* for permission to publish the *Rupert* image, and George Perry for allowing me to quote from his book *Rupert: A Bear's Life*; also the Followers of Rupert – Matthew and Margaret Heaton and John Beck for their encouragement and for assisting me with the list of books (albeit incomplete) with illustrations by AEB.

Last, but not least, I would like to thank my husband, Alan, for all the advice and help he has given me with the artwork ever since AEB died.

1

THE EARLY YEARS

Illustration for Bible bookmark (dated 1907)

ON 22 JANUARY 1986 mourners in dark suits, many wearing their yellow Rupert scarves, stood outside the sombre chapel perched on the edge of the hill. Clouds hung low, accentuating the greyness of the slate roofs and stone walls of Penrhyndeudraeth, North Wales. We, the family, arrived for the funeral of my godfather, Alfred Edmeades Bestall (AEB), who had died peacefully in the Wern Manor Nursing Home the week before. Inside the chapel, the many floral tributes included arrangements in red and yellow flowers of Rupert Bear sent by the *Daily Express*, the Followers of Rupert, and Paul and Linda McCartney. The chapel was packed and the walls resounded to the strains of Methodist hymns. The first one, 'In heavenly love abiding, no change my heart shall fear', we sang to the tune of 'Penlan', which was also the name of AEB's cottage in Beddgelert. At the end of the service we followed the coffin out of the chapel. As we reached the door, the sun came out and lit up the valley and rugged hills on the other side. The beauty of North Wales was apparent. No wonder he had loved the place.

We returned to our cars and followed the hearse along the narrow winding roads, through the Aberglaslyn Pass, to the corner from where Penlan can first be glimpsed. There we stopped and reflected. Nestling in the valley of the River Glaslyn was the village of Beddgelert, with St Mary's Church standing as it had stood for at least 700 years. Penlan lay beyond the village at the foot of the mountains, with Snowdon (*Eryri*) visible from the hill behind the cemetery. AEB was a saintly man whose faith supported him throughout his ninety-three years. His spirituality, his art, music and his love of sport and the outdoor life (not least hill-walking in North Wales) formed the bedrock of his life. The procession wound its way through Beddgelert, past Snowdon, through the bleak Ogwen Valley to the crematorium at Bangor. From there, AEB's ashes were taken to be buried in the family grave at Brookwood in Surrey, along with those of his parents – Albert Henry Arthur Bestall (always known as Arthur) and Rebecca Bestall (née Edmeades) – and sister, Mary Agnes Bestall (known as Maisie, or by AEB as 'Pop').

Alfred and Rebecca Edmeades (AEB's grandparents) about 1868

The Reverend Arthur Bestall died in Surbiton, Surrey in 1936, having spent twenty-three strenuous years abroad as a missionary. He established schools and founded the first leper home in Mandalay, as well as translating books, hymns and also the New Testament into Burmese. Rebecca Edmeades came from a large and distinguished Methodist family in Winchester and her forbears lived at Nurstead Court in Meopham, Kent. In an interview with the *Methodist Recorder* in 1963 she recalled the 'aristocratic, awesome, Victorian grandfather's presence, where a little girl of eight discovered the fascination of drawing, because her grandmother thoughtfully relieved the long prayers by providing the child with paper and pencil.' Her parents encouraged her early interest in painting and drawing, and after leaving her private school in Bristol, she attended Winchester College of Art, where she began to develop as an artist, and in which she also discovered her love for music. She shared Arthur's Christian zeal and in 1891 joined him in Mandalay, where they were married. AEB was born on 14 December the following year. Maisie was born on 11 November 1895 and in about 1897 both children were brought back to England. Mystery surrounds what actually happened to them in Burma – if anything – but, for whatever reason, AEB came back with a spinal injury and had a speech impediment and Maisie was mentally impaired. There were

Reverend Arthur and Mrs Bestall in Burma

other difficulties with life in the tropical climate, as indicated by this extract from a letter from Alfred Edmeades, AEB's grandfather:

My dear Arthur and Rebie
. . . I have for an hour been studying the 3rd chapter to the Philippians, I trust with some profit, and having closed the book I thought I ought to use the few remaining minutes to write to you, so I will begin by expressing the hope that Rebie reached home safely with the chick [Fred] . . . Rebie's last letter in which she describes briefly her feeling and experiences before she left Burma, has excited in us deep concern for her and indeed for you all, as we see the climate is evidently telling upon you . . . I have always regarded your call to Burma as God ordained, but I wish you please to fully understand that if you really think a change necessary, so necessary that you are prepared to forgo your own happiness to meet her need, you may send her home to us at once, without any hesitation and I will defray the cost of passage. Now I am satisfied I may leave this to

your judgement, and having plainly stated my wishes, you will know how to act for the future, we look forward with very much pleasure to the time when we hope in the ordinary course of things we may see each other . . .'

AEB and Burmese nurse

When Arthur and Rebecca returned to Mandalay after bringing the children to England, AEB was put in the charge of the Reverend W. Ripley Winston, a minister who had also served in Burma, while Maisie went to her grandparents in Winchester. Mr Winston's wife, Lizzie, wrote to Rebecca on 2 February 1899:

My dear Mrs Bestall

Your letter was very welcome on Saturday night with its news of the District Synod and all the missionaries and the wives . . .

Freddy has just gone to bed, he is as frisky as a little lamb and very happy. He loves to write his letters, he and Alice [presumably her daughter] have done it this afternoon. I have been out to a Busy Bee sewing meeting. They asked me to go and tell them about the work in

The Bestalls' house in Burma

Burma so I have been talking about you and Mr Bestall all the evening . . .

It has been frosty for two days and there was some attempt at snowing today. Freddy wanted to go and get a snowball but I think he would have had to scrape all round Rutland Park to get it . . .

It was my birthday on Tuesday and Freddy gave me two of his nicest pictures, dear little fellow, he thought them the most suitable in amongst his possessions and I prize his little gift very much, he was so much interested in my birthday and thoroughly enjoyed the plum pudding.

We all send much love to you and Mr Bestall.

Yours affect'ly

Lizzie Winston

PS. Freddy was greatly delighted with the account of the Xmas tree.

Rebecca with AEB and Maisie, 1903

AEB attended the local girls' high school in Sheffield (the school was proud of its Old Boy when it celebrated its centenary in 1978), but the Winstons must have been transferred to North Shields, for in 1984 AEB wrote to a friend:

I hope you do manage a visit to North Shields. I was there for a year probably 1901 and lived with a minister (and his four children), a pioneer missionary in Burma, and the Wesleyan manse was rather west of the middle of Linskill Terrace.

I used to walk to Tynemouth School (headmaster, Mr Crowe) passing a small park on the right. Of our house I remember nothing. Near neighbours were named Hogg. Years after I heard that my pal Jack Hogg had become an Evangelist and open-air preacher. For this he owed nothing to my early influence. I was a very scruffy nine year old, and our permanent desire was to watch Percy Park rugger. Admission to the ground cost a penny – and I never had a penny – so we wandered outside the fence hoping to find a spot where other malefactors had scraped away enough soil for us to wriggle through underneath.

Our favourite game as I remember was 'Pollus's Cutt'n' played at dusk or later. 'Pollus' was Tyneside for police and 'cutting' was dashing about as silently as possible using the little ginnels and snickets leading behind the houses. All completely fatuous, nobody ever got caught, because everyone was running away, no one was chasing.

I must have left North Shields when my people came back on furlough from Burma in 1902.

He was, in fact, still there at the end of the year, for on 15 November 1902 his father sent a postcard from Mandalay to Master Fred Bestall, c/o Rev. W.R. Winston, North Shields, England:

My dear Freddie

This is for your birthday and I write on this painted postcard to wish you *Many Happy Returns of the Day*. We thank God that He has spared your life to reach the first stage of ten years. We both hope God may call you to do some useful work for Him in days to come.

Much love from your affectionate Father.

The card was illustrated with an elephant 'painted by [a] Burmese man'. The artist himself sent AEB another card from Mandalay on 20 March 1905: 'Hearing you like PPC's I am sending one from your Father's station and trust you will like her royal highness the Princess with her royal white elephant.'

AEB moved from North Shields to a junior school in Southsea, going on in 1904 to Rydal Mount, a Wesleyan public school in Colwyn Bay, North Wales, but the holidays must have continued to cause problems while AEB and Maisie's parents were overseas. On 26 January 1906, when AEB was thirteen, a letter was written to Rebecca from Colwyn Bay:

Dear Mrs Bestall

Before this reaches you, the news that your son has been staying with me will have arrived. I think that perhaps a letter about him may give you a little pleasure – and so I just send you word that he went off to school last evening in high good spirits. He is looking wonderfully well and is growing so fast, and so like his Mother. He was with me at the station yesterday, meeting a new boy, and Dr Rodgers the music master spoke to him – so brightly and turning to me he said this is one of my music pupils, and a very good boy – good boy! We have quite enjoyed having Freddie with us. He is so bright and intelligent, and such a little gentleman, we feel lost without him, but he is coming across tomorrow

*Painted postcards
from Burma*

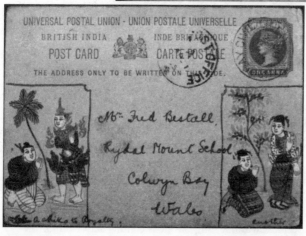

to 'cheer us up a little'. He thinks a great deal of his absent Mother. I wish you could have seen his look on Sunday morning when Corinne Feather gave him his letter! On Sunday night when we were singing hymns – Adele, Freddie and myself only – I asked for his favourite. 'Oh!' he said, 'on Sunday night "Abide with me", and it is also Mother's.' So we sang that for you, and the innocent light that boy shed on the Christian experience attained by a Mother in such circumstances as yours, by the choice of such a hymn has been a revelation – and a stimulus to me to be more and more grateful. He asked for Father's hymn next and he thought that was 'Count your blessings'. I saw Miss Matthews several times – she is simply devoted to your children; she wants to get nearer to them . . . Maisie was very well when I saw her. They are both coming for tea soon, but I cannot say so much about her, as she has not stayed with me . . .

Headmaster's House, Rydal School

It is not clear how frequently the Bestalls came home on leave, nor what effect their long absences had on their children. In 1909 the consul-general at Yokohama issued a passport to allow 'Arthur Henry Bestall, a British subject, travelling to England via Vladivostok, Siberia, Russia and other countries, accompanied by his wife Rebe Bestall to pass freely without let or hindrance and to afford them every assistance and protection of which they may stand in need'. Thus they visited the Kremlin in the days of the Tsar. The following year, 1910, Arthur was appointed to Trinity Church in Wolverhampton. AEB, meanwhile, had been quietly getting on with life at school. He won school prizes for Drawing and Classics and, in June 1911 when he took the University of London Matriculation, was placed in the Second Division in English, Mechanics, Mathematics, French and Mathematics (advanced). In December that year he was awarded a school prize for London Matriculation – appropriately enough, *Highways and Byways in North Wales* by A.G. Bradley. By the time he left Rydal Mount he was a prefect, in the first football team, captain of first XI cricket, was good at athletics, played fives, competed in the paper chase and had been involved in the artwork for school theatrical productions. The school magazine of

Rydal School Football XI 1909 (AEB is second from the left in the back row)

1910, reporting on the cricket, states: 'The fielding of Bestall at point has been one of the features of the term's play; it would be considered good in any team.' And the following year it recorded: 'A batsman of the happy-go-lucky type. Fast between the wickets. A good field.' However, it is clear where AEB's priorities lay. Writing in the Centenary edition of Rydal Mount School magazine, he explained:

My Priority No. 1 was already too well known, most of my textbooks having their margins disfigured with squiggles, caricatures and rubbish. For years some classes had been interrupted by the sharp exchange, 'Drawing again, Bestall?' – 'Yes, sir.' – 'Mark.' Sometimes the whole class would happily join in the ritual. Strangely enough, I never collected enough marks to suffer being gated, and I did not fail my exams! I just had to draw.

At the end, with London Matric looming up, my headmaster (now G.F.A. Osborn), ignoring my quick preference, made me sit three subjects allied to Maths. All went well and he strongly urged me toward the Civil Service.

But, alas, instincts just will not be denied. Within six weeks of leaving school I happened to catch a mouse in a trap, was fascinated by the subtle blend of greys that gave the contours of the tiny face, made a much enlarged watercolour painting of it and submitted that to the head of the great Birmingham Central School of Art who awarded me a three-year scholarship. Thus through a simple agency did a kindly Providence ease one O.R. [Old Rydalian] into his desired profession.

At the end of his first year AEB won a further scholarship – the sketch which gave him the award was a striking study entitled *The Strike* (see p. 16).

AEB studied at the Central School of Arts and Crafts, Margaret Street, Birmingham under R. Caterson Smith from 1911–14, travelling there from Wolverhampton. He made great friends with another art student, Harry Adams, whose parents lived in Worcester. They shared the same birthday (though Harry was two years younger). In 1912 AEB obtained first class in the Board of Education exams in the categories of 'memory drawing of plant form', 'drawing from the antique', 'geometrical drawing' and 'model drawing'.

A page from AEB's music book

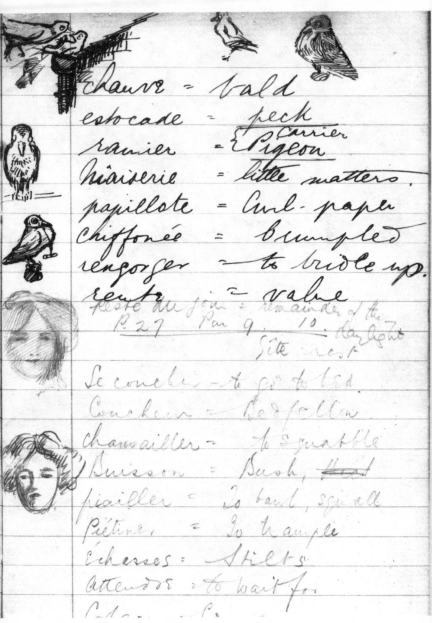

chauve = bald
estocade = peck
ramier = carrier Pigeon
niaiserie = little matters.
papillote = Curl-paper
chiffonée = crumpled
rengorger = to bridle up.
rente = value
reste du jour = remainder of the
P.27   Par 9.   10.   daylight
                  gîte nest

Se coucher - to go to bed.
Coucheur = Bedfellow.
chamailler = to squabble
Buisson = Bush, Host
piailler = To bawl, squall
Piétiner = To trample
échasses = Stilts
attendre = to wait for

A page from AEB's French vocabulary book

18 - V -12

From AEB's sketchbook, 1912

?Mother, 1912

'The Strike, June 1913, for £20 scholarship, time allowed 10 hours'

In the summer of 1912, the Bestalls took a cottage called Penlan at Trefriw in the Conway Valley, near Colwyn Bay where AEB had been at school. During that holiday he kept a journal, and spent a lot of his time walking with his dog Toby and sketching, while his father fished. The family returned to Penlan in July 1913. AEB's journal for that year as well as that for the previous year are reproduced later in this book as Wales sketchbooks . During the summer of 1914, AEB finished at art school, his parents moved from Wolverhampton to Woking, and the family probably had a third holiday at Penlan. On 16 September that year Hodder & Stoughton wrote to AEB at Penlan saying: 'We have pleasure in informing you that you have been successful in securing the second prize in our recent Poster Stamp Competition, and under separate cover are sending you the Swan fountain pen. We congratulate you on your success, and regret there has been so much delay in awarding the prizes.' On the international scene, the First World War broke out in August.

In 1915, having transferred to the LCC Central School of Art in

London, AEB began to keep a proper diary. In the front is a list of addresses for the *Tatler* and *Sphere, Bystander, Sketch, Illustrated London News, Weekly Telegraph, Punch, London Opinion, Graphic, Ideas, Cartoon, Boy's Own Paper, Passing Show, Amalgamated Press* and *Pearson's*. The first six months of the year were spent attending lectures and submitting drawings to the above journals, most of which were returned unused. However, on 6 February he submitted three drawings to *Cartoon* and on 11 February one of them, *Russian Investment*, was accepted. It was published a few days later and he received a cheque for one guinea. His father and maternal grandfather each gave him another guinea for what was his first published drawing. In May *Cartoon* rejected *Spider* but AEB accepted an offer of 7*s* 6*d* from *War Pictures Weekly*, and a few days later *Cartoon* failed. Other commissions followed. In June AEB was interviewed

Cut out from an early notebook

The Countryman (slightly mystified): " Just look at that now!
It shows the war isn't so bad as folks make out if the papers 'ave
nothing better to talk about than their furrin investments! "

AEB's first published joke drawing. It appeared in Cartoon *in February 1915 and
earned him one guinea*

by Mr John Marshall of Marshall & Snelgrove, London, about a little card
to advertise the 'Mayfair flowers' and he also did a design for the 'St
Marylebone War Hospital Depôt' poster stamp, and a drawing of a Mason
Pearson hairbrush for which he was paid four guineas (again matched by
his father). *Garibaldi* was published by *Passing Show* on 29 June and two
other sketches were published by *London Opinion* in August and September. A third was published in January 1916.

From an early sketch book

Weekends were spent with family, keeping in touch particularly with his mother's relatives at this time. (His mother's brother was Mayor of Winchester.) Sometimes AEB would go on a 'bike spin' to Newland's Corner and back. However, since the outbreak of the First World War he had been troubled by his conscience. AEB told his biographer George Perry 'For a whole year I was unable to get into the army. My chest was an inch short – in those days you had to have a full-size chest before they would allow you to go and get shot.' In 1925 the *Methodist Recorder* reported how:

At that time [1915] Fred Bestall was a delicate youth, shy and retiring, as far distant from militarist tendencies as pole from pole. His physique unfitted him for a soldier's life; but within his frail form burned the same unconquerable spirit that sent his father out as a pioneer missionary to the Burmese jungles, and after twenty-five [twenty-three, actually] years in that tropical clime inspired him to volunteer to return for another three years' term to his old field. So at the first appeal for volunteers, the young artist laid aside pencil and brush and offered himself at the nearest recruiting office for active service. The medical officer turned him down promptly as unsuitable. But Methodist ancestry and Rydal Mount training had put the iron into his blood, and he went again and again, only to be rejected. At last he said in desperation to the recruiting officer, 'Look here, you must take me; my father's been a military chaplain, and I've got to go!' Moved by the plea, the military authorities finally yielded, and put him into Mechanical Transport.

The day after being accepted AEB was sent to Osterley Park in Middlesex and at the end of September he was 'moved to Grove Park barracks with all the other first- and second-class drivers'. From Osterley Park he wrote an undated letter to his mother:

Many thanks for your PC of yesterday. I suppose you will just be thinking of returning to Woking. I discovered this morning that my last two letters to you which I had entrusted to Stevens to post were still in his pocket, so you will get quite a bunch of them after a long silence. I was at Chelsea yesterday at the school.

I suppose you know that last Tuesday's air-raid was over London. The airships passed over Hammersmith and Putney. From the camp we could hear the firing.

That being so, we were surprised last night on leaving the school in lorries at 10.45 p.m. to hear the sound of guns fairly close and, looking up, we could see the flashes of bursting shells high in the sky.

In a minute or two a huge zeppelin loomed up at a considerable height, with one searchlight playing on it, followed by another zep just above it. They were apparently just over the city and came towards us a bit before turning northwards, with the shells bursting under them. One shell apparently exploded right on the front 'gas-bag' a minute or so before it turned.[1]

They were giving off a good deal of smoke, and looked very mysterious in the pale searchlight. The night was fine, but without moon – otherwise I suppose we should have seen them more clearly. A lot of shells were being fired and bursting south of the river, but we could not see the airship in that direction.

There were crowds in the streets, who cheered and seemed impressed by the three lorries crammed with soldiers rushing along.

Please excuse more. Our spare time is quite inadequate for the amount of work we want to do.

I am putting in my pass for Sunday.

Much love to you all from Fred.

As George Perry relates, AEB told him that he was 'taken out in the charge of a bus driver, an employee of the London General Omnibus Company, the principal operator in the capital, and initiated into the mysteries of the legendary B-type engine and chassis. Many hundreds of B-types had been removed from the London streets and sent to France to be used as troop carriers, and in the early days of the war, before there had been time to repaint them in a drab military shade of khaki, homesick Tommies on their way to the front rode in red London buses still displaying advertisements for popular West End shows. Mechanically the B-type was a classic, a simple, rugged, efficient work-horse, and an early triumph of standardisation. "I became extremely fond of the B-type," AEB said, "one of the easiest vehicles I have ever driven. Even changing gear was very easy, and of course we didn't have synchromesh then. On the Albion, on the other hand, which was chain-driven, it was very much harder to change." His training complete, in January 1916 he was sent to France as a driver-mechanic.'

---

[1] Zeppelin airships raided Britain between 1915 and 1918, killing an estimated 557 people. The airship consisted of a cylindrical aluminium frame in partitions, each holding a gas-bag.

2

THE LOST YEARS

AEB in uniform

AEB SERVED IN THE 35th (Bantam) Division which, as George Perry has written, initially was meant to accommodate men below the general weight limit. 'By 1916 it had been opened up to full-size soldiers, who found themselves in the charge of bantam sergeant-majors, bantam NCOs, who [AEB] recalled ruefully, wallowed in "chucking their weight about". In the dreadful conditions of the forward areas trucks had a difficult time, and horses were still used near the front line, it being reasoned that they were more able to overcome the shell-pocked, muddy terrain. To the infantryman pinned down in the trenches the life of an army driver would have seemed like bliss, but Alfred Bestall was on many occasions under fire, and an easy target. Once in a large Thorneycroft, searching for a detached unit, he even found that he had strayed too far forward, and was confronted by a German machine gun with a crew of three, mounted in the middle of the road and aimed at him. After a momentary shock he realised that they were all dead.'[1]

AEB and company arrived in the Seine in the early hours of 28 January 1916 and disembarked at Rouen. The convoy proceeded to St Omer where very soon there was a 'raid by a German aeroplane which dropped two bombs 300 yards away, killing two English soldiers and injuring one'. They delivered many loads and maintained their lorries. In the middle of February the 'whole convoy set out for Merville which was reached in the afternoon after traversing execrable roads. Very decent big town with good shops. Went into town at night and found YMCA hut. Some men billeted in barns (we in lorries)'. Immediately there was heavy artillery bombardment, frost and snow. Soon all cameras were confiscated and sent back to England.

On one journey from Merville to Lapugnoy, near Béthune, AEB 'ob-

'Still out of reach, German Spider'
"Gott punish that fly!"
from War Pictures Weekly, *1915*
This was AEB's second published cartoon; he was paid 7/6d for it

served many interesting objects including a cart pulled by a *cow*, several pulled by dogs and an aeroplane (British) standing vertically on its nose in a

---

[1] From *Rupert: A Bear's Life*, George Perry with Alfred Bestall, London: Pavilion Books Ltd, 1985. Perry's book is hitherto the closest thing to a Rupert biography, at least as far as the Bestall years are concerned.

ploughed field near Chocques. Three kilometres out of Merville on the return we picked up eleven men and a sergeant of the North Lancs and brought them to the station. All exhausted, just out of the trenches and marching back.' The Ordnance Headquarters moved via Estaires to Bac St Maur temporarily. 'Saw several shell-battered houses,' he recorded, 'also a little English cemetery and a church of which only the tower is left (at Sailly). Slept in a disused cinema at Estaires.' On 30 March he wrote: 'Under fire for first time. Germans dropping shells at intervals over Bac St Maur. Several burst while we were there awaiting orders. One very close. Fragments whistled near and cut off twigs from tree overhanging the lorry. Aircraft and anti-aircraft very busy.' Soon after that AEB went off sick and was taken with six others in an ambulance car to a rest camp at Doulieu where his 'bed consisted of stretcher on trestles, straw palliasse and four blankets'.

Whenever possible army life was interspersed with a concert or by a football or cricket match; on one occasion he noted that Ordnance beat Signals and they also beat Armourers. In May the column started to 'rest' – that is, '[it unloaded] stuff at station for horse transport to fetch and then our troops and No. 1 have one-hour rifle drill (with bayonets) in afternoon. Full guard at night.' Only a few days later he wrote how in the evening 'we caught the tail-end of a weeping-gas attack. Humorous sight to see twenty men in billet sitting weeping. Very painful.'

In the middle of June the division moved south. Their column went to Lillers and then to Béthune. The Battle of the Somme began on 1 July, of which they were quite unaware. But on 2 July AEB recorded a 'sudden order to move at night, so having packed up, Ord. start at 11 p.m. and go through St Pol etc. to Doullens, arriving at 4 a.m. (about 45 miles). From the hill north of Pernes we had a fine panoramic view of the trenches with innumerable star shells, red and white (fire) signals, shell bursts etc. One position evidently being attacked had about a dozen star shells continually in the air. In Pernes one of our plugs burst but was soon replaced.' On 8 July they 'took load of rifles (of men killed in the advance) to railhead in afternoon. Passed many camps of artillery etc.'

Ordnance was moved rapidly around and on 13 July was at Morlancourt, a few miles south of Albert. The next day AEB 'saw lot of German prisoners. Brought load of horse-shoes. Everson missed the return route and took us nearly to Corbie, whence we returned to Morlancourt via the

Bray road. Fine views of the Somme Valley and hills and of the great church at Corbie. Constant stream of ambulances with wounded passed us. Bombardment very violent all evening and night.' The following day, on a journey to the dump, the bombardment was particularly violent. 'Some hundreds of German prisoners passed along from Bray to Corbie . . . Walked up the hill towards Méaulte in evening and had a good view of Albert and district with Mametz Wood etc. Firing on both sides very active. Germans shelling a wood near Albert very heavily to find two of our big guns, which however had been moved into a big field this side of the wood.' The next day AEB commented: 'Corbie is a delightful place with great church (or cathedral) and fine houses. At Contay we picked up the remainder of our reserve smoke helmets and returned to Morlancourt via Albert. On the way we had a look round Albert and ruins and passed right under the statue of Virgin and Child which lies horizontally away from the top of the broken church tower. Saw ruins in Fricourt and passed a lot of dug-outs and some big guns.'

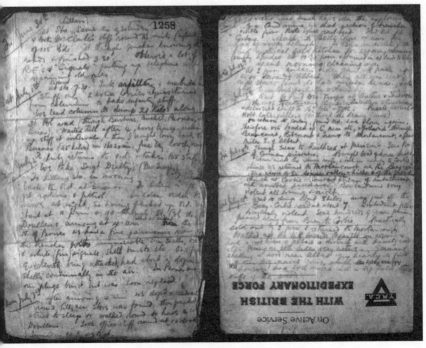

Two facsimile pages of AEB's First World War journal

A few days later, they saw large gangs of English, French and German prisoners at work repairing the roads. 'We passed some guns which were firing and dumped on a hill just behind Carnoy. Guns all round and some very close were crashing out perpetually. A walk of about 100 yards brought us to a fine viewpoint from which we could see the ruins of Carnoy and further away those of Mametz, also several woods stripped and battered. The avenue close by had also been through it severely. Several trees were smashed up and others stripped of branches. A ridge about a mile away running south-west from Mametz was being heavily shelled. Further off could be seen ridges near Bazentin. Returned slowly to Morlancourt over the shocking roads.'

On 1 August AEB recorded: 'In morning to dressing station just off the Bray–Corbie road to fetch salvage. Much of the clothing blood-soaked. While we were there seven or eight corpses were brought in from an adjoining marquee and placed on ambulances for burial. The bodies were each swathed in a blanket and covered with a Union Jack. Great heat. Had rest of day for cleaning as no truck came in at Grow Town.' There was a sudden move to Cavillon, a pretty village west of Amiens, for just three weeks, and while they were there a great number of Indian cavalry went past, westward. One evening AEB and a colleague managed to bathe in the Somme.

AEB's father was doing YMCA work in Paris, and with difficulty AEB managed to get short leave to join him, setting off at 5.15 a.m. It was a Sunday evening when they met and AEB had a 'ripping hot bath and then a big meal' before hearing Arthur preach at the Paris Wesleyan Church. He finally 'turned in between real sheets'. They had until four o'clock the next day for hectic sightseeing, after which Arthur left, though AEB was able to remain until the 11.40 p.m. train. His diary recorded: 'Last glimpse of Paris was a horrible street fight between two reprobate women.' However, he had managed to buy some ink and immediately began sketching whenever there was a lull.

Early in September they rejoined their own Ordnance again at Duisans, west of Arras. One day AEB wrote he 'saw [a] Red Cross train smashed up at Tincques – all windows broken and projecting parts torn away'. Nevertheless he was able to appreciate the countryside on his journeys: 'wonderful scenery with autumn tints, specially from Le Cauroy to Frévent'. He went to Arras one evening in November for some empty barrels. 'Managed to get a walk through some of the most ruined squares and saw Hôtel de Ville etc.', he wrote. 'No moon, but star shells nearby made it light enough to see a lot in detail.' They moved again in early December to Roëllecourt, just east of St Pol. On Christmas Day it was to the railhead as usual to collect supplies and then to Gouves, but at 3 p.m. they had a Christmas dinner. 'A previous whip round with subs according to rank had provided three turkeys and a leg of pork, also greens and potatoes.'

As a distraction from the war they tried a makeshift cinema. In January 1917 AEB recorded going to the cinema barn. However, a trial performance in the evening broke down after half an hour and he sat up all night to wind the engine and prevent its freezing. This happened time and again, but occasionally they managed to have a good show. At the beginning of February they moved south to Vignacourt and two weeks later to Caix, well south of the Somme and east of Amiens. They found crowds of French soldiers had not yet gone. A month later there was a sudden move to nearby Rosières.

AEB had a most interesting run with ammunition for the Cheshires at their new headquarters. He wrote in his diary how he went 'across old front line, no man's land and German lines (battered and shelled out of all shape) to Roye. Arrived there at the minute that a car was leaving, containing President Poincaré and Sir Douglas Haig after a visit. Hundreds of French soldiers on parade. Went on the Péronne road through Liancourt and later turned off to find the Cheshires at Curchy. Interesting to note all the German signs, notices and graves. Many fine avenues cut down for timber etc. Roads well strewn with shell holes, especially near the line, but not so bad as expected. Curchy burnt out all except the church, but Roye not so much hurt. Dumped ammunition. Picked up 800 blankets and returned after dark by same route.' A few days later there were sudden orders to move to Nesle: 'Noticed that the Germans had cut down or blazed every fruit tree in sight and nearly half of the big trees in the avenues. Nesle is a most attractive place, not too badly burnt or destroyed, with lots of inhabitants left who mostly stood in smiling clusters at their front doors watching progress of settling in of the British.' However, two weeks later the Ordnance headquarters was moved to Monchy-Lagache. Near there AEB saw the Prince of Wales pass in a big car at Tertry.

At the beginning of April Vermand and Marteville were in German hands. On 30 April AEB picked up trench covers and took them to both places as he had done a week before. 'Watched shells bursting over the front near St Quentin,' he wrote. 'Also serial battle. Then through Villeveque (of which not a wall stands) to Beauvois. Picked up rations and returned to Monchy-Lagache.' The next day there was a sudden call at 6.45 p.m. to take tents to Marteville. 'Went as yesterday. Found Germans had shelled the place all afternoon and only just stopped. A dug-out 10 yards away from where lorry had stood on two previous occasions had been shattered by shell and eight men blown to small pieces which were partially collected and laid on strips of iron for identification. Germans heavily shelling three of our planes flying close and low. Returned via Beauvois where we picked up the mails (9 p.m.).'

Ordnance moved again on 20 May, north and slightly east of Péronne, to new headquarters 'by [the] roadside near Nurlu overlooking wide view of the Bouchavesnes hills and Somme battlefield. Parked on grass by marquees. Slept on lorry.' A month later the diary entry recorded: 'Lawrence woke me at 4 a.m. and we started out with lorry to pick up some paint that had fallen off his car last night coming back from St Pol. Went through . . . to "Bullet Road" (near Sailly-Saillisel on the Bapaume road). Of Bouchavesnes and Rancourt hardly a brick remains. All has been cleared for road repairing. Every tree stripped and broken, poor road. Innumerable graves chiefly of French and Germans. Put the paint from barrel into petrol cans and returned to Ord. at 7 a.m. Did nothing rest of day except clean up.' Five days later he wrote: 'To canteen (Nurlu) in morning. With the salvage men in afternoon through Moislains and Haut Allaines to Cléry to pick up a load of shovels. Dreadfully battered about. Had a walk over part of the battlefield. Hundreds of graves all of French and Germans.' And the following week: 'At 4.30 while at Villers-Faucon saw a German biplane attack a near kite balloon (probably the one sent up from Heudicourt). Just in the nick of time he was struck by shrapnel from our anti-aircraft (near Longavesnes). He plunged right over the balloon and then nose-dived to the ground.'

In July AEB was suddenly sent on leave. He had a slow and difficult journey by lorry, train (partly in cattle trucks) and then by escorted ship from Le Havre to Southampton. On his way through London he went to

Fleet Street and met Mr McKenzie, the art editor of *Blighty*, to whom he submitted two drawings. (He was eventually paid two guineas for them.) He spent just over a week quietly at home in Woking, drawing, going for bike rides and 'motor spins', and seeing relatives.

As well as transporting goods, AEB, now back in France at Roisel, was moving prisoners around in August. On 9 September 1917 he wrote to his mother:

Another change of address! I have now been back with the Ordnance two days and am very glad to be with the old crowd for a while. It is not quite the same now that there is only one lorry on the job instead of four, but there is not too much work. Yesterday we had a ripping long run (nearly 120 miles all told), full of interest all the way and visited places I have not seen since mid-winter. Having all the rich colouring of early autumn, the places were greatly changed from the somewhat bleak and leafless spots we knew last Christmas.

The drive was longer than usual for our bumpy lorry and although we divided the driving equally, we were both pretty well washed out at the end of it, so that I was very pleased to get back at night and find a letter from you awaiting me. It was written on the 2nd from Winchester and had followed me up from the column.

You have had a much longer time with the old people than I had anticipated, and all my recent letters have been addressed to Woking, but I suppose you got them eventually.

What a weird journey Father must have had back from Havre following behind the four minesweepers! Did he make the crossing in daylight? I hope he has had an enjoyable weekend with Mr Bayliss.

I am very glad to hear that you are really better for your holiday. From the accounts in Father's recent letters it seems as though his vacation has been too strenuous to be much refreshment to him.

Now I must close as I am going with two or three others to the evening service in the headquarters church. It will be the first (excepting occasional YMCA services) that I have been able to get to for some time.

It seems quite like a visit home to get back to Ord. for a time.

Much love to you all from Fred.

Another letter survives written three days later:

Two of your letters, written on the 6th and 7th, have just come. I am glad you are all safely back from your holidays and are all the better for the change.

A big parcel has come from Evelyn [AEB's cousin] since I last wrote containing some good socks, a lot of peppermints and choc., a set of dominoes and this pad. It is wonderful what attractive parcels they make at Westminster.

You must have been surprised to get a third copy of the inoculation sketch from the Editor [of *Blighty*]. It is very curious that the August 15th number has never reached you. I will send back the page out of it and also the page out of the Summer number.

In your letter of the 7th you enquire where a certain town is and I don't know how precisely I may tell you. However it is off those bird's-eye maps of Father's and is pretty well out of the war area, south of the Somme.

We have been getting lovely weather for the past fortnight and have been running about a lot.

The second round of leave has commenced both here and on the column, so it is unlikely that anyone will have such a wait as the first.

Cheerioh.

Much love to you all from Fred.

PS. I have heard from Adams again. He is right away from the line now, having a rest.[2]

In October they moved to Harbarcq, west of Arras (with their headquarters in a château), and then again north to Arnèke, north-west of Cassel. From there they went to Proven, not far from Ypres. On 25 October AEB wrote that he 'spent day partly in hut-building and partly in laying bricks in a new stable. Went at night with six others and Corporal Adams through Boezinge and past Bard's Causeway to Bard's cottage beside Pilkem ridge on the Ypres road. Slept in a dug-out. Heavy bombardment. Hun air-raid at night.' Three days later, after a ceaseless cannonade, they were working

---

[2] Harry Adams was seriously wounded and shellshocked at Passchendaele and was very delicate for the rest of his life.

on the new stables when, as the diary recorded, 'At 5 p.m. the Germans put three over. The first dropped 100 yards off near the stables and burst harmlessly in the ground, the second burst over the same spot and the third was a dud.' Another day, 'a bomb had killed four mules close by which lay in the roadway in bits in a pool of blood'.

In December they moved south again in stages, to Arras and then Bapaume (where there was an excellent night-time concert by the 'Tonics'). On his birthday, 14 December, AEB was out at 5 a.m.; he did a lot of driving and dumping and then was 'off again with the column at 4.30. Went via Albert, Acheux, Louvencourt and Marieux to Beauquesne. Parked up there 10 p.m. Some birthday!' Then there was heavy snow and frost. They transferred to a new park in a huge farmyard on the outskirts of Ablainzevelle and two days later were on the road again. Christmas Day was described as follows: 'Energetic morning, cleaned lorries. Cleaned ourselves up in afternoon. Dinner at 5.30 . . . of turkey, ham, greens, potatoes, plum pudding etc. Very fine spread. Sing-song afterwards in the hut.'

Early in January 1918 they drove 80 miles back to their park on the

" WELL, OF ALL THE BALLY PERSPIRING COUNTRIES, THIS ——— ! " (*Deleted by Censor*).
Pte. A. E. Bestall, M.T., A.S.C.

'Deleted by Censor', Blighty, *May 1918*

Pop–Proven road. When the thaw came they were unable to take the lorries out for a bit and often had to help one another pull the vehicles out of a ditch. AEB spent an afternoon designing an Army Service Corps gravestone and in March he spent a morning on a poster for the column concert party. On 13 March he enquired about leave and three days later was back home (having crossed from Calais to Dover on the *Scotia* escorted by two destroyers). He spent his time much as before and had an hour's chat with Mr McKenzie when he took in two more drawings for *Blighty*. He also visited Harry Adams at Springfield Hospital in South London where he had been sent after Passchendaele.

When AEB returned to France at the end of March he had three nights in camp in Calais and then all the 35th Division men went by overnight train to Vignacourt. They moved around the Amiens and Somme area where one day 'halfway up hill beyond Ordnance an aeroplane apparently English turned a machine gun on us and wounded several men of the Australian transport near us. Heard afterwards that D159 Batty brought him down and found a German in one of our captured planes.' Sir Douglas Haig visited Hérissart in May but AEB did not see him. His mother wrote and told of his father's reception by the King on 7 May.[3]

AEB continued sketching for *Blighty* in spite of heavy German air-raids at times and he also completed a portrait of Sergeant Birkill. 'They soon found out that I was an artist,' he said later to George Perry. 'Drawing kept me occupied during the evenings, which could be deadly boring. I didn't drink at that time, and some of my friends would be in the bars getting so helpless that I would have to frogmarch them back. They would ask me to do sketches of their girls from snapshots, so I made a lot of portraits. Even the officers would ask me to do portraits for them.'

At the beginning of June AEB saw thousands of American infantry coming in. He was inoculated and that made him quite feverish – his temperature was 103 degrees the day before they were on the move again. They left Beauquesne on 1 July and went in stages back to the Cassel area to the north. There they were close to the shelling. In August AEB managed

---

[3] The Reverend Arthur Bestall had first met King George V in Burma, when he was Prince of Wales, and some years later the King had invited Arthur to lunch at Windsor. Of Burma the King said, 'The only thing I didn't like was the mosquitoes', to which Arthur replied, 'But I bet the mosquitoes liked Your Majesty!'.

to get a pass to visit Paris where his father was again busy doing YMCA work. AEB had a whole week for sightseeing this time, some of it with Arthur, and he bought some materials in an art shop, including Bristol board.

In October they were very close to the action. One day they retrieved seventeen German guns and brought them back to Ordnance. Then 'our lorry and Kirby's via Ypres and the Menin road and Hooge and over the ridges to fetch two German guns from Geluveld. Very exposed place in full view of a town, probably Comines or Wervicq. Just as Kirby had a gun hitched on, a salvo of little shells pitched and burst within 20 yards. No one hurt. Shelling ceased after five minutes. Other gun immovable, partly buried, so returned via Clapham Junction and plank road to Biro cross-roads and Ypres.' Four days later they were looking for the 159 Brigade which had moved. They 'followed up to the next crossroads where the advanced dressing station was. Scores of lightly wounded British and Germans crowding round for attention. Also streams of prisoners (four to a stretcher) carrying in our more serious cases. Shrapnel flying about. Could not find the brigade, so returned. On the plank road past Clapham Junction got held up two hours through a Foden skidding off. Called for rations near Zillebeke, but were unable to get any.'

The next day they had another attempt to make their delivery, but they could not get up the Menin road and the Geluveld road was impassable, so they went to the left to Terhand. 'Execrable road,' AEB wrote. 'Passed through a battery of about ten howitzers near Terhand all firing at top speed. Ear-splitting din. From Terhand took a little road to the south and were lucky to get right through to the little townlet of Geluwe which was in German hands yesterday morning. On the outskirts passed a number of dead, both ours and Germans, some by the roadside, others on the wire, and in shell-holes. Also two German machine guns in position. Just in Geluwe were confronted with a crater at a crossroads, but just managed to squeeze around it with great good luck. Thence we followed the Menin road back to the Nieuwe Kruiseecke crossroads, delivered the jerkins at the ARP [Air Raid Precautions] and came straight back. In afternoon went to draw rations near Zillebeke and to Vlamertinghe for water.'

The depôt moved east to Bissegem, on the outskirts of Courtrai. Finally, on Sunday 10 November, after a busy day: 'At 8 pm saw star shells bursting over Courtrai and heard cheering. Rushed off to the town and joined the crowd which was shouting and going mad in celebration of the armies' truce which had just been signed.[4] Went to the Grande Place to watch the bonfire of German sign-boards and the Very lights [hand-held flares] etc. Went back to depôt at 11 p.m.' The driving continued, moving salvage and so on, and at the end of the month they started the trek towards the coast.

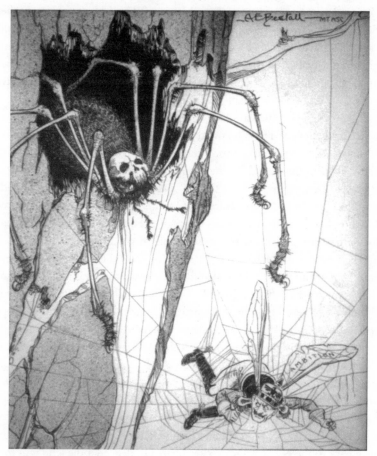

'Nemesis', a drawing of the broken ambition of the Kaiser by 'Private AEB 304 M.T. Coy ASC', c.1918

[4] Although signed on 10 November, the truce actually came into effect at the eleventh hour of the eleventh day of the eleventh month. The troops were not demobbed until several months afterwards.

Letters and a parcel from home arrived on 13 December 1918, and in his reply AEB wrote to Rebecca:

My dear Mother

It is not quite my birthday yet, but I had better begin to write and thank you for all the lovely things that have just come lest I should not be able to get it all done tomorrow.

At about four o'clock your letters of last Sunday were brought to me from Ordnance and at teatime the big parcel arrived, having been forwarded from DADOS [Deputy Assistant Director of Ordnance Services] by a thoughtful orderly.

The pocket book from Pop seemed to be a specially nice one with conveniences for everything one can want to put down. Please thank her very much for it and also for the letter enclosed in yours which I must soon answer.

The various 'goodies' in the box look fine. I have not dug into the cake or the 'pruins', but shall not be long in doing so, and will let you know in due course what they are like. I am delighted to see that you have been able to get [camera] films again. The set that you have now sent should be enough to last during the remainder of my stay out here.

Finally very many thanks for the little calendars which will be just the thing to stick on a couple of Christmas or New Year designs if I manage to finish any. The Xmas card design about which I spoke last autumn was to have been a big affair. It was during the peaceful time when we lay at the foot of Cassel that Major Stower advised me to submit a design for a Xmas card for the Army we were in. Unfortunately, as soon as I had commenced the drawing there came that fearful rush after the retreating Jerry over Hooge ridge, which left no one the opportunity to indulge in such a recreation as sketching. We had no breathing space till we got to Bissegem, near Courtrai, by which time the final day for submitting designs was long past. I was not allowed to be idle even then, for Mr McKenzie's rather urgent note turned up, and I had to get him some stuff for his Xmas number.

To turn to your letters: I am awfully sorry to hear of the death of Mr Winston [who had looked after AEB in Sheffield and North Shields] . . .

The rest of the letter is missing.

Pencil sketch for Blighty,
October 1918
*New Draft (who has reached his
battalion before an expected
advance): 'Ye'll sune learn
a'about real war-r, I'm thinkin'.'
Blasé Veteran: 'Och ay the wife
sends me the illustrated papers
every week.'*

Pencil sketch for Blighty,
April 1919
*1st Tommy: 'I wonder they don't
get the prisoners to work at
re-building these villages.'
2nd Tommy: 'Not likely. They
don't want to have all their
bloomin' houses Jerry-built.'*

On his birthday AEB managed to do some sketching for *Blighty* and go to the pictures. On Christmas Eve he had his first experience of Albion driving and on Christmas Day he wrote that he was 'supposed to be on piquet all day. Drew rations in morning and cooked them ourselves in garage. Walked to Lille in afternoon. Fine concert in YMCA at 6 p.m. by Lena Asherell party. Lena Asherell herself turned up. Bouquets to all the ladies at the close.' On Boxing Day he walked to Lille again, got some snapshots and in the evening 'joined party from workshops at the pantomime *Aladdin* at the Nouveau Théâtre. Very good. Leslie Henson and Bert Errol the star performers.' On 6 January he sent off 'panto sketches and two others to *Blighty*' and at the end of the month 'went with Lieutenant Briscoe in evening behind the scenes at the Nouveau Théâtre. Met Leslie Henson and Bert Errol etc. Did rough sketches of several characters and watched parts of the show from the wings.'

AEB had one more leave in England at the end of February, travelling via Calais and Folkestone. He had a fortnight at home, did a lot of drawing and went to see Mr McKenzie again (who returned his panto sketch from Lille). There was still much driving to be done (moving salvage) when he returned to France but at the end of May he 'transferred kit to a tent and checked the tools on the lorry. Then drove her to the Reserve Vehicle park at St Omer and said goodbye to old A1.' On 19 June he wrote to Rebecca from Somain:

My dear Mother

I am writing this from the platform of Somain station, a place I had never heard of till last night. If you have a map of the Douai district you will find Somain about 16 kilometres from that place.

Yesterday we (ten of us) left St Omer by the wrong train. We should have caught a train which got us to Lille about 3 p.m., but instead of that we took the 'Return Leave' train due to reach Lille about midnight.

First it took us back to Arques, and then meandered southwards to Aire, Berguette, Lillers, Lapugnoy and Pernes. Then just missing St Pol we ran through Roëllecourt, waited an hour for dinner at Tincques and went on into Arras!

After that we crossed the old battlefields south-east of Vimy to Vitry and Douai and stopped for tea at Montigny . . . The next stop was Somain, an important junction near the coalmining district, and hearing

'*"Aladdin". Some after-impressions of The Gaieties pantomime produced at the Nouveau Théâtre, Lille, by Leslie Henson, Season 1918–1919.' The caption next to the drawing of Leslie Henson has the words: 'Abanazar the Magician: "Four thousand years have I slept – wonder if my demobilisation papers are through"'. Leslie Henson, 1891–1957, became a distinguished English comedian.*

that there was a concentration camp here we dropped off the train at 10 p.m. and begged a bed and breakfast. The camp was in an old factory which the Germans had turned into a well-appointed barracks. The beds made of timber and wire were built in three tiers all down the sides of a long room. I chose a sound one about 10 feet from the ground. This morning we had a sort of breakfast and then missed the civilian train we had meant to catch to Lille, with the consequence that we have to amuse ourselves strolling about the little town till 3.45 when the next one goes.

The latter part of the journey was interesting as I had not been east of Arras before. One has to get to the German side of the old line to realise the importance of the Vimy ridge. Although it is of no great height it dominates a very wide stretch of the flat land towards Vitry-en-Artois.

The battlefield does not look very different from the rest of the line, and has not been too drastically 'tidied up'.

A great feature of the old lines is the display of poppies. Wherever the earth had been freshly turned – in trench parapets, shellholes, or new graves – the poppies seem to have planted themselves before the ordinary grass, and in some places one can follow for miles the irregular line of an old trench sharply defined by millions of these blood-coloured flowers growing along its edge and showing up strongly against the grey-green wilderness around.

Douai looks a fine place with fine towers. The train did not run into the town but skirted round it . . .

We shall not be sorry to get to the end of our journey. It is rather absurd to take two days over a journey that I made direct the other day in three hours with my lorry. It is rather like making a trip from Woking to Oxford and popping in at Aberystwyth and Trefriw en route.

The 8th Corps Mechanical Transport Company is stationed here at Somain and I found that their June 1915 [intake] men are just demobilised, so, if all other companies in the area are equally advanced, it will be good for my chance.

I am enclosing a few real photos of rather interesting war-area scenes which an enterprising St Omer photographer is selling.

Now I think I will close and have another look round the place.

Will write again from Lille.

With much love to you all from Fred.

10 p.m. Same day. Have arrived in Lille. Will write tomorrow. F.

The battlefield does not look very different from the rest of the line, & has not been dramatically "tidied up".

A great feature of the old lines is the display of poppies. Wherever the earth has been freshly turned,—in french Dugouts, shell-holes, or new graves, the poppies seem to have planted themselves before the ordinary grass, & in some places one can follow to Hidos the irregular line

Of an old trench sharply defined by millions of these blood-coloured flowers running along its edge & shining up strongly against the

Donai looks a fine place but the towns the train did not run into the Town but slipped round it. "Griffydans" probably knows all about it.

We shall not be sorry to get to the end of our journey. It is rather absurd to take two days over a journey that I made direct the other day in three hours with my lorry.

It is rather like making a trip from Woking to Oxford & popping in at Aberystwith & Brighton en route.

Facsimile page of a letter to Rebecca from Somain, June 1919

In another letter, written from La Madeleine, Lille, on 20 June 1919, he continued:

> I posted to you last night, and this is only just another line to say that I am in the new company.
>
> After leaving Somain between Douai and Valenciennes last evening we reached Lille in about four hours after a change and one and a half hours' wait at Orchies. The latter is a little junction and town 26 kilometres south of Lille which the Germans for some reason burnt out early in the war.
>
> On arriving at Lille the sergeant in charge of the party phoned through to our new company who at once sent a lorry to fetch us from the station out to this fine suburb of La Madeleine, 2 kilometres out on the Roubaix road, and on a hill.
>
> The company workshops are in the grounds of an enormous convent, built on three sides of a square, which probably gives its name to this suburb. The interior of the convent is badly shattered, but there are sufficient rooms still intact to make a fine dining-hall, cook-house, QM [quartermaster] stores etc. for the company.
>
> This morning they took all our particulars and gave us the rest of the day off, so we begin work in the morning.
>
> This afternoon there has at last been a good fall of warm rain which is very welcome. I walked to Lille and back in it and quite enjoyed it. I hope they are having the same thing in England. The papers say they need it badly enough.
>
> I am quite uncertain what work we shall have to do here, or even whether we shall stay here or be transferred to yet another company, but for the present please address letters to Pte. AEB 112832 – MTRASC[5] – 5th. Army Troops MT Company, Lille, Brit. Armies in France.
>
> Demob is going uncommonly well here, and we are all hoping that we shall be kept on the strength of this company and not transferred elsewhere.
>
> These workshops are going to be a fixture here for three years, and

---

[5] Mechanical Transport Royal Army Service Corps.

nearly all the personnel are 1916 men or otherwise ineligible for release, which gives us few eligible ones a good chance.

Please excuse more for the present.

With very much love to you all from Fred.

On 26 June AEB recorded: 'Order posted up for my demob.' He boarded the *Princess Victoria* at Boulogne on 3 July and had a smooth crossing to Dover. They went by train to Crystal Palace, 'put our kits in grandstand of football ground and had some dinner. Then picked up kits and handed in the various parts of our equipment at the Ordnance room. Then had pay and ration books and another meal. Left Crystal Palace at 8.30. Train to Victoria and bus to Waterloo. Had a wash and caught the 9.35. Arrived Woking 10.30.

Fini.'

AEB ended the war still a private. 'He had been offered promotion to corporal,' wrote George Perry in his biography, 'but it would have meant a desk job, and he had found that the open-air life on the road had been beneficial for his health.' No doubt his artistic talent helped him through the war and, as an article in the *Methodist Recorder* in 1962 observed, the experience indelibly confirmed him in his faith: 'Although a son of the manse, it was his army life in Flanders that finally brought him the realisation of the necessity for complete dedication as a Christian and of the privilege of belonging to our Church.'

3

THE BIG SHINIES

A CHRISTENING

For the 'christening' of a child's autograph album

WHEN AEB CAME HOME from France in July 1919 he found that his grandfather (Alfred Edmeades senior) had been living with AEB's parents in Woking since the death of his wife in April 1919. AEB soon put the war behind him and relaunched himself into the world of art, which had always been his ambition. He continued to draw for *Blighty* until the end of the year and, by February 1920, he was working full time in the Byron Studios in Farringdon Avenue, London, just after 'finishing Grandpa's portrait on litho transfer paper'. He attended evening classes at the LCC Central School of Art and in 1921 he began working independently at 36 Whitefriar's Street. He shared studio accommodation there over the years with fellow artists Fraser, Cox, Newman, Blake and James.

Alfred Edmeades (1833–1922), AEB's grandfather. Original drawing for a lithograph, 1919

AEB's life settled into a routine of working five and a half days a week, attending church twice on Sundays, going to concerts and playing or watching all kinds of sport. The Bestalls moved to Guilford Avenue in Surbiton in 1920 and AEB began a sixty-year association with Surbiton Wesleyan Church (later called Surbiton Hill Methodist Church). He sang in the choir for forty-four years and filled many roles – Sunday-school pianist, chapel steward, pew rent collector, tennis-club secretary, all offices of the badminton club at various periods, and he was a church trustee from 1928–67. The routine was interrupted in July 1922 by the death of his grandfather, a man of 'strong intellect, tireless energy and deep spirituality' who used to spend the first hour of every day with his Bible and who revelled in the hymns of Wesley.

Later in 1922 AEB drew for *Punch* for the first time – 'commenced drawing at 6 p.m. and finished at 9.45'. His work appeared five days later, realising an ambition he had held since schooldays and, furthermore, he then heard that his *Waterman Boatman* entry for the *Evening News* Waterman Pen poster competition had won first prize.

Study of a nude girl, lithograph, c.1920

In August AEB put his bicycle on the train for Torquay and had a West Country holiday with Harry Adams, his great friend from art-school days. He was reminded of that time over sixty years later when my daughter, aged twelve, on holiday in Dorset, sent him a card. He replied:

Thank you for your picture of Durdle Door. Your neat writing is just right for getting a lot on to a postcard. It took my mind back a very long way for it is just sixty-two years since I saw that piece of coast. A friend and I had not long left the army and we decided on an interesting trip, taking our cycles by train to Torquay and calling at every coastal place on the way back to Poole.

Cartoon for Punch, *1922*
Mrs Giles (ignorant of the latest form of stunt
advertising): 'Coom, Jarge, quick! One o' them
woireless messages 'as caught foire'.

At Lulworth we put up at the obvious hotel and set off to walk the downs on the east of the cove until we reached the high shelf containing large ammonites near the top of the cliff. The shelf was a few feet lower than the top of the down and we wandered there fascinated and out of sight of everybody (as we thought!) until three shells screamed just over our heads and splashed far out to sea.

Realising we must be trespassing on a firing range, we edged back keeping our heads down until we met the luckless sentry whose job it had been to prevent us going on the downs at all!

Did you get to Poole? Just over a century ago your great-great-[great-] grandparents Thomas and Sarah Edmeades lived there with their son Robert, ancestor of our many New Zealand relatives. I renovated the grave of Thomas and Sarah (who died in 1882) for the sake of New Zealanders who wanted to see it, but the weather and the birds will have made it as shabby as ever.[1]

---

[1] Thomas became a brewer and he and Sarah were received into membership of Surrey Wesleyan Chapel in 1844 – a strange juxtaposition.

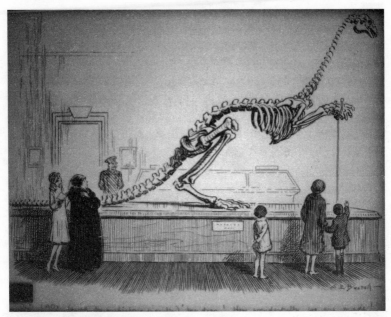

Cartoon for Punch, *1925*
Old Lady (awed by prehistoric monster): 'My dear! How wonderfully we are made!'

Cartoon for Punch, *1929*
Female (at a sale, to shop walker): 'Hi, how much is this brolly?'

Cartoon for Punch, *1924*
Young Wife (confiding in friend):
'Do you know, it's terribly hard to
convince Jack that I'm always
right.'

Cartoon for Punch, *1922*
Mother: 'Whatever are you
doing, darling?'
Peggy (who has just buried
her pet kitten): 'We we just
fought we'd ring up Heaven,
Mummy, to tell them that
Kitty's on the way.'

Cartoon for Punch, *1925*
Superior Boy *(finding brother very
sick after smoking a stolen cigar):
'Good Heavens, man what can you
expect? You've been and smoked it
with the band on!'*

Cartoon for Punch, *1935*
*'There you are, darling, you
see — we* are *going the right
way!'*

Cartoon for Punch, *1935*
'Looking for a letter, Mum, the
Professor was using as a
bookmark yesterday!'

Cartoon for Punch, *1933*
'There, look! That's the
kind of perm. I'm going to
have.'

Just before AEB went away again, this time to his beloved North Wales where he completed his first oil painting of Llyn Dinas and Moel Hebog, he 'finished *Punch* drawing but did not please Mr Reynolds with it. Must redraw'. Another one was accepted, called *Two kiddies phoning to Heaven.* He submitted three roughs on his return and found that they were to be looked at by E.H. Shepard in place of Frank Reynolds who was on holiday.

'Oh, Harold, how wonderful! And to think we forgot the glasses!'
'Well, my dear, can't we drink out of the bottles?!'
Cartoon for Tatler, 1935

In 1924 AEB's father, Arthur Bestall, who had returned to Burma in 1920, was awarded the Kaisar-i-Hind medal for public service there, and Rebecca, accompanied by AEB, went out to Egypt to meet him on his way home. AEB's journal of the ten-week journey is transcribed later in this book in the Egypt, Middle East and Europe sketchbook. On their return Arthur was appointed to Southsea, where he and Rebecca remained until 1930. AEB returned to Surbiton, living in a hotel called Sutherland House, and from time to time taking rooms in Bloomsbury.

In 1925 AEB's progress in his chosen field was described in the *Methodist Recorder*:

Practically every week in the pages of *Punch* the interested reader may discover in the corner of a delightfully executed humorous drawing the signature 'A.E. Bestall'. Mr Bestall, who is the only son of the Chairman of the Portsmouth District, whose work in the Burmese Mission-field is famous throughout the Connexion, has gained a firm foothold on the artistic ladder and may reasonably look forward to ascending to a higher place in the years that lie before him. I had the pleasure, the other day, of mounting to the sixth storey of a building just off Fleet Street where, in his little studio, Mr Bestall works, looking out westwards over the roofs and chimney-pots of the Street of Ink to the towers of Westminster and the distant Surrey hills. Turning over his portfolio of drawings, I was struck by the sound and conscientious quality of his draughtsmanship, by the happiness of his delineation of children and girls, and by the deepening note of individuality expressed in his portrayal of contemporary scenes and personalities. His work in *Punch*, whilst displaying distinctive individuality, carries on the tradition of conscientious and finished draughtsmanship and careful technique founded by Keene. His humour is clean and quiet, good-natured comment rather than satire; and he finds his best subjects in light and graceful portrayal of society figures and the denizens of well-to-do nurseries. He acknowledges many kindnesses received from the regular staff of *Punch* artists, and particularly from the present art editor, Mr Frank Reynolds, a blunt critic, but a big-hearted man.

Asked what advice he would give to a beginner in the career of graphic humorist, Mr Bestall laid stress on the necessity of preserving originality

AEB in his studio, 1925

and self-expression. 'Learn your technique at the art school, but don't stay too long' was his counsel. 'If you do, you risk losing your most precious asset, individuality, and becoming a mere reproducer of other people's ideas. Art schools turn out many admirable art teachers, but their tendency is, by immersion in technique, to overlay the individuality and power of self-expression of the student. To gain a position in the world of art, you must put your individuality into your work. Above all, avoid imitating the work of well-known people like Baumer or Bateman or Belcher. Keep on sketching from life after you have left the art school, and bear in mind that no success comes without real work.' In addition to his humorous contributions to *Punch* and other weekly papers, Mr Bestall does a good deal of illustrating work and some posters. One of the best known of the latter is a Waterman

pen advertisement representing a jolly sailor using a fountain-pen in a boat, mounting an almost perpendicular wave. But his main ambition is to be able to turn his attention to portraiture. He loves this type of work above all others, and if I may judge from the specimens he showed me, he should one day achieve a still greater reputation for his talent as a portrait artist.

AEB took holidays once or twice a year. Almost every year from 1921 he went to North Wales, staying frequently at Snowdon View Farm, Nantgwynant, near Beddgelert. After his first

Artist friend Peter Fraser, litho transfer

Joan Jenkin, litho transfer, 1928

visit he wrote in the visitors' book: 'Have received every possible kindness from Mrs Owen and family, and, with weather almost as kind to us as our fair bevy of hostesses, the all too brief fortnight has been flawless. Can only hope to come again at the earliest possible moment.' He attended St Mary's

Phyllis Bell, daughter of Bestall cousin Jessie Bell, litho transfer, 1922

Artist friend, Don Goring, 1924

Church in Beddgelert, usually on a Sunday morning, and chapel in the evening. In addition to the Welsh holidays, he went sailing twice on the Norfolk Broads with Graham Hopkins from the Byron Studios and other artist friends, he spent an Easter exploring Northumberland, he went to Devon and Cornwall with his mother and sister, and in 1926 to Scotland with his cousin, Frank, where they clocked up 1,360 miles. Shortly after that AEB bought his first car – a Singer 10.

He was not ignoring his artistic development, going to his first etching class in 1926 and rejoining the evening Central Art School life class. His own output was prodigious. Speaking of this era in 1981 he recalled 'the enormous amount of pleasure' his forty or more 'full-colour paintings for

Sketch of Nantgwynant, North Wales

Tatler' had given him. He had, however, 'a fixation with *Punch*' and contributed 112 drawings to this 'the most prestigious magazine of the period'. In a letter in 1985 he said of his work for the 'big shinies': 'My hectic, snobbish *Punch–Tatler* spell 1923–30 has just about been forgotten and, I fear, may reappear on the back of *Rupert*!' He completed *The Crevasse* for *Tatler* after his first holiday in the French Alps in 1927. His visits to his cousin Godfrey at Cambridge University between 1926 and 1930 resulted in *St John's Bridge, Cambridge, during the May Races* and *The Mill* at Grantchester.

Every May saw the beginning of the tennis season, every October from 1927 badminton started in the church hall, round Christmas time there was the Chelsea Arts Ball at which AEB and the Central Art School students did stunts. Motoring was a great interest and by Easter 1927 AEB had replaced the Singer with a Morris Oxford. He visited his parents in Southsea and frequently acted as chauffeur to his friends. He often took out the Jenkin family, for instance, and he used the Jenkin children as models in illustrations for *Magic Rhymes* by Alfred Dunning.

In 1930 AEB helped his parents (plus cat and kitten) with their 'removal from Southsea to Dorchester'. The following January he wrote to Rebecca before departing for a Swiss skiing holiday in Grindelwald with several friends from Surbiton:

My dear Mother

The tie was a great surprise this morning. It should go very well with my new suit (which, by the way, is the only suit other than dress clothes which I am taking abroad) and it was a great bit of luck your picking it up. You seem to go on taking evening work and I hope you can put up with it without entirely fagging yourself.

My week was a very social one – Adams came up on Thursday and took me away all day. We tried to get into Olympia but couldn't and played miniature golf. Then at night I took second prize at Durbin's whist drive.

Friday evening – Rampton's children's party in the primary room – about thirty there and a hectic noisy time.[2] During one game I fell over

---

[2] The Rampton family lived in Guilford Avenue and were staunch members of the Surbiton Hill Methodist Church.

and immediately had the whole lot on my chest, after which I was carried round the room (upside-down and spread-eagled) by about a dozen of the kids who yelled war-cries. Very good for the new blue suit! Durbin, who was there, had an even worse time, but the kids had a real fine beano and we were all very hoarse afterwards . . .

Tonight is the annual church meeting and that is about the last engagement before we set off on Wednesday. Our departure is from Victoria at 4 p.m., then Dover – Calais – Spiez – Berne – Interlaken – Grindelwald. The season has not been too good so far but prospects are pretty fair for more snow now, and they say that Grindelwald is never too bad having access to Scheidegg if the lower fields have thawed. I am looking forward to it tremendously.

Now for a message or two for Father relative to wirelesses. Will you please ask him to find out from several of his acquaintances:

1. Whether any particular make of wireless has *proved* most suitable in your locality; 2. whether there is any interference from the Beam station; 3. has he any great preference for a portable set; 4. is your household electricity DC or AC; 5. how much does he want to pay?

My own preference for you would be a good three-valve set with aerial (rather than a five-valve portable) as being cheaper to keep up and much purer in tone.

This sudden inquisition is the result of a visit to Jenkin yesterday. On my mentioning the subject he at once offered his help and experience. From his position he is 'in on the ground floor' with the best wireless manufacturers and has already got sets wholesale from various firms for a number of his friends. I would suggest getting one from Marconi's themselves who allow Jenkin more than a third off anyway. If he really wants to go in for a set it is an offer not to be passed by, and if he will let me have the answers to the foregoing questions when I return, I will go round with Jenkin and inspect.

Work is very scarce just now. I think the Byron [studios] have packed up trying to get me stuff to do until I come back.

I will keep you posted after we set off on Wednesday.

Much love to you all from Fred.

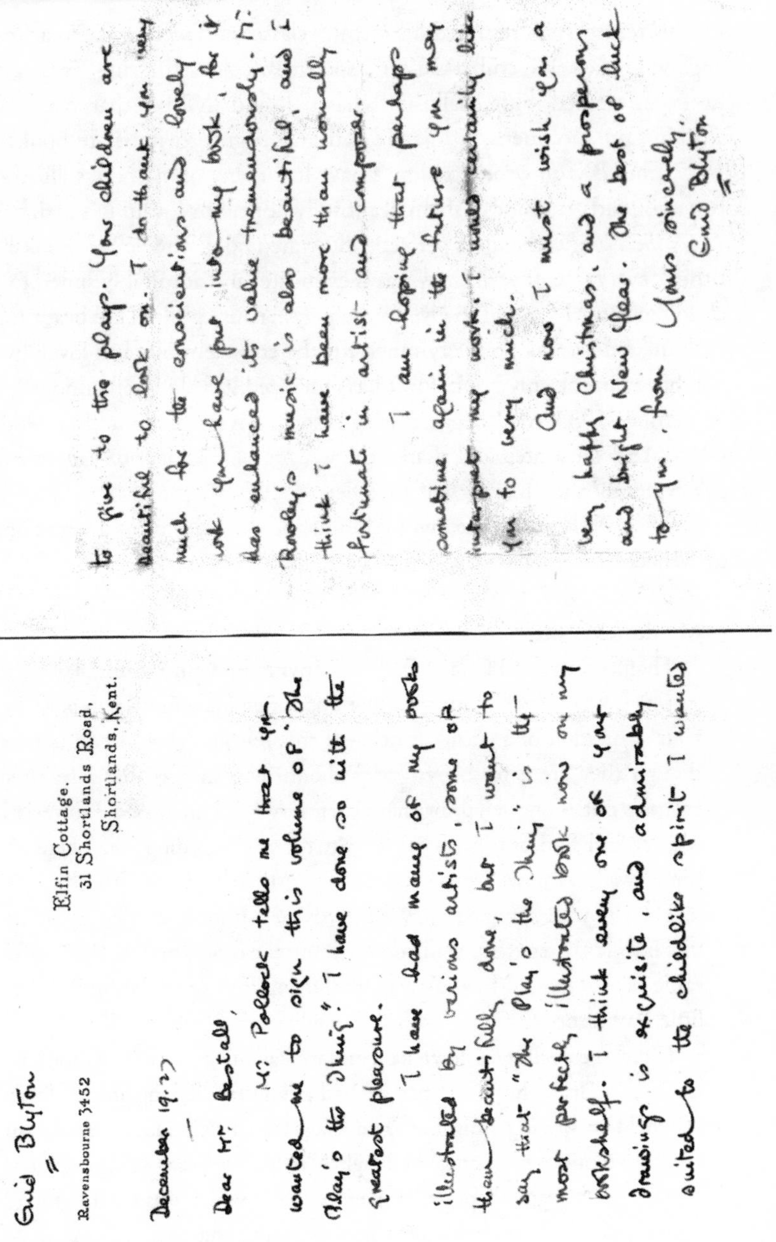

Enid Blyton

Ravensbourne 3452

Elfin Cottage.
31 Shortlands Road,
Shortlands, Kent.

December 19.27

Dear Mr. Batstall,

Mr. Pollock tells me that you wanted me to sign this volume of "The Play's the Thing." I have done so with the greatest pleasure.

I have had many of my poste illustrated by various artists, some of them beautifully done, but I want to say that "The Play's the Thing" is the most perfect illustrated book now on my bookshelf. I think every one of your drawings is exquisite, and admirably suited to the childlike spirit I wanted

to give to the plays. Your children are beautiful to look at. I do thank you very much for the enunciations and lovely work you have put into my book, for it has enhanced its value tremendously. His Rundey's music is also beautiful, and I think I have been more than usually fortunate in artist and composer.

I am hoping that perhaps sometime again in the future you may interpret my work. I would certainly like you to very much.

And now I must wish you a very happy Christmas, and a prosperous and bright New Year. The best of luck to you, from

Yours sincerely,
Enid Blyton

Facsimile of a letter from Enid Blyton

On his return AEB resumed his etching classes and went once to a wood-engraving class. He embarked on a specimen colour drawing *Sand skiing*, he experimented with chalk and charcoal, and in May that year began working on specimens in oil. He had also begun to illustrate books. In 1927 Enid Blyton wrote to him: 'I have had many of my books illustrated by various artists, some of them beautifully done, but I want to say that *The Play's the Thing* is the most perfectly illustrated book now on my bookshelf. I think every one of your drawings is exquisite, and admirably suited to the childlike spirit I wanted to give to the plays. Your children are beautiful to look on. I do thank you very much for the conscientious and lovely work you have put into my book, for it has enhanced its value tremendously.' In September 1933 AEB began a long association with the author Dudley Glass. AEB illustrated and shared the writing of *The Spanish Goldfish* and subsequently they played golf together.

In 1932 AEB was in the Swiss Alps for the second time and wrote home to Rebecca on 29 January:

My dear Mother

Thanks for your PC (and Father's 'driving bulletin'). I am glad he is getting hold of it well. I imagine that Pop is out and about again now. Re your suggestion of a cuckoo clock – there are some very nice ones here though they are a bit big to carry about. The snag is that I fear the customs duties on such things have been very much increased. However I will try and find out just what the situation is regarding tax. There are some swallows now. Do you like them little or big?

The thumb I sprained on Wednesday in a tumble swelled up pretty much yesterday so that I could do little, but the others practised skiing on some near slopes and I took a short moving film of them on Durbin's little Pathéscope.

Today the swelling is down a bit and we have all been up two thousand feet above Grindelwald whence we had a long run down through forest and field in blazing sunshine. The skies are still cloudless and the air without motion even at great height. While we were at our greatest altitude today a guide pointed out a great eagle which was circling round a mountain peak, probably in search of young chamois.

A piece of good news from the Byron – there will be about five weeks'

Photo of AEB (on the right) with his cousin, Frank, skiing, 1931

work coming through in a fortnight's time. Post is just going so I must close. Very much love to you all, Fred.

He wrote again on 4 February:

My dear Mother

Many thanks for your letter. Post takes longer than I thought, and the long interval since your last postcard made me wonder if anything had gone wrong. You seem to be keeping very active and if you are having as good weather as we are I can imagine how you like to get out of the house. Cox reports a fine week's weather and frost so doubtless you are similarly favoured. Surbiton, on the other hand, has had a succession of fogs! Father must be getting a lot of pleasure out of the car now. I hope he will not try to become a 'speed merchant'.

Maisie will be glad to feel her strength coming back. You speak of a 'little' cuckoo clock, but the little ones don't 'cuck'. The mechanism necessary for making the bird call means a large clock.

Unless you are really keen on having one I would suggest waiting until the exchange is better and the import duties not so heavy. However the holiday is not quite at an end yet and I may find just the thing before next mid-week which will probably see my departure.

If new snow comes plans may be extended, but the barometer keeps very high and steady and there seems no sign of change. I think Grindelwald will turn out the town band when the first cloud appears!

Yesterday we went up to Scheidegg and back, three of us finishing down the bob-run on luges. The run was in its fastest condition and it was difficult to check one's speed. Earlier in the day a luge carrying three had shot right over the banking.

Today most of us have been skiing on the upper practice slopes and have found it delightful. The sun has at last softened some of the snow, giving us a certain measure of control over our skis. I have been trying the slopes without ski-sticks for the first time and got on very fairly well. Less snow has improved the scenery – the general effect is not so entirely black and white as last year.

My sprained thumb was luckily the left one. I gave it one day's rest only and have been fortunate in not falling on it again. It is recovering normally though there is not much power in it yet.

We are all feeling very well and active. Hard surfaces have forced us to be cautious so that there is not the stiffness in our joints that we had last year. Food is as good as ever – also our appetites – and we only miss the rather jollier evenings when the hotel is full and dances etc. taking place. We are getting great fun out of the curling every evening, the rinks are much faster than last year. Am just off for another hour's ski practice, so will close.

Very much love to you all from Fred.

5 p.m.

Have had a jolly day's practice – only had one spill and that was this morning right in front of the cinema that Durbin was operating. It should make an amusing film. I have done most of the operating so far and therefore shall not appear in it as often as the others. Three Ramptons and I are just going curling. We have challenged four Swiss men to a match. F.

AEB went one more time to Grindelwald, in 1934, and on that occasion he went on to Italy to meet his parents in Rome. His summer holidays in the early 1930s were spent visiting his parents in Dorset and staying in Cornwall with the Rampton family, where he worked on '*Coloured Glasses* colour decoration for *Tatler* to poem by Naylor'. He frequently worked when he was on holiday, especially on wet days. In 1979 he wrote of the Dorset era to my daughter, cleverly folding the letter so that it formed its own envelope: 'Thank you so much for your card showing the church at Maiden Newton. You must have enjoyed riding in Dorset. It is a lovely county. I used to know it very well long ago, from Broadwindsor to Tolpuddle, and the beginning of the Chesil Beach from West Bay to Abbotsbury. In those days there were lots of quiet "green roads" on the high ground from Cattistock right up to Bulbarrow where one could walk (or ride) for hours and meet nobody. Do you like this fold? It was thought out by a Scottish clergyman, Revered Philip Noble, who has been a missionary in Papua New Guinea and is also a member of the British Origami Society. I hope you have been enjoying your holidays.'

AEB's father, Arthur Bestall, retired from Dorset in 1933 and he and Rebecca eventually settled again in Surbiton the following year.

There was a romantic side to AEB's life in the 1930s. The diaries frequently mention 'B' (Beatrice Nicholson from his church). He began by doing her portrait, then they played tennis and badminton together, they went to the pictures, the theatre, the proms, dances, out for long drives (as far as Studland in Dorset) and had meals together.[3]

In the spring of 1935 AEB set off by train from Paddington to Pwllheli in North Wales where he drafted the Pwllheli poster for the Great Western Railway. He did the lettering at home, worked on a St Peter drawing for the *Methodist Recorder* and did a joke for *Tatler*. But when he went into the studio after Easter, there was no work and he did just one rough before a friend called at teatime. The magazine market had slumped.

'Spring Cleaning' for a calendar for 1932

---

[3] In June 1936 an 'X' appears in the diary. Apart from a reference to one more badminton match when they played together, there is no further mention of 'B' until 1947 when AEB and his mother 'went to tea with Beatty Cole (Nicholson)'.

4

RUPERT

Drawing by Mary Tourtel, creator of Rupert in 1920

'"TELL ME A STORY." Out of that most often expressed request of every child everywhere was born *Daily Express* readers' oldest and most lovable friend, Rupert Bear, who celebrates his Silver Jubilee tomorrow,' wrote Hilda Coe in the *Daily Express* on 7 November 1945. Including some text that was cut from the original the article continued:

Since 8 November 1920, when Rupert was born, he has grown into a twentieth-century legend, comparable with the nineteenth century's *Alice in Wonderland* . . .

It was on 5 November 1920 that the editor wrote a letter to *Daily Express* children, in an easy-to-read script, beginning, 'I have splendid news for you.' He told them that Mary Tourtel, a famous picture-maker for little people, was going to tell them a picture story in verse called

Mary Tourtel's first story – Mrs Bear Sends Rupert to Market

The Adventures of the Little Lost Bear. 'His name, by the way,' wrote the editor, 'is Rupert.'

He also told them that there would be 250 prizes every week for children between five and fifteen who painted the pictures best. Three days later, on Monday 8 November, the first Rupert picture appeared, four and a half inches wide and three inches deep, showing Rupert leaving his cottage for market.

Ever since then Rupert has been the brains of every adventure – ingenious, cool, kind, confident, but not cock-sure, and mischievous enough to appeal to a child's sense of fun.

For fifteen years Mary Tourtel drew and wrote Rupert stories. Then her eyesight began to fail, and having completed 105 stories, she decided that, rather than disappoint the children by spasmodic work, she would hand over to someone else.

So Alfred Bestall, an artist who had had much experience with children's work, studied her drawings and stories, and undertook to maintain the atmosphere and tradition Mary Tourtel had established.

His first story, *Rupert, Algy and the Smugglers*, began on 28 June 1935. One thing was lacking – he could not write verse, and the youngest readers demanded verse, not once but many times. And so, early in 1936, the *Daily Express* asked me to translate Rupert into verse, and from then until war broke out [in 1939] prose and verse ran side by side.

For years Rupert was allowed two pictures a day, across three columns, but a fortnight after war began he was reduced to two columns, and on 16 April 1940 he was reduced again to his present size. But he never failed, and Mr Bestall has now finished his ninety-seventh story, and this morning you are reading number ninety-eight [*Rupert and Koko*].

*A sparrow chirps to Rupert, "Hey!
You'll have a visitor today."*

AEB's first Rupert story in 1935 from 'Rupert, Algy and the Smugglers'

Bestall thinks of most of his stories out of doors, and he has told me that they often occur to him backwards – that is, he sees Rupert in the midst of an adventure, then plans how to get him there and home again. He has only one fixed rule: Rupert's adventures must always begin and end in or near his own cottage. That helps to make Rupert's wonderland more real.

One of last year's stories, about Rupert and the darts, Mr Bestall thought of when making paper birds and frogs and darts for some little girls he knows. He likes children to give him an idea.

Bestall thinks the Rupert stories are so popular because right always wins, and that is his chief difficulty – to keep Rupert doing right without making him a prig. The other big problem is to move the story along fast enough to keep the children excited and eager for the next day's instalment.

Mr Bestall never gets tired of the little bear in his jumper and scarf. He can draw for five hours at a time, and often finds it easiest to work from about 10 p.m. to 3 a.m. the next morning.

Mary Tourtel wrote last year: 'May Rupert and his annual be a success every year, and I hope the little chap will always remain a favourite with the children.'

I'm sure he will. How many fathers and mothers are about to obey an insistent little voice that is saying 'Read Rupert' this morning?

Mary Tourtel died in Canterbury in 1948 and 20 years later an article about her by Leslie Sherwood appeared in the *Times Literary Supplement* to which AEB responded:

It is a worthy and overdue tribute to a remarkable character and may I say what a pleasure it is to find so much knowledge of the early Rupert stories and such memory of the individual atmosphere that she created. Her unerring feminine understanding of child psychology made it almost impossible for me a mere bachelor to follow her at all adequately. Stanley Marshall ('Uncle Bill' of the Rupert League) was fortunate to have such material upon which to found the club that rocketed the paper's circulation and Mary was lucky to work under the aegis of a man of such affectionate sympathy . . . Through the League she was made

Their sums are written on the wall,
And Koko scribbles on them all.

'Rupert and Koko', the picture which concluded Hilda Coe's article

perpetually aware of the success of her efforts, a position of happiness that few artists can ever have experienced. If only it could have continued! . . .

You remark that Rupert did not develop. But he did, physically. By 1935 Mary had imperceptibly aged him by five or six years over the 1920 Rupert and I tried in my poor way to reduce him gradually to the age of the figure in the picture that illustrates your article [from *Rupert and the Magician's Umbrella*]. It is from Mary's best period. However, this is wandering from the point which is to thank you for what you have so ably written about an artist of charm and complete integrity.

With kindest regards. Sincerely yours, AEB

'Rupert and the Magician's Umbrella' by Mary Tourtel

In his reply Leslie Sherwood said he particularly valued AEB's kindly reception of his article. He finished by saying:

> Back in October I was delighted to have a line from Mr William Urry, librarian of the Cathedral Library at Canterbury, with the information that Mary Tourtel was born at 52 Palace Street, Canterbury, and that the library boasts an original (pre-Rupert) animal drawing of hers.[1] I hope to see both the house and the drawing when I'm down that way later in the year.
>
> I was very glad you approved my choice of illustration – there were so many to choose from, and before finally settling on Rupert and that anxious fox I pored for a long time through the many little yellow books still in the possession of my children and their cousins.

The following year, when Rupert was fast approaching his Golden Jubilee,

---

[1] Mary Tourtel, née Caldwell, was born on 28 January 1874.

AEB wrote from his cottage in North Wales to Mr Heald at the *Daily Express*:

FHC[2] tells me that your feature on Rupert has been brought forward and that you need my memories quickly. You will have seen Leslie Sherwood's panegyric on Mary Tourtel . . . I suppose the transition from Mary to me interests you most.

My being given Rupert was a most unlikely affair – due partly to coincidence – unlikely because after four years in the first war I had spent the next twelve years illustrating as widely as possible, at least half of the output being to humorous papers rising to *Punch* and the big 'shinies', but getting serious orders too, illustrating a few classics and working for educational firms, all with a view to self-advancement. However, ironically enough, a sort of artistic claustrophobia made me want to be capable of every style and to avoid having all the eggs in one basket, so when, during a lull, I was asked to try a Rupert story (in 1935) it seemed a new line. I knew nothing of the subject, so I bought the *DE*, looked at Mary's work, and drew three specimens keeping to her simplicity of line.

Then came the coincidence. In the group who interviewed me were a features editor (possibly Rayner, I never saw him again), Arthur Christiansen, St J. Cooper (art editor), a lady who did Mary Tourtel's late verse captions (not Hilda Coe), and a man whom I recognised as having met casually at the Tavistock Residential Club. This turned out to be Stanley Marshall, the 'Uncle Bill' of the defunct Rupert League. He knew of my identity though I didn't know his and I am pretty sure he pressed for me when some people had presumed Rupert to be finished, and one man had ill-advisedly promised an agency that it could follow Mary's retirement with a photographic series of Rupert dolls. (This series had to be started in 1936, ran for 2 weeks in poor style, and was then killed by St J. Cooper).

Marshall, who had rocketed circulation in the brief life of his Rupert League, was one of nature's gentlemen, intensely anxious about Rupert's influence over millions of children and worried about trends in Mary's

[2] Frederick Henry Chaplain, who in 1952 succeeded Stanley Marshall as children's editor of the *Daily Express*.

latest work. She had always seemed to follow the brothers Grimm rather than Hans Andersen, having no humour and showing an occasional streak of cruelty in her treatment of Rupert while retaining the tenderest perfection in her drawing of animals 'in the raw'. Marshall said that [her husband] H.B. Tourtel, besides writing the verse, had been a restraining factor over Mary's tendency towards the horrific. Not unnaturally, widowhood and failing sight gradually caused Mary's stories to be even less sympathetic, stretching the arm of magical coincidence too far, and being sometimes static while complicated explanations took up a week's captions.

Anyway, that was the set-up when I came. Being only an artist, I caused consternation when I asked to be given the first story. When they asked me to do it myself Marshall took me aside and urged that I used no evil characters, no fairies and no magic. Thinking the first story must be my last I had a go and when my contract came, offering no increase for the story, I signed it, still certain that the difficulty of weaving plots would defeat me.

However, I didn't get the sack and on starting another I was given access to the children's letters. They shook me to my foundations. The way children in those days followed Rupert with affection, and as a mentor, terrified me and I frankly didn't want the responsibility but, finding my anxieties so completely in accord with Marshall's, I stuck at it and gradually ideas came. It was immediately clear that I could not match Mary's method of going from plaintive wistfulness to the edge of terror. The only method I could think of aimed at livelier action, better continuity, frequent gentle humour that the parents might or might not grasp before the children, and more chance for Rupert's initiative, while resisting the temptation to make him in any way clever.

Rightly or wrongly, I realised that it might be the most vitally important job in Fleet Street and its problems were such as to turn my outlook right round, making me regard Rupert as a major part of my Christian life. That must not sound 'pi'. Church work has always been my real background and I should have been nothing without the Methodist surroundings and atmosphere that have helped me to ignore my spinal handicap.

St J. Cooper had been producing a good annual called *The Boys' and*

Girls' Book of the Year and I put some terrible six-part Rupert pages into those for '35 and '36. In 1936 Marshall decided to produce separately several of my stories fresh from the *DE* and that was my first Rupert annual. Today Chaplain is preparing annual no. 36 and I'm still allowed to do the work in it. If only Marshall could have lived to see what his keenness led to. But he died in the bitter spell long ago when poor Asher drove us all too hard, aiming to build up a Disney-type empire with Rupert.[3]

That was the only time I was ever 'under' anybody. The introduction of quarterly booklets nearly doubled the amount of work demanded of me. I loyally tried to cope, but came so near to collapse that my doctor ordered me to give up Rupert. I therefore resigned to the surprise, I think, of Blackburn who promptly sent along the first of several assistants (for the booklets) of whom the two best proved to be Alex Cubie (then in the *DE* as general artist with Ted Matto) and Enid Ash who is drawing the current *Rupert and Dickory Dock*.

When Asher suddenly washed his hands of Rupert all the work he had organised was piled on to Frederick Chaplain who had come from the Associated Press and who was already being driven to death doing all the background work for Asher's boat-show project. How Chaplain ever survived that era I shall never know.

You won't want to wade through much more. It would be unprofitable to enlarge on the wide variations of *DE* atmosphere from the uplifting and unifying genius of Christiansen down to the discourteous boorishness of the Pickering purge which swept away the last person in the office who knew anything about Rupert: Eve Beach, who had been Marshall's secretary.

Increasing age brought increasing difficulty in inventing *new* plots. I couldn't bring myself to follow Chaplain's suggestion of going back and writing sequels to old ones, and, having written 224 for the *DE* and forty-nine for the annuals I packed up (273 altogether).

Mary Tourtel had claimed great freedom of production with big gaps between early stories, and five or six of her best adventures were repeated later so as to give her long vacations for travel. By contrast, I have never

---

[3] Albert Asher was responsible for promotions at the *Daily Express* for a time.

missed a day in over thirty years. The photo series and the press strike made unwelcome breaks. Three times Rupert has been squeezed out – once (when the *DE* was only one sheet) to give all the space to a war-time speech by Churchill, once when President John Kennedy died and once when Pope John died.

An odd thing is that no word of criticism of my work has ever reached me. Inside the office that loses its merit because no word of any sort ever reaches me – only a vast silence since we lost Marshall, Robertson and Christiansen, and I often wonder whether certain VIPs have ever read a word of any of my plots. Some outside appreciation has lately been embarrassingly warm – but an occasional slating might be salutary and might fill the vacuum.

My worst work was done, I suppose, around 1942. I was an air-raid warden from 1938 to 1945 and, in spite of those duties, the reduction of Rupert drawings to one a day gave me a trifle of leisure to revert to oil painting. Two of my pictures were subsequently hung in the Royal Academy. When the 'phoney war' ended abruptly we were often very short of sleep, and work suffered. My drawings of that year were dreadful. One gets used to anything, even the nightly clatter of doodle-bugs aimed at Eisenhower's HQ in Bushey Park, and with a quieter mind I suppose drawings became cheerful again. Anyway a government subsidy maintained Rupert in the *DE* until 1945.

AEB began working on his first Rupert story on 2 May 1935 (having just finished a Blackie job – *Girl Hikers*) and he increasingly worked at home in Surbiton. King George V's Jubilee inspired a *Tatler* watercolour entitled *Scout Beacons*, AEB having driven to Dorking and seen 'very fine bonfires at Box Hill, Newdigate and Rusper'. He also did colour sketches for the Jubilee children's book of HMS *Rodney*. Most Saturdays he continued to play tennis in the summer and badminton in the winter. He also played golf, and bridge at night which he finished on the stroke of midnight. He went several times to Poplar to adjudicate the art section of the Mission Eisteddfod and he did an endpaper for *Lax – His Book* (the autobiography of William Lax, the popular Methodist minister at Poplar, who died in 1937).

AEB's father became ill at the end of 1936 and died on 7 December. He was buried in what became the family grave at Brookwood and AEB laid a

The Reverend Arthur Bestall, AEB's father

holly wreath there every Christmas. He lived with his mother from this time on.

Towards the end of the 1930s, there were Easter holidays in North Wales with Harry Adams and once they went to Dovedale for a change. In the summer of 1937 AEB went to Scotland with the Rampton family. They boarded the *Ena* and sailed from Gourock to Fort William and back through the Western Isles. They climbed Ben Nevis and saw much wildlife. Later the same year AEB spent a lot of time working on some Dutch scenery for the church bazaar. This included a windmill, and Percy Rampton junior came up one afternoon 'to fix electric motor. Made the arms of the windmill work perfectly.' Percy senior was installed as Mayor of Surbiton.

There were rumblings of war. Even in the summer of 1936 AEB was in Bognor and 'was on the front as the German airship *Hindenburg* flew over the shore not more than 200 feet up'. At Easter in 1938 AEB and Harry Adams saw planes dropping bombs in Hell's Mouth (a big sandy beach near Pwllheli). AEB began attending air-raid precautions (ARP) lectures on Thursday evenings. In September he went on holiday to Cornwall with his cousin Godfrey, but then on the 24th a 'wire came from War Office recalling Godfrey'. AEB stayed on a few more days but noted 'news very ominous'. And again 'listened to wireless at night – Chamberlain's speech and news. England making defence preparations. Determine to return tomorrow to Surbiton.' So he did, commenting: 'Last part of journey roads very congested with outgoing traffic, army convoys etc.' The next day 'Chamberlain, Hitler, Mussolini and Daladier at Munich conference settling Sudeten dispute'. Peace was announced on 30 September. The ARP continued.

Meanwhile AEB did jury service at the Old Bailey and spent a weekend at Seasalter in Kent sailing with fellow artist Peter Fraser. He taught Joan Jenkin to drive and Peter's son, Rodney, wrote much later: 'In about 1938 when I was eighteen he [AEB] invited me to Surbiton for a few days so that he could give me driving lessons. I well remember his mother and sister. I found the former somewhat formidable in her regard for social etiquette and the sounding of a large gong for the evening meal heralded the hour to sit down to baked beans or poached egg on toast!'

In 1939 there began a long, 22-year association with Surbiton Rotary Club. Thereafter Bert, as he was known to his fellow Rotarians, attended lunch every Tuesday that he was able, and when he was away he would attend the local Rotary Club meetings. He became involved in providing transport for 'old folks', the blind and disabled.

AEB and Godfrey went on holiday together again in August. They left Tilbury in the SS *Britannia*, then travelled by train through Sweden, Finland and Norway. On 13 August AEB wrote to his mother from Viipuri in Finland:

Our stay in Sweden (four days) was most interesting. The Swedes are a calm, rich and friendly people, an astonishing number of whom speak good English, and journeying through is very easy and pleasant. The Finns are a different type. Smaller, plainer-featured, very independent, they are emerging rapidly and have the latest ultra-modern buildings in many places, but, as yet, the people themselves look out of place in them.

We did a big 'hop' yesterday: train to the capital of Finland, Helsinki, and then an hour's flight in the calm sunset over an endless archipelago of islands to this little old city not very far from St Petersburg (Leningrad).

There are three cathedrals here – ancient, modern Lutheran and Greek Catholic. Any idea we had of finding a dreamy old town half asleep was soon dispersed, for the place was crammed with troops. Our hotel housed so many high officers that we had a job to find a room and this morning we watched some of the 30,000 Finnish soldiers having their final parade here to mark the end of manoeuvres. All very surprising . . .

It is also surprising to find that we are about as far east as Athens and I think as far north as Shetland. This great heat was not expected. At dinner last night a lassie from the Finnish Salvation Army came round with a box and I have just listened to an Army meeting singing lustily in an upper room the same tunes as in England apparently, accompanied by a cello. The Salvation Army is also strong in Sweden and in Göteborg there were four Methodist churches. Today, being Sunday, lots of Viipuri girls have appeared in national costume – very colourful and becoming.

They reached Bergen in Norway on 23 August, went to bed, then 'a sudden jolt came at night. A wire arrived recalling Godfrey immediately. History repeats itself. This [same thing] happened last year when we were caught in Cornwall during the September crisis.' They left for England the next day in the *Vega*. They heard an English wireless for the first time in three weeks – 'ominous news, war very imminent. Passed beside a number of warships brightly lit up [at] 10 p.m.' They arrived in North Shields early in the morning, caught a train to King's Cross and Godfrey went straight to the War Office. AEB immediately busied himself with ARP work (he was made temporary senior warden), buying wood and preparing the house for darkening. There was a big evacuation of children from London. War was declared at 11 a.m. on Sunday 3 September 1939.

In November AEB played nine holes of golf at Tyrrell's Wood with Dudley Glass, a friend, noting in his diary: 'Nine fighting planes flew over at noon, great speed. Heard gunfire and saw trail of smoke from very high plane (reconnaissance German plane) over South London (plane later brought down over the sea).' There was a cold spell in January 1940 and the Thames was frozen over from Kingston Bridge to Pope's Ferry. It was the worst freeze-up since 1815.

When the spring came AEB was busy planting vegetables. On 10 May Germany invaded Holland, Belgium and Luxembourg and later in the month AEB did his first all-night duty at his air-raid post. *Rupert* continued, albeit reduced to one drawing per day, there was a little work for the Byron Studios, tennis when possible, Rotary lunches and church choir. On 10 June AEB recorded in his diary 'Italy enters war' and a week later 'Radio announces that the French have laid down their arms'. The evacuation from Dunkirk took place at the end of May until early June.

AEB and Godfrey went by train (with many changes and much chaos) to North Wales for a week in August. They arrived back in London in the middle of the longest air raid so far. AEB was unable to get home from Waterloo and instead slept on his studio floor. In September the London docks were set ablaze, there was a big fire near Kingston Bridge and one evening 'about 100 German planes came over – very beautiful sight. Saw bomber fall at Chessington chased by a Hurricane.' It was the time of the Battle of Britain. The Waterloo railway line was closed for twelve days because of a bomb at Clapham Junction. Another day, tennis was interrupted by an alert after which fifty or so Hurricanes passed over homeward. And so the blitzkrieg continued, with night after night of air raids. In October 'incendiaries dropped all round us 8 p.m. England's house got two. The Morrises were there, thus being bombed out of two houses on successive nights. Raid ended 2.30 a.m.'

At the end of the month AEB wrote to his mother:

The Waterloo line has been blocked again – near Vauxhall. I go up by car tomorrow to pick up another little bit of extra work. There is sadness at the *Express* office. Less than half the order for the new *Rupert* book has been delivered and now the firm of Greycaine has been bombed (they print the book) and all the *Rupert* blocks and reserve of paper have been dished, so presumably after the small stocks now in the shops are sold there will be no more. I managed to get a couple of copies in the Kingston branch of W.H. Smith. The Greycaine works are at Watford. Those street trams that were bombed last Friday while they stood in a row waiting for the traffic lights were in Blackfriars Road – not near enough to affect my office.

He wrote again on 1 November:

I wonder if you are having the heavy weather that has set in here. It was so bad last night that hardly any Jerry planes could get through and the 'all-clear' sounded at 1 a.m. Let's hope something of the sort happens tonight when I am on duty.

Have just had a letter from Frank [AEB's cousin, writing from the Malay States]. It was posted by Air Mail on the 22nd September and took therefore five and a half weeks to get here! He asks me to become godfather to the second child who was expected the first half of this month. Godfrey didn't mention the matter so probably he doesn't know how things have turned out. I shall try to cable but don't know if it is possible.

Have also heard from Rodney Fraser who has joined the mine-sweepers. Also heard from Roberts who has taken a paid job with the Home Guard – his own work having flopped. He says that his area, Purley and Coulsdon, had 2,000 bombs in September.

There is slightly better news of the Rupert book. They have reassembled the blocks etc. and have applied for a further allocation of paper and *may* be able to print off the full edition of 70,000 copies by Christmas.

Talking of Christmas, have you all thought out what you need in the way of presents?

All goes well here. Mrs Eves has cleaned Maisie's room and keeps active and cheerful. The old gardener has found his other job too heavy for his age and has returned to us. The grass has had its last cutting, two dead rose trees have been removed and he is now pruning the trees that overhang the next-door garden (no. 56). Hope you are all on the upgrade. Doubtless reaction from the strain of air raids was responsible for some of your troubles.

Much love, Fred.

The following day he wrote once more:

Your letter doesn't sound much more cheerful but I'm glad it could be fixed for M to go to Henley-in-Arden. Is the cottage mentioned also in Henley? And wouldn't the Birmingham barrage keep you awake there?

The present spells of violent weather are a godsend down here. Tonight there has been very little enemy stuff overhead (as I wrote the last words the 'all-clear' sounded). On Thursday night when I was on duty we had no raid between 9.15 p.m. and 3.30 a.m. The new multiple guns make a row like the crack of doom and apparently they are having their effect.

Today some of us contrived an afternoon's badminton. It was very jolly. Mrs Morris came along and is quite a good player. It is uncertain whether we can keep it up each week.

The old gardener has been again during the fine spells and we shall keep the garden from going back too much.

Tomorrow I go to Manor Road to fetch Mr Mitcheson B[rown] for the morning service. His road has suffered a good deal. Do you remember Cater's (on a steep slope near Jenkin's)? It was destroyed the other night, same night as Maxwell's second lot. He and his wife were unhurt in the kitchen though the front of the house was blown clean away. I saw him at Kingston Rotary lunch on Thursday. Always a most cheery fellow, he didn't seem at all changed.

I hope your bomb didn't shake you up too much. One of our wardens took his aged parent and sister to Glaisdale, a village in North Yorks, a fortnight ago for peace and quiet. Tonight's wireless says that a big German bomber has come down there! Today's air successes make happy hearing. If we really get an ascendency you might think of returning, but I don't consider it safe yet awhile unless things get past endurance in your locality.

May add a line tomorrow, but don't know – these early posts are difficult.

Much love, F.

AEB did not add a line but noted in his diary 'heard from Godfrey that Frank's second is a daughter, born October 8'.

On 14 November there was a 'tremendous raid on Coventry', on 8 December there was a heavy raid on London and three days later the raid was mostly on Birmingham (the following night the planes passed over en route for Sheffield). Just after Christmas bombs fell close by and there were eight deaths (AEB was immediately on the scene). On 29 December there was another great incendiary raid on London.

Early in the New Year Rebecca wrote to AEB:

My dear Fred

Your letter and graphic description of the happenings of Thursday has just come and I can picture every bit of it (having read it through many times) and am so thankful that you escaped unhurt. Our house too – glass and fastenings are a very small matter. It was nice of Mr Halet to go over the house with you. I wish we had been able to give some little help but *you* bore your full share for the family. The poor Englands have had a shaking up and [I] am glad you offered our house to them.

The Morrises will congratulate themselves upon escaping the terrors of that blitz! What a good thing that little Sheila had left the day before.

I am glad Mitchell's man can patch you up and keep out the rain until glass is to be had.

It *was* a good thing you were not at Winchester. I shall send your letter on for Rose [Rebecca's sister] to see.

Here everything is so quiet and peaceful. I wrote a foolish little pencil letter last night and will enclose as it is *such* a contrast to your busy days.

Much love, dear Fred, from Mother.

The bombing continued and in April AEB saw the destruction between Moorgate and Aldersgate Street. In May, during another heavy raid on the capital, Westminster Abbey was hit and thirty-three German bombers were brought down.

In February 1941 AEB began an oil painting of his air-raid post, M4, which was completed by the end of March. It was hung at the Royal Academy (one of AEB's proudest achievements) and later in the year at the Towner Art Gallery in Eastbourne. The picture was sold to the Wardens' Service, Air Raid Precautions Headquarters in Surbiton. He did another oil painting, *Conversation Piece 1941: Gas Exercise*, followed by *Post in Autumn*

AEB's air-raid post, M4, 1941. This was hung at The Royal Academy, then at The Towner Art Gallery in Eastbourne and subsequently sold to The Wardens' Service in Surbiton

and, in 1942, *Fire Guard Drill* and *Bus Stop*. His *Witch* picture was used as a stage scene at the Windmill Theatre.

One evening in August 1941 AEB wrote from M4 to Rebecca, who had gone to stay with her sister in Winchester:

My dear Mother

We have been thinking of you during the better weather recently and hope you have made what you could of it. Your PC to Maisie came this evening and we picture you now with Aunt Ada.

All goes smoothly here. Pop has been collecting for the YMCA tonight in the Coronation Cinema foyer. Yesterday she and I took Mrs Grundy and Anne to see *Target for Tonight*, a fine film.

While on the subject of the RAF, I hear that young Walters from the church has got his 'wings' and will fly a bomber. Ken Coxhead is training for the same thing.

There was tennis tonight, the first for weeks, cold and windy, but a lot turned up.

Godfrey has fixed the venue for our holiday September 15–22 – a pub of doubtful reputation called the Beetle and Wedge at Goring-on-Thames. Rather a sprightly effort on his part.

You will have read that the escaped criminal, Stanley Thurston, has been recaptured. You used to have a 'hunch' that he was prowling in our neighbourhood, but did you know that he was actually caught on Kingston Hill? The story I got tonight from Stables (who as you know is a war-time policeman) was that Thurston was burgling a house. The woman occupant, who was alone, saw him from a window when he arrived. She coolly went to the telephone, swathed it and herself in a blanket to muffle the sound and asked for 999. Having made her report she locked herself in her bathroom. Scotland Yard wirelessed the nearest police car and within minutes bobbies were round the house. They saw Thurston descend a stack-pipe and even then he managed to shin over three high walls like a cat before they took him.

Stables was in the charge room when the man was brought in and says that, while the inspector was putting questions, Thurston suddenly leapt on to the table and did a swallow-dive head first through an open window. He injured a foot in so doing and was easily retaken.

Incidentally, no one knew that he *was* Thurston until two days later when his fingerprints were compared at Scotland Yard during a remand. He, of course, gave another name. According to Stables he was very 'down' physically and had lost about three stone. A queer affair. The man apparently is not dangerous but a remarkable burglar.

I trust these details won't cause you and Aunt Ada any loss of sleep!

I'm able to write at some length as I am taking the post (on air-raid duty) all night. There's nothing much to report from home. We are eating a lot of fine beans and Muriel is 'pickling' some more. The dining-room ceiling has stuck up pretty well.

Godfrey is coming to tea on Sunday to talk 'holiday'.

I presume you will arrive by the usual evening train on Monday. Let us know if there is any change of plan.

I hope you found Aunt Ada well and are enjoying your old haunts.

Much love to you both from Fred.

After breakfast

Nothing to add. Weather turned wild in the early hours. Some very heavy rain. Now high winds and a bit of sunshine. Am going to Croydon for Rotary [Club] this afternoon. F.

Meanwhile, at Easter, AEB had taken Percy Rampton junior and his sister, Mildred, to the High School, Little Brickhill Manor, and then he designed a school badge. In 1996 one of the girls wrote to me:

I can probably only confirm what you already know – that Mr Bestall was one of the kindest men you could possibly meet.

As girls, we first became acquainted with him when he visited our boarding school, Bayfield High School, in Buckinghamshire, before [during] the Second World War. I think he was friends of the owners at that time, a Mr and Mrs Searle, whose daughter, Daphne, was a teacher there. I believe he came in the company of a friend who was courting Daphne, which later resulted in a marriage.

My first memories of him were when we played badminton with him. He was such a good sport and gave us a lot of praise and encouragement, and I rather think we had a lot of laughs. It was at this time he dubbed me 'Spider' and the name stuck. I was long and lanky, aged about ten, and according to him I had a distinct advantage over everyone. He said I didn't need to run, I only needed to stretch out my arms and legs and I was there!

He seemed to be around sometimes when we were playing tournaments both in badminton *and* tennis. He was very keen on sports.

He must have visited Bayfield a number of times, sufficiently to have established an avuncular relationship with at least half a dozen girls, for I have since learnt that he kept in touch with six other girls – probably more – for a great number of years, giving away one of the girls at her wedding in Kent. In order to do this, he had to interrupt his holiday in his beloved Wales and make the long journey there, which was very sporting of him.

From Bayfield, following a change of ownership of the school, a number of us (who were Dr Barnardo girls) were transferred to Yorkshire. I remember remaining in contact by letter with Mr Bestall and receiving a lovely letter from him with illustrations in the margin, one of those being of a sheep shivering in what he referred to as 'the wild and woolly north'.

When about ten of us were transferred south to Chawton House in Chawton (village now famous for its connection with Jane Austen), Mr Bestall visited once again and on at least three or four occasions, three of the girls (including 'Spider') were invited to visit him and his mother at home in Surbiton where he kindly provided us with lunch, courtesy of his housekeeper, or took us to a hotel.

We went on different occasions to Chessington Zoo, where he footed the bill for all our rides on various merry-go-rounds, ice-creams etc., we went rowing on the Serpentine, which was great fun, and also to his badminton club, and once to an orchestral concert. He must have had tremendous patience, but he seemed to love the outings as much as we. Presumably he paid for our rail tickets as well! We usually finished up having tea with his dear old mother, and a game of croquet on the lawn. The war was on, then, and I believe he did some ARP duty.

By this time we were all aged about fifteen or sixteen, and attended Alton Grammar School. Of course, when we left school we each went our different ways, some of us continuing to have contact with Mr Bestall from time to time.

AEB recalled his own memories in a letter to 'Spider' in 1983:

> You need not be 'astounded' by my memory of Bayfield. My being there at all was odd enough. I never knew your Miss Alice or Miss Teape. The school had been handed over to Daphne (Searle) and her fellow senior (V.N.A. Gates). The senior promptly got married, leaving the responsibility to Daphne who then demanded help from her parents. The latter, knowing of Percy's desire for Daphne, invited him for visits and he, in turn, commandeered me (and my car) to get him there. I was not a very efficient 'gooseberry' and he largely disappeared, except for badminton, leaving me to sink or swim in an unknown world.
>
> Very luckily I was accepted all round – by the youngest as a large plaything, by you in the mid-stream as a badminton player, and by certain of the near-seniors as a fellow malefactor when they planned some escapade. It soon led to small incidents that remain crystal clear in memory, some delightful, some very painful when I made insensitive blunders, some showing my initial ignorance as when a small kid grabbed my hand, out on the lawn, and came skipping along murmuring 'Daddy, Daddy, Daddy' and I realised I was being made a make-believe father for one who had never known a real one.

AEB was best man when Percy Rampton and Daphne Searle were married at Easter 1942.

At the end of August 1942 AEB and Godfrey had a fortnight's holiday at Ottery St Mary and saw the blitzed Exeter Cathedral. The following year they went, by train again, to Sidmouth. When AEB submitted a Rupert adventure to Marshall at the *Daily Express* he commented that Marshall was 'very down – seedy, without news of his son in Libya and with his wife ill'. (Stanley Marshall died in 1952.) In 1943 AEB was busy doing book illustrations between his Rupert and his ARP work.

AEB was frequently on all-night duty at the post and on 16 January 1943 his diary records 'our planes bombed Berlin'. There were reprisals, but in May the Germans collapsed in North Africa and in September Italy surrendered. However, in January 1944 the raids continued with renewed vigour. AEB did an oil painting entitled *Flares and Incendiaries*. He managed a week in North Wales with Harry Adams after planting lots of vegetables over Easter. On 6 June the D-day invasion of France began and then came the pilotless aircraft (buzz bombs), bringing frequent alerts and sleepless nights. Norman Warren, on active service, wrote on 8 July:

Dear Fred

Thank you very much indeed for your letter of good wishes and the present of books, both of which were very acceptable indeed. We do not get very much time for reading, but we do get some, and I am looking forward very much to reading the ones you sent, which have obviously been carefully selected and cover a nice wide field of choice.

We have all along had a quite astonishingly quiet time. We were not in on the assault at all, and even the original plan did not call for us to land before D+2; things however came unstuck all along the line and we didn't get ashore at all until D+5 – in fact we only beat the Prime Minister ashore by a short head, a truly humiliating state of affairs for chaps who had been trained as assault troops. Personally, ever since the figures of the Dieppe casualties came through my one ambition had been to be in debt to the Crown on D-day, with the result that I am suffering from an acute sense of anti-climax.

It is an extraordinary state of affairs, but you people at home are in much greater danger now that those infernal flying bombs have been launched, than we are here. So much so that we are using it as a threat to our ratings when they misbehave: 'If you don't behave yourselves we will send you home, where all the buzz bombs are.' Still, let's hope it won't be long before the Pas de Calais is in our hands.

We are on the whole having quite good weather, even though it was supposed to be the worst June in Normandy for forty years. We have enough work to keep us busy all day, but not too much to make life a burden. And we have the most terrific grub, all canned of course, but a very wide variety and all real food, no tinned bully beef or spam. It is a humbling thought which occurs to us quite often, that not only are the bombs which we ought to be getting falling on you people at home, but the delicacies which we are eating have only been made possible by an enormous number of people at home living on short commons for the last four years.

Please excuse this scrappy scrawl, but facilities for letter writing are very poor here. Please remember me to your people, and thank you again very much for the books.

Yours, Norman.

In the middle of September the black-out eased and on 'Battle of Britain' Sunday 'our air invasion of South Holland took place in afternoon. Brief alert for one fly bomb 8.45'. AEB did an oil painting which he called *The Intruder*. In March 1945 the flying-bomb blitz started again. However, on 22 March the last V2 bomb fell on Ilford, on 1 May the Germans announced the death of Hitler and the following day Berlin fell to the Russians and all Germans in Italy surrendered. The final surrender of Germany occurred on 7 May and VE Day was celebrated on 8 May. AEB went to London and saw the Royal Family and Churchill at Buckingham Palace.

Now that the war in Europe was over, AEB got his car into action again and drove it for the first time since 1942. Street lighting recommenced and in August he went to North Wales for a fortnight by train (petrol was still rationed) and spent some days with Harry Adams and his new wife, Margaret. The church bell ringing just after midnight on 14–15 August told of the end of the Japanese war and 'rowdy crowds paraded Beddgelert until 3 a.m.'. The next night there was a bonfire in the river bed and Welsh singing by the crowd on the bridge. From then on, AEB went to North Wales every year (except one) with Harry Adams until he bought his own cottage in 1956.

In the meantime *Rupert* generated a huge fan mail, all of which had to be answered. One such letter came soon after the war from Corporal I.G.W. Chatfield of Plymouth:

Dear Sir

I am a soldier in the Devon regiment, and have been a regular reader of the *Daily Express* for the past fourteen years. I have a son and daughter who follow *Rupert* every day and like the *Rupert Annual* every Christmas, therefore I should like to book two of these annuals for this Christmas for my children, would you be kind enough to do this for me please, as I cannot do this anywhere else.

I enclose a stamped addressed envelope for a reply informing me whether it is possible for you to do this for me, and when and where and how much, may I send the money to cover cost and postage etc.

In January 1946 AEB, Newman and Blake, his fellow artists, had notice to leave 36 Whitefriar's Street and they moved close by to 11 Seacole Lane for four years. Thereafter AEB worked at the *Daily Express* when he wanted to be in London. As well as producing *Rupert* he did a set of six cat and six dog drawings for postcards, he illustrated *The Hive* by John Crompton and in February 1947 he went to Wales to work on Welsh folklore for the little book, *Folk Tales of Wales*. It was a bitterly cold winter and London had its longest sunless spell ever known. AEB began drawing *Park Farm* for an oil painting, which was hung at the Royal Academy in 1949.

In 1947 a Mrs Gerlach wrote to AEB from Holland, to whom he responded:

Please forgive delay in replying to your letter. I have been away from home for a week. It is so interesting to know that your daughter has enjoyed the Rupert books. I shall be glad to do a drawing for you if I can get consent from the editor of the *Daily Express*. This permission has to be obtained as Rupert is the copyright of the newspaper.

With every good wish,

Yours sincerely, Alfred E. Bestall.

He wrote again in May:

I was very glad to get the kind letters from you and your daughter some time ago and to know that you liked my little drawing.

Now a most welcome parcel has arrived from Holland. There is no note with it but I am sure it must be from you, so please accept my best thanks. The butter and cheese are both delicious; we had almost forgotten the taste of pure butter and my mother (who is nearly eighty-three) particularly enjoys it.

Your country must have been lovely during the last few weeks of sunshine. Here, too, we have enjoyed seeing so many flowering trees after such a long hard winter and look forward to good crops later on.

With all good wishes and again very many thanks,

Yours sincerely, Alfred E. Bestall.

Four cat and dog postcards, 1946
'Cat's Cradle' (top left)
'Hi, you, buzz off' (top right)
'Ain't life grand!' (bottom left)
'Good morning, do I intrude?' (bottom right)

Two years later another parcel arrived from Holland and AEB put his thank-you letter inside a *Rupert and Snuffy* booklet:

Dear Mrs Gerlach

How very kind of you to think of us again. Your parcel was most welcome and the contents much appreciated by everyone here. The butter and cheese were in perfect condition.

I hope that in your country you are now enjoying more freedom from restrictions. With us things are slightly better in some ways and worse in others – but we seem to have got used to it![4]

There has been wonderful sunshine during the spring and heavy flowering on the trees which gives promise of the best fruit crop for many years.

Rupert is busier than ever and now needs two drawings every morning. Some of the old stories are being reprinted separately. I send you the first one in case you have a small boy or girl who would like to read it.

With every good wish, and again thanking you for your present,

I remain, yours sincerely, Alfred E. Bestall.

The following August he wrote again:

Dear Mrs Gerlach

You must think my behaviour very bad because I have delayed so long my answer to your kind letter of – how long ago? It is partly because you asked for a photo of my house and I had none. However, these two snapshots have, at last, been taken. There is nothing very interesting about the house. It is just an old-fashioned suburban place with a garden (too big for me to manage alone) and a good deal of fruit and flowers.

I suppose, as the *Rupert* artist, I ought to be married with lots of children but, alas, I am not. I remain a bachelor and some of my friends tell me that, perhaps, it is all for the best and that if I had a family of my own I might lose my beautiful illusions about children! I do not agree with that!

---

[4] Butter rationing did not end until 1954, although petrol came off in 1950.

My household consists of my aged mother (eighty-five), her companion and my sister who is a partial invalid.

We were lucky to escape any serious damage from bombs. They fell all around us but just far enough away for us to escape. Your reference to your experiences during those years reminds me that many people had a much worse time than we did. We, at least, were never really short of food.

It is very interesting to hear of the hobbies that your husband is able to enjoy. Two or three years ago I had to illustrate a book about bees and it made me realise what wonderful things they were. Some of my friends are bee-keepers and they seem to get completely absorbed by the little creatures. I wish I could keep some hives, but attending to them would take more time than I could spare. At present the *Daily Express* keeps me very fully occupied with new *Rupert* work and, except for a week at Easter, I can get no more holiday this year and hardly any spare time at all. I am old enough to think about retiring but, as things are going, I don't look like doing it until I am about ninety, and by that time I expect the scientists will have blown us all to atoms!

This letter is terrible – all about myself. Please forgive me – but you did ask for it.

We have had a wonderful summer with much fruit and fine crops of corn and I hope you have had equal sunshine. No, I have never visited your country. I have been to Sweden, Norway, Finland, France and the Mediterranean, but never Denmark or Holland. It is a British habit to leave the best to the last!

Enclosed is the second of my new series of *Rupert* booklets in case your little grandson is interested (they are old stories with new covers).

Again thanking you for your letter –

With best wishes, yours sincerely, Alfred E. Bestall.

The stressful period at the *Daily Express* began in 1949. AEB went to London in January and 'discussed new *Rupert* series (one story per book) with Marshall' and then he had a 'long interview with Atkins, Marshall and Best and settled on design for new *R.* series (1s)'. He signed a new contract with the *Daily Express* for three years. In November that year he 'met Mr Asher and discussed [*Rupert*] *Annual* endpaper etc.' and his rough for the 1950 annual was passed before Christmas. Enid Ash became *Rupert* assistant in 1950 and Alex Cubie joined the team the following year. Meanwhile *Don Goring* and *Fire Guard Training* were hung at the Guildhall in the 1949 City of London Art Exhibition (followed by *Peter Fraser* and *Joan* in 1950) and *Phyllis* was hung in the United Society Exhibition. Peter Fraser himself died in March 1950 and AEB asked his widow, Edith, in Seasalter to write the *Rupert* rhyming couplets from then on.

AEB's mother was eighty-eight when Muriel, the housekeeper, retired. Rebecca then learnt to cook – she even made marmalade – and she sewed curtains. There was a big celebration for her ninetieth birthday and 'open house' all afternoon. AEB had, meanwhile, purchased Penlan in 1956 and took his mother there for a week when she was ninety-two. He lent the cottage to family and friends for holidays, but he went himself six to eight times a year. He frequently broke the journey with Harry Adams in Edgbaston or Worcestershire; or, later on, at the Cobden Hotel in Birmingham. Life changed in October 1959 when Rebecca had a fall coming in from the garden and broke her left femur. She was in hospital for nearly three months and then transferred to Fallowfield, a nursing home in Surbiton. She never walked again and spent her time writing poetry. On each birthday AEB, with help, got her home in a wheelchair for tea in the garden and she played the piano. Then came her 100th birthday on 17 June 1964, ushered in with a telegram of congratulations from the Queen. Rebecca received another telegram on that day: 'On the occasion of your hundredth birthday the Methodist Missionary Society sends congratulations with deep thanksgiving for all that the name Bestall has meant to Burma.' She was interviewed and photographed for the *Evening Standard, Surbiton Borough News* and the *Surrey Comet* and an 'avalanche of flowers and post arrived'. There was a huge party in the garden, after which she was 'none the worse'. When Rebecca died, on 13 October, AEB was in Wales. It was as though he could not face his mother's passing. There was a packed funeral service,

Photo of AEB at work

Photo of AEB with Rebecca, his mother, 1964

after which her ashes were put alongside Arthur's in the family grave at Brookwood.

In January 1965 AEB recorded: 'Mr Blackburn took me to dining-room on fifth floor for fine lunch with Messrs Asher, Matto and editor "Bob" Edwards. Much flattery and kindly talk but no suggestion of relieving me on June 30! Did some *Rupert* captions in Chaplain's office.' In fact, on 8 May he 'finished *R. and the Winkybickies*' (52) (last work for *DE*)'. He did actually continue to do quite a lot of work for the annuals, but he retired from producing the daily strip. He also gave up playing badminton (tennis he continued with for two more years). He began to clear up the Surbiton house ready for sale.

Rupert with bird

5

THE LAST YEARS

AEB MOVED INTO A FLAT in Surbiton at the beginning of 1966 and took delivery of a new car also. He sold the house to one of the Barnardo girls at Bayfield who had subsequently dived for England at the Empire Games in Vancouver. Although AEB played very little tennis now, he continued to help by washing up after tea at the club and he looked after the rose beds. He also kept countless children entertained by showing them how to do origami.

Rupert Bear's fiftieth anniversary was celebrated in 1970. Anna Coote, writing in the *Observer* on 3 May, said:

The *Times Literary Supplement* has called him [Rupert] a nursery Ulysses: on the strength of two captioned pictures a day in the *Daily Express* and a colour annual which last year sold 450,000 copies, he has amassed a huge following . . . *Rupert* hasn't made Mr Bestall rich. He lives in a tiny, cluttered room, stuffed full of papers, photos, mementoes in cardboard cases, with a larder and bed behind a green brocade curtain. In a dark green tweed suit, he sat at a big table in the centre of the room, folding paper figures . . . Bestall created scores of new characters, and started a small cult in origami, with his instructions for folding paper figures which feature in every annual . . . Bestall has always fanatically guarded the Rupert image, to stop anyone from building him into 'one of these big American . . . er . . . Mickey Mouse things'. But now, at fifty, he's going to be the subject of commercial exploitation. Paul McCartney is planning a film about Rupert, aimed at the American market: a *Rupert* TV series is on the way, Century 21 Merchandising Co. is busy licensing Rupert toys, Rupert jigsaws, Rupert wallpaper, Rupert pyjama material, Rupert clocks, Rupert soaps, Rupert puppets, Rupert cereal packets . . . you wonder how *Rupert* survived without all this. Richard Culley, in charge of merchandising, is a *Rupert* man, and concerned that the exploitation should be tasteful. 'We don't want a teenage cult with T-shirts and carrier bags – he'd be dead within a year.' But Alfred Bestall is a worried man. 'I don't see how on earth they can keep the image going. You just have to get his ankles too thick and he's *all* wrong. They've made this model . . . what d'you call that bungey plastic material? . . . his head's too big, his eyes are too close to his nose, it's not Rupert at all. They've made the jigsaws in *cardboard*, you know, and as for the wallpaper, they gave the job to this quite young boy and he's made all the figures into screaming comics. Paul McCartney, he's the pick of all the Beatles . . . I gather he's settled down now, got his own baby . . . yes, he must be gaining a proper outlook on existence . . . but I don't know whether he could possibly do it. I suppose he'll have a whole lot of Americans working for him.'

AEB drew a cover for the Century 21 colouring book (he 'wrote a snorter to Cobban [at the *Daily Express*] re the Purnell *Rupert* pop-up book') and he amended the wallpaper. He then began work on the cover rough and duly delivered it to Chaplain.

As Alan Gill wrote in the *Surrey Comet* in December 1970:

You can keep your Teddy, Pooh, Yogi, Brumas, and the rest. There has only been one bear in my life and that's Rupert.

Rupert lives . . . in fact he's fifty, and what better way to celebrate than by talking to Alfred E. Bestall, the Surbiton artist and illustrator, who for thirty years was the little bear's guiding hand.

Between 1930 and 1960 [1935 and 1965], probably the most dramatic period in British history, he produced the story and pictures – two frames a day – for the *Daily Express* . . .

Rupert's founder was Mary Tourtel, wife of a former night news editor of the *Daily Express.* The legend goes that one night the editor walked into Mr Tourtel's office and said: 'We must have something for the children.' 'Easy,' replied Mr Tourtel, 'I'll get my wife to do it.'

A few days later he returned with *The Little Lost Bear.* A caption explained: 'Mrs Bear sends her little son Rupert to market.'

Since that day Rupert has had endless adventures. He has flown, using hats, umbrellas and magic shoes; visited numerous foreign countries; always returning to the rural peace of his home in Nutwood.

He has been translated and syndicated in eighteen countries in addition to the British Commonwealth, has been made into dolls and may soon be appearing in a feature film. One year his annual sold 1,500,000 copies, which brings it into the popularity class of the Bible and Mao's *Thoughts.*

Despite this Mary Tourtel was never particularly fond of Rupert. She preferred another of her creations, a little girl called Margot, who was subsequently introduced into Rupert's adventures.

From time to time she is reintroduced into the stories even today – still wearing the long dresses fashionable for children in the times of her creator.

Mary Tourtel continued to draw Rupert until 1935 when her eyesight began to fail. She was forced to retire and returned to her native Canterbury, where she died in 1948.

Mr Bestall, who was already well known to readers of *Punch,* was invited to take her place. In 1936 Rupert's adventures were expanded still further when Mr Bestall was asked to produce the first Rupert annual.

Early ones are collectors' items. A Cambridge don is believed to have the complete set. In the war years they were produced with paper covers – more likely to get torn up – which makes these issues particularly rare.

'Our little bear,' as Mr Bestall endearingly calls him, celebrated his fiftieth birthday in November with a party at the Children's Hospital, Great Ormond Street. Mr Bestall celebrates his birthday in a fortnight.

He will be seventy-eight, but producing the adventures of Rupert – some people say he even looks like the little bear – appears to have kept him young.

The son of a Methodist minister, he was born in Burma and educated in North Wales, where he developed a passion for the Welsh countryside. He came to Surbiton in 1920 and until four years ago lived in Cranes Park. He now has a small flat in Ewell Road.

His living room is lined with Rupert annuals (naturally), books on the British countryside, and others of a biblical nature.

On the mantelpiece stands a photograph of his father, in clerical collar, while nearby is an evocative drawing of a wartime street scene in Surbiton, reflecting Mr Bestall's experiences as an air-raid warden.

The drawing has been hung at the Royal Academy, as has a view of Oxted, which took his fancy many years ago and remained in his mind, 'so I painted it out of my head'.

Also dotted about the room are little figures of animals, demonstrating his skill at origami, the Japanese art of paper folding. He is vice-president of the British Origami Society, and is responsible for the paper-folding tricks included as a bonus in Rupert annuals.

A precise but kindly figure, who loves his young readers as much as he does Rupert, Mr Bestall is just the sort of person I had imagined him to be.

He counts two 'great privileges' in his life – to have

Origami elephant by AEB

belonged to Surbiton Hill Methodist Church for fifty years (he joined the congregation in the same year that Mary Tourtel founded Rupert), and to have made so many children happy. 'Thinking up the plots was the hardest. The older I got the more difficult it became.' In thirty years he never intentionally reused one of his old plots or any of those devised by Mary Tourtel.

He was always conscious of what he calls his 'appalling responsibility'. He told me: 'The thought of Rupert being in people's homes and in so many children's heads was a perpetual anxiety to me.'

He shows equal concern for technical accuracy. Take the three Surbiton [Girl] Guides and their pet cat, whose stories are related on page fifteen in today's *Comet*. Before including them in Rupert's adventures he took a series of photographs of them to make sure he got their faces and uniforms right.

Although two out of the three (and maybe the third as well) are now married with families of their own, they are still featured from time to time in Rupert's adventures today. Accuracy is such that their children can instantly spot which of the three is Mum.

Mr Bestall is particularly sorry that of the three former Guides, it is Janet who couldn't be traced for last Saturday's reunion. She is the only one of Rupert's three little friends to have fair hair.

Beryl's lanyard (a white cord draped around her chest) also caused some difficulty. Sometimes he forgot to put it in and children would complain to the editor of the *Daily Express*. To one such letter the editor replied: 'I am afraid it is very difficult to draw a white lanyard with black ink.'

What of Rupert's other friends? There's Algy Pug (one of the originals), Bill the Badger, Pong-Ping and his pet dragon, Edward the Elephant, Ozzie the Kangaroo, Margot, the Old Professor, the Chinese Conjurer and his daughter Tigerlily, and countless others.

My personal favourite was Pong-Ping. As a child I was fascinated by the lovable Peke's curly tail and also by his pet dragon. 'He keeps on cropping up as do all the others,' said Mr Bestall. He spoke as if all these little animals regularly crawl up the table legs to fight for attention on his drawing board.

He still has a voluminous correspondence from present and former readers. A greengrocer in Gloucestershire used to write and remind him if too long had elapsed without the appearance of the Old Professor.

Several children would send him ideas for stories. One request was for Rupert to go swimming, but although he experienced several duckings, Mr Bestall could never show him in a bathing costume. Rupert's arms and legs are always covered by his familiar red jumper and check trousers. He has a furry face but human hands. 'If we showed him in a bathing costume there would be problems. We would have to decide if his arms and legs were furry or not, and whether to give him feet or hands.'

As regards clothing readers are traditional. After an impromptu ducking Rupert was once shown wearing a blue jumper instead of a red one. 'That caused quite a rumpus,' said Mr Bestall.

What about the Eton suits of Bill and Algy, and the plus-fours and old-fashioned dress worn by Mr and Mrs Bear? Mr Bestall has had many letters about this . . . all favourable. The general view is that such clothing has given to Rupert a certain timelessness.

The stories also faithfully reflect the seasons. There are spring, summer, autumn and winter adventures, and Christmas must appear at Christmas, with snow in January. For two months in the summer Rupert is allowed to discard his famous scarf. In winter he is allowed to wear an overcoat.

Several times Mr Bestall has been asked by American tourists for the exact location of Rupert's home village of Nutwood. In fact it is a blend of all the nice places Mr Bestall has ever visited. 'It could be the hills of Wales, the Weald of Sussex, and maybe the Severn Valley,' he told me.

When Mr Bestall took over he was given specific instructions to introduce 'no evil characters, no fairies, and no magic'. He kept to the ruling about evil characters but found the others rather a strain. 'I introduced elves – fairies without wings – and brought along the Old Professor, who does wonderful things, and the Chinese Conjuror.' He admits it's cheating but says the children accepted the situation.

Although Rupert is fifty, he has actually been reduced in age. This was done by Mr Bestall many years ago when it was thought the little bear should be slightly younger.

Mr Bestall should have retired in 1965 but he still designs the covers, title pages, and much of the work in the Rupert annuals. The latest annual is due to appear in Holland where – a rare event – Rupert's name, considered too Germanic, is being changed to Bruintje Bear.

The adventures in the *Daily Express* are now done by several members of a team, which says much for Mr Bestall's solo efforts. Most (but not all) of the stories in the annuals are repeats of the *Daily Express* picture strips. However, since the time lag varies between four and fifteen years, not many children are likely to complain.

The *Daily Express* is rather strict on copyright and does not approve of unofficial drawings of Rupert. Mr Bestall, being a kindhearted person, occasionally cheats by putting a sketch in a child's autograph album. However, even the *Express* shows changing attitudes and there is now a puppet Rupert on TV (which Mr Bestall finds 'delightful'), and one or two advertising gambits which Mr Bestall is rather less happy about.

Paul McCartney, of Beatles fame, also has an option on using Rupert in a feature film, and has asked Mr Bestall to give a watching brief. The hippy community is the latest to have adopted Rupert as a symbol. The

Postcard to Caroline Bott's three children

underground magazine *Oz* recently had an account of a happening, 'Rupert Dancing'. Bands of teenagers were reported running through Hyde Park, flowers in their hair and joy in their hearts, to levitate Marble Arch. According to *Oz* they managed to raise it four inches.

One or two hippy leaders have made the pilgrimage to see Mr Bestall. 'They were among the gentlest people I've ever met.' The hippy community's interest in Rupert is based on the dreamworld of Nutwood in which everyone is innocent and the world is safe, peaceful and utterly secure. This is also the professed aim of the hippy underground, who feel much the same way as the countless children who write in and complain whenever Rupert, on some far-flung adventure, is away from Nutwood too long.

I asked Mr Bestall, a life-long bachelor, if he ever regretted not having any children of his own. 'Not really,' he says, 'I feel as if I've had thousands of them.'

A second article, headed 'Rupert the Bear meets his Girl Guides', related:

In 1947, three small girls, wearing the uniforms of the 10th Surbiton Guides, approached Rupert illustrator Mr Alfred Bestall and pleaded to be included in one of the adventures of Britain's most famous bear.

Mr Bestall, a kindhearted fellow if ever there was one, agreed, and a few months later the three Guides – Beryl Sweet, Pauline Coates and Janet Francksen – joined Rupert's circle of friends, together with Dinkie, Beryl's little black cat.

Daily Express readers obviously liked what they saw, and the first adventure reappeared in the 1950 *Rupert Annual.* They have been appearing in the annuals ever since (sometimes in the stories and sometimes on the covers), and are already scheduled – complete with Dinkie – for the album on sale in December 1971!

. . . The Guides celebrated their [fortieth] anniversary with a party on Saturday at Surbiton Hill Methodist Church. Mr Bestall, a worshipper at the church for most of his life, was a guest of honour, as were two of the three little girls (now somewhat older) who appeared on his doorstep way back in 1947.

To celebrate the occasion, Mr Bestall presented copies of Rupert drawings featuring the girls to Beryl, now Mrs Horrocks, married to a civil servant and with two children of her own; and Pauline, now Mrs Ellingworth, married to a Methodist minister.

In 1972, when AEB was at Penlan, he received a phone call: 'Mrs McCartney rang 5 p.m. announcing her arrival tomorrow with Paul and three children. Went to Miss Smith to book for them.'[1] The next day he 'waited anxiously until 7.45 when Paul and Linda McCartney arrived with Heather, Mary and baby Stella. I got tea for them (no food), then Paul left his Rolls-Royce and I drove them all to Miss Smith's. Much talk over dinner about the future *Rupert* film.' The next morning he recorded how he 'drove to the hotel 9.30 a.m. but Paul and co. not down. Bought paper and cards and went back 9.45 and sat with them all through breakfast mainly talking *Rupert* film. Photos at hotel door. Then I brought the three dogs [and] Heather, Mary and baby Stella back to Penlan while Paul and Linda walked. More talk and photos by me and Barbara [his next-door neighbour]. They left 11.20 and I drove to Caernarfon to pay Penlan rates.' The three dogs were an Old English sheepdog – very old – a Dalmatian and a buff-coloured Labrador puppy. In the evening AEB went next door to Bwthyn Gwyn to see Paul again in *Top of the Pops* singing 'Mary had a little lamb'. A few days later he 'drew Rupert in a kilt, with short letter, for Heather McCartney'. Paul wrote to me in 1999: 'Alfred was a wonderful, good-spirited man and I have many fond memories of him. I particularly remember a letter he sent to us after our visit to Wales in which he thanked us and included the phrase "you and your vital children". I have never forgotten this and I suspect I never will.'

Later in the year AEB received a letter from Lee V. Eastman, father of Linda McCartney, from Eastman and Eastman, Attorneys, New York. He wrote back on 9 October:

Dear Mr Eastman
    Thank you for your letter on the subject of a *Rupert Bear* film.
    It was a real pleasure to be visited by Paul and Linda and the delightful children in my Welsh hide-out and to listen to Paul's enthusiasm. I

---

[1] Miss Smith was proprietor of a hotel in Beddgelert.

AEB's cottage Penlan, Beddgelert, drawn for Caroline Bott's baby son

gathered that he did not, at that moment, wish the film to be based on any of my Rupert stories. Your suggestion of incorporating many past successes is better, if a central theme can be found to thread them all together, though your wish to 'cull all the high spots' from my thirty-seven years of Rupert annuals might lead to mental and pictorial indigestion.

I would, naturally, like to have some authority to keep the Rupert of the film as near as possible to the image I have put into children's minds and I could hope that the *Daily Express* would supply its own 'watch-dog'.

Unfortunately, since Paul's first telephone call to me two years ago, much has been done outside to impair that image. The permission given to Paul to use Rupert was one of the first ever granted. Subsequently more than fifty other licences have been issued. So few of the latter seem to aim at raising the standard of taste in the average child that I disassociated myself from nearly all, except for a little advice on stage presentation.

I am now of advanced age and occupied in extra work for the 1973 *Rupert Annual* that does not leave very much spare time. You ask for my terms in the event of my being able to help Paul with the film. The subject is rather embarrassing. It may surprise you to learn that I have never asked for money for my work in the *Daily Express*.

I have, of course, been paid a little for my artwork but I have never asked, nor been offered, anything at all for the stories which are the vital element.

When in 1935 I found myself (a bachelor and not young) suddenly in a position to influence the minds of countless children I was so shaken by the responsibility that I had to approach the matter from a standpoint of spiritual exhilaration and could never align the stories with finance.

If the forthcoming film does not similarly place the benefit to children's minds above possible monetary gain I cannot be interested.

You ask for advice as to others who could help with the film: there is now only one man with encyclopaedic knowledge of Rupert's history and atmosphere from the beginning. He is Frederick H. Chaplain . . . who has edited about twenty of my annuals and has written many Rupert stories outside the annuals, and is running the feature in the morning paper though, as a War casualty, cannot often be in the office.

On 31 October, AEB's diary recorded there was a 'conference in *Daily Express* boardroom fifth floor at 3 p.m. with Sir T. Blackburn, L.V. Eastman of New York, Paul McCartney's sec. Wendy, Tyler, Thompson, Alex Cubie and Ted Matto. Alex and I were left to get out suggestions of a story to be enlarged, possibly two. Alex took me to tea at the Golden Egg and walked to Waterloo with me.' A fortnight later AEB wrote a 'long letter to Sir T. Blackburn suggesting "R. and the Whistlefish" with "R. and the Flying Bottle" for Paul McCartney's projected film of *Rupert*, alternatively "R. in Mysteryland".' On 18 December *Rupert and the Paperfall* opened at the Royalty Theatre, London. AEB went to see it with a crowd of friends early in the New Year.

He completed the cover for the 1973 annual in April of that year. In May, when at Penlan, he received a telegram from Tyler: 'Sir Max Aitken has asked me to send you his greetings and to let you know that on looking at the *Rupert* cover for the 1973 annual with Rupert's face, hands and feet in white we find this attractive and will accordingly be arranging printing in this form. Regards and congratulations. Tyler.' AEB responded by return (and also wrote to Chaplain). He received the following reply:

Dear Mr Bestall

Thank you very much for your prompt reply from Wales to my telegram. I do entirely accept your point of view that if it had been decided in good time that Rupert's face, feet and hands were to be in white, then you would have designed the cover with this in mind and no doubt there would not have been the white area of background close to Rupert.

You are also correct in pointing out that the rather strong colouring produced by Purnells has increased the case for white in this particular cover, although this was not a development which I had myself anticipated.

You have made it very clear that you do not wish your name to appear on the cover and I have given instructions about this, which I hope will be fulfilled.

I think we must regard this year's cover as something of an experiment, in which there will undoubtedly be inconsistencies of detail, caused by the late change. We must, of course, take our decision for next year at an early stage and then you will know exactly where you are.

The first twelve days of *Rupert and the Broken Plate* had been mislaid, so on top of everything else AEB began redrawing them – a task he did not complete until 1 September – and he did two replacement drawings for *R. and the Igloo*, in addition to all the other annual work. It is hardly surprising (especially as he was by then eighty years old) that on 21 October he 'wrote long letter to F.L. Tyler re giving up all R. work'. Meanwhile, in August his solicitor Peter Cudbird had come to see him 're the will and the illegal alterations to the covers of the 1971 and 1973 R. annuals'. It was also the beginning of "political correctness" – 'Chaplain rang re eliminating Golly and substituting the Toy Cowboy (for US political reasons)' in the story *R. and the Little Bells*. In December AEB finished signing 450 Clark Brandt prints of six annual covers.

In July 1974 AEB wrote once more to Tyler:

On 22 October 1973 I wrote to you concerning the unhappy treatment of two of my paintings for the covers of Rupert annuals and I have not yet received the courtesy of a reply.

May I remind you that all the artwork done for the 1973 annual remains my property and I would be grateful if you would arrange for the originals of the cover, endpaper, puzzle pages, origami page, four half-titles and all other incidentals drawn specifically for the 1973 annual to be returned to me, either at this address or c/o Mr F. H. Chaplain.

HM Inspector of Taxes has expressed interest in my reporting no 'profits from profession' for the last financial year. Somebody in his office had probably noticed that all the pictures in the last Rupert annual carried either my name or my usual initial. I have therefore explained the situation and I gave him your name. If he writes perhaps you will kindly confirm that the *Daily Express* has sent me no money in respect of Rupert annuals since 1972.

Although he did no more covers or endpapers[2], AEB continued to contribute title and other pages to subsequent annuals until 1983.

A personal sadness at the end of 1973 was the death, following a stroke, of Harry Adams. It was the end of AEB's closest friendship, spanning sixty-two years. Four years later he left his flat in Ewell Road and was lent

---

[2] Endpapers are the pages at the front and back of a book – half of each is pasted to the inside of the cover, while the other half forms a flyleaf or the first and last page.

another by a friend until 1980. From then on AEB regarded Penlan in Wales as his first home, although he made frequent journeys back to Surbiton. On one such occasion he went to Canterbury to find Mary Tourtel's grave at St Martin's Old Church. He found it much neglected and pulled up grass and weeds.

AEB could no longer escape publicity. In November 1975 he was interviewed for the *Liverpool Daily Post*, while in Wales he was interviewed and then broadcast on *Good Morning Wales*, and in December he was on national television (set up by the *Daily Express* publicity people). The following year he received a long phone call from a lady at the *Evening Standard* for the 'Londoner's Diary'.

The publicity continued, for 1980 was Rupert Bear's sixtieth anniversary. Geoffrey Levy of the *Daily Express* called with a photographer from Woking and AEB was featured on 3 November. As soon as he returned to Penlan three TV men turned up with two cameramen hoping for an interview. AEB found himself on *Wales Today* (he thought it was dreadful!). Then Mary Cadogan wrote an article on Rupert in the *Sunday Times* and in December a reporter from the *Caernarfon and Denbigh Herald* interviewed him and took a few photos (the feature was published on 23 January 1981). AEB went to Surbiton for Christmas and whilst there was interviewed for the *Methodist Recorder*.

Terry Jones, an ardent Rupert fan and creator of *Monty Python's Flying Circus*, featured AEB on BBC TV with Jan Pienkowski, children's book author and illustrator, and Benedict Owen in June 1981. AEB was collected and taken by taxi to Lime Grove Studios. He showed six endpaper originals and then went to the make-up girl for face treatment. He was paid £75 for appearing as guest author.

On 7 September he wrote:

My last appearance on TV, though a late-night programme, brought shoals of letters, many of them lengthy and all so kindly expressed that they could not be allowed to remain unanswered, so that I was pinned to my desk in Penlan for all July and much of August. Outdoor work suffered and I am not yet back to schedule thanks to an invasion of Beddgelert by more than a dozen old friends from Surbiton! Now our connexional periodical, the *Methodist Recorder*, has given me a big splash (with photo), so more letters! I like having my work of long ago appreciated but so much personal publicity is not my line, especially as my ninetieth year is looming ahead and I have outlived nearly all my nearest and dearest who might have enjoyed sharing it.

Terry Jones gave a four-minute talk on AEB on lunchtime TV from Pebble Mill in October, and on 2 December 'Ann Saba phoned questions from Canada from 2.20 to 3 p.m. and my answers were recorded (in Toronto) for broadcasting across Canada on December 29 at 10 a.m.'.

In February 1982 AEB wrote to me:

Three weeks ago I wrote to Richard Baker [BBC Radio] asking him to include 'Shepherd Fennel's Dance' in his *Baker's Dozen*. It is by Balfour Gardiner. Oddly enough I was taught the dance by the Germans in the War. They used to broadcast a lovely English music programme, often from Stuttgart, in order to soften us up before Lord Haw-Haw started his propaganda. Other things they taught me to love were Ravel's *Bolero* and the little English dance 'Dick's Maggot'. Richard Baker answered my letter at once and last week 'Dick's Maggot' was played in his programme. A few minutes ago he included 'Shepherd Fennel's Dance' in his latest *Dozen* and quoted part of my letter (not giving my name). It has happened very quickly.

AEB made a sortie to Surbiton in March to see Paul McCartney, who 'took me into his music studio for an hour's chat. Heard "We all Stand Together" at full recording. Long chat re endpaper for 1958 (*Frog Chorus*). Paul gave me a cassette of the music. Several snaps of each other. Then was driven to St Martin's Lane to see the animators and met Geoffrey Dunbar. Walked to Waterloo.'

Back in Wales in April, Terry Jones and team (seven people) had dinner with AEB at the Tan'ronen (a hotel in Beddgelert). The next day they installed light, camera and wiring at Penlan and Terry Jones did an interview. The film was shown on Channel 4 on 12 December, after AEB had been on *Points North* (radio) and been interviewed for the *Cambrian News* and the *Liverpool Post*.

The *Daily Express* began collecting the endpapers in June 1982 for an exhibition in King's Lynn (twelve were shown). The exhibition moved on to Sheffield (where AEB returned to Rutland Park High School which he had attended at the turn of the century), Bedford, Tunbridge Wells, Birmingham and finally, in 1985, the Barbican Centre in London. AEB visited the exhibition at each venue and each time there were reporters and photographers present. He also visited the Doulton works at Longton and was presented with models of Rupert, Bill, Algy and Pong-Ping. He was interviewed and photographed for the *TV Times* with a huge Rupert Bear borrowed from Selfridges.

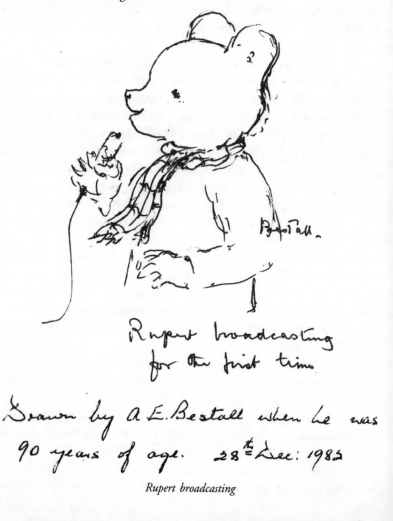

Rupert broadcasting
for the first time

Drawn by A.E. Bestall when he was
90 years of age. 28th Dec: 1985

Rupert broadcasting

It was AEB's ninetieth birthday on 14 December 1982 and the Girl Guides gave him a party in the schoolroom in Beddgelert. Idris Evans made a speech – he was the grandson of Mr and Mrs Robert Owen who were running Snowdon View back in 1921, and Idris's mother was one of the 'fair bevy of hostesses'. The following July AEB went to a Buckingham Palace garden party. 'The Queen and Prince Philip came out punctually with Princess Alexandra and Ogilvie.' He then went to Paul McCartney's house in Cavendish Avenue and was driven to the Elstree Studios where 'the "Frog" film was put through twice'.[3] AEB was by then very tired, but he changed his date of return to Wales in order to be interviewed by George Perry for a forthcoming biography.

AEB was 'south' again at the end of September to see the exhibition of his endpapers in Tunbridge Wells. He came to Sunday lunch with my family on 2 October and, while playing table tennis with my daughter Alison, he fell and broke his left hip. He was taken by ambulance to the Royal Surrey County Hospital in Guildford and had a hip replacement. When the Free Church chaplain came to visit him, AEB said he was sorry he hadn't returned the shot! After a long convalescence, he was back in Wales by the end of the year and was soon able to start doing outdoor work again. He wrote to Alison on 27 January 1984 after she had broken her wrist:

My dear Alison

The unhappy news of your accident is as painful as the fracture itself and I am writing as one old soldier to another to say how sorry I am. We can't send each other sympathy with similar backgrounds as my fall was through my own carelessness while you apparently were trying to save your brother.

It is terrible bad luck just as you are to have your first touch with my mother's old school, St Swithun's. In her day it was in Winchester and not on Mourne Hill. I do hope you can sleep properly in spite of everything – and that your fingers will soon regain their independence.

The northern blizzards have not spread in our direction. Moel Hebog is fairly well covered with snow but there is none in the village.

I am, of course, thinking of you a lot and hoping you are *not* going to

---

[3] Paul McCartney's animated film *Rupert and the Frog Song*.

try to speed your recovery. My mother broke her left wrist on holiday and became impatient at what seemed slow healing. She began moving her forearm muscles to see if the bones had joined, consequently she slightly moved the setting and the final healing meant a crooked wrist for the rest of her life, strong but unsightly.

May all go well with all your interviews at St Swithun's.

Best love to you and everybody, Uncle Fred.

He wrote again in October.

Dear Alison

Thank you for your very neat letter. It is interesting to know a little about St Swithun's and of your early work. It is splendid that you have been put straight into the first orchestra as well as the junior choir. Are you a soprano? Or can you take the lower part? You refer to fencing as 'good fun' which suggests that your brothers will have to be on their best behaviour next holidays!

As to computering – that is almost a foreign language to people of my ignorant age. And, talking of age, I am just realising that this letter will be posted tomorrow, October 2nd, which happens to be the anniversary of the last time I tried to play table tennis – which led to one of the most interesting experiences of my life and one that I am very glad to have been through.

My recovery is pretty good and there is no impairment of my ability to drive. My doctor ignored my age and has given me another year's Certificate of Fitness to Drive so I went for a 500 miles round trip recently to meet a crowd of Followers of Rupert beyond Nottingham and have to attend an Origami Conference in Birmingham next Saturday.

Terence Stamp, the actor, was here in July. He is also a Rupert fan and I want to get to Surrey in late October to see him in the new film called *The Hit* in Shaftesbury Avenue. May possibly see you if you are home for the weekend.

With best love, Uncle Fred.

Unfortunately, when he was in Surbiton he tried to go to the evening service at the church (Lord Soper was preaching) and had a fall in which he cut his head and lip and broke his left arm right at the top. He eventually returned to Wales at the end of January. In the spring he wrote to Alison:

PENLAN,
BEDDGELERT,
GWYNEDD,
NORTH WALES.
LL55 4NB

BEDDGELERT 400

14. March '85

Dear Alison,

Your letter are always welcome though my replies cannot always be given on tired punctual. Strange change keep on turning up and demanding answers. And one request (almost a demand) for a drawing has come! for the first for months except for your jealousy.

That is from the Headmaster of Rydal, a Public School in North Wales when I was from 1904 to 1911. The school reaches its hundredth Birthday this summer and he has asked for a Rupert drawing for the Centenary Magazine!! What the staff will think of a Rupert artist being the end product of a classical education I don't know. But I may find out for I have sent them a sketch

of Rupert being startled and chased by a lunatic Dolphin from the school buildings. If its first classical drama. If not - meaning my having not earned me to have one which you might - have is a lunatic Dolphin. Have you started Latin? Paul

I have just given away McCartney's "Chris Smith", the magazine containing picture of his rugby boy that was based on a Rupert Endpaper. It now too big & heavy to keep. It is sticky around. We have a few young people who like such things.

Actually this summer has been a great summer and Ceu from remarkable about Aunt "Bet". She spent her life saving for other old people but they money died, leaving her very much alone at the end, which is nearly Sad. I think she was 85 and many can be thankful to her for her services. She loved having brought to "Red leaves" on Sundays.

with best love

Uncle Fred

Letter from AEB to Caroline Bott's daughter

by Alfred E. Bestall O. R. (1904/11)

Drawn for The Centenary Edition (1885–1985) of the Old Rydalian Magazine AEB took the heraldic dolphin from the school badge, pictured to the right of the drawing

He then wrote to me:

Thank you very much for your newsy card. You emulate my paternal grandmother in the amount you can get on a card! You might try her trick of giving the card a 45 [degree] turn and writing across your previous wording, then a less turn etc. . . .

April has been consistently cold and damp except for one perfect *windless* day when friends from Hampshire were able to climb Snowdon and disrobe to sunbathe at the summit.

Easter was disappointing with fewer callers than usual, though one young publisher (head of Pavilion books) paid a visit to research my pre-Rupert period for a late autumn book. My hectic, snobbish *Punch–Tatler* spell 1923–30 has just about been forgotten and, I fear, may reappear on the back of *Rupert*!

Rupert Annual no. 50, due in September, is being kept from me as I am to be given a 'surprise'! June 28 marks the fiftieth anniversary of my first Rupert drawing to be printed. Unless my driving should deteriorate that date should find me 200 miles away at Newark, attending the delightful new, middle-aged society, Followers of Rupert, on the 29th.

The very cold April has kept me short of exercise except for a little wood-sawing but now more walking is possible, preferably with a stick on my very rough road.

I get a home help one hour a week and visits from our invaluable district nurse who lives opposite and below.

Best of love to you all, Uncle Fred.

He wrote to me again on 9 May:

It was good to have your letter and to know that you had returned from your Swiss [French] holiday without sprained ankles or other unwanted souvenirs. Was it your first experience of skiing? If so I envy you. I was nearly forty when I first tried. The snow was dry and deep and I nearly buried myself several times in the first week.

After a wet Easter we are having a dry spring with the River Glaslyn low – and the long, cold spell is yielding at last to lovely days, little wind and warmer days with – as yet – no flies!

Yesterday we celebrated VE day with a children's party. They gathered about fifty youngsters of under eleven from 'the valley' (Beddgelert, Nantgwynant and Nantmor). We are lucky to have two or three young men who run that sort of thing excellently.

The Tremadoc Christian Mountain Centre is finding me useful as an entertainment and a resting place for their children on their weekend outings. Thirty-four kids squashed into my little lounge last Sunday afternoon, thirty the previous week and thirty-four the week before, to hear about Rupert and Paul McCartney and the origin of his 'Frog Song'. It was impossible to seat such a crowd, so no origami, but I have just sent one of my own models, by request, to an exhibition in Tokyo.

Writing remains a principal occupation and the postman seldom neglects me. Last Saturday two letters came from ladies. One was your letter, the other was from Mrs Margaret Thatcher via the Principal Private Secretary. You may make what you like of that last sentence!!

With best love, Uncle Fred.

In June AEB was awarded the MBE in the Birthday Honours but sadly he developed prostate trouble and on 24 June I visited him in the Cottage Hospital at Porthmadog. He had a view of the Moelwyns from his bedroom window. On 27 August I had another letter, this time from Bangor:

I have now been shuttling between Porthmadog and Bangor for nearly three months and it is becoming tedious having no final success to report. Though down to seven stone in weight I am well and look well, with a returning appetite, but there is not much sign of regaining control of normal bodily functions.

Meanwhile Rupert's Jubilee continues with *Rupert Annual* no. 50 due to appear next week and George Perry's book on Rupert and me soon after. This illness prevented my doing many things, but George has been to see me (on holiday at Portmeirion) bringing vast proof sheets of the illustrations which may be jollier than the book itself having so much large work from my *Tatler–Punch* period (pre-Rupert), mingled with all the endpapers that have had such recent publicity.

Now it is August 30th and the surgeon has been round with his cortège of young doctors for their intimate examination and, to my surprise, expressed satisfaction with my *very* slow regaining of all personal control . . .

From the hospital I have the compensation of a great view eastward of the full line of the Carnedds from Aber to Pen-yr-ole Wen and the precipice to Ogwen, then the Glyders and the Y Garn ridge and Snowdon, most of it very undramatic compared with most Snowdon scenery.

On 8 October I heard from him once more:

This is just to tell you that I am to go to Buckingham Palace before 10.30 a.m. on Tuesday December 3rd. I am hoping that Mildred [Turner, daughter of Percy Rampton] can put me up the previous few days and provide transport and as I am allowed two companions I wonder if you would like to come too.

I am writing from Cynwyd near Corwen where very good friends have been helping my resuscitation for nearly three weeks. I am much better in general though very bad on my legs. Three and a half months' idleness in hospitals has developed a sort of painful rheumatism in muscles below the hip broken two years ago, mainly the left thigh, so I am walking whenever weather permits and fear I must use a stick on December 3! I am due to see my doctor again on the 17th and he may let me take over at Penlan and use my Metro for the short drives to the post office and shop. My steep little hill is going to pose a few problems when the winter comes.

The investiture was not to be as bone cancer was diagnosed. On his ninety-third birthday AEB received a message from HRH the Prince of Wales, which indicated that he had much enjoyed AEB's illustrations.

I saw AEB for the last time three days before that. He had been told he would not be able to return home, so he said: 'You had better have Penlan now. You'll find all my early artwork in the loft. You'll have to have a huge bonfire.' He had written to my son Simon the day before:

Dear Simon

Thank you for your joint letter with Jonathan. What varied occupations you enjoy! Is your bee-keeping welcome at school? Or are you preparing for big things at Milford?

Life is slow and progress not very obvious with me, but the hospitals provide much comfort. I have been in five great establishments so far and still cannot speak Welsh!

Very interested to hear of your summer in France and of your music, specially of Jonathan's advance on the lower register.

With love, Uncle Fred.

On 6 January 1986 AEB was taken by ambulance to the Wern Manor Nursing Home. He wrote his final diary entry on 12 January and three days later died peacefully, sitting up in his chair.

A biography of Alfred Bestall must end with his own words, written to a child. After a family visit to Penlan, when my daughter Alison was four and he was eighty-three, he wrote to her:

My dear Alison

These two pictures have come out of my camera. They show a little ancient Briton and a small girl with a smile. Can you see who they are?

It is lovely here now – lots of beautiful flowers coming out – but with no Alison to take me climbing I have to stay here and work.

Please give my love to everybody, from Uncle Fred.

Sketches of Simon and Alison,
Caroline Bott's son and daughter

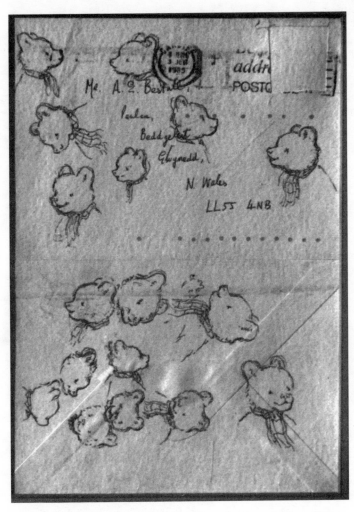

Rupert heads on a used envelope. AEB's last known drawing, 1985

Alfred Edmeades Bestall journals

Wales sketchbook: Trefriw, 1912
Wales sketchbook: Trefriw, 1913
Egypt, Middle East and Europe sketchbook, 1924

Glossary of Welsh words

afon – river
bedd – grave
betws – chapel
braich – arm, branch
bwlch – cleft, hollow, pass
cefn – ridge
coed – a wood, trees
craig – rock, crag
foel, moel – bare or bald hill
helig, helyg – willows
lan, llan – church, parish
llyn – lake
mynydd – mountain
pen – peak, top

Wales sketchbook:

TREFRIW, 1912

FRIDAY 16 AUGUST After much bustle we (Mother, Father, Pop and self, with Anna and Toby)[1] left Wolverhampton by the 1.30 train going to Rhyl without stop in an engaged carriage accompanied by Mrs Filk (sister of Mrs C.N. Knight) and her baby. At Rhyl she departed and we reached Llandudno Junction fifteen minutes late, just missing a connection. After about half an hour's stay, during which buns were munched, we left for Llanrwst, arriving at about 5.15. Once there we discharged hand baggage on to the platform and then Father sent me off to hold back the bus. The busman was pleased to take us, but was dubious about carrying anything bigger than handbags on top. However, on M's emerging forth from the station the man soon changed his opinion and agreed to take anything she liked. While the three of them settled in the bus I was despatched to hurry Father and found him standing by our pile of boxes and packages in deep consultation with two porters as a result of which they solemnly moved off to the other platform to get a trolley. F and I wheeled our bikes over and after boring through a solid crowd of tourists in correct climbing costume waiting for the return train we found Toby placidly submitting to pats by various muscular lady climbers who were amused at his wearing a label. In due (or rather *overdue*) time the luggage was towed through the crowd by the two porters and with some difficulty hoisted on to the bus. F and I rode on ahead, but on turning round I

---

[1] Pop was AEB's nickname for his sister Maisie; Anna was the family maid; and Toby was his dog.

perceived that Toby was being taken charge of by an officious porter. After
releasing him I elected to follow the bus, instead of the more direct route
taken by Father, as being more interesting and new to me. This however
led to complications as Father had paid for me at the toll, and afterwards
declared that he could not for the life of him imagine why on earth I should
ever dream of going the other way. The run was most enjoyable through
Llanrwst and over the bridge and then along the foot of a steep wooded
slope to Trefriw. Being held back by Toby I arrived somewhat late to find
the boxes strewn about the road and being tugged up a path like a little
precipice by two small boys and a portly perspiring female in an old tweed
cap to an upper road, and thence by many stone steps to the front door of
Penlan. Inside, M was talking to Mrs Marsh, F was busy trying to do
everything and arrange everything all at once, Anna was being instructed by
Mrs Marsh's maid, and Pop was helping with boxes. Eventually we sat
down to tea and boiled eggs feeling thankful that all had arrived safely and
that we were *really* at Trefriw on our holiday. After tea while M rested, F
went off to see Mr Chilton, and Pop and I went up through the almost
precipitous wood at the back of the house to explore. We succeeded in
coming out above the Conway Valley and got a good view of Afon
Cyfarwydd and Creigiau Gleision. After supper in the dining room lit and
warmed by electricity, we all retired to our much-needed rest.

Saturday 17 August dawned grey and chilly with rain; which conditions
prevailed most of the day, forcing us to take a rest of which we were all in
need after the rush of the previous days. In the morning we all read. I went
on with *The Rosary* which I had started at home. In the afternoon we all
played dominoes, after which I beat F at chess (for the first time) and he
had his revenge next game. After tea the rain cleared off and Father setting
together his fishing rod set off with it, while I accompanied him to bring
back some groceries. On entering Ellis's to buy a licence F propped his rod
up outside the shop (it was a 10- or 12-foot rod) where it was at once
surrounded by small boys, so that I had to mount guard. Leaving F fishing I
took home groceries and brought Pop to see the Fairy Falls. At supper time
F returned. He had been successful, having caught a two-pound pot of
damson jam, a bag of toffee and a bottle of vinegar, all of which he carried
home in triumph.

Sunday 18 August A much finer day. All went to the Congregational church in morning and heard a good sermon from Rev. Jones. In the afternoon Pop and I in old clothes went for a glorious walk up beyond the woods behind the house. Then on by the golf links and up till lakes Crafnant and Geirionydd were both in sight. We reached a cowshed just in time to shelter from a long and heavy shower. That was at about 1,000 feet up, and there I left Pop who was tired, while I toiled upwards to try to reach the top ridge of Cefn Cyfarwydd. This I had not time to accomplish though I reached 1,500 feet and got a view of three more lakes, namely Bodgynydd, a little one north-east of that, and one due east of the south end of Llyn Geirionydd. Toby came all the way. On our return we brought home some wild plums. In the evening F went to the Llanrwst Wesleyan chapel and met a guild party, many of whom knew him. Pop took Anna to see the falls and M and I rested quietly all the evening.

Monday 19 August was bright but there was much cloud about. F meant to go fishing and started about eleven o'clock. I determined on a full day's sketching so cut some sandwiches and set off through the woods with Toby bounding joyously in search of rabbits and other big game. After crossing a corner of the golf links I helped a luckless golfer in a fruitless search for a ball he had driven into the upper portion of the woods. I found a grand view of the Crafnant Valley which also had been found by a party of five gaunt lady artists. I pressed forward up the hill! The clouds were very threatening by this time and I managed to reach the aforementioned cowshed in time to shelter from a very heavy shower. Then I changed my plans, and hiding my paints in an unused outhouse I set off for a long tramp up Cefn Cyfarwydd with Toby. After being forced several times to shelter from the rain we reached the summit where we found a little hut or shelter, and got the first view of the sombre mountains I had so often tried to picture. The most striking feature was Pen Llithrig-y-wrach – a gloomy barren rock rising sheer up for 1,000 feet from Llyn Cowlyd and sloping away northwards to rise again in Moel Eilio before sinking to the Conway Valley. To the north-east [west?] it was connected by a ridge with Pen Helig, another steep-sided rock, and this was again continued by a sharp edge to the summit of Carnedd Llewelyn, which was enveloped at first in cloud, but which later revealed itself in all its majesty. Running north from CL was the long range of the Foels and Drum and Tal-y-fan till the sea was reached at Conway. Turning back again I perceived the Glyder range beyond Pen Llithrig, their summits also cloud-capped, and then further to the left the distance was hidden by Creigiau Gleision, the rocky eminence which was the continuation of the ridge I was on and which divides Llyn Crafnant from Llyn Cowlyd. To the left of that appeared Moel Siabod and beyond that again several mountains of Central Wales. Many little lakes towards Betws-y-coed also were visible. The view inspired me to fresh efforts and [I] determined to get up the nearer peak of Creigiau Gleision. The rest of the ascent was uninteresting till near the end, for the surface was bad and covered with heather, while marshes and swamps abounded after the recent rain. Toby found the heather difficult to get through. I gradually covered the long slope through bog and heath and rock till at last the crag was reached and we clambered up to the very summit. Then the view of the whole black length of Llyn Cowlyd opened up beneath us. It is nearly a mile long, and in a deep cleft between dark mountains. There is scarcely any vegetation near its shore. Pen Llithrig to the east [west?] rises steeply and smoothly to 2,600 feet, or 1,500 feet above the lake, while opposite to that is Creigiau Gleision with more precipitous sides and more varied by jutting rocks, but only rising 700 feet above the lake. Once at the summit we rested while a cloud passed over us, and finished the sandwiches. After taking a sketch of the Glyders and Snowdon I began the descent which was comparatively easy. At the cromlech of Cefn Cyfarwydd I made two more sketches, and then we took a shortcut down, avoiding the hut, sheltered from a shower in the cowshed and reached home at about 6.10 quite ready for a good meal and rest. Before going to bed I inked in my sketches, but they were not up to much.

Tuesday 20 August started with a good deal of rain but cleared somewhat about twelve. I tried a short walk through Trefriw and home by the embankment but found my feet very tender after the climb of the previous day. F fished but without success. In afternoon I biked to Llanrwst and then decided to go to Betws-y-coed, so went up the Denbighshire side, and back on the Caernarfonshire side of the river. In evening M, F and Pop walked to Trefriw Wells while I tried my hand at fishing without success. We had hoped to go with a guild party to Snowdon today but were spoiled by rain, so we retired early, hoping that the morrow would be better.

Wednesday 21 August was much brighter. At 8.15 we were out with the guild party waiting for the charabancs, and shortly after we started. The ride was most enjoyable, but uneventful. The hills were fairly numerous, and several times we had to get off and walk. At the Swallow Falls we all got off and descended to get a view of them. They were magnificent owing to the amount of rain which had recently been falling. At Capel Curig we got a good view of Snowdon and Y-Lliwedd which I managed to jot down a little further along the road. After walking up this side of the pass to Pen-y-pass we rode down to Llanberis. M lunched in Llanberis at a hotel while F, Pop and I had tea and tongue at the Snowdon railway station. We set off up about two minutes before the guild party. Pop soon tired, but F, not being in a very happy mood from some cause or other, rushed on ahead, but slowed down after halfway house. Thinking the atmosphere would be nicer if I were alone I pushed on ahead of him at a steady pace and passed under the railway again while he was negotiating the steep ascent to it. F saw me above the line and shouted to me to stop. He then went to a little station and after enquiring about the train signalled me to go on. I reached the summit just as a cloud covered it and so missed all the view of the Harlech district, but got the view on the way up of the Glyders, Anglesey, Moel Goch, Carnedd Goch and Braich-y-pwll. I reached the summit at 4.05 having done the ascent in 1 hour 50 minutes. After a quarter of an hour a train came in bearing M, F and Pop. M had to go down again at once to catch the charabancs back, but F and Pop remained on top. F soon started down again but Pop and I remained for rest and refreshment. In a few minutes the guild party began filing into the Summit Hotel. We waited till 5.05 and then started for Pen-y-pass. We soon got clear of the cloud and commenced the long steep descent to Glaslyn and Llyn Llydaw. We took it easily and I got three sketches of Crib Goch, Y-Lliwedd and Snowdon. We reached Pen-y-pass at 7.45 and after a rest we started back in the charabancs. It was dark before we reached Capel Curig and we arrived at Penlan for a little supper at 10.45.

Thursday 22 August was beautifully fine but we all kept quite quiet though I intended to paint a little, not feeling the slightest effects of the previous day. F fished in the morning. In the evening Pop and I went for a good walk by the embankment. F and I hoped to go to Beddgelert the next day,

Snowdon and Y Lliwedd from the road near Capel Curig

Crib Goch from the footpath down Snowdon to Pen-y-pass

DEC. 14. 1899.

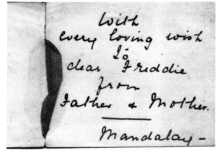

With
every loving wish
to
dear Freddie
from
Father & Mother.

Mandalay –

A seventh birthday card
from Burma made by
AEB's mother

Head of a Mouse.
This is probably the
drawing which won AEB
his scholarship to the
Birmingham Central
School of Art in 1912

Zeppelins. Drawing for a poster c.1915

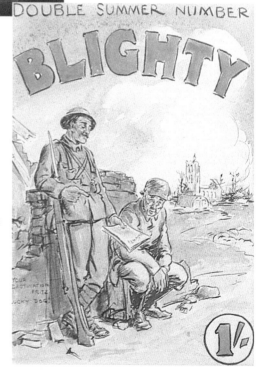

Your destination Fritz, lucky dog. Cover picture for *Blighty* c.1918. 'Blighty' is army slang for 'England' or 'home'. During the First World War the magazine was issued free for the entertainment of the troops

Dunn's Hat. Advertisement
label, early 1920s

Pleasure! Cover picture for
The Passing Show, 1924

A "Bash"ful Suitor. Cover picture for
The Passing Show, 1924

Waterman Boatman Poster. This was
published for *The Pen Corner* in Kingsway
in 1922 and it was judged the best in the
Evening News poster competition

Damascus minarets from the window of the Palace Hotel: Minaret of the Bride
in the centre and to the right 'Minaret of Jesus Christ in the Great Mosque.
Lower part used to be the belfry of the Christian Church'

Another minaret in
Damascus

Little minaret beside
the Palace Hotel,
Damascus, with Sultan
Selim mosque behind
and Mount Hermon
beyond

Baalbek. Lebanon, 1924

All in a Garden Fair. Tatler, 1925

The Coffee Stall. Tatler, 1926

Forgotten by A.A. Milne. *Eve*, 1926

St John's Bridge, Cambridge, during the May races. *Tatler,* 1927

May Queen. Rough for cover picture for *Eve*

The Pirates' Cave. Tatler, 1927

The Mill, an impression at Grantchester of the old 14th century mill
now burnt down.

> *Say, do the elm-clumps greatly stand*
> *Still guardians of that holy land*
> *The chestnuts shade in reverent dream*
> *the yet unacademic stream?* - Brooke. *Tatler*, 1928

Birds of a Feather. Tatler, 1929

The Shaded Pool. Tatler, 1928

The Legend of the Silent Pool (Shere). The story tells of a lovely peasant girl who used to bathe in the pool; King John, riding by, pursued her and she, trying to escape, was drowned. *Tatler*, 1929

Specialist (to small girl who is crying because she has overheard that she is to have her appendix taken out): 'Don't cry, Betty, it won't hurt you, I promise you.'

Betty (still crying): 'I know, b-but it will leave a nasty mark.'

Specialist: 'Oh well, nobody will see that.'

Betty: 'But ... b-but fashions do change so!'

Tatler, 1930

Le Forêt Sinistre. Tatler, 1928

No Longer on Speaking Terms. Tatler, 1930

All in Pink. Child (hearing knock at the door): 'If you come in, Uncle, you must excuse me being all in pink.' *Tatler*, 1930

This Cuckoo also comes in April, sings its song in May, changes her tune in the middle of June and in August flies away. *Tatler*, 1932

February Filldyke. Tatler, 1932

Spring. Tatler, 1932

The Last Caravan. Tatler, 1932

Our Village Cricket - fielding in the deep. Preliminary sketch and the published painting. *Tatler*, 1932

Two's Company. Tatler, 1934

(Note: the two butterflies have almost disappeared in the reproduction process)

and so retired early. During the day I inked in my sketches of the Snowdon tour – they were somewhat more successful than those of Monday.

Friday 23 August started with pouring rain which dashed all our hopes of Beddgelert and absolutely nothing was done in the morning. The rivers rose rapidly and the road just below Penlan near the shoemaker's was swamped. We all went to tea at the Chiltons where we found Rev. Jones. The male portion of the party spent all the time before and after tea by the river. F and Mr C fished. Rev. Jones translated many words for me.

Saturday 24 August was grey but rainless. Pop took the two dogs for their usual walk. I set off at 10.30 with Toby to find Llanrhychwyn Church. It was a steep walk through the pine woods and the rain had made the road very soft. From the village of Tai the road to the church lay through fields. The church itself has not a very handsome exterior consisting merely of a low building with a double-ridged roof and a bell tower on one ridge. It is surrounded by dark trees and is only visible at close range. After passing the church I determined to find the famous view of Tyn-y-bryn and looked about for a footpath which should not be so wet as the long grass and heather. Having got up some distance I saw that all the view was in clouds, so I cut down towards Llyn Geirionydd with Toby who very nearly got a rabbit on the way down. At the lake I made a sketch of it and then one of Bedd Taliesin. I took the upper path home through the woods and reached Penlan at 1.10 after running about a mile. Father went to Llanrwst after dinner and met Minthamce [from Wolverhampton] who arrived about 2.30. She rested in the afternoon and after tea we all walked to Crafnant Lake where I got in a little sketch which however did not turn out very well. F was interested in the fish which were jumping well. After a rest at the lake we all walked slowly back taking an occasional rest and admiring the varied beauty of the scenery down the valley. I retired very soon after supper with rather a bad headache and after inking in the sketch of Crafnant fell asleep a little before twelve, but a little after midnight I was again aroused by some uncanny whirring sounds in my room which at first I took to be wind in the curtain. I soon noticed that the sounds came from all over the room and it dawned on me that something was flying about, and I at once guessed – bats. Dragging myself out of bed, I first lit the candle, then pulled back the

Llyn Geirionydd from the north end

Bedd Taliesin and Llyn Geirionydd

Llyn Crafnant (evening)

curtains and opened the window wider, and then, seizing my macintosh off the door, I tried to beat them out of the window. But they flew so skilfully and so fast that none of my efforts came near to hitting either of them (there were two). After about quarter of an hour one of them got between the panes of the window, slithered down and forced itself out at the bottom. About ten minutes later the other did just the same thing. This episode had made my head considerably worse so that I got little sleep before daybreak. At breakfast I was rather a wreck and did not go to church. In the afternoon I went up and sat in the woods far away from everybody and everything and was quiet for the rest of the day.

Monday 26 August was heavily overcast at breakfast time and our intention of spending the day at Crafnant with Minthamce was quickly abandoned. I went off at about ten to get a view of Crafnant Valley. I managed to get it in spite of the light rain. Next I thought of going home by a roundabout route so as to explore the other part of the woods. On striking the Ardda path I determined to satisfy my curiosity and find out what Ardda was. Accordingly I pressed up the hill through the rain and after emerging from the

MYNYDD
DEULYN

EAGLE'S CRAG
(CLOGWYN MAWR)

CRAIG WEN

Crafnant Valley

trees and crossing two fields and a stile I reached a sort of cart road which led me to a cluster of little houses known as Ardda. Here however a cloud enveloped me, but having got so far I had to make a good walk of it, so pushed on towards Afon Ddu. To my surprise, the road instead of descending to Dolgarrog curved round the shoulder of Cefn Cyfarwydd which I was on and threatened to rise again, so I thought it best to try for a beeline to Dolgarrog and, if possible, see the falls. With this in view I cut down to the stream through a sodden field and managed to find a crossing. But on the other side I had a hard job to get clear of the scrub, for tracks, although plentiful, were necessarily muddy and the branches of the trees interlaced very low, forcing me to walk doubled up. On getting clear I saw a farm and made for it thinking to find a path thence. But the ground was very slushy with only tufts to walk on and the rain was still heavy, so it was with great relief I saw a conventional red-painted stile which meant a footpath. This I followed and found it led to the falls which were quite a fine sight, having a long drop but none too much water although it is the stream from Llyn Cowlyd. From there to Dolgarrog the path was rocky and steep so that I was glad to see the road and to start back to Trefriw. The walk back was not altogether pleasant owing to my wet condition and waterlogged boots. Once past the Wells the walk soon came to an end. After dinner we played a game of Minthamce's with dominoes called Matador. Then I inked in my sketch of the morning. In the evening M, F, Minthamce and Pop went for a walk.

Tuesday 27 August was so fine and promising that we all started off for Llyn Crafnant – F on his bike and the rest of us walking. F went on and talked to the owner of the farm by the lake about hiring a boat. I chose a position and began a sketch while Minthamce and F fished from the shore, Minthamce using a rod borrowed from Mr Chilton. We had not been there long before feeling the need of sustenance so we pounced upon the sandwiches. In the afternoon F and Minthamce fished from a boat. M went to sleep, Pop and Toby walked about and rambled, and I finished the painting which did not turn out any too well or too clean. F returned home laden with the property of the rest – M and Pop walked slowly back at about 5.30 while Minthamce and I walked slowly up Mynydd Deulyn, taking an hour over it, but enjoying it extremely and noting all the peaks as they came into view. At the top I made a little sketch and then we set about the descent. We found the slope to Geirionydd very steep indeed and crumbling, so we walked to the north end and, after much interesting scrambling, descended to Bedd Taliesin whence we followed the pine-wood track home again, having spent a most glorious day in perfect weather.

Wednesday 28 August was fine at first and after considerable hurry we got Minthamce off by the train she wished to catch. I strolled up Cefn Cyfarwydd before dinner intending to be out all day, but soon after emerging from an interesting ramble in the woods I saw a lot of rain coming over Moel Siabod, so returned home just in time for dinner. The afternoon and evening were wet, giving me time to ink in my sketch from Mynydd Deulyn and to copy my picture of Crafnant in pen and ink.

Thursday 29 August Being a fine day with broken clouds, both F and I decided to carry out certain long-planned excursions – he biking, I on foot. Accordingly at quarter to nine I cut some sandwiches and taking them

Clogwyn Mawr; Craig Wen

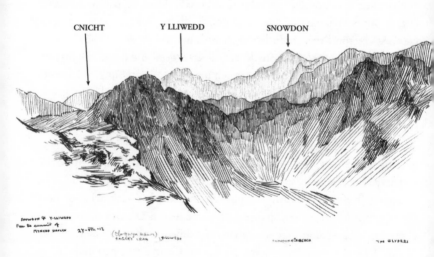

Snowdon and Y Lliwedd from the summit of Mynydd Deulyn

together with a mac, cape, my sketchbook and Toby I set off through the woods with a view to reaching Pen Llithrig-y-wrach (2,600 feet). I followed the track to the cowshed, joining the road not far from the hut on the summit which I reached in good time, although I had gone slowly in accordance with M's parting injunction. Thence the interest deepened, as the route from that point was all new. The road down to the Cowlyd stream was a pretty good one but not beautiful. Near the river I came upon a mass of rock which rose sharply out of a large tract of even and gently sloping ground. Acting on impulse I clambered up and found that there was a good view of Llyn Cowlyd and the surrounding hills from the top. This I jotted down, though with difficulty, for the wind over the lake and down the valley was very strong. The road then led over the stream and past two farmhouses, after which it dwindled down to a footpath along the edge of the lake. As that was not my route I struck off from the second farm up the hill which was the ridge between Pen Llithrig and Moel Eilio. I found it rocky and most enjoyable for scrambling. After reaching the top of a mound I found that a considerable marsh had to be crossed, but managed to do it fairly dryshod by the aid of a fence. The view of Creigiau Gleision had become very fine and from the top Carnedd Llewelyn loomed into view – no longer blue and distant but ever bold and majestic. From thence the surface was peaty and somewhat sodden, with parts worn into muddy ditches necessitating frequent more or less long jumps. Soon Llyn Eigiau

Creigiau Gleision, Llyn Cowlyd and Pen Llithrig-y-wrach

came into view – it rather disappointed me as it is artificially embanked along the east side. Clouds were now enveloping us rather often, necessitating shelter behind rocks and boulders. The last part of the climb was considerably steeper and had to be done slowly. I came upon the cairn rather suddenly. When I had nearly come up to it I was met by a hurricane of wind which nearly took me off my balance, but, struggling on, I reached it just after half past twelve. As I had expected, the whole range of Snowdon and the Glyders (excepting Tryfan) was cloud-capped, but the way up to Carnedd Llewelyn appeared quite plain but not very easy.

Pen Helig – with its many precipices and green, rounded top – looked bleak and cold, but the craggy ridge thence to CL appeared much more interesting. On the other side Creigiau Gleision, Craig Eryrod and Mynydd Deulyn stood out well, while at the foot of the precipice at the top of which I was perched, Cowlyd stretched, gloomy and desolate as ever. The view northward was most interesting: Tal-y-fan and Moel Eilio looked quite insignificant while beyond them the coast was quite clear – the Ormes and Bryn Enryn, and then the hills of the Vale of Clwyd. Llandudno pier was quite distinct and the blocks of buildings on the front looked gigantic and out of proportion to the size of the town.

On sheltering behind the cairn I found to my horror that I had dropped my waistcoat but was relieved to find it only about 100 yards down the hill. After resting a little, I conceived the mad idea of getting to the top of Pen Helig. So setting off through the gale I got some distance from the summit before I realised how deep Bwlch Trimarchog was. Then I gave up the scheme and returned to the cairn. Toby was very glad to turn and scampered back to a sheltered hollow he had found near the summit. I jotted down the view of Carnedd Llewelyn in my book, and having demolished the sandwiches between us we began to descend towards the south end of Llyn Cowlyd. It was an interesting scramble through the rocks and made the more exciting by the fickleness of the wind. Once, I walked to the edge of a 100-foot drop without realising the fact, and then had quite a struggle with the gale, eventually sitting down behind a heather tuft to save myself from being blown over. After going round another way I found the crag made a good study, so took it down, as I knew it would have additional interest on account of my escape. It was rather a nerve-shaking experience. Later on I drew another curious rock which stood on three

CARNEDD DAFYDD	PEN HELIG	CARNEDD LLEWELYN

From the summit of Pen Llithrig-y-wrach

other stones, though it was impossible to represent that fact in the picture. I reached my lowest point a good deal south of Cowlyd and was rather startled at suddenly coming across a notice to the effect that anyone found there with a dog would be prosecuted. I therefore led Toby on a string for some distance, but soon realised the absurdity of so doing, on a huge tract of land with not a soul within miles. The next stretch was quite the most

Llyn Cowlyd from south side of Pen Llithrig-y-wrach

Llyn Cowlyd and Creigiau Gleision

uninteresting of the walk, being over a long, gentle, peaty slope which led from Craig Eryrod to the valley of the Llugwy. It was excessively sloppy and the strong wind at right-angles to my direction did not add to my enjoyment. Halfway across the boggy tract I turned and got a view of Tryfan, Llyn Ogwen and Carnedd Dafydd. I also hoped to get the Elidirs,

Tryfan and Llyn Ogwen

but their summits were in cloud. At length we reached Craig Eryrod not far below Creigiau Gleision and had a good ramble there, getting a view of Llyn Mymbyr (Capel Curig preserved lakes). Crafnant also looked very fine. I found the descent into the pass leading from Crafnant to Capel Curig was very steep and I had to lift Toby several times from one ledge to a lower one. I hoped to follow the stream to the lake, but saw that the land was so boggy as to be almost impassable, so took a footpath round the eastern hump of Craig Eryrod and passed through some woods. On getting clear of these a tremendous storm of rain drove us to shelter under some hawthorn trees which were pretty plentiful just there. When that had passed we got down to a field near the first farm whence I got two views, one of Crafnant and one of the cliffs I had just descended. I got some ginger beer at the farm we had visited on Tuesday and then sauntered slowly homeward feeling quite satisfied, as no doubt Toby also was with a good day's walk. We got to Penlan at seven quite famished. Father had gone off in the afternoon and reached Capel Curig, but had had a bad time on account of the wind which had been against him on the outward journey. M and Pop had been for short walks along the road toward the Chalybeate Wells and to Trefriw.

Saturday 31 August was a very fine day, but I thought it advisable to rest. I spent all morning in mending a puncture in my back tyre and then in inking in my pictures of the previous day. The two rocky ones from the descent of Pen Llithrig-y-wrach were the most successful, while the one of Llyn Mymbyr was a decided failure, and I decided to tear it out. M and Pop went up to a farm up Crafnant Valley in the morning and up the woods behind the house (Coed Creigiau) in the afternoon to get ferns. F went off to Llandudno on his bike in the afternoon and broke his chain at Deganwy, being delayed for an hour thereby. He returned at about eight o'clock having come by train. At about 2.30 I went right to the top of the woods and began a study of a fir tree I had noticed previously, but it was so cold that I soon stopped and joined M and Pop in their fern-gathering. I was quite pleased all day that I felt no effects of the walk of the day before.

Sunday 1 September We all went to church in the morning and heard the Rev. Wynne-Jones preach – he having changed pulpits with the

Shoulder of Eagle's Crag from the north

Crafnant from the south

Rev. Henry Jones. After service M and I went in to see Mrs Henry Jones. In the afternoon I strolled up the woods with Toby. After supper I retired as I was tired. Mrs Wynne-Jones and Mrs Henry Jones came in for a chat with M and F.

Monday 2 September I got up early and went up to continue my study of the fir tree. Meanwhile F rode off at ten to meet Miss Wright who came over for the day. Then F started off for Caernarfon by train. M, Pop and Miss Wright went to Crafnant taking sandwiches. At twelve I came down from Coed Creigiau with rather a bad headache, but thought it best to follow them. After finishing the sandwiches the others went to sleep and I clambered up behind towards Geirionydd. On our return M went to the station and at nine F returned, having had a good bike run from Caernarfon through Beddgelert and Capel Curig.

Tuesday 3 September I finished mending the puncture begun three days ago. Then I packed the suitcase and helped with the packing of the holdall. Packing was the order of the day, and all endeavoured to get the house into the condition we found it in. In the evening Rev. H. Jones called to say goodbye. M and I went to see Mrs Jones as M wanted to see their house with a view to taking it next year.

Wednesday 4 September The packing and cording were soon finished. A cab came and the cabman piled our things on to it very skilfully so that little of the vehicle was left visible. M rode in the cab, Pop and Anna with Toby walked, and F and I biked, all getting to the station in good time to get the things labelled. At the station we met two of the Chiltons going to Llandudno for a week. On arriving at Llandudno Junction we found a train just departing so the others took it, intending to wait at Rhyl with Miss Wright, while I volunteered to wait with the baggage for our proper train. Finding there was half an hour I hurried out along the road to Conway and got a little sketch of the castle. At Rhyl I found the rest all waiting but Pop's box had not come with the others. (However it turned up later.) Leaving Pop with Miss Wright for a few days we journeyed on and got to Wolverhampton at two o'clock, our only stop being at Crewe. Of course Minthamce was at the station beaming with welcome. We found the house looking particularly bright, as Minthamce had been there all day. After a cup of tea M and Minthamce rested and I inked in the Conway sketch. Then Miss Thomas came in and we all had tea, followed by a quiet evening which ended our Trefriw summer holiday 1912.

Conway Castle

Wales sketchbook:

TREFRIW, 1913

O N WEDNESDAY 16 JULY, having packed Father off to conference amid the usual bustle, we (Mother, Pop and I) set ourselves to get straight for the visit to Trefriw. Auntie Ada arrived at 6.10 p.m. and during the next day gave very valuable assistance in the packing. On Friday we got ourselves ready in good time, and having deposited the keys with Mr Scott we reached the station in time to get all our packages labelled before the train steamed in. The journey was very easy and comfortable, we caught the connection at Llandudno Junction, and travelled thence first class as the train was very full. Two cabs brought us to Penlan an hour before we were expected, but we were soon engaged upon a good tea. When we had hauled the boxes to their respective rooms, I took Toby up to the woods and there met with a nasty shock. After going about 100 yards from the house I suddenly emerged into a desolate waste of land from which all the trees had been cut down. The ground was interlaced with ruts and was covered with dead branches which made progress difficult. This destruction of the forest had mainly taken place on what used to be the beautiful track to Ardda, but I found many other stretches from which all the pine trees had been dragged and the under-growth destroyed. I just went up to the old view of Crafnant Valley and then returned, not feeling specially pleased with my first discoveries of the holidays.

Saturday 19 July Rain came down lightly and steadily all morning, but we all ventured forth to see the grocer (Michael Williams) and later to show

Auntie Ada the Fairy Falls. After tea it cleared up considerably and Pop and I started out for Snowdon View or Tyn-y-bryn. On arriving at Llanrhychwyn we were directed to the quarry, and thence we made an easy ascent to the spot. The view was wonderfully clear and fine and having brought the field-glasses we were able to test their range. I was interested to see (by their aid), for the first time, Adam and Eve on top of Tryfan. After getting a sketch of Moel Siabod which looked very striking in the sunset I decided to return via Geirionydd, so we made a beeline for the lake, and after a good walk through the pine forest we arrived home at 9.15. We found that the cat [Thor] had taken a dislike to the house and had not been seen since the previous evening.

Sunday 20 July We spent a quiet day. Had a good service in morning with a fine sermon on 'Faith' by Mr Jones. After tea we all went for a walk along the embankment as far as the fourth stile and gathered various kinds of grasses etc.

Moel Siabod

Monday 21 July There was some talk at breakfast of going to the Wells, but at eleven o'clock, finding nothing settled, I determined on a big tramp to Clogwyn Mawr (Eagles' Crag). After Mother and Auntie Ada had cut me sandwiches I set out with Toby in very threatening weather through the pine forest and along the bank of Llyn Geirionydd to Tal-y-llyn Farm. Thence I followed the Crafnant track a little way but soon struck off to the left and had half an hour's very stiff scrambling on to higher ground which I found would have been unnecessary if I had kept to the path a bit longer. After crossing some very broken country (which I was glad to find quite dry) I reached a high spur and was rather taken aback at the distance it seemed to Clogwyn Mawr. A heavy shower coming on just then nearly made me decide to return, but when I had found shelter it soon passed off and I proceeded across the rough heathery surface till I came to a broad swampy valley which I crossed with the aid of a fence. Before crossing it, however, I was lucky enough to find a plant of white heather, a few sprigs of which I bore off in triumph. Beyond the swamp was another hill after which I descended to the track between Crafnant and Capel Curig, whence the scramble up the steep rocky slope of Clogwyn Mawr was stiff, but not long. At the top a strong gale was blowing, so after demolishing the sandwiches, giving Toby a dog biscuit I had brought, and making a sketch of Carnedd Llewelyn and Pen Llithrig-y-wrach, I was glad to descend and make an easy return home by road. Arrived feeling very weary, as I was not used to the weight of the new boots, which had, however, proved quite watertight and had been very satisfactory. I found that the others had been to the Wells and explored the caves. Cat still absent!

Tuesday 22 July On waking I jumped out of bed to see if the post had come. I found Pop had 'got there first'. She passed me up two packages one of which turned out to be the *Birmingham Daily Post* from Adams in which I was relieved and gratified to find I had one of the Ryland £20 scholarships. The other was my two Ordnance maps from Smith's. The day turned out quite fine and hot and we rested all morning. In the afternoon Pop and I walked to Llanrwst and back to see *From Manger to Cross* on the cinema. It was, of course, wonderfully acted, but did not strike me as being at all suitable for production in a picture theatre.

From the summit of Clogwyn Mawr

Wednesday 23 July promised to be such a brilliant day that we at once decided on a visit to Crafnant. Accordingly, at eleven we divided the parcels amongst us and set off through the valley. When at the lake we procured drinks at the first shanty and found a comfortable spot by the water where we lunched. Afterwards the others rested and read or slept, while Toby and I departed upwards towards the track we visited on Monday. After a vain search for my white heather plant we struck off still further eastward and obtained a magnificent view of the whole Snowdon range with a glimpse of Yr Aran summit just over the shoulder of Lliwedd, while Moel Hebog showed still further to the left. At our feet was Capel Curig (just out of sight) and the Llugwy Valley, and beyond was Moel Siabod, as impressive as ever. To the right of Snowdon was a fine panorama: first Gallt-y-Ogof and the Glyders with Tryfan as the most conspicuous peak, beyond which was the precipice of Foel Goch and Elidir Fawr behind. Next to that was Craig Ddu and the 'braich' leading to the summit of Carnedd Dafydd which in turn led up to Carnedd Llewelyn.[1] The peaks of Pen Helyg and Pen Llithrig-y-wrach just showed, but the Foels, Drum etc. were hidden behind the rocky eminence of Creigiau Gleision and Cefn Cafarwydd. From this point I also saw Llyn Goddion-duon – a curiously ugly strip of water – as well as Lakes Geirionydd, Bodgynydd, Tyn-y-mynydd and

---

[1] *Braich* is Welsh for an arm, limb or branch: in walking terms, a shoulder.

Snowdon from above Llyn Bychan

The Glyders from south-east of Crafnant

several smaller nameless ones. Finding from my new map that I was near Llyn Bychan I descended a little way to get a glimpse of it, after which we hurried back to find the others just going into the shanty for some tea. We had a pleasant walk back, stopping halfway at a farm where Mother made sundry enquiries about ducks etc. In the evening Mother (as previously) read some chapters of Copping's book on the Holy Land.

Thursday 24 July dawned warm but very overcast. Finding nothing planned I started with Toby for the top of Cefn Cyfarwydd. It was hot and unrelieved by any breath of wind, in consequence of which I was accompanied in triumph to the very top by a swarm of noisy flies. I found that the old hut on the summit had been removed bodily to a slight hollow where it was more sheltered. Pen Llithrig looked fine as usual as did the steep slope of Pen Helyg but Carnedd Llewelyn and most of its ridge were nearly obscured in the haze. I walked over the rough surface and across one or two brown and bitter iron streams to a rising partway to Creigiau Gleision in order to get a glimpse of Llyn Cowlyd. Creigiau Gleision looks far finer from this side than from any other, and through the misty atmosphere was most imposing. On returning I made straight towards the valley instead of going back to the hut and was surprised at the boggy nature of the whole mountain in such a dry summer. There was much heather, and Toby did *not* greatly enjoy himself. I found that none of the wood above the links had as yet been cut down. In the afternoon I felt somewhat overdone, and so rested the remainder of the day and commenced to copy my song out for Auntie Ada. The others went for a walk in the evening and Mother called on the Chiltons.

Friday 25 July Another brilliant blazing day. We spent the morning quietly about the house, some writing, and I finishing the copy of the song. We caught the two o'clock bus and went to Gwydyr Castle. After a prolonged wait outside in company with four Scots sightseers we were admitted and shown over the gardens where we gaped reverently, in wonder and in unison, at the cedar 300 years old, the clipped yew several more hundred years old, the Dutch Garden etc. The interior of the castle was so full of real interest that we found it very difficult to grasp everything that was told us by our lady conductor. I was most struck by the Gobelin tapestries and the profusion of fine old carving – examples of the latter seemed to occur in every room, and the crowning point was reached in a large and wonderfully preserved piece (old Belgian) representing St Hubert and the stag – with an extensive hunting scene, and an enormous stag underneath. On emerging thence we walked into Llanrwst and having visited the shops and collected a cheerful number of parcels we returned by bus. In the evening Pop and I took the dogs on the embankment where I got a fairly successful sketch of a bend in the Conway. Here endeth the first week of the second holiday at Trefriw.

On the Conway near Penlan, Trefriw

Saturday 26 July was another hot day, so we all decided on doing nothing, and soon after breakfast we sauntered up into the woods and found a quiet spot whereon to loll about and read. I went a short way off to get a sketch of a broad rock surface, but the foliage etc. turned out very difficult to represent. Before long the others appeared on their way home, having evidently found that their sheltered spot was not so deserted as they had imagined and having received much attention from the natural inhabitants of the glade. For my part, I also was finding the insects a nuisance, but, being interested in the sketch, I 'stuck it' for another hour after which I gave it up. In the evening Auntie Ada, Mother and I went to the shops and to look for rooms for the Pridmores.[2] We came across members of the guild party which had just arrived, and whose leader was the Rev. Evans who was much surprised to meet Auntie Ada whom he had met in Winchester only a week or two previously. He gave us the cheerful news that they were doing the Snowdon trip (which we had hoped to join) on Tuesday – the very day of Auntie's return! The event of the day, however, was still to come. We returned from the village by the river and embankment, and when just opposite the house we were attracted by a whistle, and saw Pop in the doorway holding up a black cat – our very ownest! – the wanderer who had just returned after an absence of nearly a week!

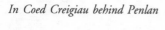
In Coed Creigiau behind Penlan

---

[2] Captain W.G. Pridmore had introduced Caroline Bott's grandfather Arthur Williams to Arthur and Rebecca Bestall in Burma in 1894. CB's grandfather subsequently married Rebecca's youngest sister, Florence, in Winchester in 1898. Arthur Bestall conducted the service and AEB was an attendant.

Sunday 27 July We all walked slowly to chapel in the morning through most overpowering heat and were relieved to find the interior much cooler. Rev. Henry Jones gave us another beautiful sermon – his texts being: 'Follow me' and 'I am come that they may have life, and that more abundantly'. The second lesson he read from the edition by Dr Weymouth. We walked back with Mrs Jones. The rest of the day we just 'mooched' about in the heat. I took Toby for one or two strolls on the embankment where he managed to get into an awful mess by scraping for rats in the mud by the edge of the river. In the evening I came across some fine bits of scenery which I determined to take down at a later date.

Monday 28 July Again we all found that the warmth was not conducive to exercise, and none of us went far from home. In the morning I took Toby to the embankment and made a sketch of one of the spots noted yesterday. There were a number of cows in the middle of the river looking very contented and, unconsciously, picturesque. Two of them formed a foreground for my sketch. After dinner I made another drawing from near the same place – this time of the village. After tea, Mother, Auntie Ada and I strolled into the village and then we all once again went beside the river and admired the many views. We met the lady artist who always seems to be with her two dogs on that particular walk.

Tuesday 29 July I was glad to notice some cloud and breeze this morning. At 7.30 we all assembled for breakfast, and at eight o'clock a cab turned up to convey Auntie Ada to the station – we were all sorry to lose her after what seemed such a short visit. I accompanied her in the cab and when she had booked her ticket I got one for Betws, intending to take a good walk from there. She got a comfortable seat, and went off a few minutes late. Three minutes afterwards I, too, was speeding off in the other direction. From Betws-y-Coed station I struck off at once for the Fairy Glen and after a good tramp along the road past the Waterloo Hotel I came to the right turning. On arriving at the entrance, however, I found it shut and no one in sight. Going back a bit I climbed a wall and somehow managed to get into the enclosure. The glen was very beautiful although there was not much water there, and, scrambling to a rock somewhere about midstream, I managed to get a fairly good sketch before the gate was opened to admit

The Conway at Trefriw

Trefriw from the embankment

Fairy Glen, Betws-y-coed

Conway Falls, Betws-y-coed

the usual crowd of trippers. Proceeding to the Conway Falls, I found them open and had to pay the legitimate 2d! This again was a fine sight, the stream dividing and making a fall on either side of an enormous jagged rock. I had an exhilarating climb round a deep basin of stagnant water in order to get a good viewpoint for a sketch, and was very thankful for the strong irons on my boots. The sun beat down on the rock very strongly and the swarms of ants and flies were a nuisance, but the sketch came out fairly well in spite of all. Next came rather a tiring stretch of very hot dusty road toward a bridge over the Machno after which I intended to return the other side of the Conway to the Lledr Valley. On reaching the bridge I was surprised to find that the old Roman bridge (which I had not noticed on the map) was also there. It was a very interesting old structure with grass all over the top, but seemed quite strong enough to last for many more centuries. The next part of the walk was very pretty, lying through the woods on Gallt-y-Pandy and past Pandy Old Mill which I did not go to see, not being quite sure whether I should have time to get to Llyn Elsi which I had in mind. Having reached the Dolwyddelan road I proceeded up the valley on another dusty road, past Giant's Head and Craig Lledr till I passed under the railway, after which I immediately turned to the right and up a steep and long grassy slope toward Llyn Elsi. Near the top I lost the path, and climbing a rock found the lake right at my feet. After a short rest I went on and took the path to the lower end of the village. Just up away from the lake a magnificent panorama showed up, though it was rather hazy. Moel Siabod, besides being the chief feature, blotted out all the Snowdon group. The Glyders and Tryfan came next, then the Carnedds with Pen Llithrig-y-wrach and then Craig Eryrod (or Creigiau Gleision). A steep and jolting descent brought me to the station where I found a convenient train and at Llanrwst I slowly sauntered back. I found Mother rather sad on account of the news which had not long reached her of the death of Miss Katie Thomas. The change of weather was now more obvious, and after supper we actually had two whole showers of rain, for which, no doubt, the surrounding districts were most grateful!

Wednesday 30 July At breakfast came a telegram saying that Miss Thomas was to be buried on Friday, so Mother decided to go to Wolverhampton today, and caught the 12.42 train. I went to see her off, walking along the embankment both ways. There had been some rain in the night, but that

Roman bridge over the Machno near Betws-y-coed

Llyn Elsi

had all cleared off and it was as hot as ever, so Pop and I did little all the rest of the day. In the afternoon she went to get some things at Michael Williams's, and in the evening I took a stroll round on both sides of the Fairy Falls, but did not make a sketch as they were not at their best with so little water in them.

Thursday 31 July The fine weather still continued, and the heat was tempered by a slight breeze. After breakfast I took up my abode amid the rushes in the field the other side of the river, and made a sketch of Penlan.

Penlan, Trefriw

The ground was somewhat moist, and the flies were a nuisance in spite of the wind, so I was glad to finish it off rather quickly and return. In the afternoon Pop wrote a letter while I mended the back tyre of my bike and afterwards mooched about the fields again. After tea Pop went to see her lady friend, Miss Jones, and to offer to take her for a toddle, while I started out for a walk to nowhere in particular and decided to let Toby lead the way wherever he thought fit. Eventually he chose the Llanrhychwyn road. On arriving at the top, we did not turn off to the village but kept straight on over the stretch of moorland, and got a fine view of Craig Eryrod and Pen Llithrig in the sunset. Descending to the small lake we took the road leading to the valley and when nearly at Gwydyr Castle we turned to the left along a road still through the wood till we joined the high road near the quarries. Reaching home I found that Thor (the cat) had got hurt in some mysterious fashion – he could not use one of his hind legs, and there was a gash on his nose. Anna said she thought he must have been run over.

Friday 1 August The brilliant sunshine of the morning brought out numbers of holiday makers in holiday garb, who gave ample evidence of the advent of August and the vacation season. All through the day cabs kept rolling in through the village piled up with luggage and bearing children. The increase in the population of the district had the effect on me of making me change my tramping suit (which was not far removed from a tramp's suit) for a more civilized costume in which I set off once more for Llanrhychwyn while Pop took Toby for a short walk. At the top I again went on to the moorland stretch and got a sketch of Tai and the mountains beyond. It was not very successful as the heat was too intense and also I had forgotten my penholder, and had to use a bit of gorse-stalk which did *not* prove a very efficient substitute. At a little after 3.30 we both started for the station along the embankment. We arrived very early and waited, only to find that Mother was not in the train, so we returned by bus. After tea we met the next bus at the church, but neither was she there. However, in a minute or two she turned up in a cab and we returned together. The rest of the evening we spent quietly – getting her things unpacked, and hearing the account of her short visit home.

MYNYDD DEULYN   CRAIG ERYROD   PEN LLITHRIG-Y-WRACH

Tai (Llanrhychwyn)

Saturday 2 August Having risen at the unearthly hour of 7.30 I set out for the station on foot to meet Auntie Chrissie who was to have come by the 8.30. On the platform was Rev. H. Jones just off to Dolwyddelan. The train arrived fairly punctually but did not contain Auntie C, so, having waited for the 9.02 with no better luck, I returned slowly through the heat to breakfast. Afterwards Pop set out, and having met two trains found the culprit and walked her all the way back as a penalty. Auntie C was, of course, considerably tired, so, after consuming her breakfast and dinner within two hours of arriving, she retired upstairs and stayed there till next morning. After tea Mother and I strolled into the village, and then I took Toby off towards Crafnant. When nearly at the lake we turned off up the path by the heather-clad slope of Mynydd Deulyn. The walk is much more beautiful than one would think at first sight, each bend bringing a new rock formation into sight while all the time there is a view of the Crafnant Valley below and the Denbigh hills beyond. After coming in sight of Bedd Taliesin I descended for the first time down the valley of the Geirionydd stream to Gwmannog Bridge and thence by the little path to Pont-y-pandy. The colours were very rich in the grass and heather, and the distances were very soft in the sunset light.

Crafnant Valley from the side of Mynydd Deulyn

Sunday 3 August We took Auntie C to chapel in the morning and heard another fine sermon from Mr Jones: this time on sin and the consciousness of sin. Mother and I stayed to Communion. There was a good deal of breeze, but in spite of that the sun was too strong to allow of enjoyable walking. In the evening we all went for a stroll on the embankment. The weather continued glorious with no sign of a break.

Monday 4 August The Bank Holiday opened distinctly cooler, and I at once saw my chance for a tramp to Eigiau which I had long had in mind. Toby and I started very soon after breakfast through the woods. The upper part of the hill seems harder to get up each time I go up – I suppose because it is so featureless. Near the hut we had a short rest, and then sauntered down towards the chapel by Afon Ddu. The valley was very desolate and marshy with broad tracts of cotton-grass. There was a good deal of cloud about, which covered the Carnedds and the Foels, and the atmosphere was misty so that the coast was not visible. After we had reached the top of the ridge beyond the chapel we struck off to the left up a rocky eminence for the sake of the view. From here I got my first sight of Bwlch Trimarchog. Pen Llithrig was much changed in shape, but still looked formidable, as did Pen

Helyg. Part of the outline of the latter was very peculiar on account of the jagged rocks giving it a serrated appearance just like a saw edge. The wind was very cold so that I was glad, after a hurried sketch, to descend to Llyn Eigiau. It was at a very low level and looked very ugly with swamps and bogs at each end and a huge artificial concrete embankment on the east side. The valley of the Eigiau stream runs right back to Carnedd Llewelyn and covers a huge tract of not uninteresting country, but after passing through the lake it emerges into what must be one of the most desolate tracts in Wales (Afon Porth-llwyd, also called 'Dead Man's Valley'). It is a broad sweep of reedy swamp, unbroken save by the long straight road to Tal-y-bont and here and there a few tiny Welsh ponies who seem to thrive in the wilderness. Its dreariness is only enhanced by contrast to the varied scenery and rugged beauty of the mountains beyond Llyn Eigiau and the suggestion of forest on Moel Eilio. While we were proceeding along the abovementioned road, the clouds lifted and before long there was a good view of the whole ridge from Carnedd Llewelyn to Drum. Leaving the road we made for the Porth-llwyd Falls and, passing beyond the wilderness, found the valley changed entirely and became quite similar to the Crafnant Valley only wilder. In a field I had the good fortune to pick up a huge horseshoe, nearly new, which evidently had not long been shed and which I triumphantly bore off. I found a footpath which took us to the falls. I made a sketch of a smaller fall (higher up) and then had an enjoyable scramble downstream on the rocks, as there was very little water, till I suddenly found myself standing on a high rock with the main fall dropping immediately below. I made the rest of the descent by the path to the

Afon Porth-llwyd (Dead Man's Valley)

Porth-llwyd Upper Fall

aluminium works and then had a tiring tramp along the dusty road past Dolgarrog and the Wells to Trefriw. I reached home at seven o'clock and was glad of supper.

Tuesday 5 August I was feeling a bit limp today, so did nothing. Spent most of the morning strumming on the piano. The others also rested and took no more exercise than a stroll on the river embankment.

Wednesday 6 August was cool and rather cloudy in the morning, but clearing later, we (Auntie C and I) decided that we would do the steamer trip to Conway which we had been contemplating. Accordingly, at 2.10 we arrived at the quay and found four boats waiting with quite a number of people already settled in them. Our boat was the third to start, leaving the quay when the second was just out of sight. The run down was perfect! The weather was ideal and the continual turns in the meandering river gave us ever-changing views, first of the Denbigh side, then the Caernarfon hills with occasional glimpses of the woods of Trefriw which we had left and over which the further heights of Pen Llithrig and Carnedd Llewelyn gradually rose. The climax of the trip was the sudden view of Conway Castle standing boldly away from its town. In Conway we had tea and afterwards went over the castle for half an hour before catching the bus from the station for Trefriw. The return ride was also most enjoyable, though shorter – the first part was the more interesting, being away from the river and round the base of Tal-y-Fan. We arrived home at 6.30.

Thursday 7 August We all arose early and made sandwiches etc. and set off quite early for Llyn Geirionydd. The first part of the walk we took through the fields near the Chiltons' to Gwmannog Bridge and thence by the main track. The day was cloudy and quite suited for walking. Having arrived in sight of Bedd Taliesin we encamped near and watched for developments. After a while Mother and Auntie C went to sleep and I descended to the monument and ascertained that the company was just going to the Mount of Song to the initiation. Accordingly Pop and I ascended thither with the crowd. On the top we found a number of people each holding a branch (stripped of leaves and twigs) forming a circle, in the centre of which were three officials, one with a cornet and another with a sword. After a good deal of impressive Welsh talk and ceremony by the three, the competitors for the prizes were led in by one of the 'circle' and their names, together with their 'noms-de-plume', were read out and each had a piece of ribbon (competition badge) tied on his or her arm. The royal harpist who was present gave two selections very well. Then the throng dispersed, most going to Isaac Williams's house by the lake for refreshments, while Pop and I woke the others up and we all lunched off sandwiches. At about two o'clock we all entered the monument enclosure and scrambled up a very slippery side of the hillock in order to get good positions for the afternoon meeting. The royal harpist again played Welsh airs and there was some very varied singing though it all sounded very well in the rugged surroundings, and the fact that we could hardly understand anything that was said only made our entertainment the more fantastic. We all came home through the pine wood which charmed M and Auntie C.

Friday 8 August In the morning came a PC from Miss Wright saying that she had spent the night at Betws and was coming on to see us. Pop and I met the 10.26 and found Miss Wright, Thelma and Miss Smallwood. We all climbed a gate and got on to the embankment which we followed down the river and on which we found Mother and Auntie C near Trefriw. The visit was short and sweet, for they left again by the bus at two. Afterwards Toby and I sauntered to Llanrwst where I got a little book on Welsh. The rest of the day we all spent very quietly.

Saturday 9 August There was rain in the morning, so we all stayed at home. After breakfast I began a pen and ink portrait of Auntie C, which I continued for half an hour after tea. Then we all went off to Trefriw Wells and gave Auntie a drink of the nectar, and, as I had never been there before, I sampled it too. Then Mother conducted us to the old baths and the cave of the well, but we did not go into either. The weather had quite cleared, so we sauntered back again, taking the high road from the hydro to the Belle-vue Hotel.

Sunday 10 August This morning we made a slight variation by going to the old church. We found it pretty high, but we enjoyed the sermon from the curate. As usual we spent the day quite restfully with nothing more energetic than a walk along the embankment,

Monday 11 August As the morning was cool and overcast, I early announced my intention of going for a tramp either up Carnedd Llewelyn or to Melynllyn and Llyn Dulyn. Thinking I might have to return by bus or train I left Toby behind, but I had not got beyond the clearing in the woods before I heard a miniature steam-engine behind me, and the dog bounded up and refused to return. The walk as far as Eigiau was easy, and on reaching the lake I turned to the left past the balanced stone on which were bottles and pots placed there by four men who were 'potting' at them with rifles from a place which looked like a club-house, close by. At the head of the lake I crossed the stream, finding the brown peat quite firm, and made for the precipitous crags leading from the lake up to Gledrffordd. I had meant to get to a little torrent I had seen and to follow it up to the summit, but found that it was next to impossible to pass the cliffs at the side of it. As I was commencing the climb a light shower came on although the sun was shining, and, looking down to a small bay in the lake, I was surprised to see a perfect rainbow in the water. This was the more unusual because there was no rainbow anywhere in the sky for it to reflect. The phenomenon lasted for about a couple of minutes and then faded. The climb was very stiff and several times I had to lift Toby on to a higher ledge before scrambling on to it myself. Eventually we reached the top and found as I had expected a vast expanse of grass and swamp still gradually rising to Gledrffordd. The climb had pretty well fagged me so I made towards Pen Helyg, intending to drop down to Cwm Eigiau and return, but after a rest I felt better and decided to go to Melynllyn and Dulyn as Carnedd Llewelyn's summit was in cloud. Pen Helig looked more majestic from this position than from any I had been in as yet, but Pen Lithrig was not so striking as from the Cowlyd side. Moel Siabod and the Glyders were in cloud. Proceeding across Gledrffordd I found it was a broad space, quite flat, and covered with shingle and stones just like a sea beach except for some patches of grass, and a few stretches of brown peat which rose slightly above the level of the rest. On one side (west) it rises to Foel Grach, while the east boundary is the grass and crags above Eigiau. At the north and south are steep grassy slopes leading down to Melynllyn and Cwm Eigiau respectively. Having crossed Gledrffordd I found myself above Melynllyn which is a nearly round lake more than 2,000 feet above sea level. There is a certain amount of crag beyond it down which rushes a little torrent similar to the one I saw running into Eigiau. I found a track leading to Llyn Dulyn which turned out to be merely the line of the pipes or aqueduct taking the Melynllyn water and pouring into the lower lake (Dulyn). Dulyn was the most striking lake I had seen, for it was partially surrounded by rocky precipices rising to about 1,000 feet above the water towards the summit of Foel Fras. Thence I took the path leading to Caerhun meaning to cross to Tyn-y-carreg Farm and thence to Porth-llwyd. But just when I reached the spot where I should have turned off I walked into a dense mist so that I could not see more than about 20 yards ahead. Toby was most surprised and disconcerted at the sudden darkness and hardly knew where to go. I immediately made for the Dulyn river across some swampy ground, and with difficulty followed it till I came to a plank which spanned it at about 6 or 8 feet above the water. This we safely negotiated and when on the other side made a beeline for Dead Man's Valley as the mist had then cleared. After reaching the road from Eigiau I took the same path as last Monday and arrived at Penlan pretty tired at 7.30.

Tuesday 12 August Did nothing strenuous today. Continued portrait of Auntie C in morning and went for a short walk on embankment in afternoon. Pop and Auntie C went to Betws after dinner and saw the Swallow Falls and the Miners' Bridge and apparently enjoyed themselves very much. After tea Mother and I went for a stroll along the Gwydyr road, turned up towards Pant-y-y-carw and back by the bridge near the Chiltons' garden.

Wednesday 13 August Finished Auntie C's portrait after breakfast. After dinner I took train to Betws and set off for Llyn-y-parc. I started on the north side of the river and soon struck off uphill by a path that led through a wood out on to some fields. After a time the path faded and, climbing some rising ground where were some very good wild raspberries, I soon found myself beside the lake. Half of it is surrounded by a delightful fir forest giving it quite a Swiss aspect, but the other half has been completely denuded of all trees. From there I climbed Allt-Wen and got a fine panorama of the district between Ro-Wen and Moel Siabod and of the distant mountains of Cnicht and the Rhinogs behind Harlech. The Glyders and Craig Eryrod looked fine but Carnedd Llewelyn was all in cloud and so was the Snowdon group except for occasional glimpses of Lliwedd. I was surprised to find that two or three

Part of Llyn-y-parc

small lakes including Llyn Ty'n-y-mynydd were nearly dry, having merely little streams trickling through the middle. On Allt-Wen I was lucky enough to get two large clumps of white heather, and I found another later on in the walk. From Allt-Wen I went due west, and after crossing the Capel Curig road and broad piece of moor dropped down to the road leading to Geirionydd. Before reaching the latter I cut across to a little tarn and thence past some mines to Llyn Bodgynydd which looked very fine in the sunset with Moel Siabod as a background. After making a sketch there I descended to Geirionydd and returned home rather hurriedly by the Jubilee path. At the Chiltons' bridge I found Mr Chilton who told me of a good walk to Ty Hyll Bridge and also told me where the Mare's-tail Falls were.

Thursday 14 August It rained a good deal in the morning so nobody did much. After dinner it cleared, so Toby and I went for a short walk towards Gwydyr and saw the Mare's-tail Falls. After tea the others went for a stroll through the village while I rested. We had supper at seven and then Mother, Auntie C and I went to the Congregational chapel to an organ recital. It went off excellently. The organist was Mr E.T. Davies, and we heard a song and an organ selection of his own composition. The singers also were very good. They were Miss Gertrude Reynolds (soprano); Mr Glynne Davies (tenor); Mr Nevin Jones (baritone). The latter turned out to be brother to our Rev. Henry Jones.

Llyn Bodgynydd and Moel Siabod

Friday 15 August This morning Mrs and Miss Jenks came by boat from Conway and stayed to lunch. The weather was fairly good and Mother and Pop took them to see the Chiltons whom they had known at Wolverhampton. After dinner Pop and I walked with them to the station to catch the 3.32. For the rest of the day we loitered around wondering when the Pridmores would turn up. At about 7.30, when we were all sitting on the wall outside, gazing towards Betws, Colonel Pridmore, alone, wandered up having left the rest of his party in the car near the Belle-vue Hotel. We all ran down, and while the others proceeded up to Bodaelog, I went with the Colonel to the Central Mews where the car was to be garaged. After a little dispute with the man in charge we managed to get good shelter for it and then proceeded to unload it. Eventually we managed to distribute the parcels between us and walked to Bodaelog to the considerable amusement of the people we passed. Having seen them safely in, we departed back to Penlan and supper.

Saturday 16 August We all did little today. In the morning and in the afternoon I helped Colonel Pridmore to swill and clean the car. In the afternoon Pop took Mrs P, Pauline and Joyce for a short walk.

Sunday 17 August In the morning we all went with Colonel and Mrs P to our Congregational chapel and heard Mr Jones again while the 'kids' went to church. In the evening all from Bodaelog came in and we had some hymns.

Monday 18 August In the morning the three strolled out to the farm towards Crafnant to try to get eggs, but found it deserted save for a rather timid little boy who knew no English, so we returned the same way. The Pridmores went for a little run in the car to see the beauties of Betws-y-Coed. At four o'clock Colonel Pridmore took Mrs P, Mother and me to the station to meet Father who turned up fairly punctually by the 4.35. He returned with the others while I waited and brought his kitbag and hamper of vegetables by bus. The rest of the evening we spent quietly, getting him unpacked etc.

Tuesday 19 August In the morning Colonel P did the act of a Good Samaritan and took a sick servant of Mrs Henry to her home at Dolwyddelan. Father accompanied him. Pop and I took Mrs P and the girls to the farm but again could obtain no eggs. The 'kids' much enjoyed going in to speak to some calves, but the 'lady' of the farm was very suspicious of us. In the afternoon all except Pop and I went to Conway by boat, saw the castle and returned by bus. We took Toby on the embankment and gave him a good swim in the river.

Wednesday 20 August This morning the four elders went off in the car for a run to Beddgelert while I took the others to Crafnant. The day was perfect and we sauntered there at a leisurely rate. At the lake we procured drinks and then went to the water's edge and demolished sandwiches, after which Pauline and Joyce had about an hour's paddling. At 2.30, when we were just preparing to ascend Mynydd Deulyn, a man appeared from Cynllwyd Farm to say that paddling was not allowed in the lake, so we departed. The climb was fairly steep and the heat of the sun made us go very slowly, but we eventually reached the post at the top and got a fine view of Snowdon. On the way up we had been fortunate enough to find three clumps of white heather. From there we went down near Geirionydd and through the pine wood, but slowly again, as the 'kids' found the wildlife too interesting to allow of a greater rate than a mile an hour. In the woods we saw a squirrel, much to Joyce's delight, as she had never seen one wild before. We all had tea at Penlan, and then, finding that the others were home again, Joyce and Pauline went to unpack their boxes which had just arrived.

Thursday 21 August was overcast in the morning, but Father intimated a desire to get to the pine woods (near Llanrychwyn), so he and Colonel Pridmore and I set off past Mr Chilton's and up the steep road. We got up in good time and turned to the right across a field surrounded by a big hedge. I eventually found a way through this and helped the others across, after which we soon got up above the woods. The clouds hid most of the view, so we descended the very steep slope, and after much sliding and scrambling, got to the beginning of the Jubilee path. It rained the rest of the day, so we did nothing.

Friday 22 August It rained nearly all day, so we merely hung about till after tea when Pop and I started out for the Mare's-tail Falls in spite of the downpour. We had quite an enjoyable walk. After supper the Ps came in for some games, and Rev. H. Jones also paid us a visit. Mother had composed a good version of the 'last letter' and with two or three other amusements we passed a very pleasant evening.

Saturday 23 August Finding the ladies disinclined for a motor run Colonel Pridmore took Father and me for a spin. I at first wished to be dropped at Bethesda for Carnedd Llewelyn but, finding that they were returning by Pen-y-gwryd, I decided to do the Glyders instead. At Ogwen we got down and all went up to Idwal along rather a wet track. I was much struck with the ruggedness of the cliffs which surrounded the lake on three sides but the others scarcely seemed to think it worth the walk. After some lunch I made for the head of the lake and decided that the Devil's Kitchen which I saw far above me between Glyder Fawr and Garn was a long way round, so started straight up the steep and slippery slope to the left towards a hollow between Bwlch-y-Ddwy Glyder and Glyder Fawr. On reaching the top of the slope found the hollow was surrounded by magnificent crags which bristled at the top with sharp perpendicular rocks and which finished off below with big boulders and long slopes of scree. Down the middle flowed a stream which had been swelled by the recent rains into a torrent. Looking back from the hollow I got a grand view of the Vale of Nant Ffrancon with the Bethesda quarries, and beyond them Afon Ogwen which terminated in the woods and tower of Penrhyn Castle. Beyond that again came the Menai Straits where were four white-winged yachts and then Beaumaris and the western [eastern] coast of Anglesey. Turning my back on these views I proceeded beside the stream and up to a steep scree which seemed to be the only reasonable exit from the hollow. It was a stiff scramble and none too safe, for the stones were continually slipping away. However, thanks to the spikes in my boots, I eventually got over the top of the cliffs and found that the climbing was finished, and there, straight ahead, were the peaks of Snowdon. These however were cloudcapped a minute or so later and I saw no more of the summit, and only a few glimpses of Crib Goch and Lliwedd. The top of Glyder Fawr is fairly flat and covered with broken stones, while several bristling and jagged clumps of rocks stood out here and there. One of the latter formed the summit, and clambering up there I suddenly got the view of the Llanberis Valley with its two lakes. Snowdon and Moel Siabod were cloudcapped, but over the shoulder of Lliwedd I saw Aran and also got a glimpse of Harlech and the sea. The Carnedds looked very fine, while to the north-west were Garn, Moel Goch and the Elidirs with Holyhead in the distance. I did not stay long at the summit as the clouds came, and it got chilly, so I made an uneventful descent down a steep grass slope to Llyn Cwm Ffynnon which I had seen below me from the summit. Finding I was in good time I ascended Foel Berfedd and then went leisurely towards Pen-y-Gwryd keeping an eye on the road to see when the car arrived. Instead of going straight to the hotel I cut across on to the Beddgelert road, and there got caught in a terrific rainstorm which nearly soaked me before I could get my cape out. After it stopped I got to the garage and tried to dry myself a bit. The car turned up in about ten minutes, and we came straight home, staying for a moment to admire the view of Snowdon (now quite clear) with Llyn Mymbyr as a foreground.

Sunday 24 August Once again we heard Rev. H. Jones in the morning and much enjoyed his sermon. All the Pridmores went to church. In the evening Mother, Father, Colonel P and I went to the Llanrwst Wesleyan chapel expecting the service to commence at 6.30. However it had begun at six, so we arrived just in time for the sermon and found Rev. H. Waterworth from Colwyn Bay was preaching. Rev. C. Isswood and Mr Thompson and his family from Ireland were in the congregation, so Mother and Father returned to Trefriw with them while I took Colonel Pridmore via the embankment.

Monday 25 August This morning I determined to get to the top of Creigiau Gleision – to the upper summit which is further south and slightly higher than the peak I ascended last year in my first climb of the district. Father was intent on a bike spin, and the Pridmores were all off to Llanberis in the car to ascend Snowdon. I took Toby by the meadow path, and soon reached Crafnant and debated whether to start climbing at the northern end, finally deciding to begin the ascent beyond the Cornel chapel. After passing through the last farm southwards we crossed the river which feeds the lake, and, taking a brief rest, we went through rather a difficult tract where the spaces between the boulders were hidden or filled up with bracken, necessitating caution. Then followed a steep rocky scramble terminated by a high loose wall which we safely negotiated. After that the going was easy up grass slopes till we reached the top of Craig-Wen whence we bore off to the right across some rather boggy grass and reached the summit of Creigiau Gleision. It proved to be one of the best viewpoints I had reached. Beginning at Llandudno which looked very clear and near the peaks were Great Orme, Moel Eilio, Pen-y-caer, Tal-y-fan, Pen-y-castell, Drum, the Foels, Pen Llithrig-y-wrach, Carnedd Dafydd, Craig-ddu, Elidir Fawr, Garn, Tryfan, Glyder Fawr, Glyder Fach, beyond which were Crib-y-ddysgl and Snowdon summit, then Gallt-y-ogof and the distant Lliwedd, Moel Hebog, Moel-ddu, the hills by Cnicht, Moel Siabod with the far Arenigs and then the Denbigh hills and Bryn Enryn and the Little Orme. At the summit I found quantities of bilberries and had a good rest before making towards Capel Curig. The view from the top of Craig-Wen was equally fine, for although Pen Llithrig hid Foel Grach and Foel Fras, yet Pen Helig and Carnedd Llewelyn came in view and the precipitous Foel Goch appeared beyond Craig-ddu. The walk to Capel Curig was swampy but uneventful, and I was glad to get to the post office for rest and refreshment. Thence the walk became tiring down the two-mile stretch to Ty-hyll Bridge, but after that it became interesting again as we struck over the hills by the old road from Capel Curig to Trefriw past various mines. The descent was through some fine woods, in the middle of which were the Hafna Mines (lead) which give the water of the Mare's-tail Falls such a curious colour. On reaching Trefriw I found the Pridmores were just back after their Llanberis spin, the Colonel and the two girls having walked both up and down Snowdon. Later on Father turned up nearly dead, having ridden to Pen-y-pass on a borrowed bike of high gear!

Tuesday 26 August was very much a repetition of one or two days last year. All the others started for Crafnant while I went to Llanrwst to see about a puncture, catching them up before they reached the lake. Once there we lunched beside a wall, after which the grown-ups read or slept and the 'kids' caught fish with a contrivance of their own (consisting of a handkerchief with a stick tied to each corner) while I mooched round looking for a sketch. We had tea in the tin hut, and then Colonel Pridmore and I set off for Geirionydd while the others started homewards. We had a very nice walk by Cyn-Llwyd Farm and across by the footpath to Tal-y-llyn Farm and Geirionydd, which looked beautiful in the sunset. After going nearly through the pine wood we crossed the fence into the lower field, and arrived home only a few minutes after the others.

Wednesday 27 August was an uneventful day. We did nothing but mooch about and gather a few mushrooms. The Pridmores went to Llandudno and had some sea-bathing.

Thursday 28 August Again we did not feel particularly energetic as it was very hot, and spent the morning and afternoon gathering mushrooms. After tea Mother went to the embankment to continue her sketch, while I was put in charge of the 'kids' who wanted to get some heather and bogmyrtle etc. Accordingly we three set off towards Crafnant and got huge quantities of heather and bogmyrtle, and also roots of honeysuckle, foxgloves and ferns which we slung on to my walking stick. It was pretty well dark when we got back, and we found Mrs P just thinking of organising a search party.

Friday 29 August Early this morning we assembled to wish the Pridmores goodbye. Colonel P took a snapshot of us all in our little strip of front garden. The heather of last night was hung on behind their car, whence it got burnt up by the heat and fumes of the engine before they reached Chester! After seeing them safely on their way Father and I wondered how we could pass the day. I decided to bus to Conway and do the Sychnant Pass, while he apparently meant to have a quiet day at home. On reaching Conway I found that the blazing heat put the Pass out of the question, so I strolled down to the Morfa and thence round by the shore road to the town again. Seeing a Llandudno bus I took it and, getting to Llandudno, spent half an hour on the pier where I got some entertainment in feeding the seagulls with bits of bread and watching the neat way in which they caught the pieces in mid-air. Returning thence I got to Conway about 4.30 and went into the castle where I wandered round a bit and then began a sketch for Auntie Ada's album. The return bus was more than half an hour late, but eventually I reached home pretty tired with the heat of the day. Father arrived home later, having been by train to Porthmadog and Criccieth, and then to Barmouth and back.

Saturday 30 August This being the day Mr Varley had fixed to take us all for a spin, we got ready early and watched for his car to come along. Just before twelve it appeared and after settling ourselves comfortably in we started off at a great rate for Beddgelert. The road from Pen-y-gwryd was all new to me and as that part of the day was nice and clear we got grand views of Snowdon and Aran and Moel Hebog. The spin down the valley was delightful, first past Gwynant lake and then past Llyn Dinas and into Beddgelert. At the top of the valley we saw the Misses Rosa and Lilian Horsey in regular tramp costume, but did not stop to speak to them and just before reaching Llyn Gwynant we saw Eric Champion, broken down (motor-bike) by the roadside and pulled up to speak to him. At Beddgelert Mr Varley took us into the Saracen's Head where we had a very nice lunch after which we went in search of Gelert's Grave. This we found to be a space fenced round, in the middle of a field, and containing an old tree and two curious old stones. On our way back to the hotel we passed through a small horse-show, where dogs and cows as well as horses were for sale and for show. From Beddgelert we proceeded south between Moel Hebog and Moel-y-Dyniewyd and over the lovely pass of Aberglaslyn. We got out at the bridge, and admired the views, after which we made off again towards

Tremadoc. When nearly there we looked back and got the magnificent view of Cnicht which so captivated Mother and Father last year. We also got a good view of the Rhinogs. From Tremadoc we took the Caernarfon road, avoiding Porthmadog which we saw about a mile to the south. The road as far as Pen Morfa was fairly steep and had a bad surface, but we did it at a great rate, and finding, later, several stretches very straight we, two or three times, got up to and above 35 mph. There was a good deal of mist about, so the Pwllheli mountains were nearly blotted out, and the summits of the nearer mountains, the Carnedd Goch range, were invisible. We passed through Llanllyfni and Pen-y-groes and so got to Caernarfon where we four hurried to see over the castle while Mr and Mrs Varley stayed and got more petrol etc. On going in we joined a party being shown round by a very vivacious conductor. After seeing Queen Eleanor's Gateway, where the present Prince of Wales [Edward VIII to be] was presented to the people at his State Investiture, we made across and climbed to the top of one of the turrets of Eagle Tower, and then while the others mooched round I explored the Chamberlain's Tower opposite the entrance. From Caernarfon we went to Bangor where we had tea at a hotel. After that we flew along the coast past Aber, Llanfairfechan and Penmaenmawr and turned south at Conway. Just after passing Trefriw Wells we heard a hiss, and the left back tyre went flat. That however was quickly remedied, and we soon were in Penlan and at supper.

Sunday 31 August This morning we heard a preacher from Swansea who was supplying for Rev. H. Jones who was on his holiday. After tea I took Father to Geirionydd as he had never seen it. From the mill we went up the steeper but shorter slope to the left. The evening was fine and we much enjoyed the views and the walk through the pine woods home again. After supper Mr Chilton came in for a chat and lent us his diary of a ten-day trip (on foot) in Wales many years previously.

Monday 1 September Today was spent in packing and getting the house straight which was no easy job seeing how much we had altered it. I managed to find time, however, to gather a few more mushrooms, but not sufficient to make it worth while to take any home.

Tuesday 2 September This morning again was full of packing and labelling and fastening. Father went off on my bike early, as he was going alone via Corwen and Llangollen. At 1.30 Mr Jones's (greengrocer) cart arrived, but could not get all the packages on board, so a cab was hailed which took the remainder as well as Mother, Pop and Anna to the station. Meanwhile I had gone to return Mr Chilton's book and to say goodbye after which I made toward Llanrwst. The carriage caught me up halfway there and I rode the remainder. The train journey was uncommonly pleasant, as, from Llandudno Junction, we had a carriage to ourselves all the way to Wolverhampton. There we found Minthamce and Father waiting for us, and, having settled about the luggage, we returned home for an early supper. So ended the second visit to Trefriw.

Penlan from top of tree in meadow opposite

Egypt, Middle East and
Europe sketchbook

1924

*S*ATURDAY 1 MARCH 3 p.m. Left 37 Bedford Place with all our
baggage for St Pancras. Were early for train and enjoyed watching
other arrivals with their possessions carrying Orient labels.

3.50. Train (*Ormonde* special) left and made a leisurely journey via
Walthamstow and Grays to Tilbury where it ran alongside the *Ormonde*.
Tickets and passports examined at barrier after which we went aboard and
discovered our cabins. We were lucky to have got single cabins very well
equipped (forward, starboard) just through the foyer of the dining saloon.
Mother next door to me (cabin 278 – Mother 279). Had tea almost
immediately.

6.00 p.m. The *Ormonde* cast off and slid gently towards the stream. Was
more than an hour getting out of the docks.

7.30. Dinner, very sumptuous, with nectarines to finish. There are 250
first-class passengers though the boat would hold 500. A great proportion
are Australians going the full journey.

8.15. On deck again. Fine starry night. Passed big places on either bank
of the river and had the usual fatuous argument with people as ignorant as
myself as to whether the places were Southend, Herne Bay etc.

10.00. Made arrangements with cabin steward about calling and baths
and then unpacked and turned in.

Sunday 2 March Did not sleep more than irregularly owing to the
constant tramping of sailors swabbing the decks etc. And the unaccus-

tomed throb of the engines (all power on this boat is oil-driven – no coal).

7.15 a.m. Called, had hot bath and dressed.

8.00. On deck. Found we were passing the Isle of Wight and that it was snow-covered.

8.30. Breakfast. Mother feeling quite fit to her surprise. Attributes it to Mothersill taken last night. Later both went on deck. High wind but very sunny. Passed quite near to Portland Bill and saw Weymouth. Heavy storm appeared south and west which we ran into and found it was *snow*. The snowstorm lasted an hour or less and then cleared suddenly. Sea was quite choppy owing to the stiff breeze, but we ran on hardly affected by it and by twelve noon had stopped in the calm waters of Tor Bay just off Berry Head (to the north of it). The sun was out and the bay looked lovely. Torquay and Paignton and the coves round to Brixham were very clear. Brixham itself looked better than from any other angle. Immediately we had stopped a tug put off from Brixham and took our pilot off (he dropped down on a rope ladder with wood steps). We then turned and headed for the dreaded Bay of Biscay. The sea got much higher when we were off Salcombe Head, but apparently it takes a lot to rock a boat of this size.

1 p.m. Lunch. One shower and then brilliant sun during the afternoon. Fine play of colours on the water. Later the sea got worse and we ran into a couple of rainstorms. I managed to take a little tea and then a sharp walk up and down deck to stave off the inevitable, but to no purpose. The pitching became too bad and I retired in disorder at 6 p.m., Mother having gone before tea.

Monday 3 March Not a very good night. There were rough seas off Ushant and later in the Bay of Biscay we rolled a lot. Dozed and slept most of day and ate a couple of apples without mishap. Cabin steward solicitous and helpful. Mother in similar condition [to me]. Some heavy rain during the day.

Tuesday 4 March Still rolling somewhat, but felt much better.

9 a.m. Got some breakfast (with very delicious grapefruit) and then rose and shaved. Mother trying to get up, very desirous of going on deck, but not feeling too well.

11 a.m. Got on deck, ship travelling well with not too much motion. Mountains of Portugal in sight to the far east. All except twenty-five of the saloon passengers had been down, but most of them seem to be up again and taking things quietly.

11.30. Mother also on deck but not feeling too spry. We both occupied our deckchairs and had lunch there. During afternoon things got much more interesting as we approached the coast more closely and could see a lot through our field-glasses. Generally the Portuguese foreshore was bleak limestone with many hamlets and little white houses with red roofs dotted about inland. A line of trees along a ridge seemed to indicate a coast road. Presently the coast became more varied and a long limestone promontory appeared to the South on the end of which was a very picturesque lighthouse looking like a church with the lantern on top of the tower. This was Cape Carvoeiro. The limestone cropped up again further out to sea making some very jagged little islands, on one of which was another lighthouse. Further south the country remained mountainous inland and quiet towards the coast and we passed the country of Torres Vedras where Wellington built his 'lines'. Further south again the town of Cintra nestled and sprawled about the lower slopes of a wonderful range of jagged peaks, on one of which was perched a palace, picturesque enough for fairyland, with turrets and spires. The jagged range ran seaward and culminated in Cape Carvoeiro which we rounded at dusk. Later up the estuary of the Tagus in the failing light we could just make out through glasses the clustered houses and spires of Lisbon. Before dark we had passed another limestone headland, Cape Espichel, and headed off for Cape St Vincent. Neither of us had much inclination for meals in the enclosed air of the saloon as the sea was still far from smooth, so we retired for dinner in the cabins. During the day we had passed one big vessel – which seemed to have no passengers – homeward bound near Lisbon, and just previously had run through a very active little school of porpoises.

Wednesday 5 March Calm weather again. Bath at seven and then on deck 7.45. Sunny and crisp. Coast of Spain visible to the north-east showing we had rounded Cape St Vincent. Mother quite OK again and rose for breakfast after which we sat on deck and watched the Spanish coast come nearer while to the south the African mountains appeared and we headed for the Straits. Games had begun and numbers of people were at quoits, ring-quoits, quoit-tennis and bull-board. Later the coasts closed in on us. We could just see Tangier to the south and then had a good view of the Cape and queer little town (with Moorish buildings) of Tarifa on the Spanish side.

Twelve noon. Came into full view of Gibraltar. To the south was a seaplane-carrier-ship with three seaplanes on its back, one of which took to flight as I watched it through the glass. We lunched at noon and then coming on deck again found we were in the sheltered waters between Gibraltar and Algeciras, gliding towards the *Valiant*. Numbers of other battleships and destroyers were behind the mole. We anchored near the mole and a tender came alongside aft to take those who wished to visit Gibraltar. Most of the passengers crowded on to her and after a wait we shot off (2s each, return) and were landed at a quay (by the Bland Line shed). Lines of weird little 'cabs' this shape [see facsimile diary page] and Ford cars waited to take those who wished to see all the sights quickly. We chose to walk and were accompanied by young Jude (a fellow just from Stamford College, Lincs, now bound for an agricultural college near Adelaide). We went through the market and then through the thick barricading walls (two) and thence through the main street. High above us the old Moorish town (the first fortification of Gibraltar) looked very imposing. The people were diverse and so were their costumes and there were many more shops and houses than I had expected to find. Through the town we came to some well-kept gardens on a steep slope and here Mother rested while we other two pushed on higher and got a fine view of the harbour and bay across to Algeciras while the African coast and Ceuta was in sight to the south. Going back through the gardens we saw many interesting things – orange trees with fruit, lemon tree in bloom, cacti, fresia, climbing geraniums and a magnificent bougainvillaea, hibiscus etc – and got back to our tender without being tempted to buy more than a few flowers at 3.30 p.m. Some of the shops were very good and the vendors importunate, but there was a very English feeling over the whole place – good streets, tarmac etc., English street names, police in nearly English costume (though with linen collars showing over their tunics and carrying huge and alarming truncheon cases on their left hips and smoking usually). Numbers of rowing boats put off and stayed around during our halt there,

Wed March 6

We anchored near the mole & a tender came alongside aft to take those who wished to visit Gib. Most of the passengers crowded on to her & after a wait we shot off (2/- each, return) and were landed at a quay (by the "Bland Line" shed) Lines of weird little "cabs" this shape & Ford cars waited to take those who wished to see all the sights quickly. We chose to walk & were accompanied by young "Jude" (a young fellow just from Stanford College, Lincs, was bound for an Agricultural College nr. Adelaide) We went through the market & then through the thick barricading walls (2) & thence through the main street. High above us the old

Facsimile diary page

selling oranges, mats, silks, postcards and brass trays etc. It was overcast all the while, so it was no good my taking photos. The Buffs, Coldstream Guards and two or three batteries of artillery were all the troops stationed at Gibraltar.

4.00. The *Ormonde* set off again in calm weather. Porpoises had bobbed up at intervals all day and were with us now, causing us much interest. To the north were the mountains of Granada (the Sierra Nevada, I think) looking very grand. One giant of over 11,000 feet was snow-capped and showed above some encircling clouds. The steeper side of Gibraltar looked very rugged though a curious effect is wrought by a large portion of the rock being smoothed and covered in concrete to form an artificial watershed. We had a quiet evening – Mother rested on deck and I played quoits etc. with four others on the boat deck – and then a capital dinner in the saloon which looked dainty with its many flowers and pink-shaded lights. Afterwards coffee in the music room while a dance was prepared outside on the wide part of deck B. The night was deliciously cool and the boat quite steady. The ship's orchestra consisted of piano, violin, two banjos and a drum-timpani. The pianist had no other job than music! Only a few couples rose to it as yet though the orchestra was distinctly a success. After watching the dancing awhile we devoured more sandwiches in the lounge and had fizzy drinks and began to be thoroughly ashamed of our appetites. Turned in at 10.30.

Thursday 6 March Bath 7 a.m. On deck 8 a.m. The Mediterranean was quite calm and the air clear and the boat steadily forging north-east. The Andalusian mountains were clear and very jagged and grand in outline. The highest were covered in snow and soared above some clouds. On our port bow appeared a picturesque cape (Cape Palos) with a little monument towards the end. We both ate ravenously at breakfast and had a peaceful day, Mother in a deckchair most of the day and I playing many games of quoits and quoit-tennis. A good many girls are on board which brightens things – some being very adept at the games. At lunchtime a big fleet of little Spanish fishing vessels came in sight, very picturesque, sailing south under full sail, almost in good enough order for a regatta. They looked almost unmanageable with one enormous three-cornered cross-sail forward and two side-sails level with the mast which had an enormous stagger forward. Gradually Spain sank from sight and during the afternoon a fine crag appeared to starboard being the south point of the Balearic Islands, Point Aguila on the island of Formentera. During the rest of the evening we steamed past the islands Ibiza and Formentera and darkness prevented our catching a glimpse of Majorca further north-east.

8.30. After dinner I joined the other people from our table (New Zealanders) in playing mah-jongg in the lounge. The idea of it soon came back to me though it was two years since I played it at Hampstead. Mother's not entirely herself yet, retired fairly early. During the afternoon

Sketch of Spanish fishing boats

while I was making a sketch of Point Aguila a gentleman came up enquiring if I were Mr Bestall and then introduced himself as Mr Campbell Dodgson of the British Museum who had bought a lithoprint of mine from the School of Art exhibition some time ago!

Friday 7 March 8 a.m. Fine morning. Ship just in the Gulf of Lyons – rolling a good deal, as a pretty high sea was running. The morning we spent

Pt. Aguila (Island of Formentera)
South extremity of the Balearic Is.
6. Mch. 24

Drawing of Point Aguila

in writing and playing quoits and tennis. At noon mountains appeared nearly ahead and after an early lunch we found ourselves just outside Toulon and entering the harbour through the narrow passage between the walls running out from either shore. It was most attractive in the brilliant light. Broken rocky hills surround the place covered in little pines and olives and the south side of the harbour is formed by a hill which is nearly an island, being joined to the mainland by a narrow neck not much wider than the main road which it carries. We anchored in the placid waters of the harbour, and, being before time, had a fairly long wait looking at the French battleships and a submarine lying near us before passport officials etc. came on. By 2.30, however, a tender was alongside and Mother and I joined it for a few hours ashore. We found Toulon much more interesting than anyone had suggested, with its tall shuttered houses and very narrow streets. After changing some money on the quay we strolled about and enjoyed it thoroughly. Passing through the Place Gambetta and the Place d'Armes we basked awhile in the Place Liberté where scores of other people were sitting about on chairs and a little carriage drawn by a donkey (for children only) was solemnly circulating. Then a stroll up the Boulevard Strasbourg took us to the fortifications whence we turned down the Rue Lafayette and up another little street and entered Ste Marie Maleure (the 'cathedral'). It is very ancient and very gloomy, having no side windows and being lit with two or three top windows and a few candles. There are several pictures in it said to be good, but the light was not sufficient to allow of their being properly seen. We went on and looked at the shops where the things were all very cheap. Exchange is now 104 francs to the pound and since this place is not a tourist centre the prices remain French prices and are not inflated as in the more popular resorts. A very bad tea at a café on the Quai Croustade and then the six o'clock tender from the same place back to the ship. The *Ormonde* looked a fairy palace being a blaze of light and, floating on the still water, threw long reflections downwards. A new moon and a clear sky and a big green light on the end of the mole completed the picture.

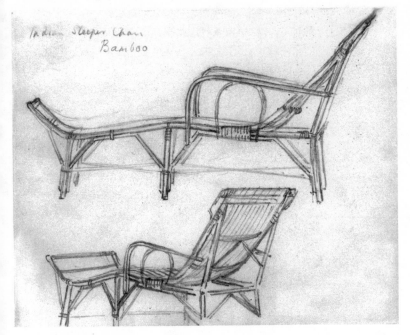

Drawings of Indian Sleeper Chairs

7 p.m. Dinner on board. Then a stroll to admire the lights of the town and the winking of the fleet's code messages. Then an hour at mah-jongg in the lounge with our table companions from New Zealand (Mrs Coombs, two daughters and a cousin) and then bed, thinking that the ship would leave at 1 a.m.

Saturday 8 March On waking we found the ship still in harbour. On deck before breakfast saw the mail being slung on board, the cradle being a sheet

being slung on board, the cradle being a sheet of canvas tied at about ten points round the edge. They say it is the biggest mail since Xmas, owing to the derangement of the recent dock strike, 4000 mail bags being taken on, some of which should have gone P. & O.

9.45 We did not waste a minute when the tenders had left & steamed straight out & got up speed quickly. The "Orient's" mail contract commences here & the Company has to pay fines for every hour late at Fremantle, so we may expect some quick travelling from now onwards.

We kept fairly well to the coast of France & aimed towards the N. Cape

Facsimile diary page

of canvas tied at about ten points round the edge. They say it is the biggest mail since Xmas, owing to the derangement of the recent dock strike, 4,000 mail bags being taken on, some of which should have gone P&O.

9.45. We did not waste a minute when the tenders had left us and steamed straight out and got up speed quickly. The Orient's mail contract commences here and the company has to pay fines for every hour late at Fremantle, so we may expect some quick travelling from now onwards. We kept fairly well to the coast of France and aimed towards the northern cape of Corsica (Cape Corse). Hyères came in sight for a while and the hills round looked attractive, but the coast soon began to run north and we headed straight across the Ligurian Sea. The sea was not smooth by any means and there was some roll. Mr Campbell Dodgson informed me that the stiff wind blowing was the mistral. With no land in sight games were popular and we played a lot of quoit-tennis and deck-quoits – mostly with the Misses Coombs and Mr Jacobs (of New Brighton). Before dinner I had half an hour's walk and interesting chat with Mr Campbell Dodgson and he showed me a print-fund report containing my name. After dinner Mr De Courcy Hamilton showed me his sketches.

Sunday 9 March Heavy rain when I woke had given place to brilliant sunshine by breakfast time and we found ourselves passing through a dead-calm sea between two islands and the coast of Italy on which was a magnificent panorama of mountains. So far the mountainous character of the countries we have passed have made England seem flat as a pancake by comparison. To the north-east of us was Monte Carlo covered in snow and an endless succession of peaks stretched southwards. After breakfast we crossed the Gulf of Gaeta and then passed between the Isles of Ischia and Procida. The ancient castle of Ischia attracted much interest as did the isle most picturesquely overbuilt. About eleven we were just in the gulf and got our first glimpse of the wonderful panorama. The day, though sunny now, was not too brilliant – distances were very blue and soft but not strong. The lower hills swept round on our left eastwards till Naples proper appeared and then the dark slopes of Vesuvius rose. Smoke was appearing lazily from its square top and mingled with a big white cloud which seemed fixed there. On the south side of the bay were fine mountains, the top of the highest being under snow and further to sea the Isle of Capri made a fantastic silhouette. (We attended a short service and Communion in the music room before breakfast and afterwards watched the approach of Naples and understood the rapturous description given by friends who had been there before.) An early lunch (twelve noon) and then we found ourselves at a quay with gangways being lowered, or rather lifted. Many other ships were there including one White Star liner and two or three Sitmar boats. Mother had suggested joining up with the Coombs party, so after changing some money (99 lire to the pound) on a quay we found a pressing guide who took us in two Fiats for a long and lovely drive. First past the palace, along the front to the aquarium where is a collection of Mediterranean fish of all sorts. Then up endless twisting roads mostly with bad surfaces over which the Fiats roared and raced in great style till we reached the very top of St Martin and the restaurant of St Elmo, whence an amazing panorama of the whole of Naples Bay at our feet. Another palace in the distance from whence Rome was said to be visible was pointed out by our official guide. In the glass room of the restaurant we had an indifferent tea with some strange and sickly cake (for 14 lire each!). The gaunt military prison was on the hilltop also, but we did not do any photographing of it. On the run back we arrived under Bertolini's hotel and our car (two Misses Coombs, Miss Andrew and I) stopped for Miss Morrison while the other car with Mother, Mrs Coombs, Miss Coombs (the cousin) and the other Miss Morrison had a further run. The approach to Bertolini's is weird, first through a passage in the solid rock to the foot of the lift-shaft whence a prodigiously long lift ride takes you right inside the hotel at the top. The view from there was superior even to that from San Elmo, as it included more of the bay and was nothing short of marvellous. Everything was clearer now. The long range of snow-covered Apennines behind Vesuvius had been indistinct in the morning but was very visible now and was mottled with cloud shadows. Miss Ella Coombs and I took more photos and also on the return spin we snapped the bay and the naval prison. The ride cost us 12s each – not cheap but worth it on such a day. We were lucky in our weather as I understand there was much rain yesterday and a storm appeared to be brewing now. On the streets we had been very interested to see the Fascisti marching in small detachments and on guard at various places, some in black shirts and caps and others in green caps with a feather and green cloaks. The police also are striking in their broad black and silver hats, long cloaks and black and red trousers; and so are the more familiar plumed Alpini. Just before we left (5.30 p.m.) a big American liner (the *President Harrison*) with a Japanese crew slid in alongside. We quickly (and regretfully) shot away from the lovely spot and just at dusk were passing inside the wild crags of Capri. Colonel Brown pointed out the remains of the palace of the Emperor Tiberius on top of one of the peaks of Capri.

Sketch of Naples police

7.00. Dinner and a feeling of change as many of our friends of a week standing – Hamiltons, Jacobs etc. – left at Naples and others are aboard. We have also taken many Italians (emigrants) in the third class bound for Australia. Our first disappointment on the voyage came now as we passed Stromboli, the Straits of Messina and Etna in the dark and saw nothing of them.

Monday 10 March was an uneventful day. The morning was fine and games were all the go. At 11 a.m. we had boat drill, all the passengers gathering at their appointed stations at a blast of the siren after which an officer told them how to don lifebelts and explained emergency measures. More games followed and we had our first game of deck-tennis (with red tennis balls) and voted it not so good as quoit-tennis. Mother basked in the sun and did not play. After tea we found a complete change – driving rain which rendered the boat deck impossible – and so we got to walking and playing card games and writing. Heard today that there had been death on board early in the voyage – an old lady suffering from heart trouble – though no one knew at the time that there had been a burial at sea. After dinner it was still pouring, but we spent a cosy time in the lounge with our usual party playing mah-jongg. Little Miss Good and another Australian girl (Miss Sprague) joined us and we had rather an uproarious couple of hours. (Did our best mileage so far – about 390 sea miles in the twenty-four hours.)

Tuesday 11 March Out on deck at 8 a.m. and found a dead-calm sea. We were just passing between the Isle of Gavdo, a sandy, quiet object, and Crete. A long distance off was a ship and through the glasses it appeared to be suspended in the air well above the horizon with a perfect reflection under it, the funnels of the reflection just touching the water like this [see facsimile diary page]: the effect was weird. The commander was walking near me and on being tackled he told me it was a mirage – a common phenomenon in these very calm waters. Within a few minutes the ship was nearer to us and was riding normally. After breakfast we found ourselves near the coast of Crete, rocky and apparently very sparsely inhabited but that disappeared soon and with a steady trip before us we gave ourselves up to games. The day was warm and sunny with a following wind and our usual party augmented by Miss Sprague (Australian) and young Mr Shaw

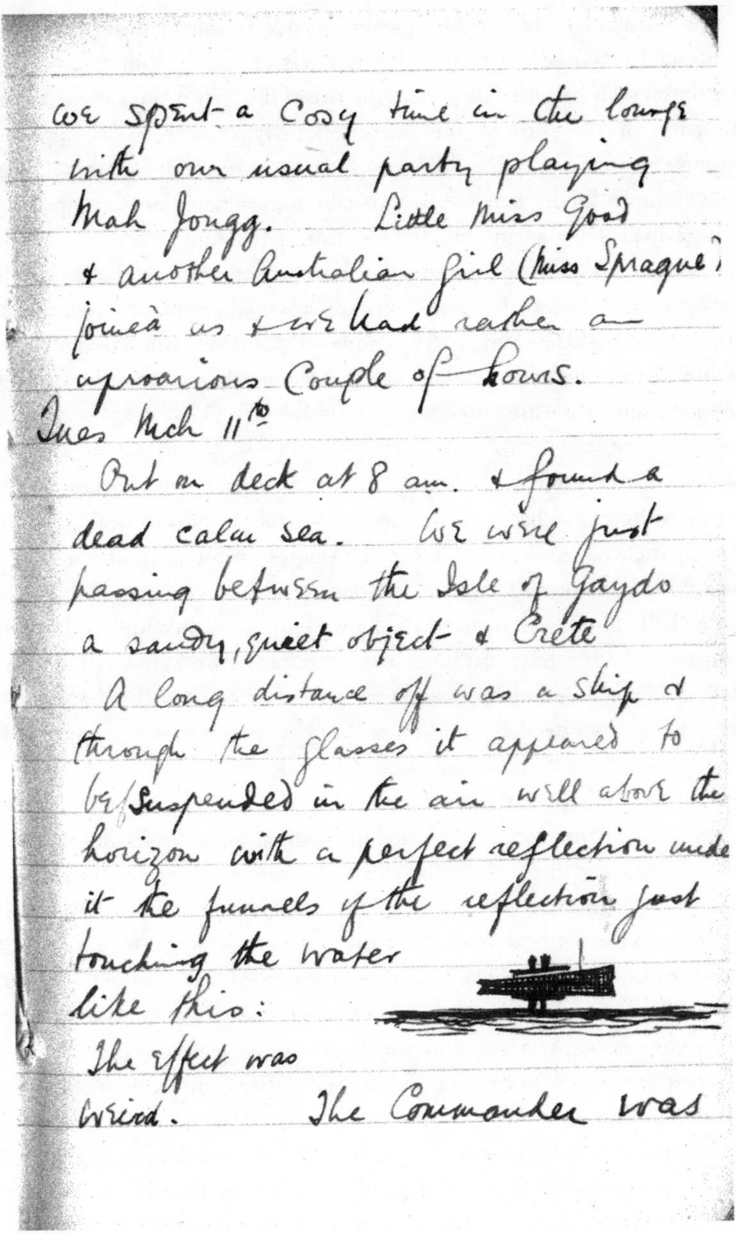

We spent a cosy time in the lounge
with our usual party playing
Mah Jongg.   Little Miss Good
+ another Australian girl (Miss Sprague)
joined us + we had rather an
uproarious couple of ~~hours~~.

Tues Mch 11th

Out on deck at 8 am. + found a
dead calm sea.   We were just
passing between the Isle of Gaydo
a sandy, quiet object + Crète

A long distance off was a ship +
through the glasses it appeared to
be suspended in the air well above the
horizon with a perfect reflection under
it the funnels of the reflection just
touching the water
like this:

The effect was
weird.   The Commander was

Facsimile diary page

(New Zealander) had many games of quoits and tennis which we thoroughly enjoyed. At teatime interest was caused by sudden boat drill for the crew. It surprised us to note the size of the crew when gathered from all parts of the ship to the boat deck. My camera has disappeared mysteriously and enquiries all over the ship have yielded nothing. Miss Ella Coombs kindly lent me hers to take some photos of the ship. After dinner mah-jongg again with the Coombs, Miss Andrew, Mrs and Miss Sprague and Ruth Good while a dance was in progress on the deck. The barber's shop on board is a well-stocked affair where one can get almost anything as well as be barbered, and today while buying other things I got a photo of the *Ormonde* and later collected a number of signatures of our friends round the edge.

Wednesday 12 March Gloriously fine and warm early. Packed before breakfast and later had two sets of quoit-tennis in greater heat than any yet experienced. Also took a few group photos on top deck of our friends with Miss E. Coombs's camera. By noon we sighted Port Said looking like a flat half-submerged island with hardly any land on either side of it. During an hour's delay just outside the breakwater we were interested in a fleet of Egyptian sailing boats and then we started to enter the channel and soon were opposite the statue of de Lesseps who stands with one hand outstretched towards his canal. Numbers of motor launches came round us mostly containing smart alert Egyptians crowned by fez caps. One or two rowing boats contained nearly naked men who shouted for us to drop coins into the sea and then dived for them and came up with them in their mouths. We steamed past the lighthouse and the busy part of Port Said right on to the oiling station. At various points men were coaling ships in gangs, or unloading coal from barges at great speed. The motor boats were now still more numerous, some official, some from Cook's and some from the leading hotels, and it was not long before passengers were disembarking and being shot back to the quay at Port Said. After getting my passport and Mother's from the purser's office I went up on deck and found a tall Egyptian, with our names on a piece of paper, who took us to Mr Charles Evans, the passenger agent who had been asked by Rev. Dwyer Kelly to meet us. With much regret we said farewell to our friends the Coombs, Morrisons, Miss Andrew, young Jude etc. on C deck and later left by motor

The Sand-skier. Publication unknown, 1931

Coloured Glasses by David Naylor. *Tatler*, 1934

The Beacons. 'In endless range those twinkling points of fire.' The Boy Scouts' Jubilee Chain of Beacons. An impression of the vast network of bonfires which was the Scout Movement's contribution to the King's Silver Jubilee celebrations. The old telegraph hills and the more ancient hills were among the sites chosen for the Beacons. The bonfires were made in the traditional conical shape of intertwined branches, old wool and rags. This picture shows one of the hillier districts, where it was possible to see many of the Beacons from one point. *Tatler*, 1935

Hallowe'en or the Witches' Frolic.
And the lightning flashed and the
                          thunder growled
and louder and louder the tempest
                          howl'd
Thomas Ingoldsby. *Tatler, 1936*

The Dragon on Guard. Tatler, 1935

Spotting a Winner. Piccadilly, 1929

The Birth of a Notion. Publication unknown

The Last of the Mow(hic)'uns.
Publication unknown

Good Samaritan: 'Can't you get on? If you've a
bit of rope I could give you a tow.'
Depressed one: 'Madam, if I'd 'ad a bit of rope
I'd 'ave 'ung myself an hour ago!' *Tatler*, 1939

Four illustrations for books. The upper pair was for Blackwood's *Omnibus Volumes* which appeared from 1947 onwards

Three silhouettes - probably for a book illustration

The Land of the Christmas Stocking by Mabel Buchanan. Rough for dust-jacket, 1948

A Sprite at School by Constance M. White. Rough for dust-jacket (the lettering was changed), 1946

Pwllheli Poster. Rough and printed posters, 1935

Night - Santa Claus. Endpaper,
Rupert Annual, 1951

Jungle. Endpaper,
Rupert Annual, 1953

Coon Island. Endpaper,
Rupert Annual, 1954

King of the Birds.
Endpaper, *Rupert*
Annual, 1952

*Rupert and Bill,
Shaded Pool.*
Endpaper, *Rupert*
Annual, 1956

Undersea. Endpaper,
Rupert Annual, 1960

Chalk Scene. Endpaper,
Rupert Annual, 1962

Nutwood Country.
Endpaper, *Rupert*
Annual, 1967

Hovercraft. Endpaper, *Rupert* Annual, 1968

Little Chinese Islands. Endpaper, *Rupert* Annual, 1969

Frog Chorus. Endpaper, *Rupert* Annual, 1958

Rupert and Pals on long Fence. Endpaper, *Rupert* Annual, 1973

Snowfight. Rough for cover, *Rupert* Annual, 1962

Blackberry. Unpublished rough for cover, drawn in 1961

Waits (Christmas Carol-singers). Cover, *Rupert* Annual, 1949

Snow, Puppy on Sledge. Cover, *Rupert* Annual, 1967

Bubble in Sky. Cover, *Rupert* Annual, 1968

Rupert and Fish. Cover, *Rupert* Annual, 1969

Rupert climbing - Snowdon and Penlan. Cover, *Rupert* Annual, 1964

Brown Face. Cover, *Rupert* Annual, 1973

Paul and Linda McCartney and family with AEB in Beddgelert, 1972

Top of Surbiton Hill from near AEB's Civil Defence Post, M4, painted in 1942

Post M4 Surbiton Hill. 'Warden Locke, formerly Town Clerk of Watchet (Somerset), keen gardener - tried to plant flowers in impossible soil under the elm trees. This was painted to put flowers where he wanted them', painted in 1942

Two Air Raid Wardens in Gas Masks. The figure on the right is AEB, painted in 1941

Park Earm, Oxted, in Winter. This picture was painted in 1947 and exhibited at the Royal Academy in 1949

Early Fireguard Training. 'Painted in 1941. The flats in the picture are fictitious but the incident took place in 1939 in Gateways flats, Surbiton Hill, near M4. District Warden - Mr English, nearer Warden - me. Girls in red tops are from Little Brickhill (Bayfield School)'

boat with our hand baggage (attaché case) and accompanied by Mr Evans and his man (tips: cabin steward 10*s*, table steward 10*s*, boot boy 2*s* 6*d* – missed bath steward).

On the customs quay Mr Evans quickly went and got our quarantine tickets before taking us into the customs house. While waiting for our cabin boxes and suitcase to arrive from the *Ormonde* he took me to a good chemist where I bought a VPK to replace the one lost on board. Mr Evans 'knowing the ropes' got our boxes straight through the customs (only one was opened and a pretence at a search made) and then we proceeded by carriage with skeleton baggage while a fellah took the boxes to Evans's office. He had accommodated me at the Sailors and Soldiers Home and Mother at YWCA. I took dinner at her place with a lady doctor named Miss Kennedy Will, and then went to my own place. On enquiry I found it was the 'Welcome' Wesleyan home under Uncle Joe and on making myself known to Captain Bothwell was welcomed warmly and listened till midnight to the story of the home for the last two years, but chiefly for the last three months during which Captain Bothwell has had charge.

Thursday 13 March Had a sound sleep although the room was very bare and unworthy of a Wesleyan 'home', and rose at eight. (Lots of hibiscus and some bougainvillaea growing in Port Said.) After breakfast went through Port Said and took Mother for a stroll before bringing her back for a chat with Mrs Bothwell. During her chat I took a few snaps in Port Said and arranged for Mr Evans to pick us up at the 'Welcome' house. It was pretty hot to us but not too warm for the average Egyptian (70 degrees in the shade). Mr Evans came for us and did all the necessary work of registering heavier baggage and saw us safely into a good seat in the train which left at 12.30 for Cairo. The run at first was beside the canal, most interesting and near Cantara we saw our first camels of Egypt. What land there was was sandy – very glaring in the sun – which made the sight of a stretch of green very welcome and resting to our eyes. At Ismailia several Egyptians joined our carriage and we struck south-west away from the Suez Canal but managed to catch sight of one of the bitter lakes through which it passes. By this time we had finished lunch on board – very tasty and curious – consisting of several courses of small things – one sardine, then savoury rice, then a few boiled peas (!), then a tiny piece of fried mutton and onions, then bread and butter and Gruyère cheese and then bananas and oranges and coffee to finish – all amazingly appetising. After Ismailia the country became increasingly green and lovely with its palms and young corn tended industriously by picturesque men and black-gowned women. Scattered everywhere were native huts, square and straight mud-coloured affairs with a plank or two across the top and then straw chucked on to that. Little mosques showed occasionally and also tiny cemeteries with graves like this [see facsimile diary page]:

Little convoys of camels appeared at intervals and in the fields donkeys and oxen but seldom houses. Everywhere were the kites, gliding and swooping and looking very powerful. Later we learnt that they had been introduced by Lord Kitchener for scavenging purposes. Soon after 4 p.m. the spires and minarets of Cairo appeared ahead with Heliopolis to the left and punctually to time the train drew in to the platform (4.20). We at once spotted Rev. Dwyer Kelly who had brought his GWK car to fetch us and who very quickly had us at the Killiney pension while heavier baggage followed in another taxi. (Should also remember that while driving from station to pension we came across a native wedding preceded by a brass band. Bride was in a taxi with drawn blinds while groom and flower-bedecked brown kiddies as bridesmaids and guests followed in other taxis. Street decorations were in progress for next Saturday's Independence Day procession.) Mrs Kelly arranged tea in Mother's room after which she unpacked a bit and I was shown to the room reserved for me at the Pension Ismailia quite near (all meals to be at Killiney House). Dinner was at eight after which all four of us went out to a lantern lecture (at the YMCA) on Cyprus by Mr Consterdine of the YMCA. Slept that night for the first time inside a mosquito curtain. First impressions of Egypt contain: the universal fez (discovered later it is a sin to call the cap a fez here. It should be called a tarbush) – the palms – the kites – the fine physique and upright bearing and smartness of the Egyptians and the unexpected lack of animosity against the British. Also the unexpected cleanliness and width of the streets both in Port Said and Cairo which put Naples to shame with its huge setts and potholed roads.

Friday 14 March Breakfast (9.00) served by a tall Berber in fez, red sash and white gown and shoes. Then we all were driven by Mr Kelly to Abbassia

Thurs Mch 13

then straw chucked on to that. Little
mosques showed occasionally & also
tiny cemeteries with
graves like this: —

Little convoys of camels appeared at
intervals & in the fields donkeys and
oxen but seldom horses.

Everywhere were the kites, gliding
& swooping & looking very powerful.
Later we learnt that they had been
introduced by Lord Kitchener for
scavenging purposes.

Soon after 4 p.m. the spires and
minarets of Cairo appeared ahead
with Heliopolis to the left & punctually
to time the train drew in to the
platform (4.20)   We at once
spotted Rev. Dwyer Kelly who had
brought his G.W.K car to fetch us
& who very quickly had us at

Camp – a huge establishment at which are two brigades at present. (The Abbassia–Heliopolis aerodrome is the jumping-off ground of the Cairo–Baghdad airline.) He stayed there for some duty while Mrs Kelly drove us on to Heliopolis, a sprawling new suburb owned by a Belgian company and planned in the modern open way though the houses are semi-oriental in design. We saw the house of one of the Egyptian princes which was surrounded by a magnificent bougainvillaea hedge in flower – a blaze of purple (iron railings served as girders to hold the 'hedge' up). Before long we had picked up Mr Kelly and he then drove us through some of old Cairo back to the station and thence over a many-girdered bridge over the Nile on to Gezira Island where he took us through the sporting club's grounds and back by another bridge by the Kasr-el-Nil barracks. Later he ran me along to Cook's to make enquiries and incidentally showed me GHQ and also the most unsavoury street in Cairo in which every house is a brothel. After lunch we all went straight across again to the Gezira Sporting Club to see the finals of the annual tennis tournament. There was some brilliant play, the star being Zerlendi from Alexandria who won the men's singles, was in the men's doubles and with Miss Alexandroff (a brilliant girl from Alexandria who has played also in England) won the mixed doubles. After a very good tea at the club restaurant we were motored to the YMCA sports ground past the commander-in-chief's house outside which we made the circuit of a large banyan tree. (In the sporting-club grounds I also had my first sight of a papaya tree in fruit, looking like a little palm with green fruit halfway between a pear and a melon growing in a cluster near the top). Lord Allenby was present at the tournament, but I only got a back view of him. The kites and the grey-hooded crows seemed extra tame and mischievous at the club. During the evening we waited in hope of a wire from Father at Port Said but none came.[1]

Saturday 15 March Egyptian Independence Day! The route from the palace to Parliament House had been decorated with festoons and flags, both in the old and the new green colours. Immediately after breakfast Mr Kelly rushed us off to Major Jamison's flat from which (on the balcony) we got a fine view of southern Cairo and the citadel. Mother stayed there rather than

[1] Arthur was on his way from Burma to meet Rebecca and AEB in Cairo.

Came across a native wedding preceded by a brass band. Bride was
in a taxi with drawn blinds while
groom & flower-bedecked brown kiddies as
bridesmaids & guests followed in other taxis.
Street decorations were in progress for
next Saturday's Independence day procession

Sat March 15th

Egyptian Independence Day!
The route from the palace to Parliament
house has been decorated with
festoons & flags, both in
the old red & the new
green colours.
Immediately after breakfast
Mr Kelly rushed us off to Major Jamison's
flat from which (on the balcony) we got
a fine view of southern Cairo & the
Citadel. Mother stayed there rather
than push through crowds while the

Facsimile diary page

push through crowds while the rest of us went to the nearest point in the line of the forthcoming procession and found surging mobs in tarbushes on the pavements while smart khaki-clad Egyptian troops lined the roadsides. Mr K managed to borrow two small ladders from a shop which, propped against a wall, enabled us to see over all heads and get a good view of things when they began. First came a brass band playing a monotonous theme followed by a small detachment of the royal bodyguard in a new uniform of bright blue with scarlet and yellow on the front – very garish. Then came a fine carriage containing two of the ministers followed by a finer one in which sat King Fouad I with Zagloul Pasha on his left. Lastly a bigger detachment of bodyguard. Later in the day I saw a detachment of 'Gyppy' soldiers playing bagpipes! After returning we found a wire from Father announcing his safe arrival and saying he was getting to Cairo at 12.40. In the meantime I got some money at Cook's and while passing the Continental Savoy Hotel was accosted by a native with scarabs for sale who showed me a couple, bluish-green and very pretty. After enlarging on their beauty he impressively offered them to me as a bargain at 4s each. I, not particularly keen, offered him one piastre (2½d) each. He insisted that he was offering them at less than the antique shops and that he got these scarabs from the natives in the off season so they must be genuinely from the tombs. On sticking to my offer I was surprised to find his price drop suddenly to 1s (5 piastre) each and almost immediately with a broad grin he offered me the two scarabs for 3 piastre! The nearest change I had was 2½ piastre and with that he closed! At 12.30 Mr K had driven us along to the station and sharp on time father's train came in and I had soon found him (trying incidentally to get out on the wrong platform). After warm greetings we returned in the car with a taxi for baggage and lunched. Much excitement and happiness and a tremendous lot to say! After lunch F and M rested while I wandered about with camera past the museum etc. After tea Father and I walked to Opera Square and for a lark took a tram which after going round in a circle for a bit brought us to the station. In the tram I brought out my scarabs and told Father about them and an Egyptian sitting near seemed to think that the price was about right (1 piastre each). Later we saw the identical things in a jeweller's near Shepheard's. The man told us that they had no genuine scarabs from the tombs but they were widely manufactured in Egypt. Father asked the price and the man said he could let him have some at 2 dollars (about 50 piastre) each! The most barefaced robbery we've struck yet. F and I also walked into Shepheard's through the lounges etc. to the far end where the American Bar is, then back through the chattering horde of visitors, inspected the visitors' book, found it nearly full of Yankee signatures and walked out again. F is very active and looks fatter and younger than when he left us three and a half years ago. After dinner we all strolled to Parliament House and to some of the government offices and ministries to see the Independence Day illuminations. Have learnt the Arabic numerals through seeing them on the taxis etc.

Sunday 16 March 9 a.m. breakfast. Father was whisked off early to take Parade Service at Abbassia Camp. We strolled at 10.30 to St John's Wesleyan church (a small edifice in Sharia Bulag rented from the French Protestant Church) and found Father and Mr Kelly had arrived first. Congregation of seventy mostly soldiers. Dr Zwemmer, an American, very great on work among Jews, took the service and spoke finely. Afterwards met Mr Gibson of Nottingham who had just arrived to push his lace and 'white' goods to Morum's and other big Cairo firms. Spent a quiet afternoon writing and then we all went over to Major Jamison's flat to have tea with Mrs Kelly's sister Edie. Tasted date jam for first time. Met Mr Bramwell (from Darlington Street) who is here in Cook's banking dept. All went to church except Edie and Father took the service. Spent evening after supper in the Kelly's lounge discussing our programme. Weather changed during the day owing to a hot wind blowing from the south-west over the desert.

Monday 17 March Hot winds still blowing from the desert and the air full of a haze of sand dimming the distances and giving one much the same impression as gazing through a drizzle of rain at home. In the morning M, F and I walked slowly through the heat to the museum but found it shut. After walking to the Kasr-el-nil Bridge we came back a bit and boarded a tram no. 1 which took us past the American University etc. right past Roda Island to Old Cairo (6 millième each). At the end a guide suddenly attached himself to us and we permitted him to lead us through some narrow, smelly streets till we emerged into a broader one and faced the great Greek church

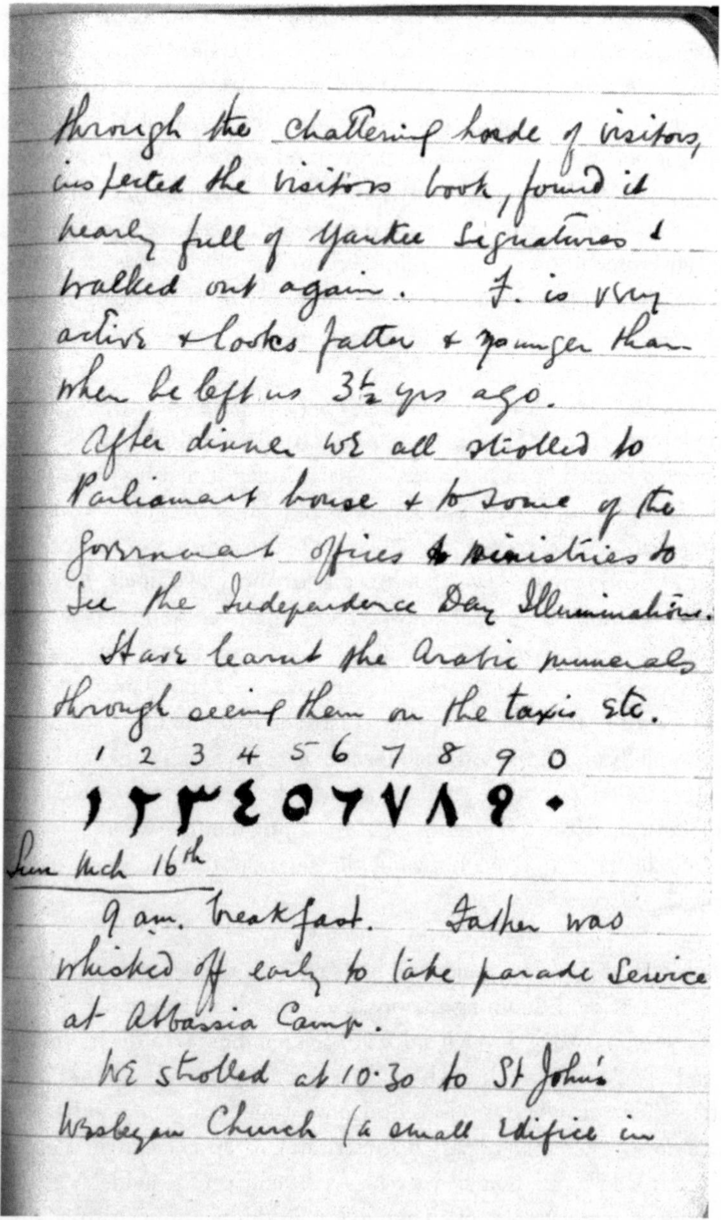

through the chattering horde of visitors,
inspected the visitors book, found it
nearly full of Yankee signatures &
walked out again.   J. is very
active & looks fatter & younger than
when he left us 3½ yrs ago.
After dinner we all strolled to
Parliament house & to some of the
Government offices & ministries to
see the Independence Day Illuminations.
   Have learnt the Arabic numerals
through seeing them on the taxis etc.
   1   2   3   4   5   6   7   8   9   0

١ ٢ ٣ ٤ ٥ ٦ ٧ ٨ ٩ ٠

Sun Mch 16th
   9 a.m. breakfast.   Father was
whisked off early to take parade service
at Abbassia Camp.
   We strolled at 10·30 to St John's
Wesleyan Church (a small edifice in

Facsimile diary page

of St George. Our guide then took us through a Roman door through the old Roman wall of Old Cairo (or Babylon).[2] The iron clasps and solid woodwork of the door were the same as in the days of Antony and Cleopatra, only the enormous wooden 'key' being renewed. Thence we walked through the tiny streets of Old Cairo past the little old houses inhabited entirely by Copts, surrounded by little grubby children clamouring for baksheesh, until we entered a very ancient church (with the dome collapsed) where there was some curious ivory and ebony inlay work. It was the church of St George and the Dragon and, though long disused, had some good pointed arches. The ancient picture of St George and the Dragon was removed from this to the newer church next door which we now entered. Under the picture is a cupboard containing a red cloth in which is supposed to be an arm of St George himself and pinned or stuck on to the cupboard are innumerable strips of cloth. The idea is that when any of the Copts is ill, he takes a strip of his clothing to the picture, leaving it there for three days, by which time his malady will have been completely cured. The altar and vestments were very primitive and dirty. Several pictures of saints on the walls were of great antiquity though of no artistic worth. Thence our guide took us to the most historic bit of Babylon – the church of St Sergius, a well-kept edifice recently renewed. The old priest was seated tailor-wise on a bench inside the church smoking a cigarette while his son, a strong fellow speaking good English, took us in tow. The altar is much better than at the last church and in front of it on either side are rich and interesting carvings of wood and ivory. On each side of the nave are pillars which with one exception were white underneath and paintings on top (some of the paint still adheres). These pillars represented the Apostles and the odd one which was of dull reddish stone, without any capital and thicker and more unshapely than the others, was Judas Iscariot! From near the altar our guide took us down to the crypt which is carved out of the solid rock. It is formed like a tiny church with a nave and side aisles

---

[2] Baedeker's *Egypt* tells us that the Greeks named the ancient city on the east bank of the Nile 'Babylon', probably in imitation of some Egyptian name of similar sound. The citadel of this town was fortified by the Romans, and under Augustus became the headquarters of one of the three legions stationed in Egypt. In AD 640 Babylon was captured by Khalif Omar's general, who subsequently established the new capital of the country there, in opposition to Alexandria, which was not so free from the disturbing Christian element.

and is the traditional place to which Joseph and Mary and the babe came during their flight to Egypt. They spent a month here. The usual altercation with our guide took place as to charge and we gave 10 piastre. Also got another little scarab (inferior) for 1 piastre (2½d) after his offering it us for 2 dollars! After lunch we were motored by Mr Kelly out to the zoo (on the left bank of the Nile across Gezira Island), a beautifully laid-out affair much more attractive than ours in London and containing a large variety. The lions, giraffes, vultures etc. naturally looked sleeker, healthier and generally more at home than those in London. We had a good tea on a delightful island in the middle of an artificial lake. In the gardens also were wonderful trees, rubber trees, various palms, cacti, mimosa, bougainvillaea. The air was still so full of sand that we could only just see across the Nile on the run back. Draughts and ludo in Mr Kelly's flat after dinner.

Tuesday 18 March In the morning we packed a box (my black cabin box) with all our unneeded things for Mrs Shrewsbury to take back to England and then went in a gharry with Mrs Kelly to the 'mousky' or native market. The mousky covers a big area and consists of endless passages in which one could easily get lost with tiny busy shops on each side. First we saw the general market where jewels, clothes etc. could be bought – next arriving at the brass-workers' department where we coveted some of the brass and pottery coffee sets. Father meanwhile was hypnotised by some big green gemstones which a swarthy dealer said were chrysophases. Later a guide took us to the gold-workers where we saw them refining the gold in a charcoal fire, polishing in fibre, working it etc. – and to the silver-workers – and through the heavy odours of the scent market and of the spice market. Our guide told us that spices are in great use among Muslim ladies who are inclined to be slender in figure, and that a pinch of certain spices every morning for a month induces that decided plumpness which is regarded out here as the chief feminine charm. Next the Algerian section of the bazaar where are the cloth-workers. We watched a man with a little frame of thin wood and coloured strings run a gaudy border along the end of a towel in very quick time. We were greatly interested in a further stroll around the tiny stalls some with busy workers, others with silent phlegmatic owners sitting cross-legged in the middle and others with one or more importunate 'scouts' outside shouting to obvious visitors and nearly

Sketches of heads and figures

dragging them inside to inspect their wares. A gharry brought us home to lunch. In the afternoon Father and I walked quietly to [Thomas] Cook's for a few enquiries and to the Lloyd Triestino offices. At night we all went to the YMCA and heard an excellent speech by Dr Mott on the student Christian movement and the work of the YMCA. Afterwards I saw Mrs Shrewsbury to her flat and gave her the key of my box which she had promised to take to England (tomorrow).

Wednesday 19 March Mr Kelly drove M, F and me early via the Bulaq Bridge to Cook's landing stage. Mrs Kelly and her sister (Miss Irwin) joined us after which Mr Kelly returned, the others of us embarked on a small launch of Cook's and set off up the river. Clouds and a headwind rendered it colder than anything in Egypt since our landing and the ladies donned furs and coats. The scenery was mainly flat, but the many *dehabiyeks* made the journey interesting as did the convict settlement. A heap of stones at the south end of the Island of Roda (opposite Old Cairo) with a few reeds and rushes growing around it was shown to us as the traditional spot for the finding of Moses! At the quay at Bedrechain (pronounced Bedresheen) we were landed and taken up an embankment covered with camels and donkeys and donkey boys. Mother and an American lady shared a sand-cart while the others took donkeys. My moke was a small willing beast which proved to be the best of the party. The donkey boy, young and friendly, thinking me to be American, said that the moke's name was George Washington. I was rather at sea on my steed at first especially when he galloped or when an unexpected whack from the donkey boy shot him forward unexpectedly, but we did not part company. At first we jogged through the dirty straggling village of Bedrechain and out along a winding road which led us to a little forest of palms which now stands over the ancient city of Memphis (Joseph's country). The first object of interest was a big statue of Rameses I [II?] lying on its back with the double crown broken off and standing upright. It was carved in fine sweeping lines and was in a good state. A few yards further was a smaller sphinx-like figure recently excavated on the spot. When found it was nearly upside-down. Yet further on we entered a house which had been built over a colossal statue of Rameses I [II?] also lying on its back. A platform built from one side of the house to the other enabled us to stand over the figure and get a splendid

Nile Feluccas   Cairo   19.III.24

Nile Feluccas

idea of the delightful sculpture of the face etc. It had broken at the ankles. Ignoring the many importunate vendors of scarabs we remounted (Mother tried a donkey for about two minutes but could not ride man-saddle) and followed the long road raised above the fields of wheat and cucumber culture and finally mounted the long ridge on which are all the Sakkara pyramids, and passing near the Step Pyramid, we pressed on to the House of Thi. Once above ground, this place is now entirely below the surface and has needed a lot of excavating. A decline led us to the entrance inside which was a courtyard beyond which were two more rooms, the walls of which were covered with carved scenes in delicate bas-relief of the very best period of Egyptian art. Mostly hunting, feasting or scenes of court life, they were amazingly vital and full of humour and entirely self-explanatory. Much of the colour – red, yellow, green and blue – remained. Thence we proceeded to the yet more amazing Temple of the Bulls. Another decline took us to the entrance and thence we walked through long passages, hewn out of the solid rock, on either side of which were deep and lofty recesses (twenty-four in all) containing polished granite sarcophagi, huge (each lid weighed 40 tons) and simple, which had held the embalmed bodies of the sacred bulls (Apis).[3] We each had a candle and the guide burnt magnesium ribbon for extra light at interesting places. We were allowed to descend one of the 'side-chapels', and, by going up some steps, peer inside a sarcophagus. These sarcophagi were so huge that we were puzzled to know how they could have been moved there. Our dragoman (guide) said they were supposed to have been floated in after artificial flooding of the rock galleries . . .

The jog back from the Step Pyramid was uneventful but the colours were good. The same road took us back to Bedrechain and to Cook's launch, where delay was caused by argument over an unexpected charge of £1 for the sand-cart. We had been three hours or more on the donkeys apart from the sightseeing and now had two hours more on the launch back to Cairo – cold! Mr Kelly joined us on the quay, motored Mother and Father back and after dinner took me to see the Spanish game of Pelota Basque. Played in a long building of considerable height, the game is much like a kind of fives, the ball being like a fives ball (a trifle larger) and bouncing prodigiously. Players (in whites) have a long curved basket (sickle-shaped) strapped to their right hands and in this they catch the ball and sling it again. The server slings the ball against the end wall so that it returns into a given area; then the other catches and slings it as hard or softly as he thinks fit, and so on. The first player to miss the ball or to send it 'out' has to retire and his place is taken by

---

[3] According to Baedeker, Apis was the sacred bull of the god Ptah.

another while his opponent scores one point. Whoever scores five points first wins the game and another is started (about six players take part). The spectators (separated from the play by a good partition and wire netting right up to the roof) sit about at little tables and take coffee etc. or deal with the bookies who scream persistently.

Pelote Basque

Pelota sketches

Thursday 20 March After our usual breakfast consisting of scrambled eggs with a tiny piece of undercooked bacon (2 square inches) very bitter and quite uneatable, followed by bread, butter and marmalade, Mother and I went to Cook's, enquired about Luxor and then quite by chance passed the office of the American Bible House. She went straight in and met the one in charge, a Rev. J. Oscar Boyd, PhD, DD, who was very friendly and recommended us to stay at the Thebes Hotel at Luxor saying it was largely patronised by missionaries and antiquarians. Thence a taxi took us to the museum where F was waiting. He had been there some while and took us to some of the best exhibits. What struck us most in the hall, after the colossal group of Amenhotep, Queen Thi and their three daughters, were the Nile boats with their paddles preserved in their proper shape from several thousand years ago. Upstairs we saw no more than the Tutankhamun relics and the mummies of the Pharaoh of the Oppression (Merenptah, son of Rameses II), Seti I and a wonderful array of coffins. The Tutankhamun chair must be unique and without price. It is of wood covered with gold and faience and inlaid with many precious stones. After lunch Mr Kelly motored us three via Giza to the great pyramids. Opposite Mena House Hotel he parked his car and we mounted four camels for the final slope. The enormous size of Cheops Pyramid (451 feet vertical height, sides 610 feet) is only realised from close to, and as we passed along one side of the base it seemed impossible that it could have been made by man in those far-off days. Our camels took us further, past some little ruined pyramids (of Cheops's daughters?) and down a long slope till the back of the Sphinx appeared. After the sight for many years of familiar photos, the Sphinx seemed very small but as we passed close to its head and then round to the front the impressions went and we could only marvel at the strength and beauty of its proportions and at the skill of the sculptors who created it from the living rock. They say that the nose was shot away by Napoleon's sharpshooters – a piece of ghastly vandalism if true. After some photos we returned to the great pyramid, were joined by Mrs K and her sister and paid off our 'Camel Corps'. We all returned for a thoroughly good tea at Mena House. Mena House Hotel is a fine spacious building in good grounds at the foot of the pyramids. Same management as the Continental Savoy in Cairo. Many good trees including eucalyptus. Have their own dark rooms and a splendid open-air swimming bath with dressing rooms etc. Part of the

Man on donkey, with Cairo in Arabic

windows are in the Persian moushrabir work (harem style) which consists of wood pierced all over in various patterns of little holes. This allows the lady inside to see out without herself being seen.

Mr K and I then walked right round the Pyramid of Khefren which still has some alabaster remaining at the top. The setting sun turned one side of this pyramid quite pink. At its base we also had a look at the curious holes and caves and inscriptions in the cliffs. Then we went to a favourite nook on the south side of the great pyramids which Mr Kelly has frequented before and sat and told yarns while the sunset disappeared and the moon (full tonight) rose. Leaving the others I climbed up the south face of the pyramid till I reached the south-east angle about halfway to the summit, not a very simple climb in the unusual light as the steps were much weathered and filled with debris left by the robbers who had taken the alabaster casing to build their mosque. It was a queer place to rest – halfway up that edifice of the dim past. The moon getting ever brighter lit up the Khefren Pyramid, while, far off to the east, Cairo twinkled. The heavy silence was only broken by the high rasping of many bats, an occasional laugh coming faintly from our party below, or very distant barking and shouting from the Arab village not far from the foot of the hill. Descending, I rejoined the others and shortly after we got up for a stroll and Mr Kelly left to get a boy to bring our supper from the car. We all descended the slope again and crossing the sand around the Sphinx dropped down into the last cup-like hollow and sat at the base of the great creature, under its chin, where we partook of an excellent meal with lemonade. The moon lit us so brilliantly that I attempted a little sketch. It was an experience never to be forgotten but we were not allowed to brood much over the ancient association of the place, the spirits and banter of the Kellys and Father making the atmosphere very light. Very reluctantly we left the enchanting scene at length and slowly made our way back past the great pyramid which now looked magical, disappearing up into the stars. The scene was helped by the sight of Venus, a brilliant light and very near the earth this year, who was low down on the west horizon. With many a backward glance we drifted to Mena House whence Father and I took a tram back to Cairo (changed at Giza) while all the others motored.

Friday 21 March After breakfast I telegraphed for rooms at the Thebes Hotel at Luxor and then Mr Kelly drove us three and Mrs K to Abbassia Camp. There he descended and Mrs K took us on for a delightful round. Skirting Heliopolis we soon reached open country, very picturesque with its long-robed workers and occasional shining mosques, though no hills were in sight except the Moqattams behind. Soon we ran through Mataria and stopped at the far end by a Red Cross station. Entered a gate into a private garden and passed through an avenue of limes whose flowers gave a heavy scent till we reached a huge old tree (sycamore) under which a man was buying lime blossom from three other people and weighing it carefully in a long scale. Nearby was a well (arranged to be worked by donkey power). Thence another gate took us to a tiny enclosed garden in the

Sketch of sphinx in moonlight

middle of which was the Virgin's Tree, a tree of great age under which the Virgin Mary is reputed to have rested on the flight into Egypt and which they try hard to preserve alive. The keeper of the garden called the tree a sycamore. Two branches were bearing leaf. The well behind was supposed to have been in existence then and the Virgin is said to have drawn water thence to wash the Child. A brilliant bougainvillaea grew near the tree and helped the scene immensely. Thence we motored further to the Heliopolis Obelisk, a beauty standing in a pool of water and clearly inscribed with hieroglyphs (all four sides the same). Returning through Mataria we found many people carrying carefully gaudily dressed dolls with tinsel and red, green, yellow etc. clothes just bought in the village, but could not find out the ceremony they were for. Then through Zeitoun to Heliopolis and out for a while on the Suez road from which I caught sight of a mirage across the desert, some distant hillocks appearing to float. In the afternoon Mr Kelly drove us to the Alhazar, a Muhammadan convent, to see the whirling dervishes. We entered through an archway, up some steps, under a vine spreading over a little courtyard and thence round to the entrance of the place – a sort of square theatre with a circular space railed off in the middle like a circus. Galleries were all round, the main one was for the ministers and musicians and one side one was protected by moushrabir work and was for ladies. The dervishes in tall brown Turkish fezes came slowly in and bowed to Mecca and silently each took a place on the edge of the circle. Lastly the sheikh entered and we noticed he had a broad black band on his fez. Taking his seat on the floor facing the musicians he sat motionless as did the others. A native flute in the gallery made sundry noises, and then a voice droned something very softly, to be answered shortly by the sheikh who with his head bowed chanted equally softly some of the Koran with his hands raised palm upwards nearly to his face. Then a man rose in the balcony and recited the Koran at some length dwelling on the various words with a nasal and somewhat dismal drone, full of runs and arpeggios and trills in a minor key. When he had gradually passed from a quiet beginning to a loud finish the band started (flute, violin and drums) for a while and then at a given signal the dervishes rose and slowly paced round their ring twice, each bowing to the man following as he passed Mecca (east). Then the sheikh stood in his place and the others threw off their black cloaks revealing white underneath – short coat and long full skirt – all

Sketch of praying man

were in white except one who was in green. Then they filed past the sheikh, each kissing his hand and immediately began to whirl with outstretched arms. The man in green whirled in the middle and represented the sun. Two men near him whirled and at the same time moved slowly round him – the planets. Several others whirled and moved faster round the edge of the circle, representing the fixed stars. The band stopped at intervals and they rested. Thence Mr K took us to the citadel and showed us the palace and harem – now a British military hospital. Magnificent high rooms and painted ceilings. Saw a Jock who had fallen halfway down the great pyramid – wonderful escape. Thence to the great mosque of Muhammad Ali. Put on yellow shoes with strings (over our own) at the entrance. Went through the courtyard and inside. Magnificent interior (said to be designed by a Greek who subsequently was blinded by Muhammad Ali) with rich carpets, gorgeous ceiling, high pulpit and myriad glass globes. Returning to Cairo we had tea and cakes under a fig tree at Groppi's famous restaurant.

Sun   all in green }
Stars + } "   " white } Brown fez
planet

Rough sketch of whirling dervish

Saturday 22 March A quiet day. M and I packed in the morning while F enquired about passports. In the afternoon F and I took tram and Shanks's pony to the Mousky where we prowled around the scent bazaar without doing business. Then we tried to find our previous tapestry shop without success till we happened to run across 'George', our previous guide, who got us there in quick time. F bought a long donkeycloth panel while I bought two small square ones and also a tarbush (fez). After tea F, M and I walked to a shop to lay in provisions for the journey of the night and F created great amusement (to us) by wearing my new red cap! As a matter of fact, instead of making him queer it rendered him inconspicuous in a city where nearly everyone else wore them. After an early dinner Mr Kelly motored M and me to the station where we got a second-class compartment to ourselves in the eight o'clock train for Luxor (return to Luxor 3 guineas each second class). It started on time and we soon spread ourselves out with rugs and cushions and got quite a good deal of sleep in patches. The full moon allowed us picturesque peeps of the Nile as we followed upstream and the silhouettes of palm trees were very effective. The dawn was wonderful in colour. Lemon yellow warmed to brilliant orange in the east while a band of dull blue over the western hills was surmounted by a mauve band which gradually became rosy pink. Then the hills caught the light and suddenly the sun came over the eastern horizon blazing and fiery yellow, not the dull red affair which usually occurs in England.

Sunday 23 March We were lucky to keep our compartment to ourselves all the way and on arrival after a broken journey in which we ate, slept and talked in spasms, we found ourselves covered in a layer of dusty sand. At Luxor station I singled out the young man who shouted 'Thebes Hotel' from the other hotel representatives and he soon had us in the hotel gharry and we were through the dirty streets of the town and in the hotel within ten minutes. The hotel overlooks some attractive gardens with many acacias (in pod and losing their leaves) and several trees which Mrs K called jacaranda covered with masses of blue blossoms of a most delicious shade. Tea came quickly and then good washes freshened us mightily, so much so that we took a stroll towards the Nile (three minutes away) and were interested by the boys filling their black goatskins in the river and the small black women and girls balancing pitchers and jars gracefully on their heads. Beside a house facing the Nile a suave old gentleman got into conversation with us and soon was showing us a valuable book with signatures of many notables in it including Rider Haggard, Roosevelt, Earl of Dudley, Henrik Ibsen, Lord Carnarvon etc. After insisting on our partaking of coffee he showed us his 'museum' and we found he was a licensed seller of antiquities. Very interesting but we did not buy. From our dragoman we afterwards learnt that our host of the museum had formerly been German consul here which would account for the large number of

German names in his great book (the book had signatures collected for more than sixty years). A good and well-served lunch followed and the afternoon was remarkable for our first spell of what M called Indian heat – still, blazing and almost unbearable – and boding ill for our stay here. After tea a long rest on the wide verandah and then dinner. The food, service and general atmosphere is nicer here than at the Killiney pension. A lizard on my bedroom wall was a new experience – but I understand I am lucky as they eat the mosquitoes. A bat got into my bedroom while I undressed and whirled round incessantly so that I was not sorry to get into bed inside my mosquito curtain. Cool night and I slept well in spite of the squawking and croaking of the frogs on the Nile banks.

Monday 24 March A pleasant breakfast fortified us for the day and our tall dark-skinned Muhammadan dragoman (Muhammad Krayim) took us off promptly at 8.30 to the Nile ferry (sail if wind enough, oars otherwise). On the other side a 'carriage and pair' awaited and we were quickly trundling over the sandy track with a barefooted runner, impervious to the heat, keeping alongside. First past some primitive mud huts where ragged children carried baby sheep and goats as an inducement for baksheesh and then on, sometimes by the irrigation canals, sometimes between fields of wheat, barley, beans, poppies or sugar canes (mostly the latter), we gradually approached the mighty Colossi standing at present in a field of barley, but shortly to be surrounded by water at 'High Nile'. The mummies of the queens proceeding to the queens' tombs rested here for the funeral service. They made the gateway to an ancient temple of Amenophis III. One had fallen by earthquake and Septimius Severus had endeavoured to rebuild it in great blocks, but the imitation is not too successful. Thence to the Ramesseum or great temple of Rameses II. Many great columns remaining with mutilated figures of Osiris and of Rameses. Along one side are the remains of the temple storehouses (discovered by Flinders Petrie) made of mud and straw bricks with the cartouche of the king stamped on each brick. These and part of the Ramesseum were built over the remains of a previous temple of Thothmes III. On a big flat wall of the Ramesseum is depicted the great battle between Rameses II and the Hittites. Beside that are the colossal remains of the biggest statue in Egypt – one of Rameses II cut out of one block of granite and weighing 1,000 tons.

It was overthrown by Cambyses, the Persian conqueror, and now is in many pieces. Thence we continued – looked in at the little temple of Ptolemy (Deir-el-Medina) and drove along the dusty road to the south of the hills. No green or grass was here and the sun getting ever hotter blazed on the barren rocks and nearly blinded us. We quickly approached the steep rocky Valley of the Queens and stopped at the tombs. The first one visited was of Queen Nefertari – a Syrian princess and wife of Rameses II (the Great). The finest tomb here. The paintings are on raised plaster and the colours are amazingly fresh. The scenes represented are of the queen before various gods but near the entrance is a painting of the queen playing draughts. She was 19th Dynasty (1250 BC). Next we saw the tomb of a little son of Rameses II. The king is shown always with the prince in the pictures which are good. Then the tomb of this prince's mother (not Nefertari) adjacent and further on the tomb of an older prince, also son of Rameses II. The heat was now overpowering and a saunter back to the carriage with our dark glasses on found us at the end of our strength and we set off back with our runner going as strong as ever beside us. We soon arrived at some palm trees with big ruins beside them called Medinet Habu. The first part of the buildings which we entered had been part of a palace and harem of Rameses III. Broken granite figures of Sekhmet were beside the entrance, and in a shady corner we seated ourselves while Muhammad unfastened our luncheon basket and then disappeared to converse with some of his fellows and to sleep. We revived after our feed and later found steps leading to the upper part of the palace. Up there we met a fresh breeze which was like a breath of life after the scorching heat, and before long clouds appeared and the day became more bearable. While we were in the upper apartment a hawk smaller than a kite flew past in the act of killing a sparrow and disappeared clutching the little bird in its talons. Rousing Muhammad we proceeded and he showed us some wonderful carvings in the other part of Medinet Habu – the temple of Rameses III. The king was depicted fighting – grasping handfuls of enemies by the hair – receiving the sword of victory from Amon Ra. Another wonderful piece of descriptive carving showed the king hunting birds, deer, wild bulls etc. while fishes were shown in the Nile. Passing into the first court between great pylons we found great pillars lining the east and west walls, those on the east having Osiris figures in front. Part of the incised pictures showed prisoners having their heads cut off. An inclined plane led to the second court, pillared all round, and the pictures on the walls showed the unfortunate prisoners having their hands and feet cut off. The hypostyle hall beyond was very dilapidated and had been the site of a Coptic church, the Copts having covered the carved remains in plaster thus destroying the colour. In somewhat cooler air we remounted our carriage and returned. The sunset colours were wonderful being almost exactly a replica in reverse of the dawn seen from the train yesterday. In the evening a mob of black-robed women and a few children moved past our hotel out towards Karnak, all crooning and singing and making weird noises. On enquiring we learnt that they were celebrating the release of a man relative who had completed a term of four years in prison.

Tuesday 25 March Muhammad Krayim awaited us at 7 a.m. and with luncheon basket we crossed the Nile in the cool of the morning and took our carriage along much of yesterday's road. Before long, however, we took another, and, leaving the Colossi far on the left, kept on towards the temple of Seti I (Temple of Kurna). Arriving there we were shown first the ancient bath (called the Sacred Lake) for the washing of mummies, which were brought straight from Karnak for a service here before burial in the Valley of the Kings (Biban-el-Muluk). In the temple eight out of a row of ten great papyrus columns remain in the first court. In the inner (hypostyle) hall part of the ceiling remains, but most of the place is dilapidated. The wall carvings have very many representations of the ram-headed god Khnum (sun god). Proceeding thence by carriage we shortly found ourselves between two slopes of rocky boulders and passing a domed residence recently occupied by Mr Howard Carter and the late Lord Carnarvon. It was the beginning of the Valley of the Kings. Quickly the character of our drive changed and the valley grew stranger. Our hot, dusty, white road wound in and out between long screes of stones at the tops of which were perpendicular cliffs which became more and more fantastic and unreal in shape as we proceeded till we arrived at a vast semi-circle of cliffs which forms the great necropolis of the kings. Nearly the first tomb we arrived at was the new one – that of King Tutankhamun – the entrance being below the present level of the ground and being now closed and well sealed and guarded always by Egyptian soldiers. A longish path past that took us to the little entrance to the tomb of Amenophis II at the base of a straight high cliff. Two flights of steps and a longish passage brought us suddenly to a vertical deep shaft with a little door at the bottom. This was the false tomb to deceive robbers and a bridge now took us across to the continuation of our passage recently discovered through the plaster on the other side of the shaft. Thence into a biggish room – turn to the left and down more steps to the final hall of the tomb. In a little room to the right we suddenly saw three unwrapped mummies, startlingly lifelike and well preserved – a man, woman and girl intended as servants to the king in the next world. Electric light enabled us to see everything very clearly and at the end of the chamber we were shown the great lidless sarcophagus, covered now with glass, in which lay the body of Amenophis II, still with flowers round it. The decorations of all the tombs were unusual and delightful, being like big pen and ink drawings on the plaster, the 'pencil' or rough marks being very discernible underneath and the bold brushwork coming on top. It was as hot and oppressive inside the tombs as outside, but the air was not so good. Thence we went to the tomb of Rameses III, a long one descending by steps to passages at three different levels. In the upper passage are several side-chambers, very tiny, each with interesting paintings inside showing slaughtering of cattle, baking, ploughing, fishing, harpists singing etc. Only half the complete tomb is visited and in that the painted work is much damaged but the design and size of the tomb is imposing. Thence to the great tomb of Seti I, the finest tomb of all, though, on account of its having been opened a long while without guard, it has been much damaged and natives have stripped much of the plaster with the freshest colour work. The tomb is of great depth (328 feet long). At the entrance the ornamentation was in bas relief cut in the smooth limestone but as we descended through room after room it degenerates to painted plaster. In the final hall of the sarcophagus the wall paintings are splendid and the dark blue and gold ceiling is extraordinary, both in design and execution being fresh as the day it was done and including the early signs of the zodiac and many scenes of afterlife. One side room was of interest being unfurnished. The designs were only in the stage of black and white outline. The rough sketch was there in a pale reddish ink and the later drawing in strong black brushstrokes. Thence to the tomb of Rameses VI built just over that of Tutankhamun presumably in ignorance of the existence of the latter. The colours on the plaster reliefs here are very good though over 3,000 years old but they are not different from the previous tombs to any marked extent. In scorching heat we remounted our carriage and returned through the blazing arid valley with its weird rock forms and noted the many marks in the screes where Lord Carnarvon and Mr Carter had excavated for years. After passing Lord Carnarvon's house we bore to the right and soon were passing between primitive mud huts of peasants. An imposing building next appeared – the house of Pierpoint Morgan who with his helpers had been excavating years ago the great rock temple of Queen Hatsu standing opposite at the bottom of a great rock face. (Queen Hatsu was daughter of Thothmes I and married her own brother Thothmes II. On the death of the latter she took the throne herself and was a powerful queen. When she died her half-brother Thothmes III reigned, and, through jealousy of her having taken the throne before him, he caused nearly all the effigies of her on temples etc. to be chiselled out or otherwise effaced – sometimes putting his own picture there instead. When Hatsu reigned alone she often caused her pictures to show her wearing a false beard. When wearing that she was called Hatshepsut. This great temple of Queen Hatsu is called Deir-el-Bahri.) To the right of the temple a precipitous track zig-zagged up to the hilltop and just beyond was the Valley of the Kings only half a mile away. The carriage road had taken us five or six miles round. Mother remained in the carriage because of the heat while Muhammad took me up the inclined approach to the ancient terraced temple. The long rows of pillars have been much broken, but renovations to the outer ones have preserved the roof part. The most interesting thing was the 'Punt Colonnade' showing boats on an expedition to and from Punt (or Somaliland) in delicate and wonderful bas relief. Much has been covered and broken by Copts, but what there is is delightful. The beehive huts on posts in Somaliland are well done and so are the facial characteristics of the blacks. There is also very perfect drawing in the fishes in the river and in the articles of trade (animals etc.) in the boats. Thence we proceeded to the village of Kurna made of the roughest mud huts and visited two of the tombs of the 'nobles', first that of Mena (or Menena or Menne), a land steward under Amenophis II, where very good paintings show him superintending work in the fields etc. Then the little tomb of Nakht, the head gardener of Amenophis IV (?), with very clear painting showing him superintending digging and tilling and also with vines and grapes. Remounting we returned straight to the Ramesseum, lunched at base of a great pillar in the second court and went strolling through the trees of the first court where we admired some brilliant-hued hoopoes and where the keeper (after baksheesh) turned over many blocks from the broken colossus of Rameses II in the endeavour to discover a scorpion underneath to show us. He was not successful. The journey back across the Nile was uneventful and after some tea we set off again and with Muhammad passed through the streets to the great open market. At the entrance a khaki-clad Egyptian tax-collector was heatedly haranguing the purchasers of two goats for trying to get out without paying the necessary tax. Then we wandered through the merchants who squatted under tiny canvas shades with their goods, beans, sugar cane, bread covered with millions of flies etc. and saw the barbers squatting on their haunches and shaving the heads of their customers. Thence through the further part where many oxen, donkeys and camels were for sale. We had quails for dinner tonight, much better than those supplied on the *Ormonde*.

Wednesday 26 March After breakfast the carriage took us and Muhammad to Karnak, the great ruined mass of temples built by many kings. Near Karnak we found we were passing through the remains of the vast avenue of sphinxes which stretched right from Karnak to Luxor Temple. These were ram-headed sphinxes 1,000 in number, 500 on each side of road, built by Amenhotep III. After passing on foot through the great pylon of Ptolemy Evergetes I, we saw the Temple of Khons, the hawk-headed god, built by Rameses III and finished by Rameses IV and Rameses XII. Fine relief carvings of the conventional scenes are still here. The carriage then took us further to the outside of the great Temple of Amon where we dismounted and walked to the west end where another fine avenue of sphinxes is, which once went right from here to the great Temple of Seti I across the Nile which we saw yesterday and which flanked the road along which the mummies of kings were taken for burial. Originally the Nile flowed to the east of Luxor so that Thebes from the Necropolis hills to here formed an uninterrupted city, but the river having changed its course has destroyed this sphinx road and now divides the Ramesseum etc. from Luxor and

Sketch of Luxor market

Karnak. Entering the great court between great pylons we passed the Temple of Seti II (to Amon, Mut and Khons) on the left, and entered the Temple of Rameses III which had an outer court (for common people) then a small higher court (for royalty) and finally a hypostyle hall and three sanctuaries (also to Amon, Mut and Khons) which are for priests only.

Then back and through other enormous pylons and into what must be the biggest piece of temple construction in old Egypt – certainly the greatest hypostyle hall. Built by Seti I and his son Rameses II, this hall contains 134 immense columns (these columns are not monoliths). In the nave are twelve columns nearly 12 feet thick and 69 feet high while all the others are over 6 feet thick and 43 feet high. We moved amongst these like little ants marvelling at the gigantic structure and I went up later through the thickness of the wall (up steps) to the top of the great girdle wall of Rameses II and tried to get a good place for photos. Rather dazed by the size of this we wandered out into the heat and sunshine through some insignificant Roman remains to the Temple of Ptah, a little one built by Thothmes III and restored by Shabaks and Ptolemies. A splendid statue of Sekhmet (standing-up position) carved in black granite is within and looks weird being lit by a hole in the ceiling though the keeper gave us candles also. Thence we walked round the great girdle walls again, watched men repairing and cementing the reliefs, saw an obelisk of Thothmes I, passed through more pylons, saw a great clean obelisk of Queen Hatsu (Hatshepsut) and the part of the temple she had built and on to the festal temple of Thothmes III, the pillars and roof of which are good though spoilt by plaster of the later Copts. Passing out to the south we watched a big gang of boys engaged in excavating and carrying baskets of earth on their heads to trolleys of a light railway and making rhythmic noises like a sailors' shanty. Further on Muhammad showed us the Sacred Lake – an unsavoury expanse of green water and slime wherein were frogs etc. (we also saw a great block of granite with a big carved beetle or scarab on top – time of Queen Hatsu) – after which we returned to our carriage and back to the Thebes Hotel where little Muhammad (the boots and waiter) rushed as usual to dust our boots and the hall porter smiled and enquired after our enjoyment and the head waiter beamed and we realised that they knew it was our last day. After lunch we settled our bill and Muhammad Krayim took us to see Luxor Temple. At the north end, whence the great avenue of sphinxes once led away to Karnak, stands an obelisk and some great granite statues (again of Rameses II) and some massive pylons, just inside which on high ground stands the Mosque of Abu'l Haggig, the founder of modern Luxor. This is in the great court of Rameses II which has a double row of papyrus columns all round and is full of inscriptions and with many damaged statues of the king, each having a miniature of the queen down by his left leg. In the next hall, smaller, our guide showed us some inscriptions of Tutankhamun and Horemheb. (Tutankhamun brought the royal residence back to Thebes and completed this temple though his successor Horemheb later put in his own name for that of Tutankhamun.) Then into the great court of Amenophis III with its many columns. Till recently these were all covered by debris nearly to the top of the columns, and houses (including the French consulate) were inside (Muhammad Krayim's own house when he was younger was here and he showed us the pillar – darkened by smoke near the top – where it was). The great hypostyle hall was cut up, part being used as sanctuary by Alexander the Great, and behind that the Copts have damaged much of the ornamentation. There is also the 'birth-room' with inscribed pictures representing stages in the divine birth of Amenophis III. Leaving the temple we were shown several shops without being much tempted to buy and then returned to the hotel for tea and final packing. At 5.15 the gharry took us to the station and we got a compartment to ourselves again (second class). A brilliant orange sunset over the hills of the ancient necropolis was our last sight of that amazing district and our three days were past like a dream. We slept quite well during the night which was not so sandy as on our journey up and consequently were fairly fresh early on.

Thursday 27 March The morning found us near Cairo. We had a good view of the long line of pyramids from Dahchour to Saccara, Abousir and Gizeh and of the fertile palm-growing tract around Memphis and Bedrechain, and arrived at Cairo at 7.30. Taxi to Killiney House and woke Father. Quiet morning. Went to lunch with Mr Gibson at the Savoy Continental Hotel. He was eager to hear about Luxor and also suggested joining us on the Palestine trip. Mr Kelly (with Father and Miss Irwin) called for me at 2.30 and we motored out through Shubra and Kaliub to the great Nile Barrage, a great piece of engineering which dams the three branches of the river. Lovely gardens with grassy lawns are laid out here and there are brilliant red, orange and purple bougainvillaeas etc. Father liked it better than anything yet in Egypt. We had tea while sitting on the grass and were entertained by some really brilliant conjuring by a splay-eyed, wandering 'golly-golly' man in a tarbush and striped robe, who did tricks with brass cups, rings, cards, balls etc.

Friday 28 March The morning was spent mostly in packing and sorting and Father went to the French consul to get our passports for Syria visaed. In the afternoon I arranged for Lloyd Triestino people to call for a trunk to be brought on our ship to Beirut and meet us there. Also took a box to Cook's to be forwarded to England. The Kellys were at a bazaar, but they turned up at the station to see us off (6.15 p.m.) as did Miss Kurban (the organist)

Luxor station

Sketches of heads at Luxor Station

"GOLLY - GOLLY"   BARRAGE GARDENS   CAIRO '27. III. 24

'Golly-golly' sketch

whose two sisters were going back to Jerusalem on the same train. We left punctually in a full train and made good time to Kantara stopping at Benha, Zagazig and Ismailia. A guide took us in hand there without being asked, and saw us to the customs shed where our things got through without being opened. Then we crowded on to the chain ferry and were hauled across to the eastern side. The baggage (containing incidentally Father's passport) was to follow later, so we waited for it while all the other passengers had their passports stamped and got health papers. We saw three boats come down the canal from Port Said with powerful searchlights on their prows (including one British India liner). At length we got through and were fixed up in our second-class compartment and returned to the buffet (Mr Gibson and I) for coffees. At midnight we left, Father spreading out on the floor and Mother and I and Mr Gibson on various seats – train not full.

Saturday 29 March We slept quite well and were thankful for the absence of the Egyptian dust and sand. When we woke we were in a green land with villages here and there, with camels and donkeys and cattle (not the huge Egyptian sort, but smaller and like our own) and children and women graceful and upright and often carrying water pots or four gallon oil tins on their heads. At the stopping places delightful children ran along outside the train with posies of wild flowers and bright smiles which were hard to withstand. With the women apparently there was freedom here – no yashmak or brass forehead-piece. The difference in the men was also marked – none of the simple nightgown costume and more of the white Arab headcloth held down by two circlets. These Arabs were leaner, more bright-eyed and alert than those seen in Cairo. At Ludd we had to change trains. Starting off again we were soon in a winding valley curling in a tortuous way between rounded hills always climbing from the lowlands along the dried valley of the brook Kedron (riverbed in which David picked up the smooth stones for killing Goliath). High up on one hill we were shown a cave going well into the earth and supposed to be Samson's cave. After stopping at Bittir we ran into Jerusalem station. There was no sign of the city there but many hotel representatives surrounded us and we went with the man from the Majestic who seemed the most importunate. Bundling the baggage into a gharry and ourselves into a taxi we went to see the Majestic and later to see the St John's Hotel within the city, deciding on the latter. The approach to the latter was a great experience for us. The Majestic is outside the Jaffa Gate through the old walls in which is the little postern gate, the Needle Gate, while the St John's is in the midst of the old city right opposite the Church of the Holy Sepulchre. Inside the Jaffa Gate carriages can only go a few yards and then the old city begins with its tiny streets always on a slope and descending by steps long or short according to gradient. The widest streets permit of perhaps four people or five abreast, while many of the narrower ones do not allow of two.

As the building of this place proceeded, thoroughfares were often arched over and homes built on top, so that a street will often become a tunnel for a long way with only a peep of daylight here and there. Crowds jostle and surge along these roads of many Christian churches and Mohammedans and Jews, the most conspicuous priests being the Greek Orthodox with their black gowns and tall black hats and those of Judaism with fur-rimmed caps and flowing gowns. Our porters who carried our baggage from the Majestic barged through and we were soon around the many corners and in our rooms at St John's which looks out on to a little square built by the Turks – about the only open space in old Jerusalem. Behind the hotel and joining the building is a Mohammedan mosque with a high minaret ringed by the usual gallery on which, later, we were frequently to see the muezzin come out and sing out his loud and tuneful call to prayer – resonant and in minor key. Beyond that was a courtyard and then the Church of the Holy Sepulchre with its great slate-coloured dome. We breakfasted in the hotel and rested till lunch when we ate again. A decent young guide came to the lounge in the afternoon. As soon as he came Mr Gibson and I went round into the Holy Sepulchre Church with him and he showed us the stone where Christ's body was anointed, then His tomb where we got candles and had rose water put on our hands by a priest. Services were going on simultaneously in various places and this together with the semi-barbarous ornamentation of the place, its many lamps and pictures and jewels, gave an unreal effect. The Greek Orthodox were having a service in the middle church, the Copts were chanting behind the tomb, while the Syrians were chanting and swinging incense in the grotto outside the tombs of Joseph of Arimathea and Zacchaeus which we next saw. Our guide took us and our candles in and out of these without fear. Later he showed us the place where the cross was found by Queen Helena, mother of Constantine (the first Christian king), also the place where Jesus was sat with his feet in stocks – also the last two stations of the cross – also the top of Calvary and the cleft caused in the rock. Many of these were covered by gaudy altars and myriad lamps of various colours put up by many churches, but there is little inducement to worship. We also saw a picture with glass eyes and loaded with jewels from many 'kings' which recently was supposed to commit the miracle of shedding tears (picture is on top of Calvary).

We went with the guide down the steps of the Street of David and through other alleys with most repulsive smells at many points till we arrived at the Jews' wailing place – a little passage along one side of which is an immense wall (the outside of the Haram Sherif) the bottom blocks of great size being some original stones of the Temple of Solomon. About forty people were facing the wall – praying, swaying, groaning or repeating the psalms of David. All were making public intercession for the restoration of their city to the Jews and it was a moving sight. Returning thence we passed through the quiet Jewish quarter (this is their Sabbath) and out through another gate (the Zion Gate) on Mount Zion and watched the sun set. It was now too late to go out for tea, so we sauntered back to the Jaffa Gate and thence into the old city and to the hotel for dinner and bed.

Sunday 30 March After a late breakfast we went to a service by the Scots Presbyterians in the fine great German Church of the Redeemer beside our hotel. A good service followed by Communion which was administered while we sat on chairs. In the afternoon we did not do much, but after an early tea a gharry drove us first down past Damascus Gate and Herod's Gate to near the Garden of Gethsemane whence we looked across the little valley of Jehoshephat to Olivet with its Russian church and gilded tops halfway up and its bigger Russian church on top. Then back to Herod's Gate and round a circuitous route to the first slope of the Mount of Olives where our soldiers' graves are. We dismounted and found the grave of a friend of Mr Oswald's. Further on we came to the big German building erected by the Kaiser and now used as our residency. We were able to enter and saw the lounge with one of the black-and-silver-clad Palestine police preceding us and also the splendid chapel with its great pictures and gallery and mosaic work. The ceiling is richly painted with saints and biblical heroes among whom appear Kaiser Bill and the Empress seated side by side, and also Barbarossa, Frederick II and various rulers of Germany! We were taken right up the tower to the belfry (Mother going halfway) from which the view was magnificent, allowing us to see for the first time the Dead Sea and the mountains of Gilead beyond. Our gharry took us to the top of

Olivet and the Church of the Ascension but we did not stay there as it was sunset. Proceeding on foot a guide took us up into the Church of the Lord's Prayer, rebuilt over an old one of the time of the Crusaders, in which the Lord's Prayer is written in thirty-two languages. We secured pieces of mosaic from the rubble recently excavated from the ancient floor of the Crusaders' church. Thence we descended to the spot where Jesus sat and wept over the city and thence down past the entrance to the Garden of Gethsemane and up the steep approach to St Stephen's Gate. Then (having looked at the map in Baedeker) I became the guide and we arrived, after traversing many strange passages and tunnels and smelly places, back at our hotel for dinner and bed.

Monday 31 March A young motor driver who had been in our hotel last evening was hired by Father to take us around today, so we set off early in a powerful car (Dodge Bros) from the Damascus Gate and whizzed past the walls and over the brook Kidron (dry) and past Absalom's Tomb and Siloam village to the hills on the south-east. Our road was good, being begun by the Turks and finished by British. The whole country as far as the eye could see was steep broken hills and our road wound constantly with no straight stretch. Roughly we followed the ancient track to Jericho, but here and there we left it to follow a longer, easier slope. It was down, down all the way for many miles, past the little huts and excavations of Bethany to the spring known as Absalom's Well, sometimes doubling on our tracks down a steep hill with two hairpin bends. Then on again uphill a little, past the ancient inn of the Good Samaritan and then many more miles downhill twisting and turning between the bleak sandy hills sparsely covered with coarse grass and tufts of a still coarser kind, till suddenly we emerged from hills to the wide expanse of 'delta' where the Jordan flowed into the Dead Sea. The latter lay and sparkled to our right with the hazy mountains beyond (to the southern end Mount Nebo where Moses was buried, and nearer to us the mountains of Jordan and Gomorrah). Across Jordan for miles were the mountains of Gilead and then to our left we saw the trees and houses of modern Jericho. Leaving that on the left we took the rough track to the Dead Sea descending gradually for 4 more miles between flat-topped sandy dunes with coarse herbage all around. The sandy soil all round became more and more baked in appearance and cracked, and over all was a white deposit of pure salt, sometimes thick. On some of the dunes it covered the tops of the slopes like snow. On one of the hillocks we noticed a couple of storks, common birds round here. The track became rapidly bad and nearly impossible in places and we jolted and tossed and twice I was bounced to the roof of the car (a canvas covering only) and sometimes the car was in first gear to crawl through the ruts and potholes. However, eventually we ran along beside the little reed huts raised on poles inhabited by Dead Sea boatmen and dismounted on the shingle foreshore. Several little sailing vessels were here and a couple of tiny 'steamers' which fetch wheat across from villages in the hills (of Sodom and Gomorrah) opposite. Although we were now 1,290 feet below sea level there was a fresh cool wind blowing and we enjoyed dabbling in the ripples. The taste of the water was intensely bitter.

The Dead Sea varies its level about 16 feet according to season (hence houses on poles), highest in April after snows melt in Lebanon. Heat is usually so great here that it evaporates as much water as is supplied by the Jordan. The sea is about 25 per cent salt and a bather can hardly get under the water.

Remounting the car we set off again by the artificial lake (made at high water to yield the salt deposit when the lake dries later in the season) and bumped along the track which was now only two wheel tracks in a soft baked desert. Passing another car in the opposite direction was dangerous but accomplished once safely, and later we ran between a stretch of thick bush in which gazelle and wild boar are still hunted and shot, and approaching another hut raised on poles found ourselves beside Jordan. Photos were taken of the stream, muddy-coloured but fringed with willows and bushes like any English river, and Mother got a bottle of Jordan water. Thence the awful track led us to modern Jericho across the plain of Gilgal. A few houses only are there and the British flag flies over the largest edifice. We saw the beginning of the good new road leading from here to Transjordania. The whole area is owned by a very rich Palestinian who, after failing to pump water from the Jordan nearby, succeeded in bringing it by pipe all the way from the Nile! Thus the land round Jericho is now fertile and full of fruit. We saw apricots and bananas growing, and there were oranges and olives and limes with their sweet heavy scent and a curious fruit with dark leaves called 'houriot' and said to be good as a purgative etc. Passing through this rich part we ascended to Elijah's fountain which had been enclosed as a pool by King Solomon. There in a high reed enclosure we ate our lunch and watched the fishes fight for our crumbs. From a nearby eminence we looked afterwards towards the western hills and saw the remains of walls and a few excavated dwellings of the old Jericho, once a place of much size and power, and now nothing but grassy mounds on which goats wandered. Near us an Arab goatherd squatted on a hillock and made plaintive runs on a little pipe of about four notes in a minor key (a pipe similar to that of the whirling dervishes. To produce sound one blows into the end of the pipe at an oblique angle. Difficult.)

OLD JERICHO.
SHEPHERD PIPING

Sketch of goatherd

Leaving there we ran back to the new Jericho and turned off to rejoin our previous road at the foot of the hills and the Dodge roared up the steep gradients in good style. We were surprised to be met soon by a hurricane of wind blowing off the enclosing hills and very hot and unpleasant. The heat of it and the dust and sand it contained made it really nasty. As we ascended it cooled somewhat but did not abate in strength. Near the inn of the Good Samaritan a plug broke, so we stopped and all except Mother ascended to the hilltop where the remains of the ancient place have been excavated. Not much to see except three arched rooms. The wind made it hard to stand still on the top so we descended and continued back to Bethany. Descended there and were shown the tomb of Lazarus and the place he rested on emerging. All down a tiny flight of steps and fairly deep into the rock. Then going past the ruins of the house of Simon the leper we got into the house of Mary and Martha of which only a few pieces of the old good stone remain. Children swarmed round us like flies for baksheesh and trying to sell us slings such as David used to slay Goliath. Some of the little chaps could throw big distances with them. We were back at the St John's by six after a stop and a rest at the Garden of Gethsemane where an old Franciscan father allowed us to walk around among the ancient olive trees. The sacred associations of that spot rather gripped us but the atmosphere was spoilt by the huge church (French) which blocks the Siloam outlook from the garden and which is not yet quite finished. We also visited the gloomy underground church and tomb of the Virgin [which was] opposite. With our usual little candles we moved through the dark chambers at the foot of the long flight of steps and marvelled at the tawdriness and dirtiness of these sacred spots under the control of the East Mediterranean Christian churches. We went behind the tomb into the sanctuary where the Greek Orthodox priests retire for Communion but it was very dark and our little lights revealed only a few good pictures and many brass lamps. A smell of stale incense pervaded all so that we were glad to get to the open air and home again.

Tuesday 1 April After breakfast (eggs are the only meat known for breakfast here) we all went down the teeming Street of David (saw three artists at work) and into the great Haram-el-Sherif or mosque of Omar. Built on the site of Solomon's temple it is a very sacred Mohammedan spot. After a few minutes during which we had bought guidebooks (these constituted tickets of admission) we ran across John Shamma (who had been one of the guides who joined our train from Ludd) with two American ladies, and joined them. He took us into the great mosque and showed us under the dome the huge rock of sacrifice on which Abraham offered the ram instead of Isaac. It is the top of Mount Moriah (the dome is called the Dome of the Rock). Inside the mosque is magnificent coloured mosaic work and the richly coloured windows all round contain no glass, every bit of them being made of stones and crystals of the purist tints in many designs. They carry out the mosaic idea perfectly and impressed us greatly. Then we went under the rock to the lower chamber and saw the hole through it by which the blood flowed down. Later it flowed on to the Valley of Jehoshaphat. In this chamber was a lovely piece of carved marble altar with twisted and intertwined pillars – very ancient and probably of the time of Solomon. A similar piece was upstairs. (Mohammed spent much time in the cavern and Muslims claim that the hole was made miraculously to allow of his ascending thence to Heaven at his death. He was unusually tall and there is a dent in the roof of the cavern which they say was divinely made to allow of his standing upright in that spot!) We went on to see the Mosque of Al Aczar with the smaller dome which to Muslims is the holiest mosque since Mohammed came to worship there. It was built by Justinian in cross form [possibly, but it was built as a mosque in the seventh century], was much damaged by earthquake, later rebuilt by Muslims, and restored again in Crusader time. It is very plain after the mosque of Omar but has rich carpets (which dragged off one of my clumsy slippers) and a good high pulpit of cedar of Lebanon. A little side-chapel, quite plain, is the real mosque of Omar where he used to come to pray and meditate. Strolling thence for photographs to the edge of the paved upper courtyard I was edified to behold, in the grassy courtyard away down below, a presumably good Muslim beating his wife while she held a baby in her arm. John Shamma then took us on to near the St Stephen's Gate where is the Ecce Homo arch and the beginning of the Via Dolorosa. Entering the convent there we saw first the room on the place where Peter warmed himself prior to the denial. Then the church on the spot where Christ was condemned, the original Ecce Homo arch being incorporated in the building behind the altar. It is a lovely little church and interesting otherwise as bare rock forms part of another wall of it. We also saw an ancient stone on which Christ probably stood for condemnation. Then we saw part of the original Via Dolorosa (which was excavated 6 feet below the present level) where Christ took up the cross and also an ancient stone in the paving with incised markings like a chessboard where the Roman soldiers played dice. Leaving the church at Ecce Homo arch we walked west, turned up towards the Damascus Gate and mooched about the interesting old shops etc. One opening proved to be a stable which contained a camel and a number of donkeys and two horses. Going inside I made a sketch of the camel in an uncomfortable squatting position while a little donkey breathed over my right shoulder, a horse's back legs were at my left, and the stable proprietor and the camel owner crouched and grunted on either side of me with their faces a few inches from my sketchbook. The odour of the place was not much like a bed of violets, so I did not stay long.

IN A STABLE IN THE
DAMASCUS STREET
JERUSALEM

Sketch of camel head

Outside I found M talking to someone from the Nile Mission Press. A good earnest chap (Syrian Christian), he was depressed at the present situation and blamed the unChristian behaviour of the western visitors and tourists for the scant successes won by Christianity amongst the Muslims and Jews. Proceeding we caught up Mr Gibson and visited the outside of Gordon's Calvary without being able to get inside.

In the afternoon our driver of yesterday took us from the Jaffa Gate down over the bridge which has the pool of Solomon on the right and the valley of Hinnom, and away up the farther hill and between the German colony and the new Zionist settlement. (Also saw the remains of Caiaphas's house and looked down the well in which the Wise Men saw the star, and also Elijah's resting rock.) Before long we reached the isolated little dome – Rachel's tomb – one of the few authenticated historical spots round here. One cannot enter, so we took photos and went on to the town of Bethlehem. It is on top of a hill the slopes of which are terraced right up with walls and little bits of garden and trees and we were struck at once by the cleanness of the whole place after Jerusalem and by the strikingly handsome appearance of the women and girls. The girls of Bethlehem wear just a 'kerchief' as head ornament, while the married women wear a high affair made of coins and brass but usually covered with a white cloth. The streets are only wide enough for one car and we fortunately got through to the big square without having to pass another, though we had to wait in one place while a complacent and ruminative donkey was dragged and shoved out of our way.

From the square a young guide took us to the Church of the Nativity – the oldest church in Christendom. We saw the remains of the three entrances, one very high, the second about 10 feet and the final one, dating from the Crusaders, about 5 feet high. This was made so small by them in order to foil the Muslims in their habits of stabling donkeys and camels inside the church. Inside we saw first the part of the church built by Queen Helena, mother of Constantine. It has about fifty pillars with many signs and paintings and inscriptions of the old Crusaders still discernible on them. A stone partition once hiding this part from the Greek Orthodox altar was taken down by Allenby. After lighting little candles we were taken down to the little grotto in the rock (now a medley of red drapery, tinsel, lamps, jewels and slabs of marble) where Christ was born and where the manger was in which He was laid. The birthplace is owned jointly by the Armenians and the Greek Orthodox and the manger by the Roman Catholics, and here on almost the most sacred spot on earth and inside the oldest Christian church it is necessary to have two of the Palestine police always on duty to prevent fighting between these sects. Outside a handsome and venerable priest rattles the offertory plate and almost demands subscriptions, and grouses if they are not high. All very depressing in such a place but making one thankful that a wider Christianity is known elsewhere. Thence we visited the rock grottoes of St Jerome and St John, the latter containing a lovely picture of the angel warning Joseph to take Mary and the child and flee into Egypt. We also saw the little place in which St Jerome (called here also St Heronimos) was for forty years and where he translated the Bible into Latin and then into Greek.

Leaving the church we went into one or two curio shops and also saw the mother-of-pearl workers at work squatting on the ground and operating large files to shape the beads etc.

We had a lovely run back in the car and Father had things explained to him by our driver with regard to the bitterness of feeling of the Arabs and Christians about the British government's favouring of the Jews and the Zionist movement.

Wednesday 2 April We did little in the morning except visit several shops for pictures and food for tomorrow's journey. Immediately after lunch we three men walked through the crowded streets and under the arches beside the clustered shops selling vegetables, sweets, bread, fruit, boots, pottery, cottons etc. to the Damascus Gate and up to the 'garden tomb' at the side of the hill-face we saw yesterday. (Sometimes this is called Gordon's Calvary because Gordon excavated the tomb itself, but others had been at work on the spot for a long while.) An Irish lady, Miss Hussey, came and showed us through first the garden with its grass, trees, lizards, flowers (and a pet lamb with a black face) and then to the excavation where in a bare rock-face is the entrance to a tomb for four persons. From the prodigality of space evidently for a rich man. Window which shines straight on to the grave. Rock seats at the head and at the feet of the place for the body. The Crusaders used the place as a stable outside and broke up part of the outer wall in their certainty that the Church of the Holy Sepulchre covered the real site.

We returned at three to the hotel where a Jewish wedding was to take place. Very interesting. Many black-hatted rabbis came. Two sat beside me and were interested and amused when I sketched a third, a young one with long curls on either side of his face but with no beard as yet. Guests sat in

Sketch of Jewish wedding guests

chairs up and down the lounge and shook hands with the happy pair (dressed much like a European bride and bridegroom). Then a little orchestra played bright music and orange quarters and lemonade were handed round (the pair sat under a little canopy on a 'throne' in the lounge and were showered with confetti and rice before going outside). Then all adjourned to the open-air court. Four men held posts supporting a piece of red and white cloth with a Hebrew inscription in the middle under which the ceremony was performed by the oldest rabbi in quite a short time and with some drinking of wine and reciting and singing (all the men – rabbis, bridegroom and guests – kept their hats on during the ceremony). The crowd surged close round while this was going on so that I did not see this part very closely. Afterwards there was talk and congratulations in the lounge and liqueur was handed round and cakes and chocolates. We were treated as guests and F and I enjoyed the liqueur though it was strong (peppermint). Then dancing began to foxtrots and waltzes etc. played by the orchestra and Mr Gibson and I left to get photos at the Jews' wailing place. Rabbis and others were again praying fervently there with much swaying and groaning and sincerity. A moving scene. Then we went back, Mr Gibson to see a shop manager and I by devious routes and tunnels to St Stephen's Gate and thence past the Garden of Gethsemane down to Absalom's Tomb where I made a couple of sketches. Crossing the brook Kidron in the gathering dusk I mounted a steep slope to near the wall of the Al Aczar Mosque and looked back at the village of Siloam spread right across one part of the hill. A little to the left the whole slope of Olivet above Absalom's Tomb and away up beyond the Russian church of the gilded domes was one vast cemetery, the graves all facing the great mosque behind me. Continuing I found the path led right round the city, for the most part under the great walls. The far-flung outlook gradually became dim and it was dark by the time I reached the top of Mount Zion and turned towards the Jaffa Gate. At the hotel the wedding party were just finishing their dancing with an arm-in-arm trot round.

After dinner I tried to hammer a few tunes out of the wonky grand piano in the lounge and had just got through 'Ar hyd y nos' when a young fellow came up – a Welshman from Aberystwyth attracted by the tune – and sang part of it in Welsh. Then he brought his friend – a Mr Jones from near Wrexham whose home was the house in which Ceiriog lived and wrote.

ABSALOM'S TOMB
FROM THE MOSLEM GRAVEYARD   2.5.24

Two sketches of Absalom's tomb

ABSALOM'S TOMB
FROM ACROSS THE BROOK KIDRON   2.5.2

We compared notes on our travels, on Welsh music, people and places etc. and he seemed much moved and quite homesick at the end, being a temporary exile and in the British section of the Palestine gendarmerie. He and his friend are stationed at Hebron and are engaged in putting down Arab bandits and car-robbers in those wild hills (Palestine gendarmerie come under the orders of the High Commissioner, but still maintain the Muslim code of law: Turkish. The British section are very largely recruited from the old Royal Irish Constabulary. Their contracts are only for one year at a time).

Thursday 3 April Have had a magnificent run today. Rose at 6.30 and by eight we were leaving Jerusalem by the Damascus Gate. While our driver was busy packing our baggage on the footboard M and F went up to see the garden tomb. Starting about 8.30 we made good going and the domes and minarets of the Holy City and the Mount of Olives soon became only silhouettes on the horizon. The road, a very good one, twisted amongst the broken hills and the first piece of new interest to us was Nob on our left, a village perched on a hill. Then entering Samuel's land we passed Mispah, his grave, with a modern church there high on a mountain to the left, and Ramah, his village birthplace, away to the right. Shortly after we ran through a little town called Ramallah, noted as the place where Mary lost Jesus. On either side recurred little grey villages with squat houses, many with domes, clustered on rock foundations. Nearly all were picturesquely placed on the tops of isolated hills, and one such was pointed out to us on the right as Bethel.

The road was winding all the time and soon we had to double [back] on our tracks with several hairpin bends down a steep hill, eventually crossing a dry stream course and entering the ill-famed Robbers' Valley. (On crossing the stream we left Benjamin and entered Samaria.) A barren rocky stretch for miles with plenty of caves and cover for evil-doers, it was easy to understand the fact that twenty years ago people had to make this journey in bands of fifty at a time, especially when one saw the rough track which used to be the only road through. Our first sight in the valley was of a large eagle perched on an olive tree. He did not budge till we were nearly under him and then flapped heavily away. A long tortuous run down the valley brought us eventually in sight of the mountains of Shiloh on the right and shortly afterwards we ran between the lofty heights of Mount Gerizim and Mount Ebal into the town of Nablus (ancient Shechem), a little place on the railway with several modern buildings and a flourishing appearance. Just before we entered the town proper we passed Jacob's well at Sychar and entered and looked down it. Away to the right we saw the tiny dome of Joseph's tomb.

Shortly after leaving Nablus we were delayed by a puncture and ate oranges under a fig tree while it was repaired. Near us were some delicate pink and white cyclamen growing wild on a pebbly slope on which were dozens of little lizards. Proceeding in considerable heat we soon came in sight of Old Samaria with the tower of John the Baptist on a hill and behind were the excavations on the sites of the palace of Ahab and Jezebel and also of King Saul. Soon the road became more and more twisting and hilly, and leaving the hill of Old Samaria on the right we zigzagged up a hill to a great height from which we could look over and see the Mediterranean far off.

The repaired tyre going flat again gave us opportunity for lunch and we sat in a barley field under an olive tree and lunched with a wide view before us of the plain of Gilboa in the district of Galilee. On the lower ground, before reaching Jenin, we saw Tell Dothan (the ancient Dothan) and were shown while we were on the move the actual spot where Joseph was sold by his brethren. Passing later through the nice little townlet of Jenin we crossed the plain of Gilboa, the country all the while becoming richer and greener, and surmounting another hill we ran down to the wide rich sweeping plain of Esdraelon, no trees but fertile and green for very many miles. Far to the west was Mount Carmel in silhouette with its steep slope down to the sea. Another eagle was on the road in front of us here but did not trouble to fly till we were nearly on to it. A Jewish colony is in the plain and we saw some of them, probably Russians or Poles, in the fields – the women in very girlish costume – white stockings and short dresses to their knees. On a hill to the right of us was the tiny village of Nain – further over was Endor, and still further was Shurem behind which rose the solitary rounded rocky mountain with two churches right on top.

Now began a long steep pull up to the top of the great ridge on which Nazareth lies. The road twisted and zigzagged ever upwards for at least two miles, giving us wonderful panoramic views over the great plain of

Esdraelon and the hills through which we recently passed. At last we entered the neat little rather modern-looking town of Nazareth with its huge French church and convent overlooking it, and got very decent tea at the Hotel Galilee (German) before going on to see the carpenter's shop, the subterranean ruins of which are now covered by a brand-new Roman Catholic church. Very little was to be seen barring the vault-like rooms of the old church which had been built there. Thence we went on to Mary's Well now equipped with taps, and were interested to watch the girls filling their earthen jars and carrying them away on their heads in dignified and graceful manner. Leaving Nazareth we surmounted the last bit of the ridge and another wide panorama opened out to the north with long sweeping valleys at our feet right down to the Sea of Galilee which we could just discern.

More curling roads took us first through the little townlet of Cana with its little stone houses, and then on and down till we were beside the Mount of Beatitudes. For many miles the country had been getting more fertile and here were masses of delightful flowers growing wild – iris, lupins, spiraea etc. and also red and white poppies. We picked a few and then continued down, past the huge cup-like hollow where Saladin defeated the Crusaders, till we were on the last slope overlooking the sea and ran into Tiberias (682 feet below sea level). After seeing the Franciscan hospice we got rooms at the Hotel Tiberias. (Tariff 80 piastre – Egyptian – per day each, good rooms and good food – better than Jerusalem. Mr Gibson had the top room with a balcony from which there was a lovely view over the nestling town with its minaret and over the calm sea with the hills of Gadara beyond. We could hear the chatter from the 'lads of the village' sitting about in the open café beside the landing stage.) For dinner at night we had fish from the Sea of Galilee – St Peter's fish – very sweet, tubby in shape and called the comb fish by the natives as the very strong spine and side-bones look like a double comb.

Friday 4 April Up at 6 a.m. All set off early in the car for a run by the sea. A lovely scene in the bright sunlight with the mountains of Gadara on the other side and, away to the distant north, Hermon with snow on its upper slopes. Keeping first close to the sea where cattle were wading and where some natives were bathing here and there, we passed the valley of

Dalmanoutha leading back to the Mount of Beatitudes and came soon to the site of Bethsaida – now only a house or two and a flour mill. (The valley was full at our end of seedy-looking camels. M suggested it was a sort of camel-hospital station.) Leaving the good Damascus road our driver now followed a track which went over fields and past Bedouin camps with donkeys and camels till we reached a high wall and entered (on foot) the old synagogue area of Capernaum. (We passed many Bedouin women with their dark faces decorated all over with tattoo marks put there in infancy for the sake of beauty. Often the marks take the form of little spots over the jaw and chin and look like a coming beard.) Nothing else of the city remains, and these excavations, carried on by the Franciscans, have shown the whole base of the synagogue built by the Centurion. Huge blocks lie about everywhere and pillars just as earthquake scattered them, and the place is to be rebuilt as it was. (Capernaum is said to be the place of the prophet Nahum and the district is also associated with Habbakkuk.) The carving on the stones is most interesting, being partly in Roman, partly in Greek and partly in Jewish symbols. A high-spirited Franciscan father showed us round and also showed us the perfect mosaic floor in the small circular church of St Peter (over the house of Peter's wife's mother) adjoining the synagogue.

Returning past the Bedouins we reached Tiberius and said goodbye to Mr Gibson and to our pleasant young driver-guide who returned to Jerusalem. Then porters took our baggage down to the landing stage and we embarked on a rowing boat with two Americans, Mr and Mrs Johnston and their guide Mr Hadad, and pushed off for Samakh. Four powerful Arabs rowed us and now and then broke into not untuneful shanties. The scenery was very pleasant, especially looking back at Tiberius and seeing the distant Hermon, but it was very hot (640 feet below sea level) and the slight breeze did not help much. We ate our food at the tiny station of Samakh and got ginger-ale at the canteen. Our train left at 1 p.m. (F electing to travel third and we second) and quickly the view down the Jordan valley disappeared and we entered the steep hills and began to climb following the picturesque Yarmuk valley. Then followed some hours of climbing up the long winding rocky gorge of the river, over high bridges in majestic scenery, a complete change from anything since we landed at Port Said. Sometimes we would follow a long valley only to cross it and return at a higher altitude. Volcanic rocks appeared after some while and we saw two big waterfalls coming from the top of a peat ridge with no mountain beyond to supply – a curious sight which was explained when we climbed to the height of the top of them and found a magical change of conditions. (We were now 3,000 feet above the Sea of Galilee.) No rocks were here, but a vast sweeping nearly flat plain almost as far as the eye could reach, with soil of a vivid burnt-sienna colour and flourishing crops. This great table-land was the country of Bashan.

Our passports were taken and stamped on the train as we were now in Syria in the area under the French mandate. We ran into Dera'a (about five o'clock) on the Hedjaz railway and continued on it northwards still over sweeping fertile land. A new and queer feature now appeared in the form of a flat rocky plain of lava on our right like a stream, wide and even flowing gradually or (as the guidebook says) like a choppy sea suddenly solidified. It rises slightly above the rest of the plain and has a clean-cut edge where the lava begins and the broken creviced surface is said to be very difficult to cross. We ran past some apparently ancient ruins at Ezra (ancient Zoroa) and soon after darkness fell we saw far off under the silhouette of a hilly range a mist of lights which we knew must be Damascus. Mr Saba, a guide whom we met at Tiberius, fetched us here and took us to the Palace Hotel in a gharry. Not too good a situation but good clean beds and good food and said to be better than either the Oriental or the Victoria (where Cook's people go). Father knocked the tariff down from £1 to 12s per diem!

Saturday 5 April Mother being fatigued did not rise to breakfast, so F and I had a stroll with a self-attached young guide past many little open shops and past the citadel (now a French barrack and prison) and through a market road which was being roofed in with semi-circular girders and corrugated iron to the Syrian Bank for Syrian money; then, returning, took a tram up to the suburb of Selhie and walked uphill to a Muslim cemetery whence we saw a lovely panoramic view of the old city with its minarets and surrounding orchards and trees and rivers and of the plain whence we came last night with mountains to the west of it. High mountains appeared well to our left which I supposed to be the Anti-Libanus. We returned by the tram again (in which the fare was 1 Syrian piastre each, or about ½d). The afternoon we spent quietly questioning our young guide and planning our stay, but in the evening we took a gharry with Mother up to Selhie again, and with the sun behind us got a much better idea of the delicate-looking city spread out below us.

The wind was very high and very cold as this part of the country stands pretty high, so we returned quickly past many orange trees laden with fruit and went through the older and poorer part of the city to the Christian quarter where was the Irish Mission. A fascinating drive down little streets only just wide enough to take us, round unexpected corners and under arches reminiscent of Jerusalem – our gharry-wallah got us through with much shouting and without destroying any of the little shops that we so nearly touched on either side, though we had to go slowly in one part where we had to follow a convoy of six camels till a broader place allowed them to get aside for us to pass. At the Irish Mission M and F went in and spoke to Mrs MacFarlane and then we returned to the hotel via the 'street which is called Straight' – a long market street covered over for a considerable distance with a semi-circular casing of girders and corrugated iron. At six o'clock a gun sounded and our guide (a Christian) immediately offered our gharry-man (a Muslim) a cigarette. The latter took one and lit up. It was the first day of the month of Ramadan during which Muslims neither eat nor smoke from 3 a.m. to 6 p.m. Ramadan lasts thirty days but very pious Muslims fast also for the previous fifteen days.

So far Damascus had not come up to expectations. There is not so much of the oriental atmosphere as in Jerusalem either in the people or the buildings. The market streets are fine broad clean thoroughfares and the shops bigger and fuller and more modern. All sorts of currency seems good here – Syrian, Egyptian, French, Turkish and English – which somewhat confuses one as the Syrian value fluctuates from day to day. One great feature of Damascus is the quantity of running water. Straight through the town runs the Barada (or the Abana of the Bible) and all over the town the water is taken by conduits and appears in sparkling streams sometimes in private fountains, or in the marble basins of a mosque courtyard, or even gushing out of little holes in the sides of houses. This renders Damascus the most prolific fruit-growing city of the country. (Nobody seems to know which of the tributary streams was referred to by Naaman as the Pharpar.)

Sunday 6 April After breakfast Mr and Mrs Holmes of California (who are booked for our boat at Beirut) asked us to join their car to the Irish mission church. We arrived as the Arab service was finishing and then took our places for ours and had a very good time. The lesson and sermon were from Acts 22 where Paul gave his account of his conversion at Damascus. The sermon by a Jew (Rev. Neumann) had fire in it. He seemed as sanguine about the conversion of the Jews as of any other non-Christian peoples. Was introduced to Rev. MacFarlane (and Mrs MacFarlane), head of the Mission. The afternoon was quiet (I made rough sketches of six minarets visible from my window – all different in design though all have the pointed top and the crescent above it, and also a gallery somewhat high up for the muezzin to call from) and then F went off to tea with Dr Brigstock of the Medical Mission Hospital (Edinburgh) whom he had met at church in the morning (the hospital is on the road to Baghdad via Palmyra). At 4.30 M and I took a gharry to the Christian quarter, picked up F and were driven, over an execrable road, but through green lands and past orchards and gardens, till we struck the Abana where there is a large house like a mill beside a grove of trees under which people drink and smoke in the summer. Very pleasant scenery here and also onwards to the walls of Damascus as we returned. A flock of dusty woolly sheep, brown and white, and some goats passed us in charge of a picturesque ragged Bedouin. Another hard-bitten Arab was behind on a donkey on which were slung a couple of young lambs, pannier-wise in a double cloth. Our young guide on enquiry found that they were from Baghdad – forty days' journey. On the great journey the Bedouin shepherds live mostly on sheep's milk. (For ordinary camels the Baghdad–Damascus journey also takes forty days, though the fine and expensive running camels – costing up to £150 each – do it in eight days. The automobile service does it by the ancient direct desert road in two days.)

Entering the old gate at the end of Straight Street we turned off and saw the house of Ananias (or St Ananias as he is called here) – a couple of vaults, one leading from the other. The smaller was said to be the ancient Christian church and a small passage leads from it underground and emerges through a hole at the bottom of the city wall. It also has a little hole in which the Bible was hid. The larger room had some forms and an altar and was used as a little Roman Catholic church. Returning outside the city walls we passed a large encampment of refugees (Armenian Christians) expelled by the Turks and cared for here by the Syrian Christians and by American and other funds. Then we saw St Paul's Gate, now blocked up, and the small window whence St Paul was let down. Afterwards we returned and saw St Thomas's Gate with its minaret at the side and jogged back in the gloaming to the hotel. Passing several cafés we saw for the first time the striped sofas of which Hichens writes and saw a number of men smoking their narghiles.

Monday 7 April After breakfast Father preferred to walk so M and I went in a gharry with 'Michael' our guide, first to the bank where I got 9 ½ Turkish gold pounds for £10 sterling (Cook's cheque). Thence we proceeded to the great mosque (the Omaiyade). Putting on slippers we entered the great courtyard on one side of which is the delicate white Minaret of the Bride while the opposite side is taken up by the great mosque. This we entered next and found a very long, pillared structure richly ornamented in many parts with inlaid wood, mother-of-pearl, ivory etc. The floors were covered entirely with little carpets and in the centre on either side of the high dome were magnificent decorated ceilings. This enormous building in the first place was a Christian edifice built by Theodosius I on the site of a Roman temple and there is a fine tomb of St John the Baptist with a lovely blue-green dome inside. It is said that when the Muslims tried to move this a voice was heard begging to be left alone. Anyhow the place is now very sacred to Muslims and many were meditating and praying there! At one end of this building is a lovely minaret, one of the finest Arab structures, while at the other end is a hybrid one of great height (the highest in Damascus) called the Minaret of Jesus Christ. The top half is very slender with a snuffer-like pinnacle while the bottom is a square tower used as a belfry in Christian times. The old Christian well and font is still in the mosque. In the middle was a low enclosure in which many old men were reclining or sitting cross-legged reading the Koran, the huge books being propped on stands before them. Many others were praying and we got many sour glances before going back to the courtyard. We saw the tomb of Hussein before discarding our slippers and going round to the tomb of Sala-hed-din (Saladin). This is the most charming spot we have yet struck in Damascus. Going through high iron gates we found ourselves in a little fragrant garden with an oval pool in the middle overhung with trees, one orange tree being heavy with fruit. Beyond was a small building with a dome at the entrance of which a venerable old man rose from a couch and gave us slippers. Two sarcophagi inside with blue turbans at one end are of Sultan Saladin and his vizier. We moved on soon and after just glancing at the museum, which did not appear interesting with its Roman carvings from Palmyra, we got in the carriage and trotted through the little streets, and through the endless yelling and energy of our driver managed to get to the Straight Street Gate without being overturned and without killing anyone. I took photos at St Paul's window and then we drove on through delightful country (past occasional mud walls) from which Mount Hermon came in sight again sparkling with its snow in the sunlight. Returning towards the walls we passed right through the great camp of Christian Armenian refugees. Crowded together these unfortunates seemed healthy and many were following their own trades. Not far from the Straight Street Gate we saw the tiny remains of Naaman's house but retired before the voluble flow of indignation (in French) of the owner of the land who suddenly appeared and was annoyed that 'Michael' had not applied to him for a 'permit to view'.

Before returning to the hotel we had a look through Nassan's great shop where amid dusty workrooms, often on bare earth, men and women and young girls worked and turned out the wonderful brass, inlaid wood, carving and carpets which are seen in all the shops of the city. One carpet, in course of making, was 13 × 12 feet and took seven months to complete (finished carpet cost £70), and one lovely table with all sorts of inlaid woods, ebony and mother-of-pearl was most ingeniously adaptable as a writing, card, chess, backgammon or occasional table. Taking one work-man some months to make, it was being sold for only £15. (Backgammon is a great game out here, chiefly in cafés. Frequently a shopkeeper may be seen playing with a friend in front of his tiny shop and paying no heed to business. Games of this kind have sometimes been interrupted to allow us to pass.)

The afternoon was quiet. We had a fine view from the hotel roof and I did a little sketching. After tea the three of us walked through many bazaars, buying donkey ornaments and looking at Arab kaffiyehs (or head-dresses) and costumes. Returning we were struck again by the amount of water in Damascus. Many little shops have running water in them and one café had a pond in the middle with a fountain around which the Damascenes recline and puff their narghiles. At night we paid 'Michael' for his services, Mother handing him two English half-sovereigns. At 10 p.m. he came to us as we were retiring and complained dispiritedly that Damascus money-changers were a difficult lot and had refused to give him anything for the coins and had even called them worthless. After I had given him a Turkish gold pound instead we examined the 'half-sovereigns' and found that she had given him two bright new farthings!

Tuesday 8 April A day of quiet mooching round the bazaars and shops and of considerable spending. Early after breakfast I made a quick colour sketch of the little minaret near us from the hotel roof – Mount Hermon in background – and the rest of the day we all wandered through the interesting and busy cloth markets, shoe markets, candy markets, brass markets, harness markets etc. and revelled in the queerness of it all. The cloth market was full of goods in brilliant colours and was a delight to the eye, the lovely tints on the stalls being set off by the uniform solid black of the women purchasers who thronged the alleys. The nose-brass and the yashmak of Egypt are never seen here, but the women are in black and have a black veil of considerable density in front, presenting a strangely corpse-like appearance. Only their hands are exposed, all the rest is solid black.

Michael tried to get us to see the Holy Carpet but it was inaccessible probably owing to Ramadan. Our purchases included some silk embroidered garments in Arab style, some Arab kaffiyehs and egals (headbands) and sundry little daggers and a kohl-pot. The Damascene traders seemed a lovable lot compared with the Egyptians or those of Jerusalem. We watched many craftsmen, harness-makers, shoemakers, narghile-tube makers etc. who smilingly showed their wares with voluble Arabic explanations none too enlightening to us. No prices of as extortionate a nature as in Cairo etc. were asked and no resentment shown when we did not buy.

Wednesday 9 April Goodbye to Damascus today. Early breakfast and then our 'fidus achates' Michael brought us our car for the journey and we settled our bill. This hotel left a very pleasant impression on us – not pretentious or grand, but courtesy from all and honesty and general helpfulness. The manager was Christian and there were apparently no Mohammedans on the staff. We went first to pick up some curios bought yesterday; then called in at the station to enquire about my topi I left at Tiberias, said farewell to Michael and turned along beside the Barada (Abana) past the Sultan Selim Mosque with its twin minarets. The road was good and our car, a big Oakland, skimmed along well till Damascus was behind and we were following the gorge of the Barada, now a sparkling river dancing through its willows and silver poplars at the foot of precipitous slopes of tawny rock. At one spot we dismounted for a photo and bathed our hands in the Abana. All too soon we left the river and mounted to the left into rocky barren country without trees and where were many flocks of goats.

Hermon was now well in view and the east and south of Anti-Lebanon. Hermon is called Jebel-esh-Sheikh and Anti-Lebanon is called Jebel-esh-Sherki. Before long we reached our top point fully 4,000 feet above sea level and entered first one dry, rocky gorge and then another longer and grander one which led us right down and out on to the lovely sweeping valley of the Litani – a wonderful fertile plain leading from here right to Aleppo. The view was delightful. At our feet the wide plain or broad valley, the soil of which was rich sienna colour and was partly clothed with green crops, bounded on the west by the majestic chain of the Lebanese mountains, snowclad for the most part, and on the east by the slightly lower Anti-Lebanon which also carried still a lot of snow in its upper hollows. Nothing so exhilarating in scenery had so far come our way and we revelled in the run over the plain. Our driver, in order to avoid a right-angle turn in the road at Stora, took us a shortcut over a bad track which meant crossing the groggiest bridge we had yet met. Providentially the car was not destroyed and we continued past Zahlek and near Reyak, the junction at which the line from Baalbek joins that from Damascus to Beirut, and stopped at the roadside for lunch at a spot from which Baalbek was just discernible. From Stora we had been running at the foot of Lebanon foothills and now we crossed the valley to the east side where is Baalbek and soon were approaching the orchard plantations in the midst of which showed the mighty ruins with the famous six columns towering over all. Almost the first place we came to was the Grand New Hotel where Saba, the guide of Mr and Mrs Holmes, had fixed us rooms, so we were soon installed. F was feeling somewhat dicky but decided to accompany us after a drink of tea to stroll round. Here again we were struck by the enchanting children though they all have learnt the appalling word 'baksheesh'. Mr and Mrs Holmes caught us up very quickly in their car and kindly offered to take us round to see a bit outside the temples. Pulling up near the entrance to the temple we walked around the edge of the old moat, beside a tiny artificial stream and under walnut trees till we reached a part of the wall where are the famous three great stones or Trilithon. Put there by the Romans on top of courses of huge stones of earlier builders, each of these is 63 feet long and 13 feet high and 10 feet thick, weighing 650 tons. How they were placed at their present height or how they were ever moved from their original quarry near our hotel is a mystery. The higher part of this wall was built by Arabs as fortifications and is made of remains from inside the temple so that carved pieces of even segments of pillars occur among the squared blocks. The strongest colour in all these ruins seems to be a fine ochre yellow – most suitable for a temple of the sun. Thence we went to see the remains of a delightful circular temple of Venus disfigured later by the Christians who made it into a church of St Barbara. Thence to an ancient Arab mosque made from granite and other columns transported from the great temple of Jupiter near at hand and then we got out beyond the ancient boundary wall of old Baalbek (or Heliopolis) and entered the catacombs or tombs of the Romans cut in the solid rock under what now is grazing ground for cattle. They say one can go for an hour or more through the passages, and that in the cold winter season, when there is 3 feet of snow on the ground here, many foxes, wolves and other wild animals (even bears) use them. Thence we drove to the ancient spring called Ras-el-ain. The Romans built it round to form a little lake and now it is surrounded by trees and is a public resort where refreshments may be got. We had tea and lemon there (at the slight charge of 1s per cup) and enjoyed watching some Arabs canter past on most perfect horses, one or two of which were shy and took fright at the standing motor. After returning to the hotel we climbed the hill behind to a little watch-tower, built by Arabs from the remains of many Roman tombs near, and sat there to watch the sunset. The whole range of Lebanon was in view stretching to the dim south and in front was the broad green and brown valley with the great ruins down at the foot of our hill glowing yellow in the warm light. To our right was a ridge in the valley (beyond which the country dipped to Aleppo) and then rose the heights of Anti-Lebanon with a little snow on it. We watched the shadow of Lebanon creep over the valley till it enveloped the six columns of Jupiter and finally the sun dipped behind the snowy top of Lebanon and we returned. As we descended, the tops of Anti-Lebanon still caught the glow and we saw their colour change from rich yellow to a deep and wonderful magenta. Our hotel, though not expensive, proved most comfortable and clean and the food better than any since we landed.

Thursday 10 April After breakfast we walked to the entrance of the great ruins and up the triple flight of steps, built by the Germans on the ancient plan, into the vast area of the Temples of Heliopolis. The day was pretty hot although we were nearly 4,000 feet above the sea and the whole temple area swarmed with lizards of all sizes from 2 inches to over a foot long.

The plan of the old architecture can be seen everywhere though earthquake has destroyed the buildings and the great blocks have been reused by old-time Arabs and built into a surrounding wall of great strength. They used the blocks indiscriminately so that sections of a circular pillar will sometimes appear laid sideways in the upper courses of the walls. Mr Coombs's discarded guide of yesterday took us round first into the hexagonal court and then through towards the old bath which still has delicate remains of carving outside it. Round here were many broken parts of huge granite pillars (two pillars were unbroken though fallen) brought in the old days from Assouan in Egypt. Next up a long flight of steps, eleven of which are cut in a single enormous stone, and into the area of the ancient Temple of Jupiter. At one time surrounded by pillars now only six remain – the famous six columns of Baalbek. The vivid yellow weather colouring, so apt in a temple of the sun, is most marked on these pillars. Each composed of three terrific blocks they tower above one to a dizzy height and support still across their capitals immense stone cross-pieces very richly carved. The method of construction is a complete mystery though our guide stated that they were put in place by means of long inclined planes and the use of many thousands of slaves. He also said that the slaves were only given a bit of black bread and a drink of water per day as it was supposed that in the building of a holy temple the gods would give the workmen strength to continue. Each pillar was nearly 6 feet thick.

We moved and picked our steps amongst the debris and sections of pillars feeling like little pygmies and gazed down great holes made by the excavators, some of which revealed subterranean passages beneath. Much of the fallen carving was perfect and we examined the care and accuracy of the work in the hard limestone which had originally adorned the highest parts nearly 100 feet up. Next we descended somewhat to the well-preserved Temple of Bacchus. Here many of the pillars remain, as well as the bulk of the building, and we noted the fine preservation of some of the ceiling which connected the pillars to the main building. Muslims had somehow defaced the heads of the figures of various gods which appeared. After walking round the outside and inside of this temple and seeing the good condition of the carving our guide took us through a wide subway under the great court and thence out of the ruins. On a stone of the ceiling of this subway was an inscription telling which legion of slaves constructed it.

After lunch we packed our goods on to the car again and left for Beirut, stopping first a few yards away to see the very ancient quarry in which lies the biggest cut stone in the world. Similar to, but even bigger than the great stones of the Trilithon, it is estimated to weigh about 1,000 tons and, though detached from the rock, was never moved from the quarry.

Our run was over the same road as yesterday as far as Stora where we commenced a tremendous uphill climb of many miles, winding backwards and forwards but always ascending till we were right up among the patches of drift-snow, 7,000 feet up, on Lebanon. Our Oakland car was not in very good condition and struggled much of the way on second speed, being handicapped somewhat by a strong headwind. It was rather a hazy day and in addition clouds of sand were blowing about, but we could well make out the fine outline of snowy Hermon till we were lost among the heights of Lebanon. Our stay among the snows was brief and soon we were dropping gradually towards the sea attended frequently by the little cog railway which had been near us up the heights and over the pass from Stora. Now we ran along a fine long ridge with a deep ravine to our right. Fine rugged scenery was everywhere and we deplored the hazy air which hid the sea. Modern houses and a look of prosperity were around us as we ran through two or three lofty villages. The last winding and picturesque descent over well-made roads led us abruptly into the outskirts of Beirut by which time the Holmes's car had overtaken us. We followed it through modern but dirty streets till we reached a little promenade on the shore and put in at the Metropole Hotel – a German affair, not too bad. Good rooms and very fair grub though not so good as the Baalbek hotel of yesterday, or as the Hôtel d'Orient next door which has an attractive sea outlook and which we visited later. Mother had tea while F and I went around, found out the Triestino office and Cook's etc. After the cold of the mountain tops Beirut was very close.

Friday 11 April After breakfast Mr and Mrs Holmes asked us to join them in their car to the Dog River. We ran northwards past part of the Armenian refugees' settlement and right away from the town, following the coast all the way till we arrived at the picturesque little rocky gorge where a rapid stream finds the sea. The feature of interest here is a number of large panels carved in the rock at many places recording the exploits of many conquerors. Some are quite obliterated, but one, apparently of the ancient Assyrians, still showed the sculptured figure of a bearded monarch. One panel was made by Napoleon and another recorded the capture of the district by our men towards the end of the war while yet another which struck us as comical spoke of the 'glorious and victorious' entry of the French some while after the Armistice. We strolled a little way up the rugged gorge and F was intrigued to find honeysuckle and maidenhair ferns. After lunch we revisited the Triestino offices and saw the office of the Nairn Transport Company whence cars run across to Damascus and Baghdad. At 3.30 Mr Holmes's car ran us all up to the American University here where we just arrived in time for a weekly assembly. A large hall was filled with young men and a few girls from Syria, Palestine, Egypt, Turkey etc. while several Americans spoke from other colleges at Cairo, Assiut and Constantinople. All spoke in English and each included some Christian appeal in the little speech. Later we were taken round other buildings by a young Syrian – a Bedouin from east of Jordan who had turned up at the college first in his native flowing dress and who now had developed into a professor of some kind of engineering.

Our boat, the Lloyd Triestino *Palacky*, was delayed at Haifa by taking up an extra large cargo, so we slept at the hotel one more night. Before turning in Mr Holmes, F and I went first to try and see some oriental dances at a

Beyrout
11. ap. 24.

Sketch of Bedouin figure

café in the Place des Canons but, being at the wrong time, returned and visited the Kensal Cinema where we saw a good Pathé film *The Five Cursed Gentlemen* very badly shown. A rather broad French comedy (domestic) was put in between the first and second parts of the film. The actors were good and full of vim, but we did not follow very accurately.

Saturday 12 April Packing in the morning while F went down to the quay, managed to board the *Palacky* and ascertained that our box sent from Cairo was safely on board. Later we found that the box had been opened and a good silk jumper of M's had been pilfered from it. The day was brilliant and the sea a royal blue as we got to the quay and through the customs. No questions were asked and nothing opened in spite of previous reports on all hands of the rigorous searching and confiscation of gold. Three minutes in a rowing boat brought us to the *Palacky* which looked a cockleshell after the *Ormonde* although still smaller boats of the Sitmar and Fabre lines were alongside. Fabre boat was a very slender little white one with red, white and blue funnel called the *Asia*. A large and capable-looking chief steward welcomed us on board and we were glad to find that English was understood. I was allotted a clean and sufficient single cabin though M and F each had a double one – F on the lower deck – all on the starboard side. The dining room, music room and smoke room all proved tiny but sufficient for our small company, as there were only about twenty-five passengers. At dinner we arranged to share a table with the Holmes and with Mrs Austen and her son and Reverend Mr Dicker (tutor and companion to the son) whom we first saw at the Tiberias Hotel. They are Australians. Very good dinner was served and we retired pretty early. The ship began to move at about midnight.

Sunday 13 April Early morning found us anchored in a vast space of calm and intensely blue water in the lee of a long ridge which ran far out to sea to the south-west of us sometimes submerged and sometimes forming little flat islands over which the waves broke high. On the farthest and largest island stood a lighthouse. Where the reef left the mainland was the new town of Tripoli with pink roofs (called El Mina). Then a wide stretch of orange plantation and then the old town crowned with its ancient citadel. Behind that rose tiers of little hills with olive trees and then the grand slopes of Lebanon, snow-capped and carrying little clouds which made a magnificent background to the sunny picture. Near us was a little British cargo boat, the *Belgravian*, unloading into barges, and towards the shore a graceful yacht painted brilliant red made a note of contrast to the blues and greens of the sea. Barges were soon round us and were having their cargoes put into our holds – mostly wheat and lemons and some bundles of brooms.

Soon after breakfast six of us entered two little sailing boats for a trip ashore. The one containing Mr Dicker, young Austen and me was controlled by a young Syrian in the usual little round white cap. He tried to make a wide detour and tack to make the landing stage but succeeded only in drifting us broadside on into two barges. At the landing stage I found I had forgotten my passport and so had Dicker. Of course as ill luck would have it, passports were needed and we were detained. However F returned and, by making himself responsible, got us out, and we strolled through El Mina. Taking a rickety little Ford bus which only just held us, we drove through the orange district with its heavy scent to the old town where we prowled for a while through the bazaars. Getting separated, the Holmeses and Dicker and I got talking to a native who was an American citizen and who was about to return to his home in Detroit. He took us up a hill to the ancient citadel still in splendid condition though it was old enough to have been besieged by Crusaders. A stone bridge now crosses the moat instead of the ancient drawbridge. We did not go in because time was short, but after admiring the gorge with its full torrent beyond the citadel and the great snowy mountains above we descended and made a slower return to the quay at El Mina on an antiquated horse-tram. While returning (all in one boat) one of our rowers amused us by explaining that a wreck whose ribs showed above the water near shore 'had been a ship one day but he die!' We steamed out at 4.30 and gradually the snowy hills disappeared. A strong wind made the little boat rock a good deal and I found it advisable to keep away from the dinner table though not actually ill. M ditto. This phenomenon of an afternoon wind after a dead-calm morning had occurred almost every day right through our holiday so far. In Egypt only a gentle cool zephyr, but in Palestine and Syria a stiff wind rising sometimes to a gale (as on the Dead Sea trip and the Baalbek–Beirut ride).

Monday 14 April At 6 a.m. we were running steadily in calm water past the great mountains of North Syria, not so high as Lebanon but more varied and still with snow on their peaks. They were the eastern border of the Gulf of Iskanderun which we had just entered, the lower hills on the north-west shore being just in sight. At breakfast time we were just gliding into the natural harbour of Iskanderun or Alexandretta, a wide sweep of calm water with a tiny enclosed harbour inside a breakwater and a tiny town nearby.

Fine hills ranged along behind the town, those to the north-east running shear down into the water. The peak of this mountain (Akba Dagh) was over 5,000 feet up.

We anchored near a great French battleship the *Waldeck-Rousseau* which had six funnels (the only ship we had ever seen carrying six funnels), and were soon surrounded by barges which took some of our cargo of cement, empty oil drums etc. And by others which brought wheat etc. to put on board. Before 10 a.m. about ten of us boarded a rowing boat and were taken into the tiny enclosed harbour whence we walked along a white road

"allo"

Old Syrian
barge loader

Alexandretta
14 - Ap. 24

Sketch of bargeloader

in much heat to the little town. After buying postcards some of us found the shore and were interested to watch a number of men and women laboriously haul in a long net which contained at examination only a few very small fishes. (Four people from on board got a car and drove over the mountains to Antioch and the waters of the Daphne and the River Orontes.)

The day was very hot, but we enjoyed the prospect of the great green slopes leading up to the cloud-capped mountains as we strolled back to our boat. Several of us took a glass of oversweet orange juice and water before embarking. In the afternoon the *Waldeck-Rousseau* steamed away with smoke pouring out of all six funnels – disappointing us of our hope of a possible visit to her. Some rain fell in the afternoon, the first real shower since we left the *Ormonde*. We steamed out about 8.30 p.m. in calm water, at which time we were spending a musical evening and I was endeavouring to play accompaniments for Mrs Hughes, a jolly English lady travelling with her husband to Cyprus.

Tuesday 15 April Awoke early and found we were in a bay as smooth as a millpond and with the usual Mediterranean purity of colouring. Mersina was spread along the shores with its pink roofs and gardens and poplars, looking very fresh, while behind rose some green hills in two rather quiet ranges over the tops of which appeared the serried peaks of the Taurus distant and dazzling white and of the Anti-Taurus farther to the east. Nearer at hand on this side was the long valley leading to Adana.

Breakfast over, we (Johnstons, Holmeses, Dicker, Austen, F and I) entered a sailing boat and gently drifted to the jetty three-quarkers of a mile away. Passports were collected (but not stamped) and we set foot for the first time on Turkish territory. The town at close quarters did not bear out the fresh appearance it had from the boat and was much like other places we have visited – open fly-covered shops – people mostly ragged. Turkish soldiers in khaki with black astrakhan caps were in evidence. The English-speaking Spanish consul whom we met told us that motors were hard to find or to hire and that the roads to Tarsus and to Pompeiopolis were very bad so we decided to see the town only. The great Greek church attracted us first and we had a great surprise on entering to find the grounds full of people with their bits of property – mattresses, frying pans and other chattels – and children. They were in groups everywhere and we learnt that they were refugees (Greek Christians) from Caesarea waiting to be repatriated under the scheme by which Greeks are being returned from here and Turks are being sent back from Greece. It was a pitiful sight – women were trying in difficulties to bake a little bread and to tend to their children, and some of the aged were lying on mattresses in the open and in the porch. A boy fetched a great key and let us into the church, the floor of which was kept ready for service though the gallery, a very high one, was full of families similar to those outside. We heard that some had been here for as long as seven months waiting for a ship.

There were a few well-painted pictures inside the church, but we could take interest in little save the people and soon left again, taking a few photos as we went. After our contact with people of Egypt etc. we were struck by the way in which the elder people preserved their self-respect and prevented their children from crowding too much round us. Although all were destitute there was not one request for baksheesh.

Thence we walked through part of the town and snapped some camels, small hairy healthy creatures, different and more furry than those of Egypt, and then on through to another part of the shore. Met a man who had been serving for many years in the American consulate. Since the departure of the American consul he had suffered much – had been beaten and imprisoned and had paid 700 Turkish pounds for his release.

Returning, the Holmeses and I became separated from the rest and visited the American Mission for five minutes. We met Miss French and Mr Romm who were in charge. The main part of the mission was closed down by the Turks under the idea that the Turkish language was not being given due prominence there over the Arabic, and the place was, for the moment, nearly idle. Before going aboard again F and I changed some money from Syrian (French) into Turkish. I got 27.30 Turkish pounds for 13 Syrian pounds (Syrian being at about 3.50 for the pound sterling). It was given us in the filthiest old notes it had been our bad fortune yet to handle.

For our journey to the ship we had to make a very long tack as the wind was dead against us which was not too agreeable to bad sailors, but we were rewarded by the interesting sight of an enormous turtle (of over 2 feet in length and brownish buff in colour) which we nearly ran down. He casually swam off to port lifting his horny head from time to time but dived quickly when one of our rowers chucked a stone at him. (The usual stiff wind rose in the afternoon higher than usual beating a high sea straight into the bay. We spent hours watching the boats and barges manoeuvre alongside and get their cargoes slung on to our ship amid very considerable danger and difficulty. A number of crates of broad beans burst open during the process.) In the evening we had more music, Mrs Hughes again singing to my accompaniment although the ship was rolling a good deal (we had left Mersina for Cyprus at 8.00 p.m.).

Wednesday 16 April Waking early I found we were running past the flat promontory which ends in Cape Andreas at the north-east end of Cyprus. One table-shaped hill and some jagged ones later broke the outline but the country looked uninteresting till we were past Famagusta Bay and approached Larnaca which lies at the west side of a quiet bay with bold mountains showing in the distance. Barges as usual were soon round us, though we again anchored pretty far out, and Cyprus military police came aboard for passport duty. We had been warned that, owing to the unsavoury reputation of Mersina and the occasional cases of typhus there, there was a possibility of those who landed there being refused admittance to Cyprus; but our passports were not even looked at and no questions were asked. Therefore our usual party went ashore at 10 a.m. and hired three Ford cars for a run to Nicosia and Limassol. First of all, however, F went to a bank and others of us went to the post office and square – afterwards starting off in Fords for a run round the little town and out to the rather picturesque salt lakes (7 feet below the sea level) from which salt is extracted. We also visited the ancient church of St Lazarus (St Lazarus after being raised from the dead came to Cyprus and was the first bishop here) in which the three fine domes had been destroyed by a former Muslim sultan owing to their being at greater height than the neighbouring minarets. An enormous gilded screen was here stretching right across the church and full of paintings. Besides paintings of St Lazarus there was one of St Barnabas who with St Paul introduced Christianity into the island. We were told that St Barnabas was a native of Cyprus and that he also was the first to carry Christianity to Britain. (Also saw a carving of the lion of St Mark. This lion recurs all over the Island.) We saw also the tomb of

St Lazarus (after his second death) but the bones have been taken to Marseilles.

It was a relief in this town to see the British flag flying and to find the streets clean and a general air of cleanliness and success among the people. Even a half-witted fellow who came to beg dumbly was well washed. The flag of Cyprus is the blue ensign with a white circle let into the blue part, and on the circle are two red lions.

Leaving at about eleven o'clock in our three cars we made fast going over a very good road to Nicosia (28 miles). Much of the way was over white country, apparently alkali and inhospitable, which was nevertheless ploughed and which yielded crops very short in stem but of substantial head. Magpies were very numerous here and also a little bird new to me with white cap, breast and tail and black wings and back (one of these joined our ship exhausted later between Cyprus and Rhodes and proved to be a sort of wagtail). Besides many hawks I noticed some blue jays and a little owl sitting on telegraph wires. We stopped at a little Greek inn halfway to Nicosia and got some wonderful oranges as big and sweet and altogether similar to the best Jaffa oranges.

Nicosia, a clean attractive spot with quite good shops and hotels, appeared at about lunchtime and we were soon at a good hotel (Greek) with a meal before us. Later we motored through a maze of intricate little streets running at every angle and saw the outside of St Sofia – a great Christian basilica of which the outside has rich carvings and the inside finely ornamented pillars. When the Muslims came into power they took away the top of it and put up two minarets. We ran round the streets of Nicosia for a while and then out to the governor's house past the ancient wall and the aqueduct. Returning some way we took a side road which led us out to the Limassol road. For much of the way we went through fertile land sparsely populated and through a curious saucer-like depression the top edges of which were the same height everywhere just as if the whole area had been dug from a flat plain. Away to our right the range of Mount Troodos was always in sight (over 6,000 feet) and the scene became increasingly beautiful as we ran through more wooded country. Many of the peasants we saw were in Greek style of costume.

After another halt at a halfway house we proceeded through hilly districts till we were near the sea and observed to our left a great monastery and church away up on a mountain top, the nearest habitations being a village right at the foot of the hill, a crooked footpath connecting the two. The scenery was now delightful with its many trees and on reaching the coast after many meanderings we had a wide sweep before us of ocean (the wide sweep of sea was Akrotiri Bay), and a cluster of ships to the right indicated Limassol harbour. Our boat had made the journey from Larnaca and was now lying near the quay and beside her was a slightly smaller boat of the Khedivial Mail Line flying the British flag (Red Ensign).

A short run round the prosperous and well-kept town of Limassol with its many modern houses and clean streets and smart-looking Greek inhabitants, and then a big motor launch took us out to the *Palacky*. We found the forepart of our ship was crowded with new 'passengers' in the form of cattle and genets, while the upper deck aft (over the second-class saloon and the rudder mechanism) was occupied by a flock of sheep, all the animals being shipped from Cyprus to Rhodes. In the sunset and the dusk Limassol with its sharp background of mountains looked romantic and we were sorry our sight of the island had perforce been so brief. Anxiety was felt at night at the absence of four passengers: Colonel Johnston (American) and Captain Frieland (British) and their wives who had gone ashore at Larnaca and not returned. However, they got to the ship at 11 p.m. and had visited both Famagusta and Kyrenia (Cyrene) in addition to our trip. We left at 11.30 and were rounding Cape Gata at midnight.

Thursday 17 April This morning the sea was oily calm and the ship going at a lazy speed through. Mount Troodos and the Cyprus coast still could be seen to the east in silhouette (the Paphos of St Paul's travels is on this coast).

The morning I spent partly writing and partly talking with Captain Frieland whose conversation proved amazingly interesting as he had spent years in Africa, partly in big-game hunting around Tanganyika on all sides, and had been in the army in France and Palestine and Egypt, being able to speak Arabic and a number of African dialects. He said that the first dialect necessary to learn was key Swahili which contains a good deal of Arabic, and is the relic of the old days when the Arabs were the aristocrats of that part of the world and carried on their slave-trading expeditions.

While we were chatting we saw a little object, shining blue and green, skim through the air near the water and plop into a wavelet and we realised it was a flying fish – the first I had seen. The rest of the day was spent in sheer idleness. The afternoon breeze freshened as usual and disturbed the smoothness of the sea but not enough to rock the boat at all. Grand mountains, snow-capped and of great height appeared after tea looking pearly grey on the lower slopes and faintly rosy where the tops caught the sun. They were Ak Dagh (over 10,000 feet high) and its satellites, the last of the Taurus range, and were in the part called Lycia in the time of St Paul, forming the western side of the Bay of Atalia. The last thing in sight at night was the revolving light on Castelorizo Island near the mainland.

Some Cypriot athletes were on board, one of whom trained part of the day running at a great rate round the ship. He was a marathon runner capable of keeping up very good speed for thirty miles. All were going to Athens for the preliminary trials for the Olympic Games and changed ship at Rhodes.

Friday 18 April (Good Friday) Before 6 a.m. we were off Rhodes harbour and anchored beside a powerful-looking American destroyer (no. 219) with four funnels. Our situation was fine. The town of Rhodes was near us with its many grey towers and walls while to the north about five miles away were the mountains of Asia Minor, rugged and steep, sweeping right round to the east where the mighty range of Ak Dagh lay under snow. Boats were as usual quickly around and our live cargo were hoisted overboard, the cattle and mules in slings, and the sheep tied each by one leg were sent four at a time from a hook. M and F were uncertain starters, so I joined the other party and we were quickly in the old harbour (by a sailing boat) with great fortified walls all round, the tops of which were new (Turkish) and castellated for guns while the base was old. We saw no sign of the great bronze Colossus of Rhodes which once straddled the entrance to the harbour or even of where it could have stood, although it was once one of the Seven Wonders of the World. On shore a stout fellow closely resembling Douglas Fairbanks offered his services as guide and was taken on though later he told us with a disarming smile that he knew nothing of the history of the place beyond that 'it was old' and had never before been in the museum! (Every flag in Rhodes and on the ships in the harbour was at half-mast on account of Good Friday.) Our first visit was to the Antico Ospedale dei Cavaliere or the ancient Hospice of the Knights of St John

Boat fare 10 lira return each (2/-)

WE saw no sign of the great bronze colossus
of Rhodes which once straddled the entrance to
the harbour or even of where it could have
stood, altho' it was once one of the seven
wonders of the World."   (This guide told us →
with a grin that the chief occupation on the island
was waiting for remittances from relatives in America.)

Every flag in Rhodes & on the ships in the
harbour was at half-mast on account
of Good Friday.

Strong smelling herb
from the garden-court
of the Knights Hospitallers

The Knights of St John of Jerusalem at Cyprus were
called the Knights of Cyprus & waged war against
the moslems. After retiring from that island
they became "Knights of Rhodes" & still later
retired further south & became "Knights of Malta"

Facsimile page of notebook with dried plant

(Knights Hospitallers), a huge and strongly built place with many rooms and
two courtyards, one of which contains lovely flowers including one which
was entirely composed of long prickles and red flowers. (The Knights of St
John of Jerusalem at Cyprus were called the Knights of Cyprus and waged
war against the Muslims. After retiring from that island they became Knights
of Rhodes and still later retired further south and became Knights of Malta.)
Part of the edifice is used as a museum and contains jars and pots from

ancient burying places nearby and also pieces of tombstones of the early Christians inscribed with the cross in a circle. I looked for, and was delighted to find, the inscribed sign of the fish used by Christians in the first and second centuries. In places all over the fortifications appear these two shields side by side with the plain and the ornate cross. Through the halls and rooms were many carvings of the Crusaders' shields and crosses and there were also tombstones of 1500–30 in Latin and English. One tombstone to a certain Thomas Newport was ornamented with the skull and crossbones, the lower jaw of the skull being shown detached from the rest.

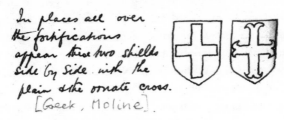

Shield illustration

Afterwards we walked through many fortifications (on which fishermen were mending a lot of nets) and passed the second harbour (full of fishing boats, mostly Italian and a few Greek) and along to the modern well-built Italian quarter. Italians have owned this island since the Tripoli war and have made it a place of delight, repairing the walls and fortifications and keeping the whole town clean and fresh (twelve years' occupation). Italy owns also eleven other big islands in this part of the archipelago. Through a lengthy Turkish cemetery we walked uphill right up to a hilltop whence we got a wide panorama over the town and its harbours and over another wide bay to the west and also over the rest of the island rising to some height at the southern end. Everywhere was rich fertility and the meadows were ablaze with flowers and the flowers were all those of England – poppies, daisies, buttercups, convolvulus etc. – an ideal spot for a holiday with its green slopes, high mountains, occasional cliffs and friendly people. Returning down the cobbled road we entered through the fortifications again. Then past the blue clocktower and a mosque and through the wide, clean semi-oriental market and to the quay again where we left our guide and sailed back to the *Palacky*.

All too soon we weighed anchor and left the beautiful spot – the most quietly charming place we have struck since F joined us – and set off at one o'clock in brilliant sunlight through water of intense blue and quite calm for our cruise into the Aegean Sea. Getting away from Rhodes we neared the coast of Asia Minor. What a contrast! Here the rugged barren mountains and hills show no sign of habitation even along their broken coastline and not till we got to the island of Symi which lies across the Gulf of Doris did we see a hut of any kind, and, even there, it appeared to be only one till we were on its western side when we saw several more. In the Gulf of Doris were some little sailing craft, and a gentleman from the Cyprus government on board (Hon. G.D. Fenn, Chief Secretary for Cyprus) told me that Symi was one of the important sponge-fishing islands. Many tiny islands bobbed up all about making picturesque scenery. Leaving the large islands of Piskopi and Niseros on our left we kept close to the mainland which ran out here and ended in the sudden rock of Cape Kris. In the far distance to our south appeared Skarpanto, a big island near Crete. Ahead was Kos, a very long narrow island flat for its southern half and high and precipitous for the northern. (Just round Cape Kris on the north and under the shelter of the final peak was a little bay with a strong old tower and a few ruins of the ancient Cnidos.) Rounding Cape Kris we passed inside Kos with the long Gulf of Kos running inland to our right. The evening sun on these limestone mountains all round and on the still sea which ran in creeks between the hills everywhere made an enchanting scene.

As we rounded the end of Kos and moved to the other side of the gulf a town appeared on the mainland with apparently a castle on a mound in a bay. On the map it was marked as Bodrum but our captain said it was the ancient Halicarnassus. (The mausoleum of Halicarnassus was the 'seventh wonder' of the ancient world. Mausoleum means the tomb of Mausolus. From its stones the Knights of St John of Jerusalem at Rhodes built the great castle of St Peter which was what we saw. With the forts of Kos and Rhodes it formed a sort of triumvirate of strongholds.) Then on the island appeared the town of Kos looking clean and prosperous with a line of strong fortifications in the middle and with richly fertile country all round gradually rising towards a great mountain, the highest point of the island which shelters the town from the south. There were many windmills there and sailing boats anchored in the harbour and every sign of peace and plenty.

In the sunset we saw the precipitous crags of Kalimnos (which is noted like the isle of Symi as a sponge-fishing centre) and of Leros. Two smallish islands but very rugged (were now sailing across the Gulf of Mandalia). After our usual very excellent dinner we went on deck and found it very mild after the quite chilly spell of the last week. It was a romantic evening in that most historic waterway. The dark islands rising abruptly from the deep and blotting out the stars with their jagged crests carried our thoughts right away from things of the moment, and seemed to breathe the hoary, classic myths and legends whose heroes all sailed and loved and fought amid their crags. We stayed up late to see Patmos and were rewarded. When we were level with the isle of Gaidaro on our right there were some small flat islands on our left beyond which were distinguishable parts of the place we wanted, for Patmos is the most westerly of the group we were passing through. By 11 p.m. we had passed the little islands, and looking back we could see Patmos, further off, spread out faintly, but quite sharply in the moonlight. Intensely interesting, though no hill of any height is there. (The full moon lit up the scene at night and gave the islands a ghostly look, and we remembered our experience at the last full moon when we were picnicking in the sand beneath the chin of the great Sphinx.) So ended Good Friday.

Saturday 19 April Retiring to bed a little before one this morning I opened my cabin 'moushrabir' window and found we were just beside the great peak of the island of Samos. In the brilliant light of the moon – just full – I could pick out many features of the mountain through glasses. On rising the scene had changed much. We were now heading east, having passed Chios, and soon turned south-east down the lovely Gulf of Smyrna with lofty green mountains on either side and several islands. We kept close to the south and west side of the gulf. After a while a wide flat stretch appeared to our left with salt works and very many salt mounds beyond which the gulf bends to the east. To avoid the shallows we hugged the opposite bank making a very wide sweep and soon were in sight of Smyrna. As we approached it the country became more and more charmingly fertile and the final wide sweeping bay is fine. It was a shock to us to note through the glasses that a little village nestling in a green and wooded valley had been entirely gutted by fire. Smyrna on close inspection was a doleful spectacle. Many good ships were in the harbour, but the long fine waterfront was lined with gutted houses, stark skeletons of what had been great buildings of a flourishing port. Little seemed to have been done to clear up the mess left by the terrible affairs of two years ago. To the left was a good-looking suburb (Cordilio) with red roofs and trees, whence a large steam ferry plied frequently to the harbour and to the right were the untouched houses of the Turk and Jew quarter rising up to the fort-crowned hill of Pagus. A few minarets in this quarter were very graceful and more slender than any yet seen in Damascus or elsewhere. They were so thin that there seemed no room for the muezzin to ascend to the balcony.

Our party consisted of the Johnstons, ourselves and Miss Daniel who had joined at Cyprus. Immediately following lunch we were rowed to the douane [customs] where our passports and cameras were removed and we went to the front where I bargained for two carriages for a run-round. Going right past the extensive ruins of the burnt Greek and Armenian quarters we followed the tramlines (one-horse trams) to the well-built railway station (made with British capital and still bearing many British signs) where our hopes of being able to get to Ephesus were dashed – no train save at 5 a.m, return 5 p.m. – 48 miles and four-hour journey! Plenty of automobiles but impassable road and brigand-infested. Thence we took a long road for miles round, first inland and then back to another part of Smyrna whence we turned up past extensive cemeteries well laid out with cypress trees and round behind the hill of Pagus. During this time we had been interested to see storks standing on their nests – one on an isolated wall and the other on the apex of a roof. Both were merely collections of sticks laid together in most exposed and inhospitable-looking places. After seeing the ancient caravan bridge we surmounted a crest and descended to the great American College with its fine square tower. Here we caught up with Mr and Mrs Holmes who had gone on alone and we saw the excellent chapel and gym. Thence we soon reached the best thing of these parts – the high curved Roman aqueduct over a deep gully. This slender structure, whose arch-supports are connected at various heights irregularly by intermediate arches, is still in perfect order and carries its full quantity of water across, feeding first a large horse-trough where our animals refreshed themselves. Then we soon struck the upper part of Smyrna and ascended by bad roads to near the top of Pagus. A short walk brought us to a cottage where was the proscenium of the great Roman stadium. The horse-shoe depression was quite clearly defined behind the cottage and even the rows where partitions between the seats had been. Here Polycarp, second Christian Bishop of Smyrna, was martyred and his grave is shown (a great plaster sarcophagus) in the cottage garden. Polycarp who died at the age of eighty-two was himself a pupil of St John. A few steps further took us to a little platform of what seemed part of the fort and from thence we got a magnificent view of the whole gulf with its mountains and of the big town beneath us with a foreground of cypresses. The burned area was quite clearly defined and stopped abruptly at the boundary of the Turkish and Jewish quarter. In the doomed area, however, the destruction was complete. Turkish soldiers prevent one going right up to the fort on the summit, but in any case we had seen enough and re-entered our carriages for the return down the steep streets and through the Jewish quarter where everyone was sitting outside the houses, as it was their Sabbath. For a while we saw over the market which had nothing of very much distinction or interest though I nearly bought a neat little Belgian revolver for 4 Turkish pounds (10s). Revolvers, ammunition and daggers were sold here with no questions asked.

On paying off carriages and boatmen, F, who as usual was our bargainer, had difficulty as the men asked for more than their bargain fees. His position was unenviable, but calling a policeman eased matters. Mr Dicker also had much trouble, being surrounded by three cut-throat-looking villains carrying knives, but he managed to get them to conclude the argument on the steamer in a safer atmosphere.

Sunday 20 April Nearly all our cargo is being removed and the roar and rattle of the derricks kept many awake last night. On the enormous lighters alongside, the quantity of cargo our ship has discharged is surprising. F and Mr Dicker conducted an Easter Service at 10.30 with Communion. Most of our fellow-passengers turned up and we had a very good time.

The rest of the morning we loafed about the decks in the sunlight watching the unloading.

In the afternoon F and I with Mr Dicker and young Austen went ashore. Dicker went off uphill to see Polycarp's tomb etc. while we other three had an hour on the water going by the steam ferry across the bay to the attractive-looking suburb village of Cordilio at the low charge of 6*d* each (return). After then wandering through part of the ruined area where desolation reigns and hardly anything seems to have been done to clean up or renew, we gathered at the quay, collected our passports and regained the *Palacky*. We steamed out at 5.30 p.m. and our last sight of Smyrna was of a widespread town quite pink in the sunset light surrounded by delicately hued hills of every shade of grey-blue and purple.

10 p.m. The great bulk of Mytilene looming up to starboard in the moonlight and a light showing on Chios far to the south.

Monday 21 April A little comedy started the day. Being due to enter the Dardanelles at 8 a.m., several people assembled on the deck, including Captain Frieland and Colonel Johnston, and right on time we were passing through a narrow strait with bleak shores on our left leading up to a high smooth mountain which Colonel Johnston who had a book and maps on the Gallipoli campaign designated as Achi Baba. He also found Morto Bay and the French battle area. However, the stream which should have marked the old no-man's-land failed to appear and we were puzzled by first the appearance of a flourishing and undamaged town and fort, then by an uncharted island and lighthouse towards the mainland and also by the absence of all traces of trenches or cemeteries. Also the Dardanelles [strait] widened unconscionably, but we did not realise we had blundered much till Colonel Johnston returned from making enquiries at the captain's office and informed us we were looking at the Isle of Tenedos, and not at the famous peninsula at all, which was still an hour's sail northwards! However, after proceeding past Tenedos and past the low hills bounding the plains of Troy and sighting through a hazy atmosphere the peaks and cliffs of Turbros (to the west), we did draw level with the tragic spot and, passing Cape Helles, entered the straits. The low scrubby hills round the point had a cluster of huts on top and something (probably a memorial statue or obelisk) swathed in scaffolding. The rusted hulls of two wrecks, one a battleship with the superstructure removed, lay by the shore just south of the beginning of Morto Bay. In the bay were many little houses of the Imperial War Graves Commission and all round were little cemeteries on the shore and on the hills, one enormous area being full of wooden crosses, some thousands, in even rows spreading across a high slope. On the Asiatic side was the little fort of Kum Kaleh, behind which stretched the plains of Troy. Passing Morto Bay and its graves, we kept near the peninsula side and reached the little stream dividing the French and Turk lines, with its scarred slopes and remnants of trenches, and kept on along the low, rubbly, scrub-covered hills which the Turks had held. Before long we passed a Bolshevik steamer (quite empty and with the propeller half exposed) and arrived at Dardanelles (Chanak Kalessi) where we anchored for two hours in the strong current which is always flowing here from the Black Sea.

Sketch of Dardanelles figure

(The Russian boat was called the *Karl Liebknecht* and their flag had a red background with white characters. The translation of 'PCCP' provided us some amusement, my only suggestion being 'Public Conveyance phor Communist Proletariat'.) Here there is a fort and a little town which during the war was shelled by the *Queen Elizabeth* from the middle of Suvla Bay in the Aegean Sea, the shells coming right over the peninsula (some houses still shattered). On the opposite coast (i.e. on the peninsula) was the highly

Facsimile of diary page

picturesque heart-shaped fort of Kilid Bahr (the 'Key of the Sea'), a massive structure at the foot of a hill and surrounded with houses.

Leaving there at 1.30 we steamed past the little town of Midos where the Imperial War Graves Commission has buildings and saw far off the Anzac Memorial perched on a hilltop – the highest and furthest point they reached from Suvla Bay. To the north another ridge ran higher, and to us it appeared that, had they been able to capture this, the whole of the rest of the peninsula southwards must have been commanded. So near and yet so far – it seemed a ghastly tragedy to have failed by so little.

FORT OF KILID BAHR
GALLIPOLI PENINSULA
21 - ap - 24

Sketch of Fort of Kilid Bahr

Over the hilltop distant mountain pinnacles appeared in the blue, probably peaks of Turbros again, or else Samothrakia. A little further up the straits we struck the second narrowest part (1,700 yards across) with the fort of Nagara on the Asiatic side. This was the ancient scene of the story of Hero and Leander. Here also Byron swam across. Thence we steamed north-east in a bitingly cold wind which made us all assume coats and wraps, passed green uneventful scenes and scrubby hills towards the Sea of Marmara. In one small bay were wrecks of three ships (one Turk steamer) run ashore. The Asiatic side was very quiet and featureless in scenery and the straits gradually broadened until the town of Gallipoli was reached on the peninsula, at which point we entered the Sea of Marmara and the coasts receded from us a good deal. We kept close to the European side till darkness fell.

Several Turkish passengers had come aboard at Smyrna for Constantinople and one little 'prodigy' of about five years caused anguish to many by continued thrumming of the stock Turkish 'tune' – a melancholy affair of about four notes without any added harmony. Packed at night in preparation for leaving the *Palacky*. At 10 p.m., with the sea dead smooth, the waning moon rose over an island in the Sea of Marmara leaving a long reflection while, to the west, Venus was setting and was so brilliant that she had a wide reflection of her own also reaching right to the ship!

Tuesday 22 April 5 a.m. We were all wakened by blasts on the siren and found ourselves just entering the Golden Horn. With much fuss and vibration we took our place near a Khedivial mail boat of the same size as ours and dropped anchor just as a rosy dawn was breaking over the hills of Asia behind Scutari and turning the glassy water pink.

After breakfast we admired the densely packed city on either side of us, bristling with minarets on the Istanbul side, and rising on the north to the big tower on the hill of Pera. The great Galata Bridge was just ahead of us. Quickly, however, we found the deck unpleasantly full of Turkish boatmen who swarmed up ropes over the side and crowded on the ship, trying to get into the saloons and corridors. An unsavoury crowd and obstinate, they staggered us by demanding a Turkish pound (2*s* 6*d*) for rowing each person to the shore nearby and we were unable to make them budge in price as they were banded together in union under certain boss men who wore red brassards. An hour or two of argument brought no benefit and to avoid further waste of time we all descended into two boats. Several of the boatmen got into each which did not make us feel any more comfortable. To add to our suspicion, they stopped the boat mid-stream and demanded their payment and, on being refused, simply rested on their oars. Captain Frieland on our boat got most infuriated and nearly came to blows with a boss man. However, a representative from the Pera Palace Hotel in our boat said that this custom was usual, so we paid.

Meanwhile F in the other boat had been accosted by a Mr Wiseman of the British and Foreign Bible Society who had come to meet him, and, calling me to the latter's boat, we returned to the *Palacky*, finished packing, and got baggages by another boat to the customs (where my Damascus curios were scrutinised and fined 4 Turkish pounds (10*s*). Mr Wiseman got us two carriages and with some difficulty we got out through a crowd of villainous-looking Turks. The extortionate charges and the insolence of the men we had come into contact with gave us the worst possible opinion of the place and made one think that there was no authority at all.

A long pull up Pera Hill to the house of Mr Wiseman at the end of Grande Rue and then we were shown our comfortable rooms by our landladies, the Misses Dunn, beneath Mr Wiseman's flat. Lunch with the Wisemans and a chat, and then into the 'Tunnel' and down again to Galata in a little train on an endless chain with Mr Wiseman as guide. On to the bridge with its surging crowd, passing the toll-men who stand across the pavement taking 1 piastre from each person on foot. Then from a landing stage on the bridge we hired a boat to row us to Sweet Water, the interpreter being Christos – Mr Wiseman's assistant and a Graeco-Turk. (The Muslim veil is discarded by the women of Constantinople. We saw not more than six during our stay. The fez and the broader astrakhan kalpak supposedly indicated official class, grey ones being worn by the police.)

For the first part the journey was past shipping, much of which was idle owing to trade depression, the result of recent political upheavals and of Turk mismanagement. After passing, on the left, the suburb of Eyoub (before passing Eyoub we also saw the remains of Valen's Aqueduct) with its nice little mosque by the water (the mosque is built over the grave of Mohammad's standard bearer who was killed by Arabs at the first siege of Constantinople), we found we had rowed right up the Golden Horn and were entering a meandering stream, the Sweet Water, so called on account of its being fresh while the Golden Horn is salt – an arm of the Bosphorus.

Through a flat valley, green and bounded by hills, we wound, beside an old wooden holiday-house of the Sultan's (entirely neglected and dilapidated), till we reached a part where the river was too shallow, and disembarked at a tea place with a refreshment shanty – a holiday resort of the people (boatman very different specimen from the customs boatmen – charged only 2 Turkish pounds (5s) for a four-mile pull carrying five people). Thence we walked through a charming tract with many trees, soon coming to the shallow stream again, now the haunt of a host of great frogs who lay with their noses just above the water and filling the air with their joyous cacophony.

Leaving Sweet Water, we turned to the right and ascended a big hill by a road and a footpath. It was a bleak lonely district but, in spite of previous reports of brigands and general lawlessness here, and of later harrowing stories of Mr Wiseman's with which he had enlivened our journey, we got no frights and saw no soul except some Mongol road-makers – cheap imported labour – till we reached the top where we struck a high road, with a wide outlook towards the hinterland, and rested awhile for coffees at a little establishment where were some enormous, but friendly, wolf-hounds.

Continuing thence slowly, for M was tired, we reached a cemetery where was a monument of freedom (representing a vertical gun, muzzle to the skies) and the fine tomb of Sefket Pasha, the great politician who was shot by Enver Bay. Outside the cemetery, on a grassy plot, I had the luck to pick up a delicately made gold-mesh ring. Walking to the suburb of Chichli, we caught a tram and returned through good-class quarters to Constantinople and passed through the Grande Rue home. The Misses Dunn had a delightfully homely dinner ready for us – the first entirely English meal for a long while – which F in particular appreciated.

Wednesday 23 April St George's Day and the day of the opening of the British Empire Exhibition is also the first anniversary of the formation of the Turkish Republic – a general holiday and an occasion for clothing Constantinople with flags. For us it has been a day of mosques and foot-slogging. Starting early, we caught a tram near the Pera Palace Hotel (as we waited for our tram two little girls in western costume came and stuck little Independence Day badges in our coats just as in an ordinary flag day in England) and rode through the gay streets, down over the Galata Bridge, up into Stambul past the ancient entrance to the Sublime Porte and the entrance to the Seraglio Palace gardens, to the mighty mosque of Santa Sophia (Santa Sophia is not a saint's name, but originally meant Holy Wisdom). This huge structure, built first by Constantine, then destroyed, rebuilt by Theodosius, damaged again and finally built by Justinian, covers a great area and would hold 18,000 people. Many trees are before the courtyard entrance and, from close up, obscure the view of the great dome and its supporting semi-domes and of the four great minarets. On entering and assuming the shoes, we were taken in tow by a guide who showed us many points of interest. Splendid mosaics and paintings are everywhere. Since the Muslims took the great edifice over they have tried to distort the

As we waited for our tram two little
girls in Western costume
came & stuck these
little Independence
Day badges in our
Coats just as in an
ordinary flag day in England.

St. Sophia is not a saints name,
but originally meant Holy Wisdom.

Facsimile of diary page

many finely painted crosses which adorn the ceilings, turning them into various geometrical forms, but the old paint is outlasting the new and everywhere the original crosses are clearly to be seen.

Around the mosque, inside, are many fine supporting pillars – nine great ones of red granite, each a single stone, are from the great Temple of Jupiter which we saw at Baalbek and twenty of grey granite are from the Temple of Diana at Ephesus.

High on one pillar was the imprint of a hand put there by a sultan during a massacre of Christians who had fled to the Santa Sophia. His horse was standing on a piled-up heap of dead bodies which enabled him to get his hand so high, and on another pillar were splintered places made by the butt of his spear and by the horse's hoof.

The place was built originally with its main window looking towards Jerusalem but the Muslims have shifted the altar a few degrees further south and all the multitude of little floor-carpets for prayer are laid at a different angle from the 'nave', so that all shall tend towards Mecca instead of our Holy City.

Passing out through gigantic doors of solid bronze, on which the cross has been changed to an arrow (near here were two medallions, much damaged, of Justinian and Theodora), we regained the courtyard and another guide showed us into two little burial chapels. One of these contains the tomb of the Sultan Selim – a big affair with a great turban at one end – and the slightly smaller tombs of his five wives and the still smaller ones of his forty-five children, the boys' tombs all being with turbans (rich blue tiles were the feature of the interior wall-decorations of these). In the other was the tomb of Sultan Murat III with his four wives and forty-six children, the Crown Prince having a tomb only slightly smaller than his father's.

Thence out to the wide square beyond which is the great mass of the Mosque of Sultan Ahmed with its six slender, tall minarets. Before entering this mosque we passed through part of the Hippodrome – a long open space with a railed-in garden containing two high obelisks, one granite one of Theodosius (Egyptian 3,600 years old) and the other of blocks, weather worn. The feature of the inside of the Sultan Ahmed is four immensely thick pillars from which the great dome was sprung. The upper part of these was richly decorated blue while the lower was fluted. Most of the other decoration was blue also and the mosque seemed very full of light while a charming view of the Sea of Marmara could be seen from one of the windows. We were interested to examine the geometrical capitals of some of the columns – these we noted again in the Sultan Suleiman Mosque. Going out again we saw the fountain of Kaiser Wilhelm, a lovely thing on the blue roof of which was rich decoration with monograms of himself and the late sultan.

After walking round the Hippodrome and looking at the obelisks, we returned by tram to Galata and lunched at the Restaurant Midi (or the 'Double D') and came back to the Santa Sophia. Then we walked up to the Church of St Irene, the only great ancient Christian church not now used as a mosque, in which is housed the War Museum, but it was closed. Outside is a very ancient tree – the Janissaries' Tree – on which a great number of the Janissaries were hanged as penalty for getting too powerful, and here we rested for a while and met Mr and Mrs Holmes. Then M and Mrs Wiseman went home while Mr Wiseman and F and I walked on to the great square outside the War Office – looked into the mosque courtyard of Bayezid where all sorts of stalls are ranged like a miniature bazaar (the 'Pigeon Mosque' – nearly all the stalls are bead stalls) and went round some side streets to reach the huge Mosque of Suleiman. This has a magnificent front flanked by two towering minarets and the whole thing shone white with the sun full on it, while dark cypresses stood out against it at intervals.

Mrs Austen and her son and Mr Dicker happened to be here, and we just had time to have a good look round the interior which was rather dark before a man began a monotonous droning chant and we were turned out. There were marvellous windows here with tiny bits of colour all over like mosaic, resembling very closely the windows made from pebble and precious stones in the Mosque of Omar at Jerusalem.

Returning, we walked through part of the meat bazaar and the spice bazaar and took the tram at Galata Bridge.

Thursday 24 April Being informed that 'permits to leave' were necessary here and were difficult to get, we sent Christos off early to begin negotiations while the others of us went through the great bazaars of Stambul. They are covered, and extend over an enormous area, but, so far as we could see, are clean, fairly wide and very well stocked. Mr Wiseman took us straight to the 'fur' area where we inspected many skins, some good, in a decent little 'emporium', without purchasing.

Returning for lunch at the 'Double D', we got some very good lamb and then descended to the Galata Bridge where Christos was waiting to say that the passport and permit people wanted us to apply personally. Going to Stambul, we found a crowd in the permit office, but discovered that the officials were quiet and civil, and got our papers nearly through, leaving Christos to get the last stamp and signature.

At Galata Bridge we caught a little steamer for Haida Pasha, a place just south of Scutari on the Asiatic side of the Bosphorus. (Scutari is Persian for a 'courier' and the correct pronunciation – 'Scootery' – rather carries out the idea!) There a gharry took us up to the British cemetery, once on the sea edge but now surrounded by gas tanks and great buildings put up by the Germans on a reclaimed foreshore prior to the Great War. Beautiful trees and flowers are there and it is well kept. We saw the obelisk commemorating those who died in the Crimean War and the long ugly hospital in which Florence Nightingale worked. Judas trees in full blossom, showing us delicate pink masses against dark cypresses, were the features of the cemetery. Another little Turkish steamer-ferry took us back to Galata.

At night a crestfallen Christos reported that he had been unsuccessful in getting our permits through after four hours' wait!

Friday 25 April Mother was tired this morning and stayed in Constantinople with Mrs Wiseman, but Mr Wiseman and F and I took the tram right up to the suburb of Bebek on the Bosphorus above which is the great American institution Robert College with its many buildings perched high on a commanding site. Nearby was the ancient picturesque fortress of Roumelie Hissar and on the opposite side of the Bosphorus was the sister castle of Anatolie Hissar. Showers had fallen on our outward journey but brilliant sunshine appeared now and our journey back along the winding strait amongst the broken green and tree-covered hills was lovely. (At one place we saw a fishing net strung to a number of poles, and a watcher sitting on a high platform raised on a pole. He would give the signal for the net to be raised to the surface, and probably was watching for swordfish.)

We disembarked at the Galata Bridge and, after lunching at the 'Double D', walked up a street of many steps to the great Galata Tower which we ascended (a strongly built round tower of many storeys made by the Genoese in the old days and used by them for business). At the top a keeper made a request for an admission fee which we had to argue and reduce. From the outside gallery the view was great. All Constantinople was spread beneath us and we could see much of the Bosphorus, Sea of Marmara, Prinkipo and other Prince's Isles as well as the hinterland and Santa Stefano. (One of the smallest islands – Plait – was once owned by Bulmer Lytton who had a big establishment there.) After taking one or two photos of the Golden Horn and the Seraglio Palace we returned home.

At night we all went to the Scottish Mission school where we saw *The Never Never Land*, an adaptation of *Peter Pan* given in English by children – mostly Jewish. Quite well done and with home-made costumes.

Saturday 26 April Yesterday being the Muslim Sunday, nothing could be done about our permits to leave, so after a little shopping, F and I with Mr Wiseman and Christos went to the office and, after some delay, got many sundry stamps and hieroglyphics added. Then we tried to get into the great museum but found it did not open till 1 p.m. – a great disappointment as this is one of the most important places. In the grounds are some pieces of Greek sculpture and some immense sarcophagi (Egyptian?).

A tram took us back to Galata where we joined Mr and Mrs Wiseman at the 'Double D' for lunch, after which Mr Wiseman and F and I went up to Pera, sent our baggage off by auto in charge of Christos, and rejoined the others before going on to the customs. There more tedious waiting while our particulars were entered (right to left in Turkish) and another stamp put in our long-suffering passports, but our baggage was not interfered with or opened and we got porters to take it along the quay to the *Praqa* which was not in mid-stream as the *Palacky* had been. (These men, though asking extortionate prices at first, were soon brought to reason and had none of the aggressiveness of our boatmen of four days ago. Indeed, the terrible impression those men had given us had nearly evaporated now owing to the amount of civility and ordinary politeness we had received from the officials and common people in the city.)

On the ship we were glad to see many of our former friends, the Holmeses, Johnstons (elder), Frielands, Miss Daniel etc. Colonel and Mrs Johnston, Dicker and the Austens were not with us, having gone to Gallipoli peninsula. Before the ship left we had a fierce altercation with a swindling money changer, but he did not do F for more than 1*s* in the end. Gliding out at dusk we cut slowly out into the Sea of Marmara over a glassy surface in which every bright star had its reflection and in which the illuminated mosques, lit for Ramadan, left their bright trails; while the only sound was the slight hiss of the foam from our prow slipping past. In every respect the *Praqa* is superior to the *Palacky*: broader, steadier, little or no vibration, better saloon and social rooms and smarter service. I was put in a double cabin with a 'stable-companion', an Englishman living in Paris but travelling for 'oil by-products' for a great American oil firm and inspecting subsidiary companies.

Sunday 27 April This morning found us in the Dardanelles steaming through a glassy sea over which our boat left a wide symmetrical trail, the ripples extending for a mile or more quite clearly. By 8 a.m. we were opposite the beautiful little heart-shaped fort of Kilid Bahr and soon had passed Chanak in brilliant sunshine. (Since entering the Dardanelles we had noticed the change in the colour of the water which had become quite green, but now we were back where it was its true Mediterranean blue.)

We passed further from the point of Cape Helles and the fighting area and soon were nearing the Strait of Tenedos where the lighthouse island is. (After passing Tenedos we had a faint glimpse of the silhouette of Lemnos low down in the west.) To the north-west was the rugged great island of Imbros and over the top of it appeared the mighty mountain peaks and crags of the island of Samothrace, looking wonderful at that large distance. In glorious sunlight and with a warm southerly breeze, we gradually lost sight of the coast and mountains of Asia Minor. By the afternoon the sea was higher, though not enough motion to rock the boat. At 4.30 the little island of Psara was to the east, a good many miles off, and still further we could see the high mountains of Chios. At sunset we were east of Skyros and before dark we were heading towards the strait between Cape d'Oro (on the long island of Enbea) and the Isle of Andros. The temperature by this time had changed greatly and was now very close.

Monday 28 April Morning 5 a.m. found us anchored amongst a crowd of gaily be-flagged vessels in Piraeus harbour near a quay. Not much work was being done anywhere as the Greeks were celebrating their Easter Monday. It was a change to see no mosques, but Christian churches everywhere with their bells ringing. After an early breakfast we prepared to go ashore and found a Greek gentleman, representative here of the British and Foreign Bible Society, was waiting to welcome us and show us round. We got straight through the customs, merely giving up our passports, and walked for quarter of an hour to the station, past much shipping, whence an electric train took us in quick time through to Athens. After walking for a few minutes through some of the splendid streets, we hired two gharries (the Johnstons accompanied us) to take us up to the Acropolis. Being Easter Monday, the Greeks had closed all their main antiquities, which was an immense disappointment to us and seemed an absurd idea. However, near the Acropolis we alighted and walked to near the top, finally being able to look at some of the ruins between the bars of massive gates. The little Temple of Victory was the most conspicuous object. Descending a little we bore to the right and ascended Areopagus or Mars Hill by the ancient steps, probably the same ones used by St Paul. Later we ascended the long slope to the memorial to Philopappus whence a splendid view of the Acropolis was obtained.

We had perforce to hurry on, and after I had got more carriages we descended to the well-preserved Theseum and then back and down again to the mighty pillars which remain of the temple of Olympian Zeus, calling on the way for a glimpse into the little theatre of Herodius Atticus where three artists were at work. Having time and inclination for a little lunch we returned to the station but found nearly everything closed for the holiday! I foraged and found one promising place but on entering we found it sold nothing except bread and milk – a kind of soured milk being their substitute for butter. However we were taken on to a little underground café run by a Smyrna refugee where we got cakes and Easter buns (a flat biscuit-like cake, very nice) and quite good ices which were most acceptable after the great heat of the day. Returning through a fine square where were palms we caught a train back to Piraeus and 'gharried' to the quay.

The boat left fairly punctually, and by three was outside the harbour and heading due south. From here the Acropolis was quite dwarfed by the picturesque crag of Lycabettus behind, while the great sweep of Hymettus was to the east. We kept steadily on past beautifully broken coast, first of the islands of Salamis and Aegina and then Cape Skyro while the eastern peninsula got further away and Cape Colonna just appeared in the haze. Past Cape Skyro we had a wonderful view of the narrow rugged island of Hydra with its precipitous cliffs. One wonderful inlet called the Mouth of Hades had sheer cliffs rising straight from the water to a height of hundreds of feet. Some of the most magnificent rock scenery we had struck was here. As that sank away in the sunset we passed inside the little islet of Belo Palo and continued in dead-calm sea and passed Cape Malea about midnight.

Tuesday 29 April Still a calm sea this morning and we were well past the last point of the 'Mulberry leaf' of Moroea and running obliquely away from the land. Away in the distance we could see the jagged snow-covered peak of Lycodemo. The boat was now quite full, many English and Americans having come on board at Piraeus, most of them probably having been there for the Byron centenary celebrations. It was a peaceful day, warm and with little wind, and at 12.30 we passed two small flat islands with a lighthouse on one of them. In the afternoon we ran past the island of Zante (on the right) with its miles of great sheer cliffs shining white and curving under at the bottom and with dozens of caves of all sizes and depths running in at the water's edge. Then crossing the strait which leads to the entrance of the Gulf of Corinth we encountered a considerable groundswell (which was not enough to cause inconvenience to anyone) and ran along the coast of the hillside of Cephalonia till darkness fell. (All these are the Ionian Islands.)

Wednesday 30 April We got early this morning to Corfu and anchored close to the big fort. A rather hazy, cloudy morning, which made the huge mountains of Albania on the east of the strait appear even bigger. Many boatmen, not extortionate, crowded on the boat and after breakfast the Johnstons and F and I went ashore and got an old car to take us round for two hours quite reasonably (here again we merely had to surrender our passports). He took us through the narrow streets of the town, over roads made of great blocks and very uneven, and out into the country. (The smell in the harbour and around the edge of the water was very objectionable.) Here also the roads were uncared for and full of holes; but the delight of the countryside, the richness of the fields and flowers and trees, made us forgive very easily the bumpy ride.

The whole land was well cultivated and men and women and children were hoeing on all sides and looked a healthy, happy race. In appearance they were all handsome, F being particularly smitten by some of the girls, much to Mrs Johnston's amusement. High mountains of striking shapes were ahead and we ascended through villages where there were many women dressed in bright colours with their queer headdress, and where sturdy children ran after us offering handfuls of roses and often throwing them into the car.

Up still further we went right to the first of the hilltops, where was the Achilleion, the palace of Kaiser Bill. Through the great gates we could see some scores of boys, refugees, cared for by the American Near East Relief. A gardener, taking us in tow, led us past the front of the building into the wonderful garden where, amongst luxurious palms, are fine statues of Phryne, Achilles and Lord Byron. Here is a glorious view (over the tops of some cypress trees growing beneath us) of Corfu island and the town with its forts, the great Albanian hills beyond, and the straits, one bay of which swept nearly to our feet. Beside the palms, there were flowers in profusion, mostly roses, bush as well as climbers, in full bloom. We were allowed to pick what we wanted and went on between the two statues of athletes, duplicates of which flank one entrance to our Embankment Gardens, into the Garden of the Muses where are more classical statues and the busts of many ancient philosophers among whom is included Shakespeare.

A descent by two terraces brought us round past more statues to the entrance again. Before leaving we were shown over the inside of the palace where are many wonderful rooms richly ornamented, some good pictures, many inferior, some striking ornaments and statuettes, and some harmonious ceiling paintings (some of the ceilings have fallen through a recent earthquake). There are two fine bathrooms with marble baths, that of the Kaiserin having good statuary. In one room under a picture of the Kaiser in yachting rig was his big brown armchair which we all tried and found comfortable. We also sat at his writing table which has a saddle instead of a seat.

Resuming our journey we ran down through enchanted scenery and after travelling through lovely country where were hundreds of ancient olive trees and cypresses and figs and oranges we arrived at another beauty spot looking out over an inlet of the sea containing a picturesque little island with the steep and wooded hills as a background. After lemonades at a little outdoor place there we returned, ran along a good promenade to the finely placed citadel, looking inaccessible on a rock jutting out to sea, and then walked by the rather plain, yellow Palais Royal back to the quay whence two cheery singing boatmen rowed us to the *Praqa.*

Soon after two we left the place and steamed northwards up the channel keeping close to the Albanian side and noting the difference between the rich fertility of Corfu and the bleakness of the opposite mountains. Just after we passed the northern end of Corfu we ran slowly into a bay on the mainland and anchored just off the dull little town of Santi Quaranta. Tracks led from the town up steep slopes of two hills, barren and grey, on the top of which were a broken Byzantine church and the remains of a fort. (In the Byzantine church were forty pious men in the early days, and under the church are said to be their cells. These were the forty saints after whom the town was named – Santi Quaranta.) One quite good road leading up between the two hills is the main thoroughfare beginning here and going right across the Balkan peninsula to Salonica. This is the only port apparently for all Albania, although it is so tiny, and all stores etc. for Janina, the capital, come here. A few ships came alongside without any badgering of boatmen, but, hearing that we should not sail till seven, F and I after tea decided to go ashore for a while to pass the time and were joined by Miss Daniel and a young American. (The boatmen here charged only 5 Italian lire each return – about half what most boatmen elsewhere had charged.)

It was a quaint temporary sort of place with two fairly good streets parallel and then the rough hillside on which a few huts were scattered with no road to join them. A few houses were good but most of the shops were in wooden shacks. We saw several Albanian soldiers in khaki with football stockings and long shoes with turned-up toes and pom-poms on them. Also some weird characters from the hills with white fez-caps above their bearded faces, and long black sheepskin cloaks and turned-up shoes. In a little post office we scribbled one or two of our Corfu PCs and got them stamped and postmarked, and then had to take them ourselves to the ship as the rest of the mail was on board her! Our prowl showed us the remains of a wide fortification, semi-circular with the flat side against the sea.

We sailed thence at 6.45. At night I had a chat with the manager of the Antwerp Museum, M. François Franck, who was one of our passengers. Incidentally, it being a very dark night, we watched the sparkling points of soft light from thousands of jellyfish which seemed to carry a phosphor-escent gleam which they could turn off or on at will.

Thursday 1 May 5.45 entered Brindisi harbour, a wide deep one which enabled us to get right up to the quayside. Set in the flattest kind of landscape, part of the harbour is surrounded by quite luxurious trees. F and I went ashore early and visited the town, finding it clean and spacious – very different from our expectations. (Exchange now just over 96 lire to the pound sterling.) At the poste restante we heard that rooms were reserved for us at Alexandra House, Naples; and after getting straight through the customs, and getting some cash at Thomas Cook's on the quay, we (with the Johnstons) took a carriage for a short drive through the streets, before taking a pea-soup lunch at the station and catching the twelve o'clock train. For the first part it was a fascinating journey through broad, flat lands of the

Hill man of albania
Santi Quaranto
30 Ap. 24.

Sketch of hill man with fez

most fertile kind, growing every kind of produce, with miles of olive orchards and vineyards and figs and almonds.

On the first hill we saw was perched picturesquely the white town of Ostuni and thereafter we ran through other villages and towns all clean and fresh and white set in rich green scenery and stopped at many places: Monopoli, Polignano, Trani, Barletta etc. (Bari was the first big place. It and one or two others were seaside towns, some perched on low cliffs.) For hours we followed the coast with the blue Adriatic in view all the time and got our first impression of the wonder of Italian colouring and landscape character. (There was a gorgeous sunset, the effect of which was heightened by a local thunderstorm over the peninsula which makes the 'spur' on Italy's 'heel'.)

We were late running into Foggia where we had to change, and it was a blow to find we had missed our train on to Naples and had to wait till midnight for the next. Our entire lack of Italian was a great handicap, but we managed to get a fair dinner in the buffet and rested on comfortable seats in the waiting room. For one hour a friendly station official (ex-soldier with one artificial leg) took us round the town and soon after midnight we left.

Friday 2 May After getting more than four hours' good sleep I woke to find we were just past Benevento running down a winding valley of great beauty at the foot of some of the Neapolitan Apennines. The stream in the wooded valley was the Calore. After passing Ponte Casalduni the scenery gradually got quieter and richer. We dropped down for many miles till a towered town was passed and then we struck the plain at Caserta and ran through very fertile flat country till Naples was reached. (None of us had ever before seen such wonderful cultivation as here. All kinds of cereals and vegetables are grown; and frequently in large areas trees are planted in even rows in the middle of a crop of corn or potatoes etc., and vines planted beside the trees with their runners strung like festoons between the trees to a height of 10 feet or more.)

Two gharries took us right through the town to our hotel Alexandra House (Via Caracciolo 14) on the northern (or western) front (English – cheap prices and clean – food adequate but not elaborate). F and I visited the GPO and Cook's in the morning, and in the afternoon we all (and the Johnstons) went up to St Elmo (St Martin) for tea on the little terrace of the restaurant. Returning by the funicular we walked through the Via Roma and through the great Arcade.

Saturday 3 May This being my last weekday with M and F a full day was planned and M and I went to Cook's at 8 a.m. and joined a party (many of whom were Germans) for the Vesuvius and Pompeii trip. Auto to the Antica Stagione and a bumpy ride before we changed and got on to Cook's own train which immediately began the ascent of the mountain. Part of the way another car pushed us up a steep slope (cog-wheel) to the Eremo Hotel. (We were interested to see the edge of the ancient volcano, Somma or Vesevo, which rings the present volcano irregularly. This was the volcano which destroyed Pompeii – Vesuvius having later sprung up inside the gigantic crater of the old one.) On each side we could see the wide lava fields which had run down during the last one or two eruptions, and we also saw the great walls erected in one long valley to stem the flow of deposit and save the villages lower down. Five minutes beyond the Eremo Hotel we changed trains and entered a funicular carriage which took us at an angle of 50 to 60 degrees up the long final slope. A short walk took us to the edge of the crater – a jagged ring of considerable circumference – whence we could look down on to the distorted plain of lava inside, part of which was a fresh black with streaks running through of glowing red where it was still molten from an outburst two days ago.

In the middle of the lava was a smallish cone, the real volcano, from which were belching clouds of dense white or sulphur-yellow smoke accompanied by continual rumbling or fitful explosions. At various points round the outer edge steam was rising, and I was interested, after slithering down a good way through the ashes (about halfway to the lava lake), to scrape away some of the side and see steam arise from there also. The descent was uneventful. At the Eremo Hotel we had a good lunch and met F who had missed the party earlier on, and descending by the same route caught another train to Pompeii.

From the station we entered straight into the excavated town and spent a fascinating afternoon walking through the straight streets with their huge blocks with the wheel-marks clear-showing on them and the frequent stepping stones (which suggested periodical floods) from pavement to pavement (like Naples the paving here is of huge blocks of lava, much like limestone). In many houses were sculptures and paintings, mostly very decadent in style and outlook but well preserved in colour (the house of the Vettii – two bachelors – was the most sumptuous and had some of the most vicious work).

It was easy in imagination to people this place and to see the crowds in the Forum and the Temple of Apollo and the Basilica and the great amphitheatre which has such a magnificent outlook over the mountains to the south. The heat was great but M stuck it all well and after a bumpy ride back to Naples on the electric railway we did a little shopping and returned to Alexandra House for dinner.

Sunday 4 May A quiet day. With F in the morning to the Italian Methodist church. Had quarter of an hour's chat with him in French and saw the great chapel, too big for its present congregation. On to the Presbyterian church, left F there and continued for service with M at the Church of England. A quiet afternoon and then an evening and supper with Mr Rae at his house above Bertolini's. The Johnstons accompanied us.

Monday 5 May M and F came to see me off by the 10.15 train to Rome (fare from Naples to Victoria – second class – was just about £6). A blazing-hot journey through very rich hilly scenery. Arrived Rome 3.15. Mr Bradford met me and we taxied to the Baldassari Pensione (Piazza di Monte d'Oro) where I put my stuff. Had tea together and then I went off and spent some time in the Forum and climbed the Palatine Hill and saw the oldest Christian church in Rome just beside the ruins of Caligula's palace. Returned past Titus's Arch and the Basilica of Constantine and back past the great memorial to King Vittorio Emanuele to meet Mr Bradford in the Via Umberto after which we went to a little restaurant to dine. Between that and bedtime he took me on a long walk through the ancient ghetto to Michelangelo's bridge and through many of the main streets. (We visited the Trevi Fountain. I threw in a halfpenny which according to tradition ensures my return to Rome some day.[4])

Tuesday 6 May Very hot, but I got through much sightseeing. First to Cook's in the Piazza di Spagna and then over a bridge and past the Palace of Justice and the great round massive Castel San Angelo to St Peter's. After taking one or two pictures in the great courtyard approach with its fountains I went inside and saw many fine paintings and some Michelangelo sculptures and the tomb of St Peter. Then I walked round the

---

[4] AEB did indeed return to Rome in 1934.

outside of the building to the Vatican galleries where was much lovely sculpture and painting. Finding at length the Sistine Chapel I spent some while with the Michelangelo ceiling paintings and the great *Last Judgment* decoration on the east wall.

After lunch in the same restaurant as yesterday I went up to the great memorial to Vittorio Emanuele with its many steps and columns and saw the coffin of Italy's unknown soldier. Then round to Trajan's forum and his amazing carved column and later went again to the Trevi Fountain. Then a taxi took me to the huge remains of the baths of Caracalla with its three divisions on the men's and the women's sides for hot, tepid and cold baths (the Romans understood and used steam heating). Then the taxi took me back to the Colosseum where I roamed awhile before returning to the Via delle Capelle to meet Mr Bradford. He took me by gharry up to the Pincio Gardens where there was a lovely view over Rome. Returning to the Pensione Baldassari time was very short and in the hurry to get clear I forgot several clothes which, however, M and F picked up later. A friend of Mr B's had kept me a seat in the train, so all went well. Travelling through the night we ran into heavy rain.

Wednesday 7 May Arrived Turin in time for breakfast in the station buffet. Pouring rain, but spent a jolly time for four hours through the long arcades. Posted the key of the house back to the Pensione Baldassari and bought a tin whistle for Cox.[5] Rejoined next train for Paris and shared my carriage with three brawny Italians who spoke broad Scots! Rain continued but in spite of it we were able to appreciate the delightful Alpine scenery through which we passed before and after the Mont Cenis tunnel and up to Modane (we were over a quarter of an hour in tunnel). Was able to get some sleep during the night. Stopped at Dijon and one or two other places.

Thursday 8 May Woke to find very flat scenery near Paris and arrived at the Gare de Lyon at about 7 a.m. Taxi to the Hotel Jacob and soon was in my room at *petit déjeuner*. Afterwards walked past the Louvre, through the Tuileries gardens to Cook's (opposite Madeleine). A strong wind was blowing and it was positively cold. Later went into the Salon for the day.

---

[5] Cox was one of AEB's artist friends, with whom he shared a studio.

Some very fine work. The paintings seemed not so good as our RA but the sculpture infinitely better. Some of it was magnificent.

After tea called on F.W. Moss (my cabin companion on the *Praqa*) who took me out to a good lobster dinner in the Boulevard des Italiens and then on to see the *Folies-Bergère*. A most spectacular show, far more extravagant than our music-hall shows but not so attractive. The place seemed mostly full of English and Americans. Anaglyph spectacles were used for one scene.

Friday 9 May Spent the morning at the Louvre, saw the *Venus* and went through the older Spanish, Flemish and Italian schools' galleries. Had lunch outside and called on Mr Allen. Met also Mr and Miss Gaskin. Back to Louvre and went through the more modern galleries. Back to Rue Roquepine for supper with the Allens and the Gaskins and two Welsh people from Llandudno. Mr Allen came with me to the Gare St Lazare and soon after eight I was en route for Dieppe. In the carriage was a young fellow looking over some sketches. He turned out to be on the staff of a Glasgow paper and was called Robin Millar. At Dieppe a porter got me straight through the customs and on to the boat where I was given a very cosy berth in the second-class saloon and was in it and asleep before the ship was far from land. Was called at Newhaven and got on deck in time to see the boat glide nose first into the quay till it fetched up with a bump. Again nothing was opened in the customs, a steward taking me straight through and getting a good seat in the London train. Millar joined me and we ran up in good style with the country looking lovely in the early light. Masses of primroses were on all the embankments. Reaching Victoria about 6.30 Millar and I had a wash and mooched around till about eight when a café opened for breakfast and we fell to. That over, he continued his journey to Scotland while I returned to my old digs at 37 Bedford Place, and afterwards went to tackle the mountain of letters that had accumulated for ten weeks at the studio.

LIST OF AEB'S ARTWORK

Abbreviations

In these lists of artwork, as chronicled by AEB in his notebooks, he used the following abbreviations:

Ad. Mag. *Adventure Magazine*; **A.P.** Amalgamated Press; **BS** Byron Studios; **B.S.** *Bystander*; **Cardigan P.** Cardigan Press; **dec.** decoration; **D.M.** *Daily Mirror*; **D.M.T.** Division Mechanical Transport; **dbl spr** double-page spread; **drg, drwg** drawing; **Eve B. Eve-Brit** *Eve and Britannia*; **G.O.P.** *Girls' Own Paper*; **G.O.S.** *Girls' Own Stories*; **G.W.R.** Great Western Railway; **hdg** heading; **illus.** illustration; **L. Calling** *London Calling*; **L.M.** *London Mail* or *Lyons Mail*; **L.O.** *London Opinion*; **M. Post** *The Morning Post*; **O.B.** *Outward Bound*; **P. & S.** *Pip and Squeak*; **P.S., P. Show** *Passing Show*; **Pic. W.** *Pictorial Weekly*; **S. Chron.** *Sunday Chronical*; **Sov. Mag.** *Sovereign Magazine*; **S.P.C.K.** Society for the Propagation of Christian Knowledge; **R.** Rupert; **R.T.S.** Religious Tract Society; **sk.** sketch/es; **S. Exp.** *Sunday Express*; **S. Pict.** *Sunday Pictorial*; **T.B., T-B** *Tit-Bits*; **W.O.** *Woman's Own*; **W. Weekly** *Woman's Weekly*; **X** author presumes X indicates an unsold artwork.

Works, Publications and Fees									
1915		£.	s.	d		Russian bear	X		
Feb.	Investment of Cracow (*Cartoon*)	1.	1.	0			£.	s.	d
Feb.	Spider & fly (*War Pictures Weekly*)		7.	6	Sep.	Route march	X		
June	Garibaldi (*Passing Show*)	1.	5.	0		Collar	1.	1.	0
Aug.	Looker on (*London Opinion*)		10.	6		Commer		10.	6
Sept.	Looker on (*London Opinion*)		10.	6	Oct.	Right – wrong	1.	1.	0
						Interpreter		10.	6
1916					Nov.				
Jan.	Looker on (*London Opinion*)		10.	6	8	Men we have not met (3)	1.	1.	0
Works for *Blighty*					**1918**				
1917					Feb.				
July					20	Civil answer	1.	1.	0
13	Inoculation					Dry land		10.	0
	Tow home	1.	1.	0		Ditched lorry	1.	10.	0
23	Joy ride		10.	6	27	Army grub		15.	0

		£	s.	d
	Allies crumplin'	1.	1.	0
Mar.				
22	Orion	1.	1.	0
	Caterpillar	1.	1.	0
May				
28	Bullets	1.	1.	0
	Looky-zee	1.	1.	0
June				
9	Kite	1.	1.	0
	Fretworker	1.	1.	0
July				
20	Centipede	1.	1.	0
	Capitulate	1.	1.	0
Oct.				
3	Real warr		15.	6
	Red 'ats	1.	1.	0
31	Strike	1.	1.	0
	San fairy ann	2.	2.	0
	Still in force		10.	6

1919

Jan.

6	King Albert	2.	2.	0
	Twins		10.	6
	Aladdin	X		
Mch.				
7	Amateurs (held over till Xmas)	1.	11.	6
	Mouthful			
	Did he? (halftone)			
	Jerry-built	5.	14.	0
12	Easter golfer			
24	Young shoes			
	Social hatmosphere			
Apr.				
20	Red Sea	3.	3.	0
	Bazaar (held over)			
	Chick (held over)			
May				
18	Dangerous links			
	Intelligent dog	3.	3.	0
June				
10	'oop			
	Bogey	3.	3.	0
18	Golf (sandhills) (held over)			
Aug.				
7	Side of a house			
	Hair dye	4.	14.	6
13	Mother engaged			
	Captain . . . modest	1.	11.	6
	Adamant			
	Baby – same pattern	1.	11.	6
27	Gwladys			
	Loss of memory	1.	1.	0
	Sundial	1.	11.	6
Sept.				
4	Awful wedded wife	1.	11.	6

	River scene (held over)			
		£	s.	d
15	Autumn tints	1.	1.	0
	Unmuzzled dog	1.	11.	6
Oct.				
1	Windfalls	2.	2.	0
	Filleted egg	1.	1.	0
14	Noah's Ark – rations			
	Cold missionary	3.	3.	0
17	White elephants	1.	11.	6
29	Christmas tree	1.	12.	6
Nov.				
3	Shower	1.	11.	6
12	Mistletoe – (brother)	1.	11.	6
14	Narrow escape – smoker	1.	11.	6
28	Anti-waist campaign	3.	3.	0

1920

Apr.   *Blighty* went into liquidation

Byron Studios

1920

Jan.

5   Rough (B.S.) 'Sergt. Mullins' poem for
St Dunstan's

6   3 sketches for 'Magpie' poem by E. Le Breton
Martin possibly for 'Royal'

7   Joke 'Sweet-shop' Windsor

10   2 'kiddy' drawings for colour printing B.S.

13   Half page joke for *Windsor* 'Curate &
old man'

15   Roughs for Persil soap

19   Joke roughs: 'Which daughter do you
recommend?' and
'Congratulations on twins'

20   Joke roughs: 'Quickest way to station'
and 'Tell her this very minute'

Feb.

2   Folding ad. (colour) for St Dunstan's
Rough for Egall Custard Powder

7   Joke: 'Suitor-profiteer for Passing Show

11   Story by P.G. Wodehouse to illustrate
for the 'Grand'

12   Advert for Siemen's

16   2 roughs for *Lyons Mail* cover. Published April.

18   Roughs for St Dunstan's poster-stamps etc.

19   Roughs for N.I.B. and pen sketch for Mr Cross

20   Covers & endpapers for kiddy books for
Renwick of Otley, Budge & Betty

21   Small illus. for *Tit-Bits*

Mar.

2   Small sketch 'Mother and child in hall' N.I.B.

3   2 sketches for Week-end novels

5   Sketch for *World's Pictorial News* for Mr Cross
Heading *Tit-Bits* 'In reply to yours'

9   2 illus. Family reader for Mr Cross, W.P.N.

10	4 illus. for Week-end novels
12	Charcoal illus. for *Woman's Life*
22	Joke for the *Captain*
23	Sketch 'Cheetah & Indian'. Not published.
24	Billiard poster for St Dunstan's
25	Jungle sketch for Week-end novels
	Serial 'Marigold Maine' for W.E.N.
26	2 uprights for *Family Reader*

Apr.

7	2 roughs *Lyons Mail* (May)
8	Rough for Am . . . (text illegible) belt
13	Drawing 'Cheetah' again
17	Cover for packet Helm chocolat-au-lait
20	Wash drg – redraw – (Indian etc.) for T.M.R. Whitwell Children's Paper
22	Roughs for *Captain*
24	Rough 'A tailor in Edinburgh'
27	2 illus. *Family Reader*
29	Illus. World's Pict. News
30	*Lyons Mail* cover (Cricket)

May

1	Sketch for Spring's Lemon Cheese
5	Illus. *Lyons Mail* short story (June)
	Hdg *Penny Mag.* story
6	Tennis cover *Lyons Mail*. Published.
7	Illus. for serial *World's Pict. News*
10	Sketches 'Park Drive' for Tom Cottrell (in Studio)
11	Altered 'Profiteer' sketch for Tom Cottrell
12	Sketch Girl-bather *Lyons Mail* cover. Published July.
13	Hdg *W. Tel.* Summer No.
	Colour rough Egall powder packet
14	6 small pen views for *War-Cry*
15	Illus. for serial *World's Pictorial News*
19	Halftone illus. for serial in *Womens' Life* (for MacMichael)
	Altered drawing by R.H. Brock etc.
20	Illus. W.P.N. serial
25	Colour page 'The Children's Lord's Prayer'
31	Half-page joke for *Windsor*

June

2	5 Silhouette illus. for *Penny Magazine* and other Cassell's work
4	Serial illus. for W.P.N.
5	Small illus. for *Penny Magazine*
7	Rough for Lyons tea poster. Not published.
9	Retouching photos for *Times Supplement*
	Joke 'Club bore' for *Windsor*
11	W.P.N. illus.
15	Heading for *Girl's Own Stories*
16	Illus. for *Red Magazine* (Tin Gods)
17	Illus. for W.P.N. serial

July

| 5 | Rough for Newnes pocket novels |

6	Booklet cover for Butcher's cameras
7	Roughs for *Lyons Mail* (August) Published cover.
10	Illus. for Cassell (upright)
12	Small sketches (figures) for *Outward Bound*
13	4 small illus. for Reg. Rigby's poem
14	Work for A.C. Cross
19	Sept. cover for *Lyons Mail.* Published.
	Roughs for 'Eyes for the Dead' story for *Outward Bound*
21	Colour rough (picnic) for Pocock's Potted Meats
23	Illus. serial in W.E.N. (Bentley Manor)
	2 pen roughs for 3 col. *Times* ads for cakes (Lyons Dundee) from pencil roughs by Oakdale
24	October rough for *Lyons Mail.* Published.
26	Xmas designs for Selfridge's bags
27	Black and white drawing from Moccasin boot poster for lantern slide
29	Rough for page ad. for Lyons for *Overseas Daily Mail*
31	Altered drg for Pratt's spirit (begun by Ernest)

Aug.

3	Rush of cheap stuff for Hulton's (W.E.N. etc.) – provincial printers' strike
4	Hulton's work – 5 small illus. and heading
6	Illus. & hdg for Stacpoole's story 'The Return' for *Outward Bound*
11	Double half-page illus. for 'The Return'
12	Cover for Dream-book (Hulton's)
13	Joke rough (bathing dress after Councillor Clarke's anti-mixed bathing campaign)
16	Illus. 'Not such a fool as he looks' Short story for *Red Magazine*
17	Put figure into ad. for Spring's Lemon Cheese
18	Rough for floor polish
19	3 little illus. for Hulton's
	2 tiny roughs for Daimler 6-cyl.
24	5 illus. for W.E.N. etc.
30	Rough for Int. Adv. Exhibn. at White City
31	Altering drawings by Miss Leicester

Sept.

1	Illus. for Newnes Comic Annual
2	Hdg & 2 illus. for Newnes Comic Annual 'From the diary of a minx'
3	Old-fashioned fashion drawing etc.
4	Joke 'Profiteer – French maid' for *Passing Show*
7	Finished someone else's cartoon for Scotch Temperance paper
8	Little figures and heading for *Scouts Annual*
10	*Lyons Mail* November cover
	Little (autumn) hdg for Selfridge's ad.

13   Retouched photo of blinded French soldier
      Small illus. to a Dudeney problem for
         Strand Xmas No.
14   3 small sketches for *All-Sports Weekly*
15   4 Art School litho. posters reproduced in
         the 'Studio'
16   Roughs for Newnes heading (*Tit-Bits*)
      Specimen illus. for Schoolgirls story
17   Border for *Outward Bound*
18   Sketch of 35th D.M.T. [Division Mechanical
         Transport] Company sign in Gt War
         Exhibition at Crystal Palace
20   2 small sk for *Boy's Sporting Paper*
      2 hdgs for *Tit-Bits* (Editor's page)
21   Halftone illus. 'A boy in the fields of
         Bethlehem' for *Outward Bound*
25   Hdg 'Who's Who & Why' for *Tit-Bits*
27   1 illus. W.P.N. etc.
29   Small group ad. 'What shall we do with
         our boy?' for?
30   Covers for Hulton's 'Beauty book' and
         'Dance book' sim. to 'Dream book'

Oct.
1   Hdg for 'The Chillerby Scoop' for Xmas
         No. of *Weekly Telegraph*
2   Illus. for above story
4   Roughs for *Lyons Mail* Xmas No.
6   1 illus. heading for *W. Tel.*
7   2 *Lyons Mail* small roughs (Dec.)
9   Rough for N.I.B. border and retouching
         print
11   Roughs for 'Ikillem' insect powder
      Border for picture by MacMichael for *The
         Beacon* (N.I.B.)
12   Joke drg for Sheffield *W. Tel.* (Young
         doctor & fiancee)
13   Series small sk for book on Jiu Jitsu and
         misc. advice etc. (Encyclopaedia)
16   Little drawings for Fru-Ju drinks
      Retouched photo of old native and boy
         scout
18   Rough for cover for *Beacon* (Xmas)
19   Roughs for Brilliantine
22   Heading and tiny illus. for *Penny Magazine*
26   Bleach out for 'Little Folks' & for photo
         of Mr Moulding – Heading for Home
28   Rough for *Penny Magazine* cover (mostly
         script)
29   Pussyfoot cartoon for Scottish Temperance
         paper (Canute)

Nov.
2   Joke rough (little girl & cat)
3   Rough for Phillip's rubber soles and heels
4   Rough for *Lyons Mail* (Dec.) of Cenotaph
      Small illus. for Cassell's (The women that
         men hate)

6   Joke rough 'Profiteer & piano'
10   Cover for W.E.N. book of Christmas
         cheer
11   Halftone illus. for Cassell's Sat. Journal. Not
         published.
12   Retouched small head for Direct Photo
         Ltd., also boy's head for ad.
15   Roughs *Lyons Mail* (Jan.)
16   Rough for Cassell's *Sat. Journal* cover
      Heading for *Girl's Own Stories*
17   Illus. for *G.O.S.*
      Illus. for *Red Magazine* story 'Making his
         name famous' by James Barr
18   Joke rough 'Girl people look round at'
19   Rough for Scooter ad.
      Bleach out photo for Hulton's
20   2 sketches Philip's maps
24   2 small drawings for G.O.S.
26   2 illus. for 'Ideas'
      Joke drg 'Train with 5 min. start'
         L.O. Published 18.12.20.
27   Hdg for Cassell's mag. (Love – Sometimes)
30   Bart Kennedy story for *Outward Bound*
      Altered 5 drawings for Campbell Cross

Dec.
2   Specimen for Newnes cheap weeklies
3   Little sketch for Newnes Pocket novels
7   Roughs for *Lyons Mail*
8   Put figures into an ad. for the Trocadero
9   Jan. cover for *Lyons Mail* (fox)
10   Hdgs for Newnes Pocket novels
13   Small designs for Cassell's 'Children's
         Encyclopaedia'
14   Altered drawing for Cottrell
15   Headings for 'Ideas' etc
16   Cartoon rough for *Comrades Journal*
         (Gt War)
18   Retouched photo for Mr Marr (Georgian
         & Caucasian people) for O.B.
21   Halftone Philip's maps
24   Drawing for Campbell Cross for G.O.S.
      Altered 2 covers by R.H. Brock for
         Newnes Adventure novels
28   Little sketches for Cassell

1921
Jan.
3   Spec. pen & ink sketch for Ovaltine
4   Headings for *Ideas*
5   Joke (old gent & toffee) for Cassell
6   Rough for *Lyons Mail* (Feb.) Seascape
         cover
7   Joke drg for *Windsor* (Anonymous baby)
8   Landscape drg for children's puzzle
      2 silhouettes for *Penny Magazine*
18   Joke drg (Artist & yokel) for L.O.

21	3 (half-page) illus. to 'Treasure Royal' for Cassell's
24	Kiddy & squirrel sketch for Cassell (in brown & green)
27	Made up plot for more kiddy stuff for Cassell
28	Rough for *Boy's Paper* (cover)
29	Silhouettes for *Penny Magazine*

Feb.

1	Coloured cover for Treasure Trove library
2	Tiny sketches (N.I.B.) to help Mr Marr
3	Fairy Map for endpaper of children's book (Oxford Press)
7	2 drawings for W.T., heading for 'Ideas'
10	Drawing of Jurybox for Blue-band Margarine Fashion drg of overcoat for Mr Holden
11	Illus. for W.E.N.
12	Rough for Cassell's technical books W.T. Novels cover 'The White Hen'
15	Joke rough (Professor & Costen)
16	Cover (W.T.) for 'The Greater Claim'
18	Drawing 'Spring is Coming' for Passing Show
21	Finished 'Merry Moments' drawings for Mr Jenner
22	George Robey's Annual 'Riddle of the Sands'
24	Joke drawing 'pie' for Windsor 2 silhouettes for *Penny Magazine* (What a husband wants)
25	*Lyons Mail* cover (Washing Day). Published.
28	Illus. for *Red Magazine* & also tiny initial sketch for Cassell's

Mar.

1	Roughs for 6 headings for Cassell's children's book of knowledge
2	Illus. for *Red Magazine* (seashore) Began to re-draw Cottrell's sketch for *Gaiety*. Not published.
9	Page drawing for *Gaiety*
10	Finished page for 'Puck' for Jenner
12	Rough sketches for N.I.B. pamphlet Drawings for John Mackay (Kolacafe) (Knights in armour)
14	3 roughs for Cassell's headings
19	Drawing for Selfridges to advertise pyjamas
22	Headings for W.E.N. – *Lyons Mail* etc.
30	Roughs for *Lyons Mail* (May)
31	Small halftone diagram sketches for Cassell's (children's book of knowledge)

Apr.

1	4-part comic for 'Bubbles' Diagram sketch (Red Indian outfit) for Cassell's
4	Line illus. for 'Chums'
5	Joke for W.T.
8	Merry Moments front page (for Mr Jenner)

| 14 | 2 illus. for *Outward Bound* |
| 15 | Illus. for 'Bubbles' for Miss Balchin Drawing of Prince of Wales' head |

36 Whitefriars Street
1921

Apr.		**£.**	**s.**	**d**
18	Chalk illus. 3 Chinese figures for *Tit-bits* BS 947	2.	2.	0
19	Head of Napoleon – crayon – *Tit-bits*	1.	1.	0
	2nd. line drg – 'Tai-hoa' – *Outward Bound* begun at BS	2.	1.	9
22	'Usco' drawing. *Lyons Mail* BS 738 No. 4	2.	12.	6
25	Chalk illus. for 'The Beast-Man' *Tit-bits* BS 198	2.	2.	0
	Line illus. 'Competition' *Red Magazine* BS 953	1.	11.	6
29	Roughs for N.I.B. Folder 'Jack Wilson, Farm Hand & Hero' BS 1046	X		

May				
2	Pen sketch (T-B) Man under Water 1054	2.	2.	0
4	Roughs for 2 T-B cartoons 'Tip-cart' and 'Papa's lost keys' Ideas C.C. Stretton	X		
5	T-B crayon illus BS 1080 (Girl kneeling)	2.	2.	0
	T-B crayon illus BS 1093 (Man & girl on cliff)	2.	8.	0
6	2 Set Comic for 'Bubbles' (Merlin & Hive)	1.	10.	0
7	Pen drg. Mackay's Mr Veryfit 1078	1.	1.	0
	Pencil rough ditto (Golfing) 1078			
9	Silhouette 2 men BS 1122	2.	2.	0
10	ditto altered			
	2 roughs for cover of 'The British Legion' BS 1032	X		
11	Roughs for heading and illus to first instalment 'Concerning this Woman' T-B BS 1144			
	4-part Merlin Comic, spade & pail BS 1125	1.	10.	0
12	T-B line illus Cobra etc. BS 1166	2.	2.	0
17	T-B Serial illus (1) BS 1144	2.	2.	0
	Butterfly drg for Label BS 1205		17.	6
18	2 sketches for T-B serial heading BS 1144	1.	12.	6
20	T-B serial illus (2) BS 1144	2.	2.	0
	3 silhouettes 'The Archdeacon's daughter' Cassell's Mag. BS 1222	3.	3.	0
23	Cartoon 'Drat that Cat' (idea by Evens) for Popular View BS 1232	1.	1.	0

		£	s	d
24	12 roughs Cassell's 'Words & their origins' Children's Encyc. BS 1267			
	3 roughs *Lyons Mail* cover			
27	4-part, Molly & Peeko BS 1290	1. 10.	0	
	T-B serial illus (3) BS 1144	2. 2.	0	
30	6 small sketches Cassell's Children's Encyclopaedia BS 1267	2. 2.	0	
	Roughs for tennis article (T-B) BS 1308			
31	5 pen sketches tennis article (T-B) BS 1308	2.. 10.	0	
	Children & goat, heading M.M. BS (?) (The Runaways)	8. 0.	0	
June				
2	T-B serial illus (4) BS 1339	2. 2.	0	
3	4-part Molly & Peeko (Soapsuds in teapot)	1. 10.	0	
6	*Lyons Mail* cover (Yachts) BS 1277	X		
	T-B serial illus (5) BS 1339	2. 2.	0	
8	Dentist joke (Windsor) BS 1306	2. 2.	0	
	4 roughs (Swimming) T-B BS 1394			
	5 roughs (Cricket) T-B BS 1396			
9	Alterations to 738 (4) (of April 22) & 1267 (May 30)			
10	4 pen sk (Swimming) T-B BS 1394	2. 0.	0	
	5 pen sk (Cricket) T-B BS 1396	2. 10.	0	
13	3 ad. drawings for Aerlite Bivouacs BS 1416 (B. D & E)	3. 18.	9	
	Cartoon rough (Lloyd George & traffic)	X		
14	2 roughs *Chums* title page	X		
15	T-B serial illus (6) BS 1449	2. 2.	0	
	Line drawing for Cottrell's serial 'Secrets' in 'Playtime' (Boy & Girl-cricket-pan)	X		
16	Joke drawing W.T. (Girl on floor & Aunt)	2. 2.	0	
17	T-B serial (7) BS 1449	2. 2.	0	
July				
6	T-B serial (8) BS 1449	2. 2.	0	
	Merlin 4 part BS 1560	1. 7.	6	
7	4 roughs Lipton's tea BS	1. 11.	6	
	2 roughs *Lyons Mail* (Autumn)			
11	T-B serial (9) BS 1449	2. 2.	0	
12	2 line illus, W.E.N. serial (1st instal.) BS 1663	2. 2.	0	
13	1 line heading W.E.N. serial BS 1679	18.	0	
14	3 small sketch (Punting) (2 used) BS 1668	1. 0.	0	
	Merlin 4 part BS 1664	1. 7.	6	
	Colour rough for Younger's Ale BS 1682			

		£	s	d
18	T-B serial (10) BS 1675	2. 2.	0	
	4-part Peeko (Seed cake) BS 1709	1. 7.	6	
20	4-part Merlin (School Cinema) BS 1723	1. 7.	6	
21	3 roughs W.T. Xmas No.	X		
	3 roughs cartoons for 'Popular View'			
22	Line drawing of Ku Klux Klansman BS 1758	1. 0.	0	
	T-B serial (11) BS 1675	2. 2.	0	
25	3 line cartoons 'Popular View' BS 1776	5. 5.	0	
27	4 part Merlin (Well & Aeroplane) BS 1773	1. 7.	6	
	4 part Peeko (Pram) BS 1772	1. 7.	6	
28	T-B serial 12th (last) illus. BS 1675	2. 2.	0	
Aug.				
2	4 roughs for 1st instal. & heading to T-B serial 'Vengeance' BS 1831	X		
3	2-colour cover 'Buffalo Bill' BS 1829	2. 2.	0	
4	4 more roughs 1st instal. and heading BS 1831			
5	Colour drawing 20″ × 30″ of boat & wave for Waterman's Ideal pen BS 1613	6. 18.	0	
8	2 roughs for 'Kijja' showcard BS 1864	X		
9	2 headings 'Vengeance' T-B, 2 illus. 1st instal. 'Vengeance' BS 1831	6. 6.	0	
11	4 part Peeko (Doll's clothes) BS 1871	1. 7.	6	
12	T-B serial 'Vengeance' 2nd BS 1899	2. 2.	0	
15	T-B serial 'Vengeance' 3rd BS 1899	2. 2.	0	
16	2 colour roughs Nestle's 'My hobby'			
	Heading for *Red Magazine* 'The eye of Sekhet' BS 1918	1. 5.	0	
17	T-B serial 'Vengeance' 4th BS 1889 (1899?)	2. 2.	0	
	Rough for Cassell's colour ad. BS 1928			
	Roughs (2) Politics (Popular View) or Bystander	X		
19	1 colour rough Younger's Ale (1682?)			
22	*Lyons Mail* cover (Sept) BS 1949	4. 4.	0	
	Page ad. (colour) Robinsons Patent Barley for Cassell BS 1928	2. 16.	0	
24	T-B serial 'Vengeance' 5th BS 1937	2. 2.	0	

		£.	s.	d
	2 roughs T-B Football Competition BS 1968			
	1 rough 'Crocodile' toothpaste			
25	1 rough (*Popular View*) St George etc. BS 1975			
	1 rough 'You ask we answer' T-B	X		
26	Cartoon (St George) (*Popular View*) BS 1975	4.	4.	0
	Wash drawing man's head (small) T-B BS 1981		10.	6
	Rough (*Popular View*) LI.G. as Drake BS 2004			
29	Finished Robin House sketch for F.M.L. BS 1997		10.	6
30	Page cartoon *Popular View* (LI.G. as drake) BS 2004	4.	4.	0
31	Illus. *Red Magazine* 'The Woman who helped' BS 1994	1.	11.	6
	3 roughs T-B Mascot Competition BS 2016			
Sep.				
1	2 roughs L.M. Oct. Cover	X		
	T-B serial 'Vengeance' 6th BS 1937	2.	2.	0
	Tiny figure for T-B football heading BS 1968	1.	0.	0
2	Colour rough 'The Quest' Reids Stout (?)	2.	2.	0
	Figure for T-B 'Mascots' heading BS 2016	1.	0.	0
	Younger's Ale rough (altered) BS 1682?			
6	3 roughs T-B 'Mascots' Competition BS 2070			
	Pencil rough 'Drummer Dyes' BS 2053	X		
7	Pencil rough Mackintosh's BS 2053	X		
	Pencil rough Pascall's BS 2053	X		
8	T-B Mascots headings (cat) BS 2070	1.	0.	0
	Pencil rough (Jacksons') BS 2053	X		
9	T-B Mascots heading (Dilliken) BS 2070	1.	0.	0
	T-B Mascots heading (Cat & horseshoe) BS 2070		17.	6
	Joke rough 'Autumn leaves'	X		
	T-B serial 'Vengeance' 7th BS 1937	2.	2.	0
12	1 rough *Lyons Mail* cover (Colleen)	X		
	1 rough Phosferine (pencil) BS 2092	X		
13	T-B serial 'Vengeance' 8th BS 1937	2.	2.	0

		£.	s.	d
15	Colour rough (Burglar) Reid's Stout (?)	2.	2.	0
16	Pencil rough (New Imperial Motor Cycle) BS 2144	X		
	Rough L.M. cover (Girl & pigtail)			
22	T-B serial 'Vengeance' 9th BS 2134	2.	2.	0
23	Line illus. 'Money for Nothing' (Red) BS 2149	1.	11.	6
	L.M. cover (Oct.) BS 2089	4.	4.	0
	Rough for 'Popular View' (Castle) BS 2212	X		
27	Halftone rough 'Eventide' (N.I.B.) BS 2194			
30	'Eventide' finished	2.	2.	0
Oct.				
3	Nestle's 'My hobby' poster figure BS 1908	8.	8.	0
4	T-B serial 'Vengeance' 10th BS 2134	2.	2.	0
5	W.T. heading 'A Couple of Crumpets' BS 2269	1.	17.	0
6	W.T. heading 'Journey's End in the Wilderness' BS 2269	1.	17.	0
7	T-B serial 'Vengeance' 11th BS 2134	2.	2.	0
	T-B serial 'Vengeance' 12th BS 2336	2.	2.	0
17	Halftone page for Paton's laces	5.	0.	0
	T-B serial 'Vengeance' 13th BS 2336	2.	2.	0
21	*Lyons Mail* (Nov.) Cover BS 2440	4.	4.	0
25	*Lyons Mail* Dec. roughs (2)			
27	T-B serial 'Vengeance' 14th BS 2336	2.	2.	0
Nov.				
7	Line cartoon 'Britain's Bulwark' BS 2551	3.	13.	6
	Line cartoon 'The Taskmaster' BS 2551	3.	13.	6
8	Showcard (colour) 'Youngers Ale' BS 1682	6.	16.	6
11	2 roughs *Lyons Mail* (December)	X		
	2 roughs Luntins tobacco			
	Joke for *Gaiety* 'Love – low tide' (R. 143) BS 2546 (or 3546?)	3.	3.	0
14	3 joke roughs R.144 & 167 & (D's barber)	X		
15	Joke rough (Bishop & barber)			
17	*Lyons Mail* cover (December)	4.	4.	0
18	Daily Mirror serial – Man's head Halftone	2.	2.	0
	2 joke roughs R.178 & 182	X		
23	2 joke roughs 56 (acc) & 88	X		

		£	s.	d
28	L.M. Jan. cover 2 roughs			
	Rough for Story Hour book (colour)			
	BS 2654	X		
Dec.				
5	Line ad. (Hulton's) Small & heading			
	'This Man & this Woman'			
	BS 2790	1.	2.	6
6	Heading 'Children & Woman at table'			
	(A.P.) BS 2764	1.	1.	0
8	L.M. cover (Jan.) BS 2828	4.	4.	0
	Ad. for McDougall's Flour (Mather			
	& Crowther) BS 2804	X		
9	*Red Magazine* illus. 'Devil-may-care			
	MacRae' BS 2756	1.11.		6
13	McDougall's ad. (see 8th) redrawn			
	BS 2804	2.12.		6
14	Heading and; 2 tiny sk. 'Sunday Night's			
	Supper' (A.P.) BS 2806	1.	1.	0
17	MacRae No. 2 *Red Magazine* BS 2926	1.11.		6
20	McDougall's ad. (No.2) BS 2804	2.12.		6
24	MacRae No. 3 *Red Magazine*			
	BS 2926	1.11.		6
28	'Dawn of Intelligence' W.T.			
	BS 2793	1.17.		0
30	Heading & 1 tiny sketch 'Vegetables'			
	(A.P.) BS 3000	1.	1.	0
31	MacRae No. 4 *Red Magazine*			
	BS 2926	1.11.		6
1922				
Jan.				
3	MacRae No. 5 *Red Magazine* BS 2926	1.11.		6
5	Line illus. 'Janiere du Dragon'			
	BS 2998	1.11.		6
7	T-B heading 'Trumps' BS 3073	1.	0.	0
10	Line illus. 'Long lost Treasure'			
	(Boy's Own Adventure Annual)			
	BS 2998	1.11.		6
	Rough for Skipper poster (bathing girls)			
11	*Lyons Mail* cover (Feb) BS 3117	4.	4.	0
12	Heading W.P. (Woman buying apples)			
	BS 3104	1.	1.	0
16	Drawing W.P. (2 children at table)			
	BS 3136	1.	1.	0
18	2 sketches & heading 'Everywoman's story'			
	BS 3158	3.	3.	0
20	MacRae No. 6 *Red Magazine* BS 3003	1.11.		6
24	Heading W.P. 'Poor old potatoes'	1.	1.	0
Feb.				
1	2 (Halftone) drawings 'Tamati's Revenge'			
	BS 2998	4.	4.	0
2	Trumps' heading T-B BS 3330	1.	0.	0
3	2 sk for L.M. cover (March)			
6	Line illus. 'Roberta's Mascot'			
	BS 3341		15.	0

		£	s.	d
7	Line illus. 'Fair Exchange' (*Chums*)			
	BS 3352	2.	2.	0
8	*Lyons Mail* (March) cover	4.	4.	0
13	Line illus. 'The leakage' (*Scout*)			
	BS 3403	1.	5.	0
15	Dedication page – Oxford Press			
	BS 3400			
17	Rough for cover 'The Summer			
	Camp' BS 3280	X		
22	5 tiny sk. (D. Mirror) BS 3527	2.	1.	6
27	3 tiny sk. (D. Mirror) BS 3581	1.	6.	0
28	Line illus. *Chums* BS 2546			
	(or 3546?)	2.	2.	0
Mar.				
3	Cover *Scout* BS 3541	2.	2.	0
7	Small drawing 'Tamil the trainer'			
	BS 3662		10.	6
8	*Lyons Mail* cover (April) BS 3648	4.	4.	0
	Title page 'On the trail' (Oxford			
	Press) BS 3800			
10	Tiny sketch *Sunday Pict.* Boy & dog			
	BS 3716		10.	6
15	Camp Fire stories (title page)			
	BS 3400	X		
17	Chums cover (Sculling) BS 3774	3.	3.	0
21	Contents page 'Scout punch'			
	BS 3807	2.12.		6
23	Title page 'The Boy's Own Book'			
	BS 3400			
24	Title page 'The Golden Book'			
	BS 3400	X		
28	Title page 'Pluck & Daring'			
	BS 3400	X		
Apr.				
3	Rough cover 'Ayres of Studleigh'			
	Oliphant BS 3867			
6	Finished drawing 'Ayres of Studleigh'			
	(Oliphant) BS 3867	3.	3.	0
13	Tiny sketch (D. Mirror – Chinese			
	pirate) BS 4026		15.	0
	Lyons Mail cover (May) BS 4035	4.	4.	0
25	2 title pages (Oxford Press) BS 3400			
26	7 drawings 'Millers Exercises' BS 4021			
27	3 more ditto	6.	6.	0
28	Wrapper drawing & Spine 'A lost Ideal'			
	(Oliphant) BS 3976	3.	3.	0
	Wrapper drawing & spine 'The gates			
	of Eden' (Oliphant) BS 3976	3.	3.	0
May				
3	2 coloured roughs Antizol			
	BS 4026	X		
9	2 title pages (Oxford Press)			
	BS 3400	16.16.		0
10	Rough also finished sketch for			
	'. . . & Palm' BS 5046	3.	3.	0

		£.	s.	d
12	*Lyons Mail* cover (June) BS	4.	4.	0
24	Cover 'Who Shall Serve?' (Oliphant) BS 3976	4.	4.	0
29	Cover 'Maitland of Lawrieston' (Oliphant) BS 5145	3.	3.	0
31	Cover 'The Guinea Stamp' (Oliphant) BS 5145	3.	3.	0
June				
1	Joke for *Gaiety* (pacer) BS 5316	3.	3.	0
8	Halftone illus. for *Popular Wireless* BS 5408	2.	2.	0
10	2 page decoration 'Success' (Cassell) BS 5349	3.	3.	0
12	7 roughs (Cricket) Andy Ducat article – Cassell			
13	*Lyons Mail* July cover BS 5405	4.	4.	0
15	Scout cover (wolves) BS 5424	2.	2.	0
16	4 diagrams Cricket (Cassell's Ducat's article) BS 5407	4.	4.	0
24	2 tiny sketch 'Vantage All' (Cassell) BS 5539	1.10.		0
26	Cover & spine 'St Veda's' (Oliphant) BS 5398	3.	3.	0
27	Rough for Wembley Tennis booklet	X		
	MacRae story (No. 7) *Red Magazine* BS 5518	1.11.		6
30	Heading for 'Golden Lilies' BS 5560	2.	5.	0
July				
3	6 heads for Luntin tobacco	15.15.		0
5	Cover & spine 'Hands across the Sea' (Oliphant) BS 5573	4.	4.	0
6	2 tiny tennis sketch (T-B) BS 5644	1.10.		0
12	*Lyons Mail* cover (Sept.) BS 5570	4.	4.	0
13	Tiny sketch 'Lawn Love' T-B BS 5709		15.	
	Another rough for Wembley Tennis booklet	X		
17	Half-page joke 'Keep to the Left' (Gaiety) BS 5704	3.	3.	0
20	2 tiny tennis sketches T-B 'Killing Strokes' BS 5751	1.10.		0
26	Half-page line illus. 'The edge of the Unknown' (Hutchinson) BS 5780	2.	5.	0
	Upright joke drawing 'Eyebeards' (*Tatler*)	4.	4.	0
27	Joke for bank hol. cover W. Tel. BS 5852	4.	4.	0
28	Joke (Baby & Gent.) *London Mail* BS 5713	2.	2.	0
Aug.				
1	2 tiny sketch for 'Woman's Weekly' BS 5868	1.	3.	0

		£.	s.	d
2	2 tiny sketch for T-B tennis BS 5897	1 10.		0
3	Half-page illus. (Hutchinson) BS 5895	2.	5.	0
4	Half-page joke (Fur) *Gaiety* BS 5844	3.	3.	0
26	Half-page joke (park-keeper) *Gaiety* BS 6172	1.12.		6
28	Illus. for *Red Magazine* BS 6186	1.11.		6
29	Man & Elephant illus. for *Scout* BS 6196	1.	5.	0
31	Cartoon for *Bystander* 'attab(u)oy sa..!'	2.	2.	0
Sep.				
5	Illus. & heading for *Yellow Magazine* story BS 6225	2.12.		6
	Joke drawing Tatler 'Me thrown in' BS 6174	4.	4.	0
Oct.				
3	Joke drawing *Gaiety* page BS 6530	4.	4.	0
8	Illus. Hutchinson (Remarkable Husband) *Adventure Magazine* BS 6575	2.	5.	0
10	Joke drawing Tatler 'Dustman' BS 6565	4.	4.	0
13	Illus. Hutchinson *Adventure Magazine* (13th chair) BS 6619	2.	5.	0
14	Illus. Hutchinson *Sovereign Magazine* (The Crystal Death)	2.	2.	0
16	Joke to Hutchinson (tooth-brush) BS 6607	2.	2.	0
27	Joke to P. Show (broadcasting) BS 6798	1.11.		6
30	Joke to *Gaiety* (letter) BS 6837	4.	4.	0
Nov.				
9	Illus. *Green Magazine* Bull & Blackman BS 6932?	1.11.		6
15	Illus. Hutch. *Adventure Magazine* 'The Eyes' BS 6986	2.	5.	0
20	Joke to *Tatler* (Lych-gate) BS 6961	4.	4.	0
23	Joke to *Gaiety* (I want to marry Bobby) BS 7046	4.	4.	0
25	Illus. 'Romance' half-page BS 7109	2.	2.	0
27	2 illus. 'Romance' (page and half page)	6.	6.	0
28	Joke drawing *Passing Show* (Red Tape) BS 4962	1.11.		6
Dec.				
5	Joke drawing *Tatler* (Vaccination) BS 7188	4.	4.	0
13	Half-page illus. 'The Captive' (*Sovereign Magazine*) BS 7236	2.	5.	0
14	Half-page illus. 'Justitia' (*Sovereign Magazine*) BS 7238	2.	5.	0
18	Joke (Pierrot) to *Bystander* BS 4960	2.12.		6

		£.	s.	d
19	Page and half-page illus. 'Romance' BS 7273	6.	6.	0
27	Half-page joke 'Bushel'	3.	3.	0

1923
Jan.

		£.	s.	d
1	Joke drawing (*Tatler*) 'Face on it' BS 4961	4.	4.	0
2	Joke drawing (*Passing Show*) 'Amateur Orchestra' BS 7254	2.	12.	6
4	Joke drawing (*Bystander*) 'Capital levy' BS 4963	2.	2.	0
8	Joke drawing (*Tatler*) 'Jiffies' BS 7528	4.	4.	0
23	Joke drawing (*Gaiety*) 'Huh' BS 7524	4.	4.	0
	Joke drawing (*Gaiety*) 'Rugger' BS 7673	4.	4.	0

Feb.

		£.	s.	d
5	Joke P.S. 'Wireless' BS 7809	3.	13.	6
	Half-page illus. (Sovereign) 'The Poison Cup'	2.	5.	0
	Half-page illus. (Sovereign) 'Outside the Verdict'	2.	5.	0
	Half-page illus. (Sovereign) 'The hour of doom'	2.	5.	0
12	Joke drawing (*Gaiety*) 'Boots' BS 7834	3.	3.	0
14	Heading and 2 illus.	5.	5.	0
17	Joke drawing (*Gaiety*) 'Opera' BS 7873	3.	3.	0
21	Heading and 3 drawings 'Strange boy next door' BS 7961	4.	4.	0
24	Joke (*Gaiety*) 'Boiled Cod' BS 8054	3.	3.	0
27	Heading and illus. 'The Borderline' (*Yellow Magazine*) BS 7996	3.	13.	6
	Joke drawing (London Mail) 'Samson' BS 8031	1.	11.	6

Mar.

		£.	s.	d
5	3 sketches 'Shadowing' (*Detective Magazine*) BS	2.	2.	0
	Joke 'April 1st' (L.O.) BS 8128	1.	11.	6
8	Joke 'Ticking Kitten' (P.S.) BS 8030	3.	3.	0
12	Rough for cover (Heinemann) BS 8184			
	Rough for Scott's Porage ad. (children)		7.	0
14	Cover for Heinemann's 'According to Gibson' BS 8184	5.	5.	0
20	Heading and illus. 'Valparaise Dreams' (*Yellow Magazine*) BS 8245	1.	13.	6

Apr.

		£.	s.	d
6	Half-page illus. 'Pharaoh's treasure' (*Adventure Magazine*) BS 8891	2.	5.	0

		£.	s.	d
10	Heading and illus. 'Mystery of Mr Abbs' (*Yellow Mag.*) BS 8974	3.	12.	0
13	Illus. to 'The Lotus flower' (Hutchinson) BS 8984	2.	5.	0
16	Heading & 3 illus. 'The Magic Carpet' (Pip & Squeak Annual) BS 9014	6.	6.	0
23	Joke (Landlady) for *Happy Magazine* BS 9113	1.	12.	6
	Joke (Line Engaged) for Eve BS 8317	2.	2.	0
24	Half-page illus. 'Pharaoh's treasure' (2nd) (Adventure Mag.) BS 8985	2.	5.	0
25	Joke drawing *Gaiety* (Outdoor Sea) BS 9055	3.	3.	0
30	Heading and illus. 'Nancy from Nowhere' (W.T.) (Instal. 1) BS 9168	4.	4.	0

May

		£.	s.	d
4	Illus. for 'Nancy from Nowhere' (W.T.) (Instal. 2) BS 9168	2.	2.	0
11	Illus. for 'Nancy from Nowhere' (W.T.) (Instal. 3) BS 9168	2.	2.	0
14	Joke for P.S. ('Obbs) BS 9350	3.	3.	0
18	Illus. 'Nancy from Nowhere' (W.T.) (Instal. 4) BS 9218	2.	2.	0
28	Illus. 'Nancy from Nowhere' (W.T.) (Instal. 5) BS 9218	2.	2.	0
	Illus. 'Nancy from Nowhere' (W.T.) (Instal. 6) BS 9365	2.	2.	0

June

		£.	s.	d
8	Joke to P.S. (Daffodil Charabancs) BS 9406	3.	3.	0
9	Illus. 'Nancy from Nowhere' (W.T.) (Instal. 7) BS 9579	2.	2.	0
12	Illus. 'The fool wins' (*Sovereign Magazine*) BS	2.	5.	0
15	Illus. 'Nancy from Nowhere' (W.T.) (Instal. 8) BS 9579	2.	2.	0
	Illus. 'Nancy from Nowhere' (W.T.) (Instal. 9) BS 9612	2.	2.	0
	Joke to W.T. (sheep) BS 9048	2.	2.	0
16	Joke to W.T. (Children take after their parents) BS 9048	2.	2.	0
19	Page joke (Bowlin' broadcastin') Gaiety BS 9677	4.	4.	0
22	Illus. 'Nancy from Nowhere' (W.T.) (Instal. 10) BS 9612	2.	2.	0
25	Illus. 'Nancy from Nowhere' (W.T.) (final) BS 9740	2.	2.	0
26	Joke for P.S. (Steeple) BS 9678	2.	12.	6
28	Page joke for *Gaiety* (distemper) BS 9813	4.	4.	0
29	Joke for *London Mail* (Clothes line) BS 9828	2.	12.	6

July

		£.	s.	d
23	Joke for *Tatler* (Mountaineering) BS 10007	3.	3.	0

		£.	s.	d
24	Joke for P.S. (Sunburn) BS 10089	3.	3.	0

Aug.

		£.	s.	d
1	Double page (posters) *Gaiety* BS 10154	7.	7.	0
2	Small head and shoulders (naval officer) for patch on Serge ad.	X		
8	Page joke (heat) *Gaiety* BS 10253	4.	4.	0
9	Drawing for 'Ideas' (Harem) BS 10273	1.	1.	0
29	Drawing for 'Ideas' (Confessions) BS 10451	X		
31	Page ad. 'Swiss Hotels' (L.O.) BS 10481	4.	4.	0

Sep.

		£.	s.	d
1	Page joke (*Gaiety*) 'Ticklish' BS 10480	4.	4.	0
3	Line illus. 'The Target' (*Mystery Magazine*) BS 10472	2.	5.	0
4	Joke 'Perpendicular' *Bystander* BS 10454	2.12.	6	
6	Border dec. 'Our Dream Corner' BS 10490	1.11.	6	
10	Joke for P.S. (String of Pearls) BS 10470	3.13.	6	
	Chalk drawing Rhinoceros charging BS 10547	2.	2.	0
18	Line drawing 2 figures seated BS 10654	X		
20	Joke drawing 'Moderato' (P.S.) BS 10534	4.	4.	0
24	*Gaiety* cover (Gone to Ground)	9.	9.	0
27	Joke 'Doctor & Plum Pudding' (L.O.) BS 10688	1.11.	6	

Oct.

		£.	s.	d
1	Page joke 'Charlady' (*Gaiety*) BS 10751	4.	4.	0
	Page joke 'Public Golf Course' (*Bystander*) BS 10817	5.	5.	0
3	2 sketches (*Bystander*) 'An Episcopal Error'	4.	4.	0
5	Half-page and page illus. 'Derring do' (*Sovereign Mag.*) BS 10793	5.15.	0	
8	Joke (Hard-boiled egg) Reeves Shaw BS 10897	3.	3.	0
12	Joke (Trussed) L.O. BS 10883	2.	2.	0
15	Joke (Sour cow) *Gaiety* BS 10985	4.	4.	0
17	Joke (Organ blower) L.O. BS 10988	2.	2.	0
25	Joke (Youthful) *Lyons Mail* BS 10984	3.	3.	0
30	Joke (Spine) *Gaiety* BS 12149	4.	4.	0
31	Joke (Counter attractions) *Gaiety* (page) BS 12071	7.	7.	0

Nov.

		£.	s.	d
2	Joke (Ceylon) P.S. BS 12148	2.12.	6	
7	Joke (Celebrating) P.S. BS 12072	2.12.	6	
27	Half-page drawing 'Vaudoux' (*Mystery Magazine*) BS 12498	2.	5.	0
	Joke (*Tatler*) 'Daily bread' BS 12138	3.	3.	0
29	Joke (P.S.) 'Angels nighties'	2.12.	6	

Dec.

		£.	s.	d
14	Coloured plate (witch) Hulton's Girls' Annual	5.	5.	0
	Joke 'Hard Life' P.S. BS 12241	3.	3.	0
21	Heading and 2 sketches 'Girls not allowed' P. & S. Annual	4.10.	0	
31	Heading, page sketch and tailpiece (*Scouts*) Oxford Press BS 523	4.19.	0	

1924

Jan.

		£.	s.	d
3	Joke 'Parsnips' (P.S.) BS 12241	3.	3.	0
15	2 illus. and heading 'The Witch of Whitestones' (Hultons) BS 867	3.	3.	0
17	2 colour Music cover 'Give me the right time' BS 857	3.	3.	0
18	Heading 'Astrology' BS 980	1.	1.	0
21	Joke 'Church-fit' (L.O.) BS 987	2.	2.	0
	Joke 'Did he?!' (*Gaiety*) BS 984	4.	4.	0
22	Joke 'Lift' (*Windsor*) BS 12607	1.12.	6	
28	Joke 'Peeve' (P.S.) BS 12582	3.	3.	0
29	Joke 'Extinguished' (Gaiety) BS 1066	4.	4.	0
31	Joke 'Counter-irritant' (*Gaiety*) Double page BS 1125	7.	7.	0
	Joke 'Mixed Infant' (*Gaiety*) Half-page BS 1099	3.	3.	0

Feb.

		£.	s.	d
1	Joke 'Squeak' (P.S.) BS 805	4.	4.	0
15	Joke 'Thumb-mark' (P.S.) BS 1746	3.13.	6	
29	Joke 'Runabout' (*Humourist*) BS 1766	3.	3.	0
	Heading and 2 illus. 'Water, Water Everywhere' (P. & S. Annual)	3.	0.	0

May

		£.	s.	d
16	4 tiny sketches for Sausage ad. folder (Penton) BS 4034		5.	0
19	Half-page illus. 'The Law of the Sea' (Adventure Mag.) BS 4024	2.	5.	0
28	Cover *Gaiety* (July) BS 3863	9.	9.	0
30	Half-page illus. 'Return of 'erb' (*Sovereign Mag.*) BS 4062	2.	5.	0

June

		£.	s.	d
2	Joke 'Crimson Wembler' (*Tatler*) BS 3881	4.	4.	0
3	Joke 'Crippen' (*Gaiety*) BS 3864	4.	4.	0

		£.	s.	d
4	Joke 'Chinese Children' (P.S.) BS 3883	3.	3.	0
6	Joke 'What Auntie Saw' (*Red Mag.*) BS 3918	3.	13.	6
10	Joke 'Wants Eatin' (*Gaiety*) BS 3953	4.	4.	0
12	Joke 'Steeped in Crime' (P.S.) BS 3883	3.	13.	6
14	Joke 'Wave-length' (*Red Magazine*) BS 5001	3.	13.	6
19	Heading and 2 illus. 'Pirates & Smugglers' (A.P.) BS 5013	5.	0.	0
23	Joke 'Hampstead 157' (*Gaiety*) BS 3999	4.	4.	0
24	Coloured cover 'The Silver Lining' BS	5.	5.	0
26	Joke 'White Elephants' (W.T.) BS 5069	2.	2.	0
	Joke 'Witching Wares' (P.S.) BS 5014	3.	3.	0
30	Joke 'Rose' (*Tatler*) BS 5080	4.	4.	0

July

1	Heading and illus. 'Horseshoe for luck' (*Yellow Magazine*)	3.	10.	0
3	*Gaiety* double 'Divers & Sun-dry' BS 5070	7.	7.	0
4	P.S. cover 'Bashful Suitor'	10.	10.	0
11	Jamboree programme cover (2 col.) BS 5916	6.	6.	0
15	Illus. 'Dawn of Day' serial (1st) 'Her will & her way' BS 5076	4.	4.	0
17	Joke 'Felix' (*Tatler*) BS 5924	4.	4.	0
18	2 illus. 'Stodge Burke' (Crusoe) BS 5918	5.	5.	0
22	P.S. cover 'Pleasure' BS 5947	10.	10.	0
23	1 illus. 'Military honours' (*Mystery Magazine*) BS 4290	2.	5.	0
24	Joke 'Worm' (*Writers Pie*)	7.	7.	0
25	Joke 'Wrong room' (P.S.) BS 5925	3.	3.	0
28	Joke 'Explosion' (P.S.) BS 5925	3.	3.	0

Aug.

12	Serial 'Dawn of Day' (2nd) BS 5076	4.	4.	0
13	Joke 'Snapshots' (P.S.) BS 6211	3.	13.	6
15	Joke 'Toodles' (*Bystander*) BS 6213	2.	12.	6
25	Joke 'Ten Commandments' (*Happy Magazine*) BS 6238	4.	4.	0
28	P.S. cover 'Height of Ambition'	10.	10.	0

Sept.

2	Joke 'Outer' (*Tatler*) BS 6342	2.	12.	6
	Joke 'Outskirts' (P.S.) BS 6289	4.	4.	0
3	Joke 'Father Xmas – white hair' (Newnes) BS 6344	4.	4.	0
8	P.S. cover 'Cash with order' BS 6391	10.	10.	0
	Joke ''Ere's luck' (P.S.) BS 6434	3.	3.	0

		£.	s.	d
10	Serial 'Dawn of Day' (3rd) BS 5076	4.	4.	0
11	Joke 'Bilge for Babies' (P. S.) BS 6272	3.	3.	0
18	Joke 'Arabic . . . telephone' (P.S.) BS 6434	3.	3.	0
23	Joke 'Second-hand' (Reeves Shaw) BS 3504	3.	13.	6
25	Joke 'Woad' (Reeves Shaw) BS 3504	3.	13.	6
27	Joke 'I know better' (Reeves Shaw) BS 3504	3.	13.	6
29	Joke 'Prayers wasted' (P.S.) BS 6482	3.	3.	0
	Joke 'So sudden' (*Gaiety*) BS 6483	4.	4.	0

Oct.

2	*Gaiety* cover 'Providence' BS 6647	9.	9.	0
10	Joke 'Joking apart' (*Tatler*) BS 6597	3.	3.	0
15	Joke 'Unrepentant child (*Tatler*) BS 6617	3.	3.	0
20	Joke 'A bit deaf' (Reeves Shaw) BS 6504	3.	13.	6
	Joke 'Arctic Explorer' (P.S.) BS 7158	4.	4.	0
28	Joke ''Iccups' (Reeves Shaw) BS 6554	4.	4.	0
31	Joke 'Stopping train' (*Gaiety*) BS 7294	4.	4.	0

Nov.

3	Joke 'Three times' (P.S.) BS 7204	4.	4.	0
12	Heading and 3 illus. 'Melton Chase' (P. & S. Annual) BS 7111	6.	6.	0
15	Joke 'Yokel – aerial' (P.S.) BS 7391	3.	13.	6

Dec.

4	Joke 'Artist – burglar' (*Tatler*) BS 8211	3.	3.	0
8	Heading and illus. 'Luck's Flag Day' (*Merry Magazine*)	3.	3.	0
15	Joke 'Bridge' (P.S.) BS 7772	3.	3.	0
22	Joke 'Policeman for Cook' (*Printers Pie*) BS	7.	7.	0

1925

Jan.

5	Joke 'Jade' (*Gaiety* half-page) BS 7959	3.	3.	0
	Joke 'Purse' (*Gaiety* page) BS 7959	4.	4.	0
7	Joke 'Amazon' (P.S.) BS 7854	3.	3.	0
8	Illus. 'An Interrupted Programme' (*Red Magazine*)	2.	2.	0
12	Joke 'Billiards or Snooker' (*Tatler*) BS 8022	4.	4.	0
13	Joke 'Monday Car' (P.S.) BS 8021	3.	3.	0

		£	s.	d
16	Joke 'Young Once' (*Tatler*) BS 8103	3.	3.	0
20	Joke 'Nighty' (P.S.) BS 7470	3.	3.	0
23	Joke 'Right lung' (P.S.) BS 8178	3.	3.	0
26	Joke 'Censured devil' (P.S.) BS 8178	3.	3.	0
30	Joke 'Car burglar' (W.T.) BS 8240	2.	2.	0
Feb.				
3	Joke 'Muffler' (P.S.) BS 8293	3.	13	6
5	Joke 'Non-plussed' (*Gaiety*) BS 8351	4.	4.	0
10	Joke 'Loudspeaker' (Cassell) BS 8309 or 8389	2.	2.	0
16	Joke 'Striker – Spring Clean' (P.S.) BS 8350	3.	13.	6
19	Joke 'Bear race' (P.S.) BS 8499	3.	13.	6
23	Joke 'Shorthand writer' (*Gaiety*) BS 8496	4.	4.	0
24	Joke 'Meringues' (P.S.) BS 8415	3.	13.	6
27	Joke 'The Crowd' (*Gaiety* double page) BS 8575	7.	7.	0
Mch.				
2	Joke 'R.S.V.P.' (*Gaiety* page) BS 8575	4.	4.	0
5	Joke 'Can sit out' (P.S.) BS 8293	3.	13.	6
10	Joke 'Valve set raided' (P.S.) BS 8635	3.	13.	6
12	Joke 'Polish' (Reeves Shaw) BS 8721	4.	4.	0
23	Joke 'Ought to tell him' (P.S.) BS 8576	3.	13.	6
	Joke 'Count Zblicz (W.T.) BS 8808	2.	2.	0
	Joke 'Stockings a yard' (Gaiety) BS 8761	4.	4.	0
30	Joke 'A bit hotter' (P.S.) BS 8908	3.	13.	6
	Joke 'Emu – Ape' (*Gaiety*) BS 8884	4.	4.	0
Apr.				
3	Joke 'A run on the Bank' (*Gaiety* double) BS 8954	7.	7.	0
6	Joke 'Bathroom scenes' (P.S.) BS 8802	3.	13.	6
14	Joke 'Dentist' (P.S.) BS 8958	3.	13.	6
17	Joke 'Cricket pitch up' (Reeves Shaw) BS 8810	4.	4.	0
20	2 illus. (page) 'King of the Surf' (Crusoe) BS 8974	4.	4.	0
24	Joke 'Professional' (*Tatler*) BS 8728	4.	4.	0
27	*Gaiety* cover (Wholesailor) BS 686	9.	9.	0
May				
4	*Gaiety* page joke 'Funeral' BS 611	4.	4.	0
	Gaiety page joke 'Left handed' BS 769	4.	4.	0
	Gaiety page joke 'Marmalade' BS 530	4.	4.	0
7	Joke 'Man run over' (P.S.) BS 532	3.	13.	6
8	Joke 'Cricket-shower' (P.S.) BS 702	3.	13.	6
9	Joke 'Pat-Mike' (Windsor) BS 511	2.	2.	0
	Joke 'Library' (Windsor) BS 511	2.	2.	0
14	Joke 'Bathing dress – photograph' (W.T.) BS	2.	2.	0
	Joke 'Hooter-siren' (Reeves Shaw) BS 918	3.	13.	6
17	Joke 'Shaving-soap' (Reeves Shaw) BS 918	3.	13.	6
	Joke 'Vandyke' (*Tatler*) BS 934	4.	4.	0
25	Joke ''Alf me seat' (P.S.) BS 612	3.	13.	6
27	Joke 'Mixed bathing' (*Sketch*) BS 1015	3.	13.	6
	Joke 'Holidays early' (*Bystander*) BS 1035	3.	3.	0
June				
2	*Gaiety* cover (Rouge et Noir and border) BS 1072	12.	12.	0
3	Joke 'Car breakdown' (P.S.) BS 935	3.	13.	6
4	Joke 'Professor – knot' (*Gaiety*) BS 1140	4.	4.	0
	Joke 'Bathroom door' (*Gaiety*) BS 937	4.	4.	0
9	Joke 'The Set' (*Tatler*) BS 934	4.	4.	0
11	Joke 'Algebra' (P.S.) BS 1005	3.	13.	6
12	Joke 'Average' (Reeves Shaw) BS 1220	5.	0.	0
23	L.O. cover 'The Silencer' BS 1919	X		
24	Joke 'N. Latitude 52' (P.S.) BS 1141	3.	13.	6
26	*Gaiety* cover 'The Early Bird' BS 1369	8.	8.	0
30	Joke 'Silly old fool' (*Gaiety*) BS 1326	4.	4.	0
July				
1	Joke 'Between drinks' (*Gaiety*) BS 1370	4.	4.	0
2	Joke 'Singing flat' (P.S.) BS 1386	3.	13.	6
3	Joke 'Wit's End' (Reeves Shaw) BS 1309	5.	0.	0
13	Joke 'Bastion' (P.S.) BS 1386	3.	13.	6
17	Joke 'Singing loud' (*Tatler*) BS 1566	4.	4.	0
	Joke 'Inte'urupt' (P.S.) BS	3.	13.	6
21	Joke 'Holiday packing' (*Tatler*) BS	6.	6.	0
27	Joke 'Conscience' (*Tatler*) BS	4.	4.	0
30	2 illus. 'The Cheval-Glass Club' (*Strand*) BS 1384	9.	9.	0
Aug.				
17	Joke 'Xmas Cards' (P.S.) BS 1827	3.	13.	6
18	Joke 'Stag-beetle' (*Tatler*) BS 1730	4.	4.	0
20	Joke 'Pad well' (Reeves Shaw) BS 1881	5.	0.	0

		£.	s.	d
21	Joke 'Male Girl-guides' (P.S.) BS 1862	3.	13.	6
22	Joke 'Quod-wear' (Allied Newspapers) BS 9738	3.	3.	0
27	Joke 'Can't lick it' (*Tatler*) BS 1789	6.	6.	0
28	Joke 'Woonter Willies' (Royal) BS	2.	2.	0
31	Joke 'Verbatim' (Reeves Shaw) BS 2037	5.	0.	0
Sept.				
3	Joke 'A bit of tact' (W.T.) BS 1936	2.	2.	0
9	Joke 'Mercy on your Soul' (Newnes) BS 1881	5.	0.	0
11	Joke 'She may miss' (*Tatler*) BS 2190	4.	4.	0
14	Joke 'Bad skater' (Newnes) BS 2193	5.	0.	0
21	Joke 'Monkey' (*Tatler*) BS 2359	6.	6.	0
	Joke 'New Year – wasn't looking' (Newnes) BS 2193	5.	0.	0
25	Joke 'My God' (*Tatler*) BS 2202	4.	4.	0
30	Joke 'Book' (*Tatler*) BS 2065	6.	6.	0
Oct.				
5	Joke 'Tuning up' (P.S.) BS 2510	3.	13.	6
12	Colour page 'Virginia' (*Tatler*)	15.	15.	0
13	1 illus. story by Dean Inge (*Strand*) BS 2646	4.	4.	0
20	Joke 'Encourage' (Newnes) BS 2524	5.	0.	0
22	Joke 'Quite a kid' (*Tatler*) BS 2359	6.	6.	0
26	Joke 'Butler' (*Tatler*) BS 2695	6.	6.	0
29	Joke 'Village meeting' (Newnes) BS 2647	5.	0.	0
30	Joke 'Dentist-tummy' (P.S.) BS 2991	5.	5.	0
Nov.				
2	Joke 'Entomology' (Newnes) BS	5.	0.	0
6	Joke 'Bad words' 2-colour (*Tatler*) BS 2522	7.	7.	0
9	Fan design for Eve (Fairy)	15.	15.	0
12	Joke 'Believer' (*Tatler*) BS 2929	4.	4.	0
13	Joke 'Give in – Xmas' (Newnes) BS 2973	5.	0.	0
16	Joke 'Lifelong friend' (P.S.) BS 3166	5.	5.	0
19	Joke 'Saturdays only' (Newnes) BS 2961	5.	0.	0
24	Joke 'Never met' (*Tatler*) BS 2432	5.	5.	0
	Joke 'Outlook unsettled' (Newnes) BS 3288	5.	0.	0
28	Joke 'Earlier train' (Newnes) BS 3288	8.	0.	0

		£.	s.	d
Dec.				
3	Joke 'Hear you coming' colour (*Tatler*) BS 3343	15.	15.	0
	Page 'Last bus' (*Oojah Annual*) BS 9862	2.	2.	0
14	Colour double page 'Coffee Stall' (*Tatler*) BS 2951	26.	5.	0
	Joke 'Central heating' (P.S.) BS 3431	5.	5.	0
17	Joke 'Cromwell Rd' (*Tatler*) BS 3513	5.	5.	0
18	Joke 'You know what doctors are' (*Tatler*) BS	5.	5.	0
21	Joke 'Blind Man's Buff' (P.S.) BS 3598	5.	5.	0
31	Heading and 7 sketches 'Butterfly Express' (Oojah) BS 5085	10.	10.	0
1926				
Jan.				
4	Joke 'Ear trumpet' (*Tatler*) BS 3638	5.	5.	0
15	6 illus. 'A rolling stone' (Wide World) BS 3730	12.	12.	0
20	Joke 'Sheep' (Tatler) BS 3868	5.	5.	0
28	Heading and 2 illus. 'Winnie the Pooh' (Eve) BS 3828	10.	10.	0
Feb.				
2	Joke 'Red Indians' (Newnes) BS 3761	5.	0.	0
5	Joke 'Beg pardon Dod' (*Tatler*) BS 3868	4.	4.	0
22	Joke 'Shady side' (Newnes) BS 3952	5.	0.	0
Mar.				
1	Joke 'Tough' (*Tatler*) BS 3573	7.	7.	0
	1 illus. Girls Story (Blackie) BS 5266	3.	3.	0
4	Chelsea Arts Ball page (*Bystander*)	6.	6.	0
19	4 page illus. Hans Andersen etc. (Nelson) BS 5285	21.	0.	0
24	Joke 'Chewing-gum' (*Tatler*) BS 3936	5.	5.	0
25	Joke 'Bridge party' (*Tatler*) BS 3452	4.	4.	0
31	Joke 'Clap-hands' (*Tatler*) BS 6076	4.	4.	0
Apr.				
8	3 little illus. Fathers & children (*Home Magazine*) BS 6482	5.	5.	0
9	Joke 'Partner's lead' (P.S.) BS 6517	5.	5.	0
12	Joke 'Tennis Balls' (Newnes) BS 6527	5.	0.	0
15	Joke 'False hair' (*Tatler*) BS 6089	4.	4.	0
16	Joke 'Hobbs' (Newnes) BS 6527	5.	0.	0
26	Full colour drawing 'The Alchemist' (*Tatler*) BS 2929	15.	15.	0

		£	s.	d
30	3 illus. 'A splash of publicity' (*Strand*) BS 6564	15.	15.	0
	Joke 'Pick up sides' (Windsor) BS 7054	2.	2.	0
May				
7	Joke 'Pichfork' (Windsor)	2.	12.	6
	Joke 'All up' (Newnes) BS 6683	5	0.	0
20	Joke 'Golf-blush' (*Tatler*) BS 6635	5.	5.	0
June				
10	6 page decorations (Ethel Mannin's poems – Eve) BS 7040	37.	16.	0
July				
2	3 illus. 'The Latitude of Propriety' (*Eve*) BS 7339	10.	10.	0
6	1 illus. 'The Mare's Nest' (*Eve*) BS 7435	4.	4.	0
7	1 illus. 'The Roadmenders' (Blackie) BS 5597	2.	12.	6
8	2 illus. 'The Blotting-paper dog' (Blackies) BS 5597	5.	5.	0
9	Joke 'Sun-burnt meat' (Newnes) BS 6582	5.	0.	0
15	Joke 'Bald-head-nude' (*Tatler*) BS 7021	4.	4.	0
21	Joke 'Bus-conductor' (*Tatler*) BS 6652	4.	4.	0
22	Joke 'Eggs' (*Tatler*) BS 7653	4.	4.	0
Aug.				
12	Joke 'Warm overcoat' (*Tatler*) BS 6304	4.	4.	0
19	2 colour drawing 'The Plotters' (*Sketch*) BS 8292	7.	7.	0
25	Colour drawing 'In possession' (*Tatler*) BS 7070	15.	15.	0
	Joke 'Half the bed' (*Tatler*) BS 6398	6.	6.	0
Sept.				
14	2 colour drawing 'EKUA AMIOU' (*Eve*) BS 7614	7.	7.	0
15	Joke 'Quiet Wedding' (*Tatler*) BS 9016	4.	4.	0
24	2 page 2-colour decoration 'Forgotten' by A.A. Milne (*Eve*)	12.	12.	0
30	6 page decorations Ethel Mannin's poems (*Eve*) BS 7826	37.	16.	0
Oct.				
1	3 silhouettes Children's Salon (Eve) BS 8431	5.	5.	0
6	2-colour page joke 'Mummy do it' (*Tatler*) BS 3239	10.	10.	0
9	2 illus. 'Mrs Thompson's daughter' (Mackies)	6.	6.	0
13	2-colour Xmas card sketches (*Eve*) BS 8430	4.	4.	0

		£	s.	d
14	Joke 'Horse-gee-gee' (*Tatler*) BS 8460	4.	4.	0
29	Certificate design (*Eve*, Girls Salon) BS 8432	6.	6.	0
Nov.				
20	Joke 'Bills, bills, bills' (Newnes) BS 541	5.	0.	0
	Joke 'Cigars for Xmas' (Newnes) BS 541	5.	0.	0
27	Joke 'Stradivarius' (P.S.) BS 545	5.	5.	0
30	Joke 'Coughed & waited'	4.	4.	0
Dec.				
2	Page decoration 'Handy man' (*Home*) BS 554	5.	5.	0
3	Joke 'Prayers like Daddy' (*Tatler*) BS 674	4.	4.	0
6	Joke 'Puppy food' (P.S.) BS 708	5.	5.	0
18	2-colour line cover 'New Health' BS 9374	8.	8.	0
	Joke 'Hole in glove' (*Tatler*) BS 707	5.	5.	0
21	Joke 'Pedigree' (Newnes) BS 887	5.	0.	0
22	Heading and 1 illus. 'The Red thread of honour' (Nelsons) BS 9332	5.	5.	0
28	Heading and 5 illus. 'The 3 golden apples' (Nelsons) BS 9364	15.	15.	0
30	1 illus. 'Pirates' Fancy dress article (*Eve*) BS 882	5.	5.	0
31	Joke 'Your husband' (*Tatler*) BS 957	5.	5.	0
1927				
Jan.				
3	Joke 2-colour 'Appendix' (*Tatler*) BS 674	10.	10.	0
10	Joke 'Mayfair 7287' (Newnes) BS 1063	5.	0.	0
11	Joke 'Betting' (Newnes) BS 1092	5.	0.	0
12	Joke 'Dead aliens' (*Tatler*) BS 1069	5.	5.	0
14	Joke 'Little boys' (*Tatler*) BS 1147	5.	5.	0
20	3 illus. 'Supposing' (*Eve*) BS 1148	15.	15.	0
24	Joke 'Four wheel brakes' (*Tatler*) BS 1147	5.	5.	0
25	Joke 'Rainbow' (Newnes) BS 1260	5.	0.	0
31	Joke 'Neck & crop' (*Tatler*) BS 1311	5.	5.	0
Feb.				
14	Colour page 'Pirates' Cave' (*Tatler*) BS 1226	15.	15.	0
	Joke 'Better luck next time' (P.S.) BS 1390	5.	5.	0
	Joke 'Half-hour ago' (*Tatler*) BS 1311	5.	5.	0
21	Fashion border decoration (*Tatler*) BS 1554	5.	5.	0

		£.	s.	d
22	Joke 'Flu germs' (*Tatler*) BS 1555	5.	5.	0
Mar.				
2	Colour page 'Fairy Prince' (*Tatler*) BS	15.	15.	0
4	Joke 'Auntie singing' (P.S.) BS 1472	5.	5.	0
9	Page 'Red poppies' (*Eve*) BS 1645	6.	6.	0
11	Page 'Foxgloves' (*Eve*) BS 1645	6.	6.	0
15	Page 'Fogbound' (*Eve*) BS 1645	6.	6.	0
21	Joke 'Pretty teeth' (*Tatler*) BS 1555	5.	5.	0
25	Joke 'Lost a child' (*Sketch*) BS 1902	6.	6.	0
Apr.				
5	Colour page 'Wave' (*Tatler*) BS 1553	15.	15.	0
13	Joke 'Pipe on fire' (P.S.) BS 1941	5.	5.	0
19	Half-page joke 'Spell believe' (*Sketch*) BS 1902	5.	5.	0
25	Colour page 'Bridge of Sighs' (*Tatler*) BS 2099	15.	15.	0
May				
27	2 illus. 'The House with the Hedge' (Blackie) BS 5371	6.	6.	0
	2 illus. 'The Frock' (Blackie) BS 5371	6.	6.	0
June				
2	2 illus. 'In those days' (Stock Exch. Annual) BS 2538	10.	10.	0
7	2 illus. 'Romance' (*Tatler*) BS 2133	10.	10.	0
10	1 illus. 'All along London' (Blackie) BS 5465B	3.	3.	0
	3 illus. 'Timity & the Tartan dress (Blackie) BS 5465A	9.	9.	0
28	2 illus. 'The Invasion (cello)' (*Tatler*) BS 2675	10.	10.	0
July				
25	Colour page 'The Crevasse' (*Tatler*) BS 3119	15.	15.	0
27	2 page decoration 'Motor bus' (Stock Exch. Annual) BS 3012	6.	6.	0
Aug.				
4	2 illus. 'The Kingdom of Elfin' (*Eve*) BS 2971	12.	12.	0
8	2 illus. (small) 'The Flood' (Blackie) BS 5556	5.	5.	0
	4 illus. (small) 'Shut out' (Blackie) BS 5556	7.	7.	0
9	Joke 'What sort of grace' (*Tatler*) BS 1069	5.	5.	0
10	Joke 'Flapper-golf' (*Bystander*) BS 3942	3.	3.	0
12	Joke 'Little Jane in it' (*Tatler*) BS 7284	4.	4.	0

		£.	s.	d
15	Joke 'Older still' (*Tatler*) BS 3315	5.	5.	0
Sep.				
5	Line drg 'Round pegs & square holes' (*Home Notes*) BS 3479	5.	5.	0
29	Heading and illus. 'Chinese Doll' (*Eve*) BS 3576	10.	10.	0
Oct.				
3	1 illus. for Dudeney's Puzzles (*Strand*) BS 6191	3.	13.	6
10	24 page drawings Enid Blyton's Plays (Newnes) BS 3388	105.	0.	0
11	3 illus. 'Sybil Thorndyke (1st instal.) (Strand) BS 6272	15.	15.	0
13	3 sketches 'Peter, the Pram, & Me' (*Sketch*) BS 4040	6.	6.	0
21	3 sketches 'Bunty's Secret' (*Sketch*) BS 4041	6.	6.	0
25	3 sketches 'Bunty's Sinnema' (*Sketch*) BS 4042	6.	6.	0
28	3 sketches 'Peggy & the Pictures' (*Sketch*) BS 4156	6.	6.	0
Nov.				
3	3 illus. 'Sybil Thorndike (2nd instal.) (*Strand*) BS 6272	15.	15.	0
9	3 sketches 'Meeting Richard' (*Sketch*) BS 4335	6.	6.	0
14	3 sketches 'Bunty's House' (*Sketch*) BS 4295	6.	6.	0
	Joke 'Good time' (*Tatler*) BS 3316	5.	5.	0
15	Endpaper 'The Play's the Thing' (Newnes) BS 4539	7.	7.	0
22	Heading and 2 illus. 'Eve' story for Nursery No. (Peacocks) BS 4478	15.	15.	0
	Wash ad. 'Children in snow' (Erwin Wasey) BS 4514	10.	10.	0
29	Joke 'Grow sideways' (*Tatler*) BS 3662	4.	4.	0
Dec.				
13	Colour cover and 33 illus. 'Magic Rhymes' (Blackie) BS	50.	0.	0
15	Joke 'Kind of him' (*Tatler*) BS 3956	4.	4.	0
16	2 line illus. 'She goes to Church' (Nelson) BS 6566	5.	5.	0
19	Wash ad. (Nestle's Milk) 'Homework' BS	10.	10.	0
28	Wash illus. 'The Odd Room' (*Tatler*) BS 5050	5.	5.	0
1928				
Jan.				
16	Colour page 'The Shaded Pool' (*Tatler*) BS 144	15.	15.	0
	Joke 'Pipes' (*Tatler*) BS 235	5.	5.	0

		£.	s.	d
24	Joke 'Coward-magician' (*Tatler*) BS 346	5.	5.	0
	Joke 'Boat-race' (Arkell) BS 327	5.	5.	0
27	Joke 'Short skirts' (*Tatler*) BS 234	5.	5.	0
30	Joke 'New dress' (*Tatler*) BS 349	5.	5.	0
	Colour page 'Grantchester' (*Tatler*) BS 2099	15.	15.	0
Feb.				
1	Joke 'Sixes' (Newnes) BS 447	5.	0.	0
2	Joke 'Only just' (*Tatler*) BS 236	5.	5.	0
6	Joke 'Sun set' (Newnes) BS 499	5.	5.	0
8	3 line & tone sketches 'The Average Man' (*W. Journal*) BS 439	10.	10.	0
10	Joke 'Two ears' (Arkell) BS 643	3.	3.	0
16	Joke 'Devilled kidneys' (Arkell) BS 619	3.	3.	0
17	Joke 'Swum the Channel' (Newnes) BS 500	5.	5.	0
20	Joke 'Tenor or baritone' (Arkell) BS 642	3.	3.	0
21	Joke 'Capital punishment' (Arkell) BS 715	3.	3.	0
23	Joke 'Clue' (Newnes) BS 618	5.	5.	0
28	Joke 'Claret glass' (Arkell) BS 714	3.	3.	0
Mar.				
1	Joke 'd . . . d bus' (*Tatler*) BS 825	4.	4.	0
6	Colour rough for Folder (Cardigan Press) (Underwear)	2.	12.	6
7	Joke 'Epstein doll' (Newnes) BS 826	5.	5.	0
9	Illus. 'Unseen fingers' (*Tatler*)	5.	5.	0
14	4 sketches 'Bear in the Midi' (Nelson) BS 6888	12.	12.	0
26	Colour page 'Fairies Gold' (Blackie) BS 6815	6.	6.	0
29	2 line sketches 'Beggars & Brides' (Novel) BS 1143	6.	6.	0
Apr.				
3	Joke 'Little Lamb' (Arkell) BS 716	3.	3.	0
17	Joke 'Divinely stagnant' (*Tatler*) BS 793	5.	5.	0
18	Joke 'Tooth-paste' (P.S.) BS 1332	5.	5.	0
30	Joke 'Umbrellas' (*Tatler*) BS 859	4.	4.	0
	Colour page '*Le Foret Sinistre*' (*Tatler*) BS 1387	15.	15.	0
May				
14	Colour page 'Charabanc' (*Tatler*) BS 1287	15.	15.	0
	3 illus. 'Educating Janet Dodd' (A.P.) BS 1643	6.	16.	6
18	2 illus. 'Daffy Fleetwood's Job' (Blackie) BS 7137	6.	6.	0
	2 illus. 'The finger of fate' (Blackie) BS 7138	6.	6.	0
	2 illus. 'From top to bottom' (Blackie) BS 7139	6.	6.	0

		£.	s.	d
	Joke 'Bogey' (*Tatler*) BS 1331	5.	5.	0
	Joke 'Cheating' (*London Calling*) BS 1666	5.	5.	0
July				
2	1 illus. 'Josey gets going' (Blackie) BS 7450	3.	3.	0
	Colour page 'The Ogre' (*Help Yourself*)	8.	8.	0
10	14 Headings 'Reading & Thinking VI' (Nelson) BS 7262	44.	2.	0
12	2 illus. 'The beautiful balloon' (Blackie) BS 7311	6.	6.	0
25	Joke 'Swimming bath' (Newnes) BS 2400	5.	0.	0
26	Joke 'When I was young' (*London Calling*) BS 2467	4.	4.	0
Aug.				
2	Illus. 'Lazy Wives' (*Sunday Dispatch*) BS	8.	8.	0
10	Illus. 'Gold diggers' (*Sunday Dispatch*)	8.	8.	0
13	Heading, 6 illus., & colour plate 'A couple of guineas' (Blackie)	29.	18.	6
16	Illus. 'The golf widow' (*Sunday Dispatch*)	8.	8.	0
24	Label 'Witch Hazel Jelly' (Cardigan Press)	3.	11.	0
25	3 chalk illus. 'Sybil Thorndike' 3rd instal. (*Strand*) BS 7669	15.	15.	0
29	Page dec. 'Neo Georgian' (*Eve*) BS	6.	6.	0
	Page dec. 'Modern Youth (*Eve*) BS	6.	6.	0
30	Joke 'Which days' (P.S.) BS 2399	5.	5.	0
Sept.				
10	Dec. 'Sailmaker' (Britannia) BS 3071	5.	11.	0
13	2 chalk illus. 'Sybil Thorndike' last instal. (*Strand*) BS 7725	10.	10.	0
26	Halftone heading to Puzzle page (*Xmas Strand*) BS 7849	3.	13.	6
Oct.				
1	Page decoration 'Ekthalamion' (*Eve*) BS 3241	6.	6.	0
2	Joke 'Panto' (P.S.) BS 860	5.	5.	0
4	Winetraid ad. (line) 'Toast proposer' BS 887	6.	6.	0
8	Joke 'Deflated' (*Tatler*) BS 899	5.	5.	0
10	2 halftone figures John & London heading BS 7891	2.	2.	0
11	Joke 'Early Xmas' (*London Calling*) BS 986	5.	5.	0
12	Joke 'Castor-oiled' (Newnes) BS 982	5.	0.	0
15	Illus. 'Her Xmas Holiday' (T.B. Xmas) BS 7888	4.	4.	0
16	2 poster roughs (colour) 'Kodak' (Cardigan Press) BS	2.	2.	0

		£.	s.	d
18	Joke 'Lost children' (P.S.) BS 984	5.	5.	0
22	Joke 'New femininity' (P.S.) BS 1130	5.	5.	0
24	Illus. Bransby Williams article (T.B. Xmas) BS 7968	4.	4.	0
	Illus. 'The Ancient Call' (T.B. Xmas) BS 7969	5.	5.	0
	2 thumbnails 'Sledge & Prayers' (T.B. Xmas) BS	2.	2.	0
	Joke 'Snowdrift' (*Sketch*) BS 1190	5.	5.	0
29	Joke 'Like a native' (Newnes) BS 1129	5.	0.	0
	Joke 'Miles from anywhere' (Newnes) BS 1193	5.	0.	0
30	Joke 'Ignition' (P.S.) BS 1194	5.	5.	0
31	3rd rough for Kodak poster 'Green interior' (Cardigan Press) BS	1.	1.	0
Nov.				
1	3 illus. 'Gold horns & sandals' (Merry) BS 1198	10. 10.		0
5	Joke 'How p-pretty' (Newnes) BS 1269	5.	0.	0
7	Joke 'Boy Cinema star' (P.S.) BS	5.	5.	0
8	Joke 'Look up to you' (*L. Calling*) BS 1283	3.	3.	0
	Joke 'Your old Cook' (*L. Calling*) BS 1284	5.	5.	0
9	Joke 'Can't get to sleep' (P.S.) BS 1196	5.	5.	0
13	Joke 'Oversmelt' (Newnes) BS 1360	5.	0.	0
14	Joke 'No heart' (*Tatler*) BS 1267	5.	5.	0
15	Joke 'Oxford-dancing' (P.S.) BS 1195	5.	5.	0
22	3-colour cover 'My wife poor wretch' BS 7966	5.	5.	0
26	Joke 'Boy Scout' (Newnes) BS 1360	5.	0.	0
27	3 pages 'Home interior', 'Garden', 'Fairy-tale character' (Nelson) BS 7944	15. 15.		0
29	Joke 'House on fire' (Newnes) BS 1535	5.	0.	0
Dec.				
7	Joke 'Look where I'm going' (*Tatler*) BS 1672	5.	5.	0
11	Joke 'Picture-Bazaar' (P.S.) BS 1651	5.	5.	0
31	Joke 'Mephistopheles' (P.S.) BS 1650	5.	5.	0
	Joke 'Pore rabbit' (*Tatler*) BS 1693	4.	4.	0
1929				
Jan.				
3	Joke 'Rice pudding' (*L. Calling*) BS 1742	5.	5.	0

		£.	s.	d
9	3 illus. 'Sybil Thorndike' (*Strand*) BS	18. 18.		0
	3 illus. 'Women & Divorce' (S. Exp.) BS	4. 14.		6
11	2 headings 'The Wheel of Life', 'The Book World' (J. o'L.)	4.	4.	0
18	Cover 'Another pair of shoes' (S.P.C.K.) BS 4113	5.	5.	0
23	Joke 'Noo tap' (*Tatler*) BS 2014	5.	5.	0
	Joke 'Visitor's book' (Newnes) BS	5.	5.	0
25	Joke 'Not looking' (*Sketch*) BS 2151	5.	5.	0
	Joke 'Give your mind to it' (Newnes) BS 2016	5.	5.	0
28	Joke 'Young Married Women' (*London Calling*) BS 2272	5.	5.	0
	Cover 'Lucky Fool' (Besant) BS	5.	5.	0
29	Joke 'Jim's watch' (P.S.) BS 2271	5.	5.	0
Feb.				
12	Cover 'Simon Wisdom' (Besant) BS	5.	5.	0
25	Colour page 'Silent Pool' (*Tatler*) BS 2182	15. 15.		0
Mar				
12	Joke 'Bathing-dress fashion' (P.S.) BS 2675	8.	8.	0
19	3 drawings (colour) 'Fairy Magic' (*Eve*) BS 2878	6.	6.	0
20	Cover 'The Shadow on the road' (Besant) BS 2689	5.	5.	0
22	Heading 'The Fun Fair' (*Eve – Britannia*) BS 2928	5.	5.	0
28	Colour page and 1 illus. 'Plain Jane' (Blackie) BS 4448	8.	8.	0
Apr.				
2	Heading 'Wedding presents' (A.P) BS 2995	2. 12.		6
	2 roughs colour Kodak Summer booklet	2.	2.	0
4	46 line headings and 8 colour pages 'Myths' (Nelson) BS 4067	100.	0.	0
5	Joke 'Shylock' (P.S.) BS 2757	8.	8.	0
8	Line decoration 'Her choice' (*Red*) BS 3120	3.	3.	0
16	Joke 'Cricket – Kent' (P.S.) BS 3198	5.	5.	0
17	Colour page 'Swans' (*Tatler*) BS 3264	15. 15.		0
19	Joke 'Uncle Peter – puppy' (*Tatler*) BS 3196	5.	5.	0
23	1 illus. (colour) 'Weather permitting' (*Eve-B.*) BS 3305	5.	5.	0
	Heading and 2 (colour) 'Talking trees' (*Eve-B.*) BS 3304	10. 10.		0
29	Joke 'Clemenski-Sopelminoff' (*Tatler*) BS 3265	5.	5.	0

May		£.	s.	d
2	Joke 'Jack of Spades' (*Tatler*) BS 3195	5.	5.	0
10	Joke 'five fifty-five' (*T-B Annual*) BS 3468	4.	4.	0
14	Joke 'Grannie Channel swimmer' (P.S.) BS 3468	5.	5.	0
17	Colour sketch 'Fairy Cat' (*Britannia Eve*)	5.	5.	0
24	Colour drawing 'birds of a feather' (*Tatler*) BS	26.	5.	0
June				
4	2 illus. 'Vic & the Bolshy Crew' (Blackie) BS 4796	6.	6.	0
10	Joke 'Music room' (*Tatler*) BS 3790	5.	5.	0
13	Heading (2nd) 'The Fun Fair' (*Britannia*) BS	5.	5.	0
17	Colour illus. 'A lost B . . .' (*Britannia*) BS	5.	5.	0
26	Joke 'Cricketer-Journalist' (P.S.) BS 3886	5.	5.	0
28	Joke 'Draughts in pub' (P.S.) BS 3887	5.	5.	0
	Cover 'Evergreen' (Besant) BS	5.	5.	0
July				
4	Joke 'Tipster' (P.S.) BS 5042	5.	5.	0
11	Cover 'Jack & Jill Annual' (Collins) BS 4876	6.	6.	0
15	Page dec. (colour) 'Rainbow End' (*Tatler*) BS 5184	10.	10.	0
	Colour sketch 'Puppy's first Collar' (*Britannia*) BS 5200	5.	5.	0
	Joke 'Cannot but fail' (Newnes) BS 5185	5.	0.	0
27	Joke 'Top notes' (Newnes) BS 5259	5.	0.	0
	Double spread colour 'Reed boat' (Piccadilly) BS	18.	18.	0
Aug.				
8	Hdg 'Shadow' (*Britannia*) BS 5415	5.	5.	0
14	Joke 'Xmas Decorations' (P.S.) BS	10.	10.	0
19	Joke 'Initial Outlay' (Newnes) BS 5566	5.	0.	0
	Joke 'Fice' (Newnes) BS 5567	5.	0.	0
22	Illus. 'Children' (*S. Dispatch*) BS	7.	7.	0
27	Page joke 'Superstition' (*Tatler*) BS 5696	10.	10.	0
Sep.				
10	Page joke 'Ski-costume' (*Tatler*) BS 5565	10.	10.	0
	Cover 'Barrier' (*Co-op Journal*) BS 5764	12.	4.	6
	Illus. (colour) 'Puppy's removal' (*Eve Britannia*) BS 5750	5.	5.	0
	Joke 'King George' (Piccadilly) BS 5751	5.	5.	0

		£.	s.	d
12	2 colour pages 'Spotting a winner' (Piccadilly) BS 5750	8.	8.	0
13	Halftone illus. 'John' (*Lady*) BS 5828	5.	5.	0
17	Cover 'Girls Adventure Annual' (Collins) BS 4828	5.	5.	0
23	Joke 'Bride's health' (*Tatler*) BS 5697	5.	5.	0
	Joke 'Doctor-drink' (P.S.) BS 5963	5.	5.	0
Oct.				
4	Joke 'Understand a Woman' (Novel) BS	3.	3.	0
	Joke '3rd Party Risks' (Novel) BS	3.	3.	0
	2 illus. 'A divided Xmas' (Novel) BS 6119	6.	6.	0
8	Joke 'Wears it at yer' (*Tatler*) BS 5698	5.	5.	0
15	7 sketches 'Round the World in a baby car' (Part i) (Wide World) BS 2213	8.	15.	0
	1 sketch 'A Happy Xmas' (T-B) BS 2198	3.	3.	0
	Heading 'Fun-fair' (snow) (Eve-Britannia) BS 6245	5.	5.	0
16	2 sketches 'Polka' (T-B Xmas) BS 2205	4.	4.	0
17	3 sketches 'The Witch of Wookey' (T-B Xmas) BS 2266	4.	4.	0
	3 sketches 'On the Phone' (*Happy Magazine*) BS 6203	6.	6.	0
21	Joke 'Watteau' (*Sketch*) BS 6246	5.	5.	0
24	Little sketch 'Family Singing' (*T-B Xmas*) BS 6246	1.	11.	6
26	Joke 'Infantile' (*Sketch*) BS 6247	5.	5.	0
Nov.				
1	Conte sketch 'Song that haunts' (*T-B Xmas*) BS	2.	2.	0
	Joke 'Mucked it up' (*Sketch*) BS 6405	5.	5.	0
12	7 sketch 'Round the World in a baby car' (Conclusion) (Wide World) BS 234	8.	15.	0
19	Joke 'Magneto trouble' (P.S.) BS 6644	5.	5.	0
22	Joke 'All the children we've got' (P.S.) BS 6713	5.	5.	0
Dec.				
2	Joke '2 radiators' (*Motor Owner*) BS 6674	4.	4.	0
3	Cover 'Runaway Caravan' (S.P.C.K.) BS 6678	5.	5.	0
10	Joke 'Got Set' (P.S.) BS 6645	5.	5.	0

1930

Jan.		£.	s.	d
14	14 pages and 19 small sketches 'Tales from Many Lands' (Arnold) BS 33.	33.	9.	0
Feb.				
6	Cover 'Poor Man's Pepper' (S.P.C.K.) BS 7465	5.	5.	0
28	Joke 'Stamps' (P.S.) BS 7721	5.	5.	0
Mch				
5	Joke 'Fishmonger' (*Tatler*) BS 7718	5.	5.	0
12	Joke 'Furnish Well' (*Tatler*) BS 7827	5.	5.	0
25	Colour Page 'Bluebell Wood' (*Tatler*) BS 7955	15.	15.	0
	Joke 'Child in punt' (Newnes) BS 7881	4.	4.	0
31	Joke 'Rat poison' (*Sketch*) BS 8022	5.	5.	0
	Joke 'Tennis Umpire' (*Sketch*) BS 8023	5.	5.	0
Apr.				
8	Joke 'Twins' (Newnes) BS 8092	4.	4.	0
11	Joke 'Flapper learning to drive' (P.S.) BS 8205	5.	5.	0
	3 Elizabethan (redrawn) line drawings (Longmans) BS 8059	6.	6.	0
23	Joke 'Light hand at pastry' (Newnes) BS 8267	4.	4.	0
May				
6	Joke 'Plant fried potatoes' (Novel) BS 8440	2.	12.	6
9	34 sketches 'True tales of an old Shellback' (Longmans) BS 8068	50.	0.	0
13	2 redrawn sketches (Roundhead & Sedan chair) (Longmans) BS 8388	4.	4.	0
19	Showcard 'Brettle's leglets' (Cardigan P.) BS 8513	12.	0.	0
	2 line drawings 'The Enchanted Door' (Blackie) BS 2739	6.	6.	0
	1 line drg 'The Skipping Song' (Blackie) BS 2740	3.	3.	0
	2 line drawings 'Mutton Annie' (Blackie) BS 2737	6.	6.	0
	2 line drawings 'Felicity & the wonderful bag' (Blackie) BS 2738	6.	6.	0
29	Joke 'Stealing fruit' (*Tatler*) BS 8684	5.	5.	0
June				
5	Joke 'Acrostic' (*Tatler*) BS 8685	5.	5.	0
18	2 sketches 'The Springs of humour' (Quiver) BS 8975	4.	4.	0
	2 sketches 'What constitutes humour' (Quiver) BS 8975	4.	4.	0
July				
1	2 sketches 'The Challenge' (Blackie) BS 2955	6.	6.	0

		£.	s.	d
7	2 sketches 'Steel partitions' folder (for J. Pike) BS 9144	5.	15.	6
15	Colour page 'Dragon on Guard' (*Tatler*) BS 8985	15.	15.	0
	1 sk. 2 colour 'Nursery Rhymes' (Britannia) BS 9236	5.	5.	0
16	4 small sketches 'Rita & last minute' (Blackie) BS 2984	6.	6.	0
22	Joke 'Publicity stunt' (Novel) BS 9297	3.	3.	0
	Joke 'For better or worse' (Novel) BS 9297	3.	3.	0
	Joke 'Washing – telegraph pole' (Newnes) BS 9334	5.	5.	0
28	Joke 'Beast Nanny' (Newnes) BS 9334	5.	0.	0
Aug.				
8	Colour page 'Ghost Story' (*Tatler*) BS 9479	15.	15.	0
11	Joke 'No seam' (*Tatler*) BS 9313	4.	4.	0
12	2 colour sketches 'Nursery Rhymes' No. 2 (*Eve-Britannia*) BS 9497	5.	5.	0
14	Joke '39 articles' (*Sketch*) BS 9577	5.	5.	0
18	Joke 'Wireless Beethoven' (*Sketch*) BS 9576	5.	5.	0
22	Joke 'Mr Fawkes' (Newnes) BS 9630	5.	0.	0
27	Joke 'Turkeys migrate' (Newnes) BS 9632	5.	0.	0
	Heading, 3 sketches and colour page 'Mrs Woman' (*D. Mirror Annual*) BS 9550	13.	13.	
Sep.				
1	Joke 'Edgar Wallace Fairy Tales' (Newnes) BS 9631	5.	0.	0
8	Co-op cover (2-colour) 'Surprise in Store' BS 9751	12.	1.	6
10	Joke 'You'll do' (P.S.) BS 9718	5.	5.	0
16	2 colour sketch 'Nursery Rhymes' No. 3 (*Eve-Brit.*) BS 9883	5.	5.	0
17	Heading 'First aid in Camp' (Blackie) BS 3157	3.	3.	0
24	Double spread 'Speaking terms' (*Tatler*) BS 9828	26.	5.	0
25	Joke 'Week-end' (*Tatler*) BS 9929	5.	5.	0
29	Joke 'Bargain basement' (P.S.)	5.	5.	0
30	Joke 'Give you the pleasure' (*Tatler*) BS 131	5.	5.	0
	Joke 'Shan't keep Xmas' (Novel) BS 167	3.	3.	0
Oct.				
1	Joke 'Twiddly-bits' (Leader) BS 211	2.	2.	0
6	Joke 'Dentist-bombs' (Novel) BS 168	3.	3.	0
	Joke 'Prayers to Santa Claus' (Novel) BS 169	3.	3.	0

		£.	s.	d
	Joke 'Full stomach' (Novel) BS 170	3.	3.	0
8	Joke (Colour) 'All in pink'			
	(*Tatler*) BS 130	15.	15.	0
10	2 colour sketch 'Nursery Rhymes'			
	No. 4 (*Eve-Brit.*) BS 284	5.	5.	0
13	8 sketches & 1 halftone 'Two			
	wanderers in Jugo-Slavia' (Wide			
	World) BS 3221	11.	11.	0
16	Showcard Brettles Gloves			
	'Tweedestria' BS	9.	15.	0
22	Illus. 'Ursula Bloom article'			
	(*T-B Xmas*) BS	3.	3.	0
27	Joke 'Dressmaker-portrait' (*Sketch*)			
	BS	5.	5.	0
	Joke 'What is it?' (*Tatler*) BS 300	5.	5.	0
31	Heading and 4 sketches 'Sleepy Hollow'			
	(Nelson) BS 3173	5.	15.	6
Nov.				
11	2 col. page 'Scrum-half – Melon'			
	(*Tatler*) BS 630	10.	10.	0
18	Col. page 'Coquette' (*Tatler*)			
	BS 651	15.	15.	0
Dec.				
9	Colour page 'Spring' (*Tatler*) BS	15.	15.	0
22	Joke 'Lost little girl' (*Tatler*)			
	BS 1967	5.	5.	0
1931				
Jan.	2 decorative sketches 'Jewelry' (*Woman &*			
	Beauty) BS 117	2.	2.	0
Feb.				
18	Halftone illus. 'Bill is ruined'			
	(M. Post) BS 1492	4.	4.	0
Mar.				
10	Joke 'And how!' (Newnes) BS	5.	0.	0
	Joke 'Snappy egg' (Newnes) BS	3.	13.	6
	Joke 'Daylight saving certificate'			
	(Newnes) BS	5.	0.	0
17	Joke 'In the deep' (*Tatler*) BS 1826	5.	5.	0
19	Halftone illus. 'Bill' No. 2 (M.			
	Post) BS 1918	4.	4.	0
27	Joke 'Seasickness' (Novel) BS 1965	3.	3.	0
	Joke 'Lower animals' (Novel)			
	BS 1966	3.	3.	0
	Halftone illus. 'Bill' No. 3 (M.			
	Post) BS 1975	4.	4.	0
Apr.				
1	Joke 'Bowl for catches' (Newnes)			
	BS 2003	3.	13.	6
24	Joke 'Over exposed' (*Tatler*) BS 5094	5.	5.	0
	2 sketches 'Pal' & 'Constantine'			
	(*S. Exp.*) BS 5194	6.	6.	0
May				
1	Halftone illus. 'Bill' No. 4			
	(M. Post) BS 5230	4.	4.	0

		£.	s.	d
23	3 halftone sketches 'Man who shook			
	cake' (R.T.S.) BS 3880	7.	7.	0
June				
4	Halftone sketches 'Bathing Belle'			
	(T-B) BS	3.	3.	0
9	Colour double spread 'Astronomers'			
	(*Tatler*) BS	23.	12.	0
17	Colour page 'Achievement'			
	(*Tatler*) BS 5651	14.	3.	6
22	Joke 'Titan' (*Tatler*) BS 5867	5.	5.	0
	Halftone illus. 'Bill' No. 5			
	(M. Post) BS 5652	4.	4.	0
July				
21	Colour decoration 'Fairies in the bread'			
	(*Tatler*)	14.	3.	6
Aug.				
10	Joke 'Canned' (Newnes – L.O.)			
	BS 6401	5.	0.	0
11	Heading 'Children by fireside'			
	(Newnes) BS 4089	2.	12.	6
	Heading 'Bridge party' (T-B) BS 4094	3.	3.	0
17	2 drawings 'Spring thunder' (London)			
	BS 6325	14.	14.	0
18	Joke 'Teething' (*Tatler*) BS	5.	5.	0
24	Joke 'Tailwagger' (P.S.) BS 6484	2.	12.	6
31	Joke 'I am a pig' (P.S.) BS 6483	5.	5.	0
	Joke 'Sound in wind' (Newnes)			
	BS 6485	5.	0.	0
Sept.	Line drawing 'Traffic' (T-B) BS 4221X			
10	Joke 'Xmas cheque' (*Sketch*)			
	BS 6624	5.	5.	0
17	Joke 'Died in perfect health'			
	(*Sketch*) BS 6625	5.	5.	0
25	Halftone illus. 'Bill' No.6			
	(M. Post) BS 6752	4.	4.	0
28	Joke 'Old girl's colours' (P.S.)			
	BS 6824	5.	5.	0
	Joke 'Postman – presents' (P.S.)			
	BS 6826	5.	5.	0
29	Joke 'Nobody's wife' (Novel)			
	BS 6841	2.	12.	6
	Joke 'Not such nothing' (Novel)			
	BS 6841	2.	12.	6
	Joke 'Empire Free Trade'	2.	12.	6
30	Cover 2 colour 'Xmas Cracker' BS	12.	0.	0
Oct.				
1	Halftone sketch 'Child & envelope'			
	(S. Pict.) BS 6882	5.	5.	0
5	2 halftone illus. 'Halcyon Journey'			
	(London) BS	14.	14.	0
13	Double page 'The last Caravan'			
	(*Tatler*) BS 6804	23.	12.	6
15	Joke 'Apathy' (*Tatler*) BS 6804	5.	5.	0
	Joke 'Is it British?' (*Tatler*)			
	BS 6943	5.	5.	0

		£.	s.	d
20	Joke 'Bluebottle' (P.S.) BS 7021	5.	5.	0
	Joke 'Edgar Wallace' (P.S.)			
	BS 7020	5.	5.	0
	Line sketch 'Mabel Constanduros'			
	(T-B) BS 4348	3.	3.	0
21	Joke 'Dole' (*Tatler*) BS 7043	5.	5.	0
22	Halftone sketch 'The Invitation'			
	(S. Pict.) BS	5.	5.	0
27	Joke 'Airman's fiancee' (Newnes)			
	BS 7094	3.	13.	6
29	Joke 'Driving signals' (P.S.)			
	BS 7093	5.	5.	0
Nov.				
6	Joke 'Rainbow' (*Tatler*) BS 7143	5.	5.	0
10	Joke 'Modern Clock' (Newnes) BS	5.	0.	0
23	Joke 'Floodlit' (*Sketch*) BS 7324	5.	5.	0
24	Joke 'Truculent hiss' (*Sketch*)			
	BS 7323	5.	5.	0
Dec.				
2	Cover 'Mystery of the Sinclairs			
	(S.P.C.K.) BS 7284	5.	5.	0
8	Joke 'Chairing the Captain'			
	(*Tatler*) BS 7389	8.	8.	0
15	Halftone illus. 'Nurse & Children'			
	(S. Chron.) BS	5.	5.	0
17	Line illus. 'Princess & Swineherd'			
	(*Tatler*) BS 7576	5.	2.	6
31	Colour page 'February filldyke'			
	(*Tatler*) BS	14.	3.	6
1932				
Jan.				
22	8 page illus. (line) '3 Musketeers'			
	(Nelson) BS 4231	26. 17.		7.
Feb.				
18	Line cover 'Mystery of the Sinclairs'			
	(S.P.C.K.) BS 7948	2.	2.	0
	Page line decoration 'Sundowner' (*Tatler*)			
	BS	14.	0.	0
Mar.				
16	Colour page 'Cuckoo-hiker' (*Tatler*)			
	BS 8118	14.	3.	6
18	Joke 'Porter – Waterloo (*Tatler*)			
	BS 8170	5.	5.	0
Apr.				
26	Joke 'Where's your gun?' (Novel)			
	BS 8464	2.	12.	6
	Joke 'Daily Bread' (Novel)			
	BS 8465	2.	12.	6
29	16 line illus. 'Black Tulip'			
	(Nelson) BS 4685	62.	0.	0
May				
4	Joke 'Dr Wilkinson' (Newnes)			
	BS 8323	5.	0.	0
31	Joke 'Be good' (*Leader*) BS 8725	2.	2.	0

		£.	s.	d
June				
2	2 sketches 'The Prince's Socks' (*D.M. Annual*) BS 8739	3. 10.		0
13	Line sketch 'Baby in train' (*Express*)			
	BS 8889	3.	3.	0
30	Colour double spread 'Fielding in the			
	deep' (*Tatler*) BS 8900	23.	2.	6
July				
19	15 line drawings '————?' (Nelson's)			
	BS 5091	34.	2.	6
26	Page 'frame' decoration 'Sandy mac' (*D.M. Annual*) BS 8989	2.	2.	0
Sept.				
3	Joke ' "No carol" board' (Novel)			
	BS 9481	2.	12.	6
7	Joke 'Egg-fish' (*Leader*) BS 9530	2.	2.	0
	Joke 'Not cricket' (*Leader*)			
	BS 9531	X		
8	Joke 'Love at first sight' (Novel)			
	BS	2.	12.	6
9	Heading 'Taxi Sir' (*D.M. Annual*)			
	BS 9435	1.	11.	6
Oct.				
10	1 sketch for Graham Simmons			
	(*Happy Magazine*) BS 5426	4.	4.	0
11	2 sk. 'Puddings' (*T-B Xmas*)			
	BS 5399	3.	3.	0
	2 colour dec. 'Xmas Story'			
	(*T-B Xmas*) BS 5400	5.	5.	0
23	Double spread 'Concentration'			
	(*Tatler*) BS 9358	23.	12.	6
Nov.				
1	Joke 'Commissionaire' (*Tatler*)			
	BS 9866	5.	5.	0
3	2 double spreads 'All square' (London)			
	BS 9864	16.	16.	0
8	Joke 'S'yoursh' (Newnes)			
	BS 9967	5.	0.	0
Dec.				
9	Cover and spine 'Forest Hall'			
	(S.P.C.K.) BS 234	5.	0.	0
30	Joke 'religious views' (*Tatler*)			
	BS 207	5.	5.	0
	Cinema hoarding' (Newnes)			
	BS 309	5.	0.	0
1933				
Feb.				
17	2 halftone double spreads 'Journey of			
	Life' (*Wife & Home*) BS 700	12.	12.	0
Mch.				
7	Line cover for S.P.C.K. book			
	above BS 790	2.	2.	0
17	Halftone half page 'Teaching			
	Granny' (*Wife & Home*)			
	BS 879	3.	3.	0

		£.	s.	d
20	Line drawing 'Woman next door'			
	(*Lady's Comp.*) BS 929	3.	3.	0
31	Line decoration 'Now & then' (*Tatler*)			
	BS 938	7.11.		2
Apr.				
3	Halftone sk. 'Cosmetics & lady'			
	(M. Post) BS	4.	4.	0
10	Joke 'Butler – smile' (*Tatler*)			
	BS 1048	5.	5.	0
25	Joke 'Again tomorrow' (*Tatler*)			
	BS 1152	5.	5.	0
28	Line decoration 'Ghosts' (*Tatler*)			
	BS 1048	7.11.		2
May				
9	Joke 'Being watched' (Newnes)			
	BS 1231	1.13.		6
18	3 line and 3 halftone sketches			
	'All because of a bucket'			
	(*Wife & Home*)			
	BS 1319	12.12.		0
24	Joke 'Ramblers-hikers' (*P. Show*)			
	BS 1362	4.	4.	0
June				
9	Joke 'Wife's trousers' (*P. Show*)			
	BS 1472	3.	3.	0
28	Joke 'Water diviner' (*Tatler*)			
	BS 1471	5.	5.	0
July				
4	Joke 'Leaky hose' (*Tatler*) BS 1649	5.	5.	0
12	Colour page 'Two's Company'			
	(*Tatler*) BS	14.	3.	6
Aug.				
6	Colour decoration 'Coloured glasses'			
	(*Tatler*) BS 1809	7.11.		2
	Joke 'Fromage' (Newnes) BS 1868	5.	0.	0
21	6 small sketches 'Rag Bag talks' (*Wife*			
	& Home) BS 1927	6.	6.	0
Sep.				
22	Page decoration 'Repercussion' (*New Pic.*)			
	BS 2158	3.	3.	0
	Line drawing 'Snakes & ladders' (*Lady's*			
	Comp.) BS 2156	X		
Oct.				
14	Border decoration 'The Manager'			
	(Quiver) BS 2336	4.	4.	0
20	Border decoration 'Weather wise'			
	(*D.M. Annual*) BS 2184	1.15.		0
Nov.				
13	Decoration and illus. 'Radio oracle'			
	(*D.M. Annual*) BS 2542	3.	3.	0
22	Joke 'Hiccough-change-gear'			
	(*Tatler*) BS 2525	4.	4.	0
Dec.				
14	Double spread 'Skating' (*Tatler*)			
	BS 2377	18.10.		0

1934				
Jan.		£.	s.	d
29	Cover and spine 'The Rubies &			
	the Ring' (S.P.C.K.) BS 2984	4.	0.	0
Feb.				
28	Joke 'Litter' (P.S.) BS	3.	3.	0
Mar.				
8	Border decoration 'Queen of the Roses'			
	(*D.M. Annual*) BS 3230	2.	2.	0
12	Joke 'Horn out of order' (*Tatler*)			
	BS 3256	4.	4.	0
	2-colour p.c. 'Child at table' (Krake)			
	BS 2357	1.10.		0
21	Page decoration poem '2nd Sight' (*Tatler*)			
	BS	7.11.		2
Ap.				
27	Small sketch 'Price on his head'			
	(*Mirror*) BS 3528		10.	6
May				
18	Halftone sk. 'Giving Ann a treat'			
	(*Wife & Home*) BS 3606	5.	9.	3
June				
11	Poem sketch 'If you must go' (*W.*			
	Weekly) BS 3731		17.	6
20	Poem sketch 'Curious' (*W. Weekly*)			
	BS 3751		17.	6
22	Halftone sketch 'Weather Forecast'			
	(*Pic. W.*) BS 3812	2.12.		6
25	Poem sketch 'Tea-time' (*W. Weekly*)			
	BS 3801		17.	6
July				
2	Poem sketch 'Concealment' (*W.*			
	Weekly) BS 3801		17.	6
10	Poem sketch 'I do not like' (*W.*			
	Weekly) BS 3801		17.	6
16	Halftone sketch & 2 line sk. 'Please			
	adopt H.R.H.' (*Wife & Home*)			
	BS 3867	4.	4.	0
17	Poem sketch 'This is the street'			
	(*W. Weekly*) BS 3801		17.	6
18	Double spread 'Goodbye Summer'			
	(*Tatler*) BS	23.	2.	0
19	2-page border decoration 'Pooh!' said			
	Isabelle (*D.M. Annual*)			
	BS 3779	3.10.		0
24	Poem sketch 'Unchanged' (*W.*			
	Weekly) BS 3801	X		
31	5 sketches colour Electricity triple			
	folder BS	26.	5.	0
Aug.				
7	Joke 'Night life' (*Tatler*) BS 3829	4.	4.	0
17	2 sketches 'Bwoke Dolly' (*Wife &*			
	Home) BS 4041	5.	5.	0
Sep.				
11	Joke 'Hawker or Circular' (Xmas			
	Cracker) BS 4187	3.13.		6

		£.	s.	d
30	2 page frame border 'Holiday Snaps'			
	(*D.M. Annual*) BS 4291	4.	4.	0
Oct.				
12	Page decoration 'Xmas Carol' (Quiver)			
	BS 4338	4.	4.	0
	Thumbnail 'Woman at window'			
	(*W. Weekly*) BS 3801		17.	6
Dec.				
10	5 line sketches 'Caesar & the Pirates'			
	(Nelson) BS 8523	15.	15.	0
17	Halftone illus. 'Mister Magpie'			
	(*Wife & Home*) BS 4734	4.	4.	0
19	Joke 'Terra firma' (*Tatler*) BS 4751	5.	5.	0
27	Halftone sketch 'Riviera' (M. Post)			
	BS 4845	5.	5.	0

1935

Jan.

8	Line sketch 'St Sophia' (Nelson)			
	BS 8645	3.	3.	0
	Line sketch 'Gertrude Bell' (Nelson)			
	BS 8644	3.	3.	0
9	Heading and 1 sketch 'Too much Marzipan'			
	(*D.M. Annual*) BS 4696	3.	0.	0
23	2 illus. (halftone) 'Back Numbers'			
	(*Home Notes*) BS 4986	8.	8.	0
29	Joke 'View – bottles' (*Tatler*) BS 5008	5.	5.	0
Feb.				
11	Joke 'God knows' (*Tatler*) BS 5039	4.	4.	0
	Heading and 1 sketch 'Snowbound' (Wilfred's			
	Annual) BS 5069	3.	0.	0
25	Halftone sketch 'Elm tree, etc.' (*Wife*			
	& Home) BS 5091	3.	3.	0
26	Joke 'Reference – Poster' (Newnes)			
	BS 5074	4.	4.	0
Mar.				
4	Colour page 'Scouts bonfire' (*Tatler*)			
	BS	12.	12.	0
8	2 line sketch 'Jubilee decorations'			
	(*Wife & Home*) BS 5195	1.	10.	0
25	Line sketch 'Ideal Husband' (*Wife &*			
	Home) BS 5349		15.	0
Apr.				
9	Page decoration (colour) 'My Lord, the			
	Carriage waits' (*Tatler*) BS 5363	7.	11.	2
16	Poster 'Pwllheli' (G.W.R.)			
	BS 5251	26.	5.	0
	Joke 'Cross out sentence' (*Tatler*)			
	BS 5425	4.	4.	0
July				
1	Joke 'Bucket' (Newnes) BS 5742	4.	4.	0
25	Joke 'Jam-roll – lost' (*Tatler*)			
	BS 5862	4.	4.	0
	Joke 'Head or tail' (*Tatler*)			
	BS 5861	5.	5.	0

		£.	s.	d
Aug.				
30	Colour page 'Hallowe'en' (*Tatler*)			
	BS 5756	15.	15.	0
Sep.				
26	1 halftone illus. 'Keep smiling'			
	(*Woman's Magazine*) BS 1168	5.	5.	0
Oct.				
24	Cover & frontispiece 'Wit's End'			
	(R.T.S.) BS	6.	6.	0
Nov.				
8	2 halftone illus. 'Mr Timpson'			
	(*Woman's Magazine*) BS 1357	5.	5.	0
22	Cover & frontispiece 'Bunny & the			
	Aunt' (R.T.S.) BS 1393	6.	6.	0
Dec.				
	Cover & frontispiece 'The 3 halves			
	(?)' (R.T.S.) BS	6.	6.	0

1936

Jan.

23	Joke 'Les Miserables' (*Tatler*)			
	BS 6706	4.	4.	0
	2 halftone illus. 'Drusilla' (*Woman's*			
	Magazine) BS 1531	5.	5.	0
Mar.				
11	Joke 'Little pudding' (*Tatler*)			
	BS 6995	4.	4.	0
May				
8	Halftone dble spr. 'Bough breaks'			
	(*Wife & Home*) BS 7306	6.	6.	0
	Heading and double spread 'The Pet haunt'			
	(*Woman's Own*) BS	6.	6.	0
July				
7	Double spread halftone illus. 'Debut			
	of Eddie' (*Wife & Home*)			
	BS 7592	3.	3.	0
29	Joke 'Horse guards' (*Tatler*) BS	4.	4.	0
Sep.				
17	Cover and frontispiece 'Stella's			
	Victory' (S.P.C.K.) BS	6.	6.	0
Oct.				
	Page dec. 'Sam's Roman Ancestor'			
	(*T.B. Xmas*) BS 2370	6.	6.	0
	2 illus. 'Young man in search of			
	Xmas' (*T.B. Xmas*) BS 2428	8.	8.	0
Nov.				
	Cover and frontispiece 'Sally of			
	the 4th form gang' (R.T.S.)			
	BS 2517	6.	6.	0
	Border des. 'Greenwich Pensione'			
	(Newnes) BS 2481	X		

1937

Jan.	Colour page 'Fancy dress shop'			
	(MacMillans) BS	5.	5.	0
Feb.	Cover and spine 'Daman's at			
	Dorothy's (S.P.C.K.) BS 4413	5.	5.	0
Mar.	3 roughs for Electricity Calendar			
	(Cardigan Press) BS 4539	3.	3.	0

		£	s.	d
Apr.	1st painting Elec Calendar 'Child & dolls & fire' (Cardigan Press) BS 474	10.	10.	0
	Decoration for poem 'A fishy affair' (T.B.) BS 1358	7.	7.	0
June	Heading and 3 thumbnails (wash) 'The Shepherd' (R.T.S.) BS 1977	3.	13.	6
July	Heading and 3 thumbnails 'Maggie Dean's first place' (R.T.S.) BS 2046	3.	13.	6
Sep.	Heading and 3 thumbnails 'Entertaining a stranger' (R.T.S.) BS	3.	13.	6
Oct.	Heading & 3 thumbnails 'Maggie Dean's Courtship' (R.T.S.) BS 2290	3.	13.	6
Nov.	4-page decoration 'Sam de Bouf' (T.B. Xmas) BS 2314	6.	6.	0
12	Heading and 3 thumbnails (wash) 'Story of Eliza Day' (R.T.S.) BS 2388	3.	13.	6
Dec.	Heading and 3 thumbnails (wash) 'Andrew's chair' (R.T.S.) BS 2599	3.	13.	6

1938

		£	s.	d
Jan.	Odd sketches to 18 ads for 'Crawford's' BS 2368	30.	4.	10
Feb.	Double page halftone 'Little Lou' (*Wife & Home*) BS 6462	6.	6.	0
May	Large decoration 'The Old 'un' (T.B. Summer) BS	5.	17.	7
Oct. 4	Large decoration 'The Old 'un's Ghost Story' (T.B. Xmas extra) BS 3590	7.	7.	0
10	5 thumbnails 'Roderick Tweedie' ad. BS 3664	4.	4.	0
28	Page decoration 'George's Ghost' (T.B. Xmas no.) BS 3739	6.	6.	0

1939

		£	s.	d
Mar.	Joke 'Bit of rope' (*Tatler*) BS 8353	3.	7.	2
May	Double page decoration 'Holiday in 20 countries' (T.B. Summer) BS 1169	7.	7.	0
Sep.	Joke 'Scot & Kids respirators' (*Tatler*) BS	4.	4.	0
Oct.	Heading, 2 full pages and 1 half page 'Strange adventure with a pony' (Univ. of London Press) BS 9288	4.	10.	0
31	3 line sketch 'A Rum Go' (T.B. Xmas) BS 1532	4.	4.	0
Nov.	Page decoration '3 Services Books' (*The Field*) BS	4.	4.	0
Dec.	Line sketch (Grecian) 'Is this really 1943?' BS	2.	2.	0

1940

		£	s.	d
Jan.	Colour Xmas card 'Scouts' (R.T.S.) BS 9642	4.	4.	0
Mar.	Decoration for poem 'Fish & chips' (T.B. Summer no.) BS 1921	6.	6.	0
26	Colour cover and frontispiece 'One too many' (R.T.S.) BS	5.	5.	0
Apr.	Line and wash heading 'Sundial' (*Wife & Home*) BS 623	1.	2.	6
May	Line sketch 'Holidays with books' (T.B.) BS 723	2.	2.	0
Sep.	2 colour decoration 'Fall out the Cooks' (T.B.) BS 2024	3.	3.	0
	Line sketch 'Fatigue Party' (T.B.) BS 2019	2.	2.	0
Oct.	4 halftone sketches (3 children) (*Woman's Weekly*) BS 2032	3.	3.	0

1941

		£	s.	d
Nov.	Line sketch 'Prince wished too often' (T.B.) BS 2419	2.	2.	0

1942

		£	s.	d
July	Page decoration 'The garden in the Square' (G.O.P.)	1.	11.	6
Aug.	Halftone drawing 'Moldavian black on rose' (G.O.P.)	2.	2.	0
Oct.	Halftone drawing 'Twin beeches' (G.O.P.)	2.	2.	0
Nov.	'Queen by Proxy' 1st instal. (G.O.P.)	3.	3.	0
Dec.	'Queen by Proxy' 2nd and 3rd instal. (G.O.P.)	3.	3.	0
10	'The boy next door' (Newnes) [accounted for on a] loose sheet			
15	2 page decoration 'Sailormen's Tales (G.O.P.)	2.	2.	0

1943

		£	s.	d
Jan.	8 woodcut tailpieces for 'The Village & us in Wartime' (Lutterworth)	16.	16.	0
Feb.	Double page decoration 'The Lay of the little tune' (Lutterworth)	3.	3.	0
19	Queen by Proxy (4 & 5)	6.	6.	0
Mch.	8 more tailpieces 'The Village sk.' (Lutterworth)	16.	16.	0
15	Queen by Proxy (6)	3.	3.	0
Apr.	Queen by Proxy (7 & 8)	6.	6.	0
May	Suzette's Family (32 illus. and cover) (Newnes)	42.	2.	0
June	Colour drg '2 a dozen' (*Woman's Magazine*)	6.	6.	0
17	Queen by Proxy (9)	3.	3.	0
Aug.	2 p. dec. 'Seasonal recipes' (*Woman's Magazine*)	3.	1.	0

		£.	s.	d
30	Queen by Proxy (final)	3.	3.	0
Sep.	Page decoration 'Travellers' tales' (Printers Pie)	5.	5.	0

1944

Jan.	Line sketch 'Saloamn the mouse' (B.B.C.)	1.	11.	6
31	Book 'The boy next door' (Newnes) BS 2785	78.	15.	0
Mch.	5 illus. 'Kenilworth' (Arnold's) BS 573	13.	12.	6
Apr.	Page decoration 'Heard at the Zoo' (Playways)	2.	2.	0
May	Page decoration 'Enchantment' (G.O.P.) BS	2.	2.	0
July	'Last of the Mohicans' 4 pages halftone (Arnold)	10.	10.	0
Aug.	Johnny Mouse of Corregidor (full book) (Hutchinson)	75.	1.	6
18	'The Pathfinder' 4 pages halftone (Arnold)	10.	10.	0
Sep.	Double page decoration 'Nicholas Claus Esq.' (Lutterworth)	5.	5.	0
19	'The Borrowed Garden' (full book) (Lutterworth)	50.	0.	0
Oct.	'Thalaba the Destroyer' 4 pages halftone (Arnold)	10.	10.	0
Dec.	'The Black Tulip' 5 pages halftone (Arnold)	13.	2.	6

1946

May	'A Sprite at School' Cover, frontispiece 4 line illus. (Hutchinson)	32.	15.	2

1947

Apr.	'Folk Tales of Wales' 20 illus. (Nelson)	16.	16.	0

1948

Jan.	3 illus. each for 'Chatterbox Jack', 'Father Christmas' & 'Coat of Many Colours' (McDougalls)			
Apr.	4 illus each for 'Sambo & Topsy' and 'The Five Black Boys' (McDougalls)			
May	Coloured cover and spine and 10 line illus. for 'The Land of the Christmas Stocking' (Latimer House)	60	18	
June	Heading 'Mr Nobody' and hdg and small illus. for 'Learning to fly' (McDougalls)			

Principal Books Illustrated by A.E. Bestall

*denotes books that are not mentioned in Artwork

1927 'The Play's the Thing' by Enid Blyton (Music by Alec Rowley) (Newnes). All scenes and costumes for 12 Plays for Children

c1927 'Magic Rhymes' by Alfred Dunning (Blackwood) Coloured cover and frontispiece

1927 'Lax of Poplar' by Himself (Sharp)*

1929 'Let's go to Poplar' by Lax of Poplar (Sharp)*

1927–30

'Literary & Dramatic Readings' (Schofield & Sims) 7 vols shared with the Brocks & G.S. Dixon – some coloured

'Reading and Thinking' Book VI (Nelson)

'Bright Story Readers' (Potted Classics) (Arnold)

'Tales from Many Lands' Book I (Arnold)

1930 'Myths & Legends of Many Lands' retold by Evelyn Smith (Nelson). 8 coloured plates & chapter headings

1930 'True Tales of an old Shellback' by Stephen Southwold (Longmans)

c1932 'Mother Goose's Book of Nursery Rhymes' (Warne) including cover and 4 colour plates

c1932 'The Black Tulip' by Alexandre Dumas (Nelson) including coloured cover

c1933 'The Three Musketeers' by Alexandre Dumas (Nelson) including coloured cover

1933 'The Disappearing Trick' by Agnes Frome (Warne) including 2 colour plates

1934 'The Spanish Goldfish' (writing shared with Dudley Glass) (Warne)* including cover & 4 colour plates

1934 'The Fleeters' by Walter Wood (Warne)

1934 'The Haunted Holiday' by Hylton Cleaver (Warne) including cover & coloured frontispiece

1935 'Samples from the Bookshelf' (Books of Delight) (Nelson)* With other illustrators

'The Apples of Youth' from 'Myths & Legends of Many Lands'

'A Legend of St Sophia' Traditional

'Cuchullin & the Morrigu' from 'Myths & Legends of Many Lands'

'A Tremendous Performance' from Eleanor Scott: 'Adventurous Women'

'The Deeds of Perseus' from 'Myths & Legends of Many Lands'

'The Capture of Julius Caesar by Pirates' from Henry Gilbert: 'The Book of Pirates', 'Sleepy Hollow' from 'The Times'

1937 'Lax his Book' Autobiography (Epworth Press)*

1937 'The Pilot Prefect' by Hylton Cleaver (Warne)*

1930s 'The Children's Story Book' by Many Famous Story-Tellers (Univ. of London). Edited by Rodney Bennett – with other illustrators

'Strange Adventure with a Pony' by Dorothy Ann Lovell

1939 'The First War-time Christmas Book' – same as above

c1940s 'Round the Mulberry Bush' edited by Rose Fyleman (Partridge)*. With other illustrators

'Princess Melinda' by E.K. Woolner

'Spring Cleaning' by Barbara Euphan Todd (1 colour)

c1942 'Professor Twinkle's Puzzle Book' (R.A. Publishing Company London)*

1943 'Salute to the Village' by Fay Inchfawn (Lutterworth Press)

1943 'Suzette's Family' by Harriet Evatt (Newnes)

1944 'The Boy Next Door' by Enid Blyton (Newnes) including coloured cover

1944 'Thalaba the Destroyer' by Robert Southey (Arnold)

c1944 'Johnny Mouse of Corregidor' by Marion Johnson (Hutchinson)

c1944 'The Borrowed Garden' by Kathleen Fidler (Lutterworth Press)

c1944 'Kenilworth' by Sir Walter Scott (Arnold)

c1946 'A Sprite at School' by Constance M. White (Hutchinson) including coloured cover and frontispiece

1947 'The Hive' by John Crompton (Blackwood)* including 1 colour plate

1947 'Folk Tales of Wales' by Eirwen Jones (Nelson)

1948 'The Land of the Christmas Stocking' by Mabel Buchanan (Latimer House). Coloured cover & 10 line illustrations

1936–73 inclusive, all 'Rupert' Annuals (mostly reprints from the *Daily Express* but incl. 49 specially written and drawn stories)

Covers only by AEB

c1923 'According to Gibson' by Denis Mackail (Heinemann)

c1929 'The Shadow on the Road' by Alice Massie (Besant)

c1929 'Lucky Fool' by L.C. Gould-Fleme (Besant)

c1929 'Simon Wisdom' by Hilary March

1947 'Countryside Tales from Blackwood' (Blackwood)*

1949 'Animal Tales from Blackwood' (Blackwood)*

1950 'Strange Tales from Blackwood' (Blackwood)*

c1951 'A Thorny Wilderness' by J.B. Welman (Blackwood)*

The Big (Bumper) Budget for Children

'Zammy the Zebra'

The Big Budget for Boys

c1932 Cover with marquee & 3 boys hurdling

c1934 Cover with 5 boys on mountain top

The Big Budget for Girls

c1932 Cover with mountains & 9 figures

'A Double Triumph' by Shirley Grey

'Which Switch?' by J.Y. Thomson

'Something Happens' by Irene Boyd

'Biddy's Bogeys' by Helen Everest

'Up the Tower Stair' by Lilias Small

'Cousin Leslie' by Enid Barclay

'The Mouse' by Irene Boyd

Blackie's Children's Annuals

1929 'A Couple of Guineas' by Eleanor B. Simeon. Including colour plate

1930 'Plain Jane' by E. Maslin Kearsey. Including colour plate ('You Miss Peggy')

1938 'Magic Farm' by Susan Buchan

c1939 'A Present for Uncle John' by Agnes Grozier Herbertson

'The Model Cabin' by Lorentz Gullachsen

Blackie's Girls' Annuals

1929 'Daffy Fleetwood's Job' by Evelyn Smith

'The Finger of Fate' by Lady Middleton

1930 'Outwitting Aunt Maud' by Margaret Middleton

'Vic and the Bolshy Crew' by Agnes Adams

1931 'Mutton Annie' by Alison Graham

1932 'Serenading the Burglars' by Iris de V. Forth

'Aunt Eliza is not Prepared' by Sybil Haddock

1933 Colour frontispiece 'The Swan Maiden'

'Two Old Comrades' by Marjorie Beven

'An Anonymous Party' by Jessie McAlpine

'A Wet Day and a Walk' by Dora M. Hardisty

1934 'A Previous Engagement' by S. Beresford Lucas

'Much Pleasure in Accepting' by E.M. Defubert

'Bill's Bomb' by Alice Massie

1935 'Stop me and Buy One' by Frances Joyce

'A Castle in Spayne' by Blanche Hunt

1936 'Daughters of Gentleman' by A.E. Seymour

1937 Colour cover – 2 girls hiking, one with map

'The Crown of the Road' by Marjorie Miller

'The Babes in the Wood' by W. Kersley Holmes

'The Sun-dial Syndicate' by A.E. Seymour

1938 'Money Musk' by Violet M. Methley

1939 'The Patchwork Counterpane' by Phyllis I. Norris

1940 'The Younger Sister Mystery' by Dorothy Wilding

'Just Luck' by J. Paterson Milne

'Follow in Father's Footsteps' by Ann Beverley

'Lady Louise' by Margaret Turvey

Blackie's Little Ones' Annuals

c1930 'Skipping Song' by Margaret E. Gibbs

1930s 'Ambition' by Margaret E. Gibbs (in colour)

1930s 'Shut Out' by Agnes Grozier Herbertson

1930s 'Mrs Thompson's Daughter' by Arthur Groom

A Book of Girls' Stories

'Bill's Bomb' by Alice Massie

'A Previous Engagement' by S. Beresford Lucas
'Has Much Pleasure in Accepting' by E.M. de
    Foubert
'A Castle in Spayne' by Blanche Hunt

The Dandy Book for Children
'Zammy the Zebra'

Droll Folk
c1937 Colour frontispiece 'The Swan Maiden'

The Girls' Budget
c1927 'The House with the Hedge' by Margaret
    Middleton
'The Frock' by Alice Massie
c1928 'From Top to Bottom' by Alice Massie
c1930 'The Tuppeny Cup' by Ethel Talbot
c1933 Cover and 'The Open Door' by Mary Vivian
?   'Miss Sylvester's Standard' by Evelyn Smith
c1934 'The Blue Butterfly' by E.C. Brereton
'Not Cricket' by Jessie McAlpine
c1934 'Felicity & the Wonderful Bag' by Violet M.
    Methley
'Not Cricket' by Jessie McAlpine
?   Frontispiece 'On the Trail'
'On the Trail' by W. Kersley Holmes
'The Rhododendron' by Evelyn Smith
?   'The Ginger Cat' by Felicity Lowe
'Specimens' by W.K. Holmes
'The Turret Room' by Irene Boyd
'Selina – and her Soap' by Laurie Munro
'The Growing up of Rosamund' by Primrose
    Cumming
?   'The Pink Glass Epergne' by Phyllis I. Norris
?   'Damaris Forgot!' by Jean Callender
'A Pair of Madcaps' by Irene Boyd

The Golden Budget for Girls
c1928 'Josey gets Going' by Stan Hope

Good as Gold
'Puzzled' and 'Missed it'

Lucky Girls Budget
?   'Fuscia Buds' by E. S.

The Prize Budget for Girls
c1933 Cover (Skiing)
?   Black and white frontispiece (not cricket) and
    'The Frock' by Alice Massie

1936 'From Attic to Ground Floor' by Alice Massie
1940 'On the Trail' by W. Kersley Holmes
    including coloured frontispiece
    'The Enchanted Door' by A.M. Sterling
?   'The Rhododendron' by Evelyn Smith
    'On the Trail' by W. Kersley Holmes
1942 'On the Trail' by W. Kersley Holmes (reprint)
    'From Attic to Ground Floor' by Alice Massie
        (reprint)
    'The Wrecker' by M.W. Kays

Read a Story
'The Other Three Bears' (1 colour)
'In London Town' (1 colour)

Thrilling Stories for Girls
c1934 'The Luck of Glenmore' by Jane Stirling

Other Annuals
c1921, Hulton's Girls' Annuals (Allied Newspapers Ltd)
24   'The Mysterious Island' by Mrs A.S. Lawrence &
    'The Witch of Whitestones' by Katharine L.
    Oldmeadow
c1923 Pip & Squeak Annuals – 'The Magic Carpet'
c1923 The Red Book for Scouts ed. by Herbert Strang
    (OUP) – 'Running' by P. Longhurst
1923 The Schoolgirls' Annual ('Play Up School!') –
    cover & 'A Cavalier's Daughter' by Ada
    Crundall
1924 The Schoolgirls' Own Annual ('An Easy First') –
    cover & 'The Girl Queen of Campana' by Ada
    Crundall
1925 The Schoolgirls' Own Annual ('Voted the Best!')
    – cover & 'Anne and the Little Admiral' by
    Ada Crundall
1926 The Schoolgirls' Own Annual ('Wall Ahead') –
    cover & 'Afraid to Own Up' by Freda Graham
1927 The Schoolgirls' Own Annual ('Off for the
    Holidays!') – cover & 'A Girl of Old London'
    by Ada Crundall
1928 The Schoolgirls' Own Annual ('The Heroine of
    the Hour') – cover
1929 The Schoolgirls' Own Annual ('Full of Good
    Things!') – cover
c1925 Oojah Annuals – 'Last Bus' & 'Butterfly Express'
c1926 on Nelson Annuals
c1928 The Chummy Book (Nelson) – 'She Goes to
    Church' – poem by T. Cynon Jones
1929 Jack & Jill Annual (Collins) – cover
1935 Bo-Peep's Bumper Book

Bestall Contributions to Punch 1922–1935

1922	14 Jun	16 Aug	13 Sep	20 Sep	1 Nov	22 Nov	29 Nov	
1923	24 Jan	11 Apr	4 Jul	3 Oct	17 Oct	21 Nov	28 Nov	
1924	16 Jan	30 Jan	13 Feb	26 Mar	16 Jul	23 Jul	20 Aug	
	3 Sep	24 Sep	1 Oct	8 Oct	15 Oct	22 Oct	5 Nov	
	12 Nov	26 Nov	26 Nov	3 Dec	17 Dec	17 Dec		
1925	21 Jan	28 Jan	11 Feb	18 Feb	25 Feb	4 Mar	11 Mar	18 Mar	25 Mar
	1 Apr	22 Apr	29 Apr	6 May	20 May	3 Jun	15 Jun	29 Jul	12 Aug
	9 Sep	16 Sep	23 Sep	7 Oct	21 Oct	4 Nov	2 Dec	23 Dec	
1926	13 Jan	20 Jan	10 Feb	17 Feb	10 Mar	1 Dec		
1927	19 Jan	26 Jan	9 Mar	23 Mar	6 Apr	22 Jun		
1928	9 May	20 Jun	22 Aug	19 Sep	26 Sep	7 Nov		
1929	23 Jan	6 Feb	4 Sep	2 Oct	9 Oct	9 Oct	13 Nov	
1930	9 Apr	28 May	6 Aug	20 Aug	1 Oct	12 Nov	24 Dec	
1931	29 Apr	26 Aug	16 Sep	23 Sep	11 Nov			
1932	27 Apr	29 Jun	27 Jul	21 Sep	9 Nov	28 Dec		
1933	25 Jan	8 Mar	22 Mar	3 May	8 Nov			
1934	31 Oct	7 Nov						
1935	30 Jan	1 May						

Rupert Covers

Endpapers

	Rupert Covers	Endpapers
1936	R. & kite – loose cover	
1937	Pals on a bridge	
1938	Staircase in tree	
1939	Beppo & kite (last red back)	
1940	Rupert's graffiti	
1941	Rupert & paddle	
1942	R. on castle roof	
1943	R. & black butterfly	
1944	Pals up a tree	
1945	R. on flying bicycle	
1946	Flapping bird	
1947	R. chasing dragon	
1948	Rainbow	
1949	Waits	
1950	Shell & gooseberry fool	1 Imp on willow tree
1951	Ice scene	Night – Santa Claus, Imps' house in tree
1952	R. & arrows	King of the Birds, R. on bird's back
1953	R., B. & Algy on fence	Jungle
1954	Orange sky, black snowman	Coon Island, distant magic boat
1955	R., B. & Algy approaching over a ridge	Chalk scene (1). Hare on hillside
1956	Sledge – green sky	R. & Bill, shaded pool
1957	R. riding below balloon	Pine Ogres
1958	Leapfrog	Frog Chorus
1959	Big R.	Copper bird, sunset
1960	Snow falling – lantern	Undersea
1961	Swing	Seascape, Imps & roots
1962	Snowfight	Chalk scene(2). Box Hill, Pong-Ping, Podgy
1963	Merboy in net	Noah's Ark – Aurora
1964	R. climbing – Snowdon & Penlan	Tree house, Ash Hill
1965	Snow, Xmas tree	Scarecrow & Castle, flat colour
1966	Flying saucer	Waterfall (not mine)
1967	Snow, puppy on sledge	Nutwood country. R. in helicopter
1968	Bubble in sky	Hovercraft
1969	R. & fish	Little Chinese Islands
1970	Snow climb, Swiss lake	Big tree. R. as bandit on a rock
1971	R. entering cave	Gomnies underground
1972	Bird bringing letter	Imps in pine tree, Moel Hebog
1973	White face	R. & pals on long fence. Long lake

Paper-folding

1946	Flapping Bird		1966	Sara's furniture
1947	Paper Kettle		1967	Paper Hare
1948	Hobby Horse		1968	Tall Lily, Fish
1949	Chinese Junk		1969	Xmas Tree (Harbin), Pagoda
1950	Paper Plane		1970	Light ship, Standing bird
1951	Paper Man		1971	Hobgomnie, Swimming bird
1952	Elephant		1972	Cave Hopper, Cave Lantern
1953	Snapper, Paper Ball		1973	Salad Plate
1954	Sealion, Penguin, Canoe		1974	Sailing Boat (Toshie Takahama)
1955	Cat's head, Work basket		1975	Sampan
1956	Spill-holder, Spark-man		1976	Humming bird shape, Three Monkeys
1957	Paper Scottie, Glider		1977	Sleeping Goblin
1958	Paper Frog, Water Lily		1978	Seagull (John S.)
1959	Party Cap, Copper bird		1979	Philip Shen's Bowl, Paper Weaving
1960	Donkey & panniers		1980	Tortoise
1961	Paper Chain, Hearthrug		1981	(Nil)
1962	Shaun's Glider		1982	Horse's head (Martin W.)
1963	Paper Kangaroo		1983	Baby Rabbit (Thea Clift)
1964	Paper Star, Butterfly (Yoshizawa)		1984	Cicada
1965	Fireside seat, Notecase (Stift)		1985	Repeat 1946

Rupert Bear in the *Daily Express*

No.	Date of starting	Annual Xmas	Days run	Title
1	28 June 1935	1937	54	Rupert, Algy and the Smugglers
2	30 Aug. 1935	1936	54	Rupert's Autumn Adventure
3	1 Nov. 1935	1936	43	Rupert, Bill and the Pearls
4	21 Dec. 1935	1936	8	Rupert's Christmas Adventure
5	2 Jan. 1936	1939	43	Rupert's Adventures in the Snows
	(Interval for experimental photographic series)			
6	7 March 1936	1936	54	Rupert and the Wonderful Kite
7	11 May 1936	'36 & '53	54	Rupert, Algy and the Cannibals
8	13 July 1936	1937	36	Rupert and Dog Toby
9	24 Aug. 1936	1938	23	Rupert and Bill in the Tree Tops
10	19 Sept. 1936	1937	26	Rupert and the Flying Bottle
11	20 Oct. 1936	1937	26	Rupert and the Chinese Cracker
12	19 Nov. 1936	1937	28	Rupert and the Little Men
13	22 Dec. 1936	1939	12	Rupert and the Goblin Cobbler
14	7 Jan. 1937	1937	26	Rupert and the Snow Machine
15	6 Feb. 1937	1937	28	Rupert in the Floods
16	11 March 1937	1938	28	Rupert and the Daffodils
17	14 April 1937	1942	16	Rupert and the Fire
18	3 May 1937		12	Rupert and the Coronation
19	17 May 1937	1938	40	Rupert and Pong-Ping
20	2 July 1937	1938	24	Rupert, Edward and the Paper Chase
21	30 July 1937	1938	24	Rupert and the Ruby Ring
22	27 Aug. 1937	1938	32	Rupert and Peter
23	4 Oct. 1937	1939	23	Rupert and the half-crowns
24	30 Oct. 1937	1939	31	Rupert and the strange Airman
25	6 Dec. 1937	1938	24	Rupert and the Cuckoo Clock
26	5 Jan. 1938	'38 & '53	28	Rupert in Mystery Land
27	7 Feb. 1938	1940	24	Rupert and the Pedlar
28	7 March 1938	1940	24	Rupert and the Silver Trowel
29	4 April 1938	1939	32	Rupert, Beppo and the Kite

Rupert Bear in the *Daily Express*—(contd)

No.	Date of starting	Annual Xmas	Days run	Title
30	12 May 1938	1940	24	Rupert and the Air Smugglers
31	9 June 1938	1939	36	Rupert and the Courier-bird
32	21 July 1938	1942	28	Rupert at Sandybay
33	23 Aug. 1938	1940	28	Rupert and the Iceberg
34	24 Sept. 1938	1940	28	Rupert and Uncle Bruno
35	27 Oct. 1938	1939	26	Rupert's Bonfire
36	26 Nov. 1938	1941	25	Rupert and Baby Badger
37	27 Dec. 1938	1939	22	Rupert and Jack-in-the-box
38	21 Jan. 1939	1940	36	Rupert and King Frost
39	4 March 1939	1941	29	Rupert and the Sugar-bird
40	8 April 1939	1940	20	Rupert, Bill and the Bluebells
41	2 May 1939	1940	38	Rupert's marvellous Bat
42	15 June 1939	1942	22	Rupert and the Old Ruin
43	11 July 1939	1941	30	Rupert and the lost Boat
44	15 Aug. 1939	1942	46	Rupert and the Seaserpent (War: size reduced 18 Sep.)
45	7 Oct. 1939	1941	32	Rupert and the Mystery Pond
46	14 Nov. 1939	1941	33	Rupert and the little Woodman
47	22 Dec. 1939	1942	24	Rupert and the Wrong Presents
48	22 Jan. 1940	1941	28	Rupert and the Forest Fire
49	23 Feb. 1940	1941	36	Rupert and the Red Egg
50	6 April 1940	1942	40	Rupert and Odmedod (reduced to 1 drawing per day 16 Apr.)
51	23 May 1940	1942	27	Rupert and the Cartwheels
52	24 June 1940	1943	37	Rupert and Tigerlily
53	6 Aug. 1940	1943	42	Rupert and the Banjo
54	24 Sept. 1940	1943	34	Rupert's Good Turn
55	2 Nov. 1940	1943	38	Rupert and the Piper
56	17 Dec. 1940	1944	15	Rupert and the Dutch Doll (1 drawing added for Annual)
57	6 Jan. 1941	1943	36	Rupert's Birthday (Rupert comes of age, 7 Jan. 1941)
58	17 Feb. 1941	1943	42	Rupert and the Iron Key
59	12 April 1941	1942	32	Rupert and the Little Plane
60	20 May 1941	1943	46	Rupert and the Black Moth
61	12 July 1941	1943	30	Rupert and the Circus Dog
62	16 Aug. 1941	1943	48	Rupert's Big Game Hunt
63	11 Oct. 1941	1943	30	Rupert's River Adventure
64	15 Nov. 1941	1943	40	Rupert and Golly
65	6 Jan. 1942	1944	46	Rupert's Strange Party (2 drawings added for Annual
66	2 March 1942	1944	30	Rupert's Rainy Adventure (2 drawings added)
67	7 April 1942	1944	38	Rupert and the tiny Flute (2 drawings added)
68	21 May 1942	1944	56	Rupert and the Mystery Voice
69	27 July 1942	1944	54	Rupert and Rollo (2 drawings added)
70	29 Sept. 1942	1944	42	Rupert and the Old Map (2 drawings added)
71	18 Nov. 1942	1945	54	Rupert and the Reindeer (2 drawings removed)
72	22 Jan. 1943	1945	56	Rupert's Winter Journey
73	29 March 1943	1944	40	Rupert and Granny Goat
74	15 May 1943	1945	52	Rupert and the Cuckoo
75	15 July 1943	1945	38	Rupert and the Turnips (2 drawings removed)
76	28 Aug. 1943	1945	43	Rupert and Jock
77	23 Oct. 1943	1945	40	Rupert and Willie
78	9 Dec. 1943	1945	60	Rupert's Fairy Cycle
79	19 Feb. 1944	1945	36	Rupert and the Music Man
80	1 April 1944	1946	52	Rupert and Rastus
81	2 June 1944	1946	56	Rupert and the Blue Mountain
82	7 Aug. 1944	1946	52	Rupert, Beppo and the Duck

Rupert Bear in the *Daily Express*—(contd)

No.	Date of starting	Annual Xmas	Days run	Title
83	6 Oct. 1944	1946	36	Rupert and Podgy
84	17 Nov. 1944	1946	52	Rupert and the Magic Dart
85	19 Jan. 1945	1946	32	Rupert and Bingo
86	26 Feb. 1945	1947	36	Rupert and the Top Hat
87	10 April 1945	1947	52	Rupert and the Black Cat
88	11 June 1945	1947	52	Rupert and the Young Dragon
89	10 Aug. 1945	1947	44	Rupert, Bill and the Merboy
90	1 Oct. 1945	1947	48	Rupert and Koko
91	26 Nov. 1945	1947	44	Rupert's Christmas Tree
92	18 Jan. 1946	1948	60	Rupert and Jack Frost (My hundredth story)
93	29 March 1946	1948	32	Rupert's Puppy Hunt
94	7 May 1946	1948	56	Rupert and the Sleepy Pears
95	12 July 1946	1949	48	Rupert and Uncle Grizzly
96	6 Sept. 1946	1949	49	Rupert and the New Pal (contained 52 drawings)
97	2 Nov. 1946	1949	32	Rupert, Algy and the Bee
98	10 Dec. 1946	1949	56	Rupert and Ninky
99	15 Feb. 1947	1949	52	Rupert's Island Adventure
100	18 April 1947	1949	52	Rupert and the Young Imp
101	18 June 1947	1950	48	Rupert and the Jumping Fish
102	13 August 1947	1950	56	Rupert and the Three Guides
103	17 Oct. 1947	1950	40	Rupert and the Big Bang
104	3 Dec. 1947	1950	40	Rupert's Silver Trumpet
105	21 Jan. 1948	1951	52	Rupert and Dr Lion (Rupert helps Dr Lion)
106	22 March 1948	1950	56	Rupert and Margot (Rupert and Margot's House)
107	27 May 1948	1951	48	Rupert and Ting-Ling (began signed drawings)
108	22 July 1948	1951	52	Rupert and Mr Punch
109	21 Sept. 1948	1951	56	Rupert's Elfin Bell (and the Elfin Bell)
110	25 Nov. 1948	1951	40	Rupert and the Live Toys (Runaways)
111	13 Jan. 1949	1952	56	Rupert and the Arrows
112	19 March 1949	1951	45	Rupert's Queer Path (60 drawings, 2 pictures per day 25 April on)
113	12 May 1949	1952	48	Rupert and the Mare's Nest
114	7 July 1949	1953	29	Rupert at Rocky Bay
115	10 Aug. 1949	1952	46	Rupert, Beppo and the Caravan
116	3 Oct. 1949	1952	30	Rupert and the Snuff Box
117	7 Nov. 1949	1954	42	Rupert and the Dragon Pills
118	28 Dec. 1949	1953	46	Rupert and Miranda
119	20 Feb. 1950	1954	46	Rupert and the Back-room Boy
120	15 April 1950	1954	32	Rupert and the Sketch-book
121	23 May 1950	1956	46	Rupert's Climbing Adventure
122	15 July 1950	1954	48	Rupert and the Castaway
123	9 Sept. 1950	1955	46	Rupert's Autumn Primrose
124	2 Nov. 1950	1955	34	Rupert and the Blue Firework
125	12 Dec. 1950	1955	44	Rupert and the Coughdrop
126	3 Feb. 1951	1958	42	Rupert and the Ice-flower
127	26 March 1951	1956	46	Rupert and Simon
128	18 May 1951	1956	40	Rupert and the Sorcerer
129	4 July 1951	1957	50	Rupert and the Lion Rock
130	31 Aug. 1951	1957	38	Rupert and the Pine Ogre
131	15 Oct. 1951	1958	30	Rupert and the New Bonnet
132	19 Nov. 1951	1959	42	Rupert and the Toy Scout
133	9 Jan. 1952	1957	40	Rupert and the Windwhistle
134	25 Feb. 1952	1959	32	Rupert's River Rescue
135	2 April 1952	1958	44	Rupert's Spring Adventure

Rupert Bear in the *Daily Express*—(contd)

No.	Date of starting	Annual Xmas	Days run	Title
136	24 May 1952	1959	40	Rupert and the Butterflies
137	10 July 1952	1960	48	Rupert and the Diamond Leaf
138	4 Sept 1952	1960	44	Rupert and Morwenna
139	25 Oct. 1952	1959	30	Rupert and the Hazel Nut
140	29 Nov. 1952	1962	32	Rupert and the Robins
141	8 Jan. 1953	1958	32	Rupert's New Year Adventure (R. & the Train Journey)
142	14 Feb. 1953	1962	42	Rupert and the Bad Dog
143	6 April 1953	1961	32	Rupert and the Pepper-Rose
144	13 May 1953	1960	44	Rupert and Ozzie
145	3 July 1953	1962	42	Rupert's Coral Island
146	21 Aug. 1953	1963	36	Rupert and the Lost Cuckoo
147	2 Oct. 1953	1961	32	Rupert and the Black Spark
148	9 Nov. 1953	1964	34	Rupert and the Compass
149	18 Dec. 1953	1966	48	Rupert and the Magic Ball
150	15 Feb. 1954	1966	38	Rupert and Billy Goat
151	31 March 1954	1966	46	Rupert and the Spring Chicken
152	25 May 1954	1962	36	Rupert and Niagara
153	6 July 1954	1961	52	Rupert at Greyrocks Cove
154	4 Sept. 1954	1963	48	Rupert and the Inventor
155	30 Oct. 1954	1975	32	Rupert and the Broken Plate
156	8 Dec. 1954	1961	40	Rupert and the New Boat
157	25 Jan. 1955	1963	34	Rupert and the Cold-cure
158	5 March 1955	1964	44	Rupert & the Distant Music (interrupted by long strike)
159	21 May 1955		46	Rupert and Dinkie
160	14 July 1955	1972	56	Rupert's Deep Sea Adventure
161	17 Sept. 1955	1963	38	Rupert and the Gold Acorn
162	1 Nov. 1955	1983	42	Rupert and the Black Circle
163	20 Dec. 1955	1969	36	Rupert and the Old Chimney
164	2 Feb. 1956	1965	46	Rupert and the Winter Woolly
165	27 March 1956	1968	50	Rupert and the Firebird
166	25 May 1956	1964	42	Rupert and the Dog-Roses
167	13 July 1956	1969	42	Rupert and the Fishing Rod
168	3 Aug. 1956	1964	42	Rupert and the Rock Pool
169	19 Oct. 1956	1976	46	Rupert and the Windy Day
170	12 Dec. 1956	1975	42	Rupert and the Thinking Cap
171	1 Feb. 1957	1968	44	Rupert and the Rolling Ball
172	25 March 1957	1965	46	Rupert and the Old Hat
173	18 May 1957	1968	46	Rupert and the Fiddle
174	11 July 1957	1965	52	Rupert and Rusty
175	10 Sept. 1957	1977	48	Rupert and the Silent Land
176	5 Nov. 1957	1967	52	Rupert and the Lost List
177	7 Jan. 1958	1967	40	Rupert and the Jackdaw
178	22 Feb. 1958	1971	44	Rupert and the Early Bird
179	16 April 1958	1967	46	Rupert and Floppity
180	9 June 1958	1967	56	Rupert and the Carved Stick
181	13 Aug. 1958	1966	48	Rupert and the Secret Boat
182	8 Oct. 1958	1970	52	Rupert and the Blunderpuss
183	8 Dec. 1958	1968	46	Rupert and the Truant
184	2 Feb. 1959	1969	38	Rupert and the Snowball
185	18 March 1959	1969	40	Rupert and Raggety
186	4 May 1959	1970	58	Rupert and the Outlaws
187	11 July 1959	1969	54	Rupert and the Whistlefish
188	12 Sept. 1959	1978	46	Rupert and the Squire

Rupert Bear in the *Daily Express*—(contd)

No.	Date of starting	Annual Xmas	Days run	Title
189	5 Nov. 1959	1971	56	Rupert and the Windies
190	12 Jan. 1960	1975	32	Rupert and the Winter Sale (R. 40 years old, 7 Jan. 1960)
191	18 Feb. 1960	1985	40	Rupert and the Snowstorm (repeated 28 Nov. 1978)
192	5 April 1960	1971	48	Rupert and the Gomnies
193	1 June 1960	1970	56	Rupert and the Ske-boat
194	5 Aug. 1960	1975	56	Rupert and the Purple Star (changed to 'Blue Star')
195	10 Oct. 1960	1972	56	Rupert and Gwyneth
196	14 Dec. 1960	1970	38	Rupert and the Paper-Fall
197	30 Jan. 1961	1973	48	Rupert and the Housemouse
198	27 March 1961	1972	48	Rupert and the Rugger Match
199	23 May 1961	1974	54	Rupert and the Secret Path
200	25 July 1961	1971	54	Rupert and the Pop-weed
201	25 Sept. 1961	1973	54	Rupert and the Flying Boat
202	28 Nov. 1961	1973	48	Rupert and the Bouncers
203	25 Jan. 1962	1984	44	Rupert and the Igloo
204	17 March 1962	1972	42	Rupert and the Learner
205	7 May 1962	1973	54	Rupert and the Waterfall
206	9 July 1962		52	Rupert and Prince Crab
207	7 Sept. 1962	1976	52	Rupert and the Hot Water
208	7 Nov. 1962	1974	52	Rupert and the Little Bells
209	9 Jan. 1963	1974	52	Rupert and the Icicles (or Jenny Frost)
210	11 March 1963	1975	44	Rupert and the Little River
211	2 May 1963	1977	50	Rupert and Septimus
212	29 June 1963	1974	52	Rupert and the Iron Spade
213	29 Aug. 1963	1977	50	Rupert and the Fire-lighter
214	26 Oct. 1963	1978	51	Rupert and the Rivals
215	27 Dec. 1963		42	Rupert and the Last Cracker
216	14 Feb. 1964		54	Rupert and the Unicorn
217	18 April 1964		50	Rupert and the Tree-house
218	16 June 1964		50	Rupert and the Weatherman
219	13 Aug. 1964	1981	49	Rupert and the Wrong Sweets
220	9 Oct. 1964	1976	50	Rupert and the Jumping Man
221	7 Dec. 1964	1978	39	Rupert's Odd Party
222	23 Jan. 1965	1976	50	Rupert and Kevin
223	23 March 1965	1982	52	Rupert and the Umbrella Boy
224	24 May 1965	1977	52	Rupert and the Winkybickies (ended 22 July)

Extra Stories

Boys & Girls Book of the Year for 1936
Boys & Girls Book of the Year for 1937
Boys & Girls Book of the Year for 1938 & Annual 1950
Boys & Girls Book of the Year for 1939
Rupert Book for 1944–5

Rupert Book for 1945–6
Rupert Book for 1946–7

Rupert Book for 1947–8

Rupert Book for 1948–9

(Not used in the *Daily Express*)

12 2-colour 6-part adventures
Ditto
1 Rupert & the Travel Machine (32)
2 Rupert & the Red Box (32)
3 Rupert & Snuffy (56)
4 Rupert & the Yellow Cloak (28)
5 Rupert and Bingo's Trail (40)
6 Rupert & the Rocket 'Plane (52)
7 Rupert on Coon Island (56)
8 Rupert & the Prince of China
9 Rupert & the Woffle-fly (64)
10 Rupert's Paper Kettle (40)
11 Rupert & the Wavy Wand (36)
12 Rupert & the Blue Balloon (48)
13 Rupert & the Magic Sock

Extra Stories

Rupert Book for 1949–50

Rupert Book for 1950–51

Rupert Book for 1951–2

Rupert Booklet No. 8
(Plots suggested by Caydon)
Rupert Booklet No. 9
(Plots by Marshall)
Rupert Booklet No. 10
Rupert Booklet No. 11 (Plot by Miss Ash)
Rupert Book for 1952–3

Rupert Booklet No. 12 (Miss Shane Heale)
Rupert Book for 1953–4

Rupert Book for 1954–5
Rupert Book for 1955–6

Rupert Book for 1956–7
Rupert Book for 1957–8
Rupert Book for 1958–9
Rupert Book for 1959–60
Rupert Book for 1960–61
Rupert Book for 1961–62
Rupert Book for 1962–63
Rupert Book for 1963–64
Rupert Book for 1964–65
Rupert Book for 1965–66

(Not used in the *Daily Express*)

14 Rupert & Rosalie (48)
15 Rupert & the Rainbow (40)
16 Rupert & Cedric (44)
17 Rupert and the Hobby-Horse (40)
18 Rupert's Magic Top (44)
19 Rupert and the Twins (36)
20 Rupert and Pong-Ping's Party (40)
21 Rupert and the Gooseberry Fool (36)
22 Rupert and the Paper 'Plane (32)
23 Rupert and the Mystery Cottage (40)
24 Rupert and the Lucky Man (52)
25 Rupert's Dull Day (56)
26 Rupert and the Wicked Uncle (52)
27 Rupert's Good Resolution (36)
28 Rupert and the New Rose (44)
29 Rupert and the Ticking Box (44)
30 Rupert and the Stray Puppy (44)
31 Rupert and the Little Tree (44)
32 Rupert and the Elephants (56)
33 Rupert and the Sea-sprites (60)
34 Rupert and the Silent Dog (38)
35 Rupert and the Missing Pieces (56)
36 Rupert and the Green Buzzer (52)
37 Rupert and the Friendly Sea-Lion (56)
38 Rupert and Poll Parrot (36)
39 Rupert and the Unknown Journey (36)
40 Rupert and the Blue Moon (80)
41 Rupert and the Crackerjack (76)
42 Rupert and the Waterlily (60)
43 Rupert and the Copper Bird (52)
44 Rupert and the Crystal (84 + whole page)
45 Rupert and the Hearthrug (64)
46 Rupert and the Dragon Fly (76)
47 Rupert and the Birthday Present (60)
48 Rupert and the Dover Sole (64)
49 Rupert and Gaffer (96)

EDMEADES FAMILY TREE IN 1986

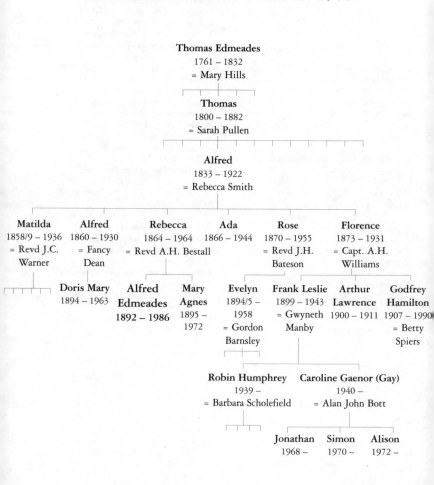

INDEX

Page numbers in *italic* refer to illustrations